THE PLANNING POLITY

The RTPI Library Series

Editors: Cliff Hague, Heriot Watt University, Edinburgh, Scotland
Robin Boyle, Wayne State University, Michigan, USA
Robert Upton, RTPI, London, England

Published in conjunction with The Royal Town Planning Institute, this series of leading-edge texts looks at all aspects of spatial planning theory and practice from a comparative and international perspective.

Planning in Postmodern Times
Philip Allmendinger

The Making of the European Spatial Development Perspective
Andreas Faludi and Bas Waterhout

Planning for Crime Prevention
Richard Schneider and Ted Kitchen

The Planning Polity
Mark Tewdwr-Jones

Shadows of Power
Jean Hillier

Forthcoming:

Sustainability, Development and Spatial Planning in Europe
Vincent Nadin, Caroline Brown and Stefanie Dühr

Planning and Place Identity
Cliff Hague and Paul Jenkins

Public Values and Private Interests
Heather Campbell and Robert Marshall

Urban Planning and Cultural Identity
William J.V. Neill

THE PLANNING POLITY

Planning, Government and the Policy Process

MARK TEWDWR-JONES

Routledge
Taylor & Francis Group

London and New York

First published 2002 by Routledge
11 New Fetter Lane, London EC4P 4EE

Simultaneously published in the USA and Canada
by Routledge
29 West 35th Street, New York, NY 10001

Routledge is an imprint of the Taylor & Francis Group

Typeset in Akzidenz Grotesk by Wearset Ltd, Boldon, Tyne and Wear
Printed and bound in Great Britain by Biddles Ltd, Guildford and King's Lynn

British Library Cataloguing in Publication Data
A catalogue record for this book is available from the British Library

Library of Congress Cataloging in Publication Data
A catalog record for this book has been requested

ISBN 0-415-28654-9 (HB)
ISBN 0-415-28655-7 (PB)

CONTENTS

TABLES

As a student of planning in the mid- to late 1980s, I was fascinated by the way in which the political process shaped, manipulated and implemented spatial planning decisions. Within education, I had been taught that town and country planning was predominantly a scientific process, utilising technical expertise, professional values and rational judgement. I had long felt uneasy about these parameters. I knew that public sector planning occurred through the democratic process, and that there was a partnership between professional planners and elected political representatives. I also acknowledged that the public had reasonable rights of consultation within both plan-making and development control. But I was nevertheless intrigued, possibly even bewildered, by the extent to which politics impinged on planners' work, and how planning affected the attitudes, behaviour and actions of political actors. As far as I could identify from my own observations of the town and country planning process, assisted by deep reading of the theoretical contributions that existed at this time, planning was actually in the crucible of a contested arena that involved the creation of winners and losers.

On the one hand, planning seeks to involve and attract developers and property companies to specific areas of land that are suitable for development or redevelopment. On the other hand, planning is also answerable to local people and seeks to involve the public in the policy- and decision-making aspects that form part of the determination, scrutiny and analytical processes within government. It did not seem feasible to me that these were mutually compatible exercises. Professional planners, advising political actors of the 'most appropriate' form of action, would inevitably have to make judgements about right or wrong, environmental protection and development, public versus private interests, the interests of local and strategic concerns, and so on. Although Patsy Healey is right in remarking that it is not helpful at all to look at the world in terms of dualisms, my educational – and later professional practice – experience only consolidated this perspective. Planning, for me, equated to political choice, and it was not only within local environments that these decisions had to be framed and resolved. I learned quickly that while a planner may resolve a contested matter locally, there was the added complication of taking on board the political preferences and planning stances of other tiers of government. Planning was therefore not only attempting to reconcile so many varying interests horizontally between local actors arguing over specific sites or policy proposals, it was also attempting to reconcile local versus regional and national interests. Associated with these two axes, there was a third dilemma: how to deliver varying economic, social and environmental sectoral (and ultimately political) objectives.

Could the town and country planning system, as it had evolved in the UK in the decades after the post-war period, really be expected to deliver everything it was being asked to do? Planners were increasingly being told from varying quarters to deliver or facilitate economic growth, environmental protection, social and community justice, sustainable development, private sector developments, public consultation and participation, local political objectives, to make strategic and regional contributions, and to reflect national (and even European) interests. And planners were being encouraged to act as both judge and jury, encouraging the public to get involved locally in the planning system but reminded that they had a duty to approve development schemes where they could; the final decision on the small matter of in which direction to plump for, ultimately, would be for the elected politicians, assisted by the rational, technical and professional opinions of individuals who provided the necessary advice.

I entered the world of planning practice post-education with a great deal of trepidation to say the least and it was little wonder why so many of my contemporaries decided within a few months of experiencing these dilemmas to pursue other careers (of the 17 of us graduating from Cardiff, within two years nine remained within local government, two went into higher education research, two worked in environmental voluntary groups, one had entered the teaching profession, one worked in transport, one entered the world of home insurance, and one had become a sales and marketing manager with a motorcycle manufacturer). Part of the fault, of course, was with our planning education. There was nothing inherently wrong with a good degree in planning from Cardiff University; the fault lay more in the contents of the degree programme that the Royal Town Planning Institute had required planning schools to follow at this time: a concentration on the technical and insufficient attention paid to public administration, politics, government, policy-making processes, bargaining and negotiation, the pressure from public and community desires, and financial management.

Within a few years of returning from local government planning practice to the safe haven of higher education, I was fortunate enough to be able to participate in the redesign of the degree programme curriculum at Cardiff to include elements relating to politics and administration that had been excluded previously to enable students to gain a better understanding of the bureaucratic and strategic contexts within which planning resides. If anything, though, I have to admit that this element of the programme was overplayed to some extent as the appetite for more planning practice issues within the degree intensified for the purposes of students' gaining an upper hand over their 'competitors' in their knowledge of the 'real world' and in the employment stakes upon graduation (upon discovering that admission, my former students are free to bombard me with rotten eggs the next time they see me taking to the podium for a public lecture). It is clearly a matter of balance; my contemporaries and I considered that we had had insufficient preparation for the political world of resource allocation, elected members' requirements, and public administration prior to entering planning practice. Later students may criticise degree programmes for insufficient regard for more academic or theoretical learning that considers the purpose and role of a town and country planning system (students are also in the habit of creating dualisms between planning practice education (good) and planning theorising (bad), even though they are clearly inseparable matters). Planning is not just about the political or statutory framework within which it exists; but then neither should it be thought of solely in terms of social, economic or environmental objectives and outcomes, for the latter may be determined partly to the political process. Both elements need to be considered simultaneously.

My research work centred on the politics of development, the politics of decision-making, and political conflicts between agencies and individuals within planning, and these themes have remained with me to this day. This book is therefore the culmination of ten years of research and analysis in the field of the British town and country planning process. A great deal of change has occurred throughout those years, both within planning and the political and governmental processes within which it is set, and it has been difficult to ascertain both the planning impacts on political policy- and decision-making and the political leanings on the planning judgement process over many years, across various political and geographical settings, and from a variety of perspectives. Nevertheless, I hope this book will prove useful in order to instil a recognition of the political and administrative world of planning practice into the teaching and learning process, and to further enhance the interests of academics, political scientists and practitioners. I readily agree that it is not the only aspect of planning, and nor should it be treated as such.

The planning polity, which I take to mean the political, administrative and governmental contexts within which town and country planning policy-making is placed and the tensions and conflicts between each of those various tiers, scales and agencies, needs to be highlighted and examined for many reasons. First, let us dispel a myth that planning is essentially technical and value free; it is neither, and anyone within practice who thinks they are performing such a job are deluding themselves and others. Second, let us not pretend that public sector planning is all about the interests of one group of political actors; planning, even within individual communities and local areas, masks a whole series of conflicting webs between different levels of government and different political actors that have to be reconciled. Third, the amount of discretion that appears to exist within public sector planning at the local and regional levels is often circumscribed by the requirements of a national political agenda or the sheer administrative and bureaucratic bloody mindedness of officials; local planners and politicians, even with the best of intentions of ameliorating the economic, social and environmental problems of their administrative areas, may be constrained into ways of acting by higher political and governmental requirements even before they negotiate with developers and listen to public opinion. Fourth, and finally, what one hand gives another takes away in the planning polity: more room for differentiation between agendas of different tiers of policy-making can be constrained even where it appears initially to allow greater flexibility and discretion on the part of implementing variant planning policies within some public agencies. These four issues form the basis of the book.

The British town and country planning system is one of the most centralised processes in the world. Despite the majority of planning matters being undertaken at the local level, central government has always kept a tight rein on the planning activities of local government. At the initiation of a town and country planning system, particularly in the post-war era of 1945–50, it was perhaps desired and inevitable that the nation-state would seek to co-ordinate and set the parameters for planning locally. The country was eager to rebuild itself physically and economically after the devastation caused by the Second World War, and planning was awarded a central role in that task. National co-ordination and physical rebuilding were issues enthusiastically pursued by the post-war Labour government after 1945. In addition to implementing a process of development planning, planning regulation, land development and acquisition, the government created the first steps towards urban redevelopment, environmental and countryside protection, green belts surrounding urban areas for the purpose of urban containment, national parks, the distribution of industry, and new towns. In essence, these features mark the creation of the modern planning system, and could only be proposed and established at the national level as political imperatives.

The provision of national planning policy from central government to local government to shape land use policy and development has therefore been a cornerstone of the town and country planning system in Britain since the 1940s. While the original role of national planning policy was to provide strategic direction and co-ordination in the spirit of the post-war era, central government retains a role to provide strong central guidance to local government and others on the form, nature and operation of planning at the regional and local levels, even though one could say that its political purpose remains questionable these days. We rarely build new towns, we have witnessed the ascendancy of private sector property interests to determine the location of new developments such as housing, retailing and industry, the countryside remains protected, and local government has been afforded more power to prepare development plans locally to respond to local issues. Nevertheless, central government retains its overriding duty to ensure national co-ordination of planning issues and to ensure consistency in the ways in which planning is operationalised across various spatial, geographical and political scales. In practice, the nature and political purpose behind this remit has meant greater control by central government over planning matters in the last 20 years or so. It occurred prominently in the Thatcher era, as Andy Thornley comprehensively examined in his excellent *Urban Planning Under Thatcherism* book ten years ago, and reached new heights under the Major government even though planning was supposed to be in a new decentralised era after 1991. The Blair government has continued the tradition of previous governments in maintaining an overarching control over planning policy matters locally, and even under more recent proposals to enhance a regional tier of planning in England and to award devolution to Scotland, Wales, Northern Ireland and London the national co-ordination and consistency remit over planning of the UK government remains sternly in place.

Since 1991, a desire to create more certain conditions for local authorities, developers and the public, through the use of local development plans and local policy-making has – perhaps somewhat bizarrely – decreased discretionary decision-making on the whole but also shifted it from some parts of the planning process to others. Since 'consistency' and 'certainty' have continued to form the underlying political tenet to changes to the planning system after 1991 and found policy expression through national planning policy, the planning polity structure and operation in Britain could now be situated at the juncture of an unhappy ideological conflict between the discretionary nature of town and country planning (enshrined in a system of local planning policy-making to deal with local problems) and the more certain, less pragmatic forms of planning policy formulation operated after 1991 (reflecting, initially, a New Right rule of law ideology and lately a New Labour determination) to 'keep control' at the national or central level. This book considers the role and significance of central government in the town and country planning system of Britain since 1991 and simultaneously provides one of the first in-depth examinations of the apparent discretion available to local planning and local government and regional governance policy-makers under both the Major and Blair eras.

The key issues I want to consider in presenting this work are:

- How has central government utilised its national co-ordination and consistency remit to impact upon policy-making at local and regional tiers of government, and to what effect?
- To what extent is a national co-ordination and consistency role of central government over the planning policy activities of regional and local levels of government both desirable and ethically feasible in a decentralised and devolved United Kingdom?

The book is structured to reflect these arguments. Following an introduction, Part 1 considers political ideologies, policy relationships between government tiers and the planning system as they have evolved over the last ten years. This concentrates on some of the recent theorising to establish the nature of relationships and reliances within government at different levels, and discusses – separately – the politics of planning policy under both the Major and Blair governments to establish ideological positions towards government, central government, and the town and country planning system. The final chapter of this part discusses in a detailed way the nature of the planning process from a policy perspective, in order to examine the stresses and strains between different government levels inherent within policies and decisions that affect the operation of town and country planning and its implementation at different spatial scales. This discussion includes a detailed examination of statutory and policy changes within planning between 1991 and 1997 and since 1997 to the present day.

Part 2 discusses the tensions and conflicts within government relationships and policy-making that affect the town and country planning system by examining each level of the planning polity: national, regional, and local. These chapters encompass discussion of how planning policy is formulated and the role of other tiers of planning within these processes. A final chapter in this section discusses another scale of planning polity relationship, the historical links and conflicts within town and country planning between two countries and how the UK government's national co-ordination and consistency remit impacts on the emergence of separate policy agendas.

Part 3 turns attention to developments in policy-making since devolution in 1999 by considering the formulation of differentiation and the clearly separate political and planning agendas by new institutions of governance in Wales and Scotland, but also how these are operationalised in the context of the UK government's desire to implement a national approach to planning. A chapter is also devoted to addressing what town and country planning issues might be considered to be so significant nationally as to warrant a UK government retaining its national co-ordination and consistency remit over not only the activities of local government but also those of the devolved and decentralised administrations. A final chapter summarises the debate, by returning to some of the key themes: the issue of national consistency, certainty and local discretion within the planning polity as it now exists and how feasible and desirable this may be; the changing role and nature of the state with regards to devolution and decentralisation and how planning is developing and could develop in future within this structure; and the changing political ideology towards the state, sub-national government and the town and country planning process.

ACKNOWLEDGEMENTS

As the product of a long gestation period, I am indebted to a great number of individuals in academic, professional and social circles over the last ten years for their inspiration, critical comments and perceptions, experiences, and support towards both the progression of the book and my work more generally. I hope readers will forgive me for providing a perhaps lengthier-than-usual acknowledgements page but I do believe that expressions of gratitude should be given where warranted.

At university, my research interests and planning obsessions were duly supported by Jeremy Alden, Mick Bruton, Mike Batty, Phil Cooke, Chris Yewlett, Richard Davies, Ian Bracken, Neil Wrigley, Cliff Guy, Carole Rakodi, Roy Cresswell, Gareth Rees, John Brookes, Huw Williams, Rob Imrie, Chris Webster, Paul Longley, Alan Hooper and Sam Romaya. From my own period in planning practice I owe a great deal to John Eaton, Lee Bray, John Oakes and Graham Swiss for showing me the ropes, correcting my mistakes, keeping me out of trouble and providing good humour when I needed it most. Returning to CPLAN in Cardiff for research, I am grateful to my colleagues for their encouragement, many of whom are listed above, but I would also wish to record thanks to Robin Hambleton, my initial Ph.D. supervisor, Neil Harris, Huw Thomas, Sue Essex, Jon Murdoch, Bob Smith, Peter Williams, Stephen Crow, Steve Littler, Gary Higgs, Nick Phelps, Dave Valler, Sean White, Sheryl Jones, Kev Morgan, Richard Walker, Terry Marsden, John Punter, Kevin Bishop, Adri Stoffaneller, Diane Tustin, Ruth Leo, Geraldine Bousie, Andrew and Jan Edwards, Jane Melvin and Phil Boland, all of whom provided a stimulating and oft-times political research environment in which to work. Apologies if I have inadvertently excluded anyone.

Colleagues and friends at Aberdeen University and at UCL have also assisted by forcing me to consider planning from different perspectives to those that I had been used to. This has proved valuable, and I must record thanks to David Adams, Adam Barker, Selina Stead, Cath Jackson, Neil Dunse, Mark Shucksmith, Craig Watkins, Arlene Heron, Steve Tiesdell, Anne-Michelle Slater, Aileen Stockdale, Liz Cordy, Lorna Philip, Andy Cumbers, Dave Newlands, William Maloney, Bob McMasters, Harminder Bhattu, Michael Keating, Peter Sloane, Hayden Lorimer, Danny MacKinnon, Jon Shaw, Will Walton, Peter Hall, Harry Dimitriou, Claudio de Magalhães, Mike Edwards, Lisa Turner, Alan Mace, Judith Hillmore, David Banister, Matthew Carmona, Sue Batty, Jo Williams, Richard Oades, John Zetter and Robin Thompson.

Phil Allmendinger, Jon Murdoch and Nick Gallent deserve special mention as my co-authors for their academic insight, support, and friendship over many years, and I acknowledge their ideas and suggestions as influences on the development of this book.

Within the academic community I am indebted to many scholars for their words of encouragement over the years, among whom I wish to name (in no particular order) Greg Lloyd, Taner Oc, Patsy Healey, Geoff Vigar, Gwyn Williams, Cliff Hague, Keith Hayton, Lyn Davies, Richard Williams, Peter Roberts, Andy Thornley, Yvonne Rydin, John Forester, Enid Arvidson, Jean Hillier, Cecilia Wong, Mark Baker, Heather Campbell, Bob Marshall, Mike Bingham, Mark Pennington, Dave Shaw, Vince Nadin, Angela Hull, Simin Davoudi, Donald McNeill, Ted Kitchen, Ernest Alexander, Margo Huxley, Mark Oranje, Phil Harrison, Bent Flyvbjerg, Tim Richardson, Andy Gilg, Mike Kelly, Urlan Wannop, Nigel Thrift, Gordon MacLeod, Martin Jones, Bill Edwards, Richard Munton, Peter Wood, David Sadler, Kwang Syk Kim, Klaus Kunzmann, Peter Ache, Louis Albrechts, Mike Breheny, Bill Lever, Martin Elson, Peter Fidler, Bob Bennett, Victor Moore, Paul Cloke, Peter Batey, Moss Madden, Dylan Phillips, Simone Abram, Tony Crook, John McCarthy, Barbara Illsley, Suet Ying Ho and Glen Bramley.

In the world of planning practice, many people have given me the impetus for writing and researching in the field of planning and politics, and these individuals are employed at all levels of government and private practice across England, Scotland and Wales. I wish to single out for particular thanks Karime Hussan, Ian Gatenby, Chris Offord, John Clotworthy, Richard Jarvis, Mike Flynn, Vince Goodstadt, Robert Upton, Martin Shaw, Graham U'ren, Owain Wyn, Kay Powell, Mark Behrendt, Eifion Bowen, Eric Bowles, Matthew Quinn, Adrian Haddon, Chris Chiverton, Claire Forster, David Rose, Jon Barker, Dave Hodges, Patrick McVeigh, Janice Morphet, Adrian Thomas, Alan Jones, Jan Dominguez, Paul Robinson and Helen Williams. I would also like to pay tribute to my planning students at Cardiff (1992–8), Aberdeen (1998–2000), and at UCL (since 2001) for influencing the development of my thoughts on the subject of town and country planning, and for their critical engagement with some of the issues. I believe the learning was a two-way process.

Finally, but by no means least, my family and friends – other than those already mentioned – have always provided support and good humour both within and outside higher education. Among my closest friends who have provided frequent escape routes for me (often to the bar but not always) are Rui, Gregor (alias Dr Lovely) and Alex, Stevie, Geoff (alias Dr Splendid) and Jen, Johnnie and Kathy, Donald, Adrian, Roger and Sheena, Dean and April, Piers and Kate, Chris, Gary and Doug, Phil and Claudia, Adam, Steve, Nick and Anna, That Patrick, Pauline, Growler Phelps, Higgsy, Earl, Valler, Ian, Nik, Mike, Rob, Graeme, Alistair, Tracey,

Asi, and Jeremy and Brenda. They have been fantastic, as have my family, for opening up my eyes to the non-planning world of art, music, cinema, real ale and fine wines (but not together or necessarily in that order), good conversation and exceedingly enjoyable company. I owe them a great deal and I hope this goes part of the way to show them how much I appreciate and care for them.

I acknowledge the editors and publishers of journals for permission to utilise two of my previous publications for use as part-chapters within this book. Aspects of Chapter 10 were published in *European Planning Studies* (2001, volume 9, number 4) and parts of Chapter 11 were published in *International Planning Studies* (2001, volume 6, number 2). I am also grateful to the BBC for permission to print extracts of a script from *Yes, Prime Minister*.

The editors of the RTPI Library series, Robert Upton, Robin Boyle and Cliff Hague, and their referees, have been extremely supportive during the writing. Caroline Mallinder, Helen Ibbotson and Jenny Geras have been amazing, as always, at Spon/Routledge, and I am grateful to my copy-editor Alan Fidler and Claire Dunstan, my production editor, for the speedy and smooth production of the manuscript from draft to publication. All the mistakes and typos, if any remain, are mine.

Mark Tewdwr-Jones
Bloomsbury, London
December 2001

ABBREVIATIONS

AWC	Assembly for Welsh Counties
CPS	Centre for Policy Studies
CSD	Committee for Spatial Development
CWD	Council for Welsh Districts
DCPN	Development Control Policy Notes
DEFRA	Department of Environment, Fisheries and Rural Affairs
DETR	Department of the Environment Transport and the Regions
DoE	Department of the Environment
DoT	Department of Transport
DRDNI	Department for Regional Development Northern Ireland
DTI	Department of Trade and Industry
DTLR	Department of Transport Local Government and the Regions
ERDF	European Regional Development Fund
ESDP	European Spatial Development Perspective
EU	European Union
GDO	General (Permitted) Development Order
GLA	Greater London Assembly
GORs	Government Offices for the Regions
GOSW	Government Office for the South West
IOR	Institute for Operational Research
ITFT	In Trust for Tomorrow
LGR	Local government reorganisation
MINIS	Management Information Service for Ministers
MPG	Minerals Planning Guidance
MWWSPG	Mid and West Wales Strategic Planning Group
NAW	National Assembly for Wales
NPG	National Planning Guideline
NPPG	National Planning Policy Guideline
NSPF	National Spatial Planning Framework
NWPG	North Wales Planning Group
ODPM	Office of the Deputy Prime Minister
PGW	Planning Guidance Wales
PPG	Planning Policy Guidance
PPW	Planning Policy Wales

RDA	Regional Development Agency
RPG	Regional Planning Guidance
RTPI	Royal Town Planning Institute
SERPLAN	South East Regional Planning Conference
SEWSPG	South East Wales Strategic Planning Group
SWWSPG	South West Wales Strategic Planning Group
SP	Scottish Parliament
SPG	Supplementary Planning Guidance
TAN	Technical Advice Note
TPO	Tree Preservation Order
UCO	Use Classes Order
UDC	Urban Development Corporation
UDP	Unitary Development Plan
WDA	Welsh Development Agency
WDDC	West Dorset District Council
WO	Welsh Office

'POWER TO THE PEOPLE'

HACKER: Now tell me, what is wrong with local government?

DOROTHY: Well, it's a 'them and us' situation. The local authority ought to be us.

HACKER: Us the people or us the government?

DOROTHY: It's a democracy, it ought to be the same thing. They ought to be running things for us, they ought to be part of us, but they are not. They are running things for them, for their power, their convenience, and their benefit. So what's to be done?

HACKER: Abolish them! Invest all power in the central government.

DOROTHY: That's exactly what Humphrey would say ...

*   *   *   *

SIR HUMPHREY: Once you create genuinely democratic local communities, it won't stop there. Once they get established, they'll insist on more power, and the politicians will be too frightened to withhold them, so you'll get regional government.

BERNARD: Would that matter?

SIR HUMPHREY: What happens at the moment if there's some vacant land in, say, Nottingham and there are rival proposals for its use – a hospital, a college, or an airport?

BERNARD: We set up an inter-departmental committee, ask for papers, hold meetings, propose, discuss, revise, report back, redraft.

SIR HUMPHREY: Precisely. Months of fruitful work, leading to a mature and responsible conclusion. But if you have regional government, they decide it all in Nottingham! Complete amateurs!

BERNARD: It is their city ...

SIR HUMPHREY: And what happens to us? Much less work, so little that ministers may be able to do it on their own, so we have much less power.

BERNARD: I don't know if I really want power.

SIR HUMPHREY: Bernard, if the right people don't have power, do you know what happens? The wrong people get it! Politicians, councillors, ordinary voters.

BERNARD: But aren't they supposed to in a democracy?

SIR HUMPHREY: This is a *British* democracy, Bernard!

Antony Jay and Jonathan Lynn

Yes, Prime Minister, BBC Television, 1987

Polity *n.* Form or process of civil government; organised society; State; (arch.) condition of civil order.

CHAPTER 1

INTRODUCTION

The British planning system is unique in Europe. As Newman and Thornley (1996) highlight in their overview of planning systems and policy across the European territory, the British planning process stands in isolation from other European countries. This is a consequence of its development within the legal process that has derived from Common Law, a system that has relied on pragmatism rather than a defined written constitution and bill of civil rights. An unwritten constitution proves flexibility, of course, but it also guarantees no formal rights whatsoever. The relationship between central government and local government, for example, is problematic in this regard since there is no protection if one tier decides to withdraw duties necessary for the other tier to function. Local government authorities in Britain traditionally undertake functions on behalf of central government; they do not possess power over their own affairs as of right, a situation in marked contrast to other European countries where local authorities possess power under the doctrine of general competence. Within these countries, central government will only interfere in the activities of local government if local levels are unable to undertake their functions.

In Britain, local authorities – although separately elected to central government – are agents of the government. Central government sets the financial and legal parameters and monitors the activities of local authorities. Local government is able to raise its own tax to fund local services, but most funding is derived from block grants received from central government. Equally, central government is able to remove powers from local government, or to define tight parameters for the delivery of local services. Bulpitt (1983) has described the relationship between the two levels of government as a 'dual polity', where officials tend to be employed distinctly in one level or the other. This also assists in explanations for conflicts and divergence between the functions and expectations of each tier over particular services, such as planning.

Planning is a government functional that sits across the dual polity. In recent years the issue of policy development and governmental relationships within the town and country planning process has been one of the dominant issues concerning professional planners, researchers and political scientists. A plethora of planning research textbooks have been published devoted to assessing the transitory nature of the British land use planning system and its place in contemporary socio-economic and environmental change in the new millennium (see, for example, Allmendinger,

2001a; Allmendinger and Thomas, 1998; Blowers and Evans, 1997; Booth, 1996; Chambers and Taylor, 1999; Cullingworth, 1999; Greed, 1996a, 1996b; Healey, 1997; Kitchen, 1997; Pennington, 2000; Tewdwr-Jones and Williams, 2001; Thomas, 1997; Thornley, 1993; Vigar *et al.*, 2000). For a system that was under a perceived threat of virtual abolition by the Thatcher governments in the 1980s, planning as a governmental activity has received a renaissance in the 1990s under the Major government and more so since the election of a New Labour government, thanks to the emergence of the environmental agenda, a change in attitude on the part of the British government towards both planning and local government, and a recognition of the system's ability to both facilitate and promote economic development and environmental protection and encompass a range of political aims and objectives as a form of state co-ordination. This planning renaissance has received widespread attention by academics and policy analysts over the last ten years, although very few of these critiques have provided a detailed assessment of the nature of the renaissance from a governmental, political and institutional perspective that focuses on policy format, scope and relationships between the separate but interrelated spheres inhabited by the agencies of planning (see Table 1.1).

The critiques can be categorised as falling within three broad camps:

1   The conceptual and theoretical basis of, and for planning and its manifestation into practical policy possibilities (Allmendinger, 2001a; Allmendinger and Chapman, 1999; Healey 1997; Vigar *et al.*, 2000).
2   The ideological framework of planning and its manifestation as a political process (Allmendinger, 1997; Allmendinger and Thomas, 1998; Pennington, 2000; Thornley, 1991, 1993).
3   The practical and policy nature of planning and its manifestation as a governmental process and profession (Greed 1996a, 1996b; Kitchen, 1997; Tewdwr-Jones, 1996a; Tewdwr-Jones and Williams, 2001; Thomas, 1997).

Table 1.1 Academic critiques of planning in Britain

Nature of critique	Manifestation
Conceptual/theoretical	The scope and role of planning, explanations of the planning process, assessment of its purpose and intentions
Ideological/political	Political ideology underpinning changes to planning and policies, and review of those policies
Practical/professional	How planning operates as a professional activity and in implementation; assessment of processes and outcomes

Source: author

These three broad camps of critiques have provided students and researchers of planning with an array of material, evidence and assessments of the trajectory of the planning system in England, Scotland and Wales in the 1990s and the new millennium. And while they have proved valuable as explanations for and of planning change, there has simultaneously been a dearth of research evidence that has empirically explored how these changes are manifesting themselves into both the governmental and political processes of the state and the policy-making contexts of planning practice. In other words, an assessment is required of the planning system in England, Scotland and Wales that attempts to bridge the second and third analytical camps and present conceptual findings that will assist the first analytical camp; to combine a review of and understanding for the ideological framework of planning and its manifestation as a political process since the early 1990s with an empirical focus on how this ideological underpinning has caused the development of structures and policies within the practical and policy world of planning and government. It is this desire to combine political ideology, multi-level government activity and planning policy analytically that forms the distinctive contribution of this book and its overall aim. The time is certainly opportune for such an analytical assessment.

The principal state agencies of planning currently comprise the national UK government; the devolved governments in Scotland and Wales; the government's regional offices in England, that are responsible for both delivering the government's planning objectives through national policy guidance and ensuring consistency across local authorities on an intra-regional basis; regional assemblies, that are taking responsibility increasingly for forming regional policy; and local government, comprising county councils, district councils, and unitary authorities in certain areas (that combine the functions of counties and districts) and are charged with preparing local planning policies (see Table 1.2).

This planning polity is relatively recent. Prior to the establishment of these administrative and political tiers, planning policy was formulated before 1997 by a relatively small number of agencies. These comprised the national UK government; central government offices in the English regions and in Scotland, Wales and Northern Ireland; and local government. Devolution to the Celtic countries and decentralisation to the English regions since 1997 has complicated the planning polity landscape.

The town and country planning system is formulated and implemented at all these levels of the planning polity. Central government, the county councils and the district councils, and the unitary councils are all elected independent of each other but largely implement a planning policy process that is interdependent. Regional government is an emerging process in England at the present time, but a regional planning policy nevertheless exists and is formulated by strategic local authorities

Table 1.2 Principal state agencies of British planning: the planning polity

Britain	UK central government
England and Wales	UK central government (primary legislative powers, secondary legislative powers, policy powers)
England	Regional chambers
	Government offices for the region
	Unitary local authorities (metropolitan and certain provincial cities)
	County councils (non-metropolitan areas)
	District councils (non-metropolitan areas)
Scotland	Scottish Parliament (primary legislative powers, secondary legislative powers, policy powers)
	Unitary local authorities
Wales	National Assembly for Wales (secondary legislative powers, policy powers)
	Unitary local authorities

Source: author

within each region or regional assemblies. The government established a revised framework for planning policy at the national, regional, county and local levels in Britain under the provisions of a so-called 'plan-led' planning system within the Planning and Compensation Act 1991. This revised framework, by giving enhanced weight to locally formulated planning policies, appeared to provide the local levels of the planning polity with greater authority, to a degree, in planning policy formulation (MacGregor and Ross, 1995; Tewdwr-Jones, 1994a, 1994b). This followed the centralising tendencies of the Thatcher governments in the 1980s (Thornley, 1993, 1996), but was nevertheless implemented by a New Right government that believed in continuing with a centralising theme that directly impacted upon the nature of the relationships between policy at different levels of government (Allmendinger and Tewdwr-Jones, 1997b; Allmendinger and Thomas, 1998).

Central government-formulated planning policy in the latter 1980s and early to mid-1990s appeared to be having a considerable effect on planning policy formulation at the lower levels of the planning framework, despite the rhetoric provided by ministers implementing a local plan-led process (Tewdwr-Jones, 1997c; Ying Ho, 1997; Baker, 1999). Associated with the provisions of this plan-led system that was introduced to achieve more national consistency and certainty in planning policy across England, Scotland and Wales, the amended planning polity framework seemed to result in new forms of central rule of law occurring to limit local authorities' discretion.

The key issues that formed the basis of the research within this book were that:

- The planning policy formulation process operated in England, Scotland and Wales since the early to mid-1990s has been determined to a significant extent by central government's national planning policies in its quest for national consistency and certainty across Britain.
- The national consistency remit enjoyed by central government militated against any sub-national alternative planning policy agenda promoted by local authorities and has been at variance with the locally formulated plan-led spirit of the Planning and Compensation Act 1991.

The key questions that arise in order to test these themes are:

1   How has central government used its legal planning remit to provide national consistency and certainty while promoting locally led planning agendas within local government?
2   To what extent do the changes to the British planning process of the late 1980s/early 1990s actually provide for sub-national and local authority policy alternatives and differentiation in formulating planning policies in the spirit of the plan-led legislation?
3   What were the political ways in which, first, the Conservative government and, lately, the Labour government, created new forms of national control over the formulation of local policy agendas; how have these been in the spirit of New Right and New Labour ideology, and how might answers to these questions assist us in conceptualising the planning relationship between central government and local government at this time?

This book takes as its starting point the existing literature and policy framework, and from this position pursues four objectives:

1   The development of the incidence and characteristics of planning policy formulation at different levels of government (that I refer to as the planning polity).
2   The assessment of the different dimensions or scale of planning policy relationships that exist between national agendas, regional concerns and local policies.
3   A detailed examination of planning policy tensions and conflicts between these governmental levels since the implementation of the Planning and Compensation Act 1991, in the pursuit of national consistency and certainty, regional compatibility and local discretion.
4   An assessment of the impact of these planning relations and tensions on the nature and operation of the planning policy process, based on the findings in objective 3.

The substantive focus of these objectives rests on each of the levels of planning administration within the planning polity. The emphasis of the literature review is on the planning policy dimensions of both central and local government in the latter 1980s, but more especially the 1990s. This is a necessary preliminary task in order to establish the interconnected nature of planning policy relationships occurring at multi-levels of government in England, Scotland and Wales and sets a context for the assessment of the tensions between national consistency, regional certainty and local discretion in planning policy formulation. In pursuing this assessment, extended discussions are devoted to considering the operation of the town and country planning system in Britain, and the alterations to planning caused as a consequence of changing governmental relations, changes to planning legislation and policy, changes to the political and administrative map of Britain as a consequence of devolution, and changes to the discretion available to local planning authorities.

From a theoretical perspective, the research attempts to place the 'post-Thatcherite' (Allmendinger and Tewdwr-Jones, 1997b) changes to the planning policy process in Britain in the context of New Right and New Labour ideologies. The Thatcher governments of the 1980s had implemented a New Right or neo-market policy towards urban development with the consequence that local authority public sector planning had been gradually watered down in favour of greater market determination, less local state intervention and discretion, and the centralisation of policy-making at a national level. The Major governments of 1990–7 followed with many of the Thatcherite policies, but implemented many new measures in the planning policy area. The New Labour government since 1997 has adopted many of the policies of the New Right in addressing planning policy matters, but with a greater emphasis towards a regional renaissance. The key question to consider is: to what extent did New Right ideology continue to form an underlying rationale for policy changes affecting planning in the late 1990s and beyond? Were the changes made by central government between 1990 and 1997, and 1997 and 2001, within the ideological parameters set by New Right thinkers?

During the period of Margaret Thatcher's premiership of 1979–90, it is possible to identify and examine the legal and policy amendments undertaken by central government that reflected New Right thinking, including the centralisation of policies, the reorientation towards the market, and the requirement for speedy, efficient processes to assist the private sector. These changes are most evident in the plethora of national policies released, changes to development control, the fostering of an 'appeal-led' planning process by reducing local authorities' discretionary powers, and in the deregulation of planning. The period after John Major acceded to the premiership coincides with a changed climate for the planning process. The introduction of a plan-led planning process, the incorporation of the environmental agenda, the striking of a policy balance between environmental and market concerns, the fostering of competitiveness as a component of government policy, and a reorientation towards public sector quality and standards, is in marked contrast with the market-orientated approach of Major's predecessor. The election of the Blair government in 1997 promised a commitment to town and country planning (DETR, 1998c), with an enhancement of both the European and regional levels of planning policy, support for the plan-led system and planning control, and interest in utilising financial instruments within planning. But to what extent do these changes from both 1990–97 and 1997–2001 reflect New Right ideology, and do they represent a similar ideological vein to the New Right changes in the 1980s, or do they amount to an ideological difference away from New Right thinking? Although the research discussed within this book is restricted to analysis of the planning policy dimension, there are significant conceptual and theoretical issues that arise from the study, and these will be addressed later in the work.

Before proceeding with this programme, some important groundwork must be covered. It is necessary, first, to establish the institutional framework of the town and country planning system with particular reference to the 1980s and 1990s. This will provide an introduction to the administration of the planning polity in Britain and indicate the relationships between planning and government, and planning policy and legislation, as a function of central and local government. This section will also highlight the potential significance of formulating national, regional and local planning policies as an area of concern. The chapter then outlines the changes to the planning polity that have been implemented since the late 1960s to contextualise the focus of the research.

THE INSTITUTIONAL FRAMEWORK OF PLANNING POLICY

INTRODUCTION TO THE ADMINISTRATION OF PLANNING POLICY

The planning process operates in England, Scotland and Wales as a predominantly administrative system. Planning agencies and organisations responsible for the management of the built and natural environment agree on policies and programmes to instigate change, promote sites and prepare for development. Fundamental to this administrative role of planning agencies in facilitating or enabling is the preparation and implementation of policies, the allocation and organisation of goals, and the mediation of conflicting interests by those organisations competing for the allocation of scarce resources (e.g. land).

The planning policy process is therefore concerned with the preparation of land use plans and the control of development. Although planning, broadly defined, is something much more than plan-making and policy control, Britain has experienced a planning framework devoted almost entirely to a quasi-legal administrative system concerned with policy and control. Since the implementation of the Town and Country Planning Act 1947, when development plans and development control were formally introduced, successive governments have laid particular emphasis on the need to prepare land use plans and ensure state control of the physical environment. These roles have been delegated to local government, with advice from central government and legal parameters established by courts of law. Even today, the main substance of the planning system is administered by governmental professional planning officers, either within forward planning teams (responsible for preparing planning policies) or development control teams (responsible for determining applications for planning permission by individuals and organisations).

Development plan preparation allows the community and those interested in physical change to participate in drafting policies of promotion or conservation. The resultant policies within development plans must be viewed therefore as an agreed set of principles to guide decision-makers on the future of the built and natural environment and as a means through which development opportunities are advertised to the private sector. Planning in Britain equates to physical land use development, and the promotion and control of that development rests with government. Planning policy, consequently, is fundamental to the future social and economic well-being of any spatial area since it is the essential nexus between the state's requirement to review the need for physical change in an area while controlling unacceptable development and conserving the best landscapes.

Given that planning policy can affect the future economic prosperity of an area, it cannot be viewed as an independent statutory function of the state; it is inherent in all governmental activities. Government, either centrally or at the local level, certainly prepares policies, redrafts plans, negotiates with other interested parties and with developers. But planning policy is more than an administrative exercise: it is a product of a long process of bargaining, negotiation and political compromise that encompasses the views and activities of a wide range of organisations, including central government, local planning authorities, statutory bodies, the market and the public. All these agencies influence the planning policy process in some respect at various stages of policy formulation and implementation. The extent of influence wielded by these different interest groups varies between governments and between different situations and groups within government. Policy planners will attempt to draft and implement the most appropriate policies for the administrative area they are responsible for, having taken into account the different opinions voiced, but ultimately a plan containing those policies can never be used as a blueprint: there will always be scope for amendments, for other factors to be taken into account, and for exceptions to the rule, a clear sign of the political component that is so intrinsic in the British planning system.

Planning policy is closely tied to the fields of public administration and politics. It operates as a means of negotiation between market choice (the desires of the individual) and political choice (the desires and actions of the state). The activity of selecting and amending policies as part of the formulation and implementation of plans can never be a technical problem-solving exercise undertaken by professional urban and regional managers possessing perfect knowledge and high skills with community backing. Planning policy marries the technical issues of physical land use planning with behavioural actions and choices between different options. Policy planning, as a political process, encompasses both the technical and the ethical; values underlie decisions to an equal extent as technical characteristics. Given this relationship, it is inevitable that conflicts frequently occur – between different arms of the state, between interested organisations, and between individuals. If anything characterises the turbulence of planning policy it is the source of argumentation over land use. Within this introductory section, the context for the chapters that follow is briefly outlined, indicating the administrative framework of planning policy and the changing political actions that have affected the process since the creation of our present form of planning policy process in 1968.

THE DEVELOPMENT OF STATUTORY PLANNING SINCE 1968: THE CONTEXT

The town and country planning system currently operating in England, Scotland and Wales emerged following the report of the expert Planning Advisory Group of 1965 (Delafons, 1998) and the enactment of parliamentary legislation in the Town and Country Planning Act 1968 (for a review of the statutory planning system prior to 1968, see Cullingworth and Nadin, 2002). To accompany the new planning system in Britain, the provisions of the Local Government Act 1972 enacted a three-tier system of local authorities: within England and Wales there were 47 county councils and 333 district councils, with numerous community, town or parish councils at the lower level. Within Scotland, the Local Government Act 1973 created autonomous local authorities. With the exception of the parish or community councils, all these local authorities were responsible for a range of state services upon which specific powers were conferred. The planning framework operated by these local authorities was introduced by the Town and Country Planning Act 1968, subsequently being replaced by the Town and Country Planning Act 1971 (1972 Act in Scotland) to bring the system in line with the revised structure of local government. This legislation introduced new forms of development plans to be formulated and implemented by the county/regional and district local government structure. County and regional councils were required to prepare structure plans, broad strategic documents containing policies on a range of issues to apply across the county (Cross and Bristow, 1983). District councils were encouraged to prepare district plans, detailed forward planning and development control plans containing policies for specific land use allocations. The district plans could comprise numerous types of different documents, including district plans, action area plans, and subject plans, according to the needs and development pressures existing for each area (Bruton and Nicholson, 1987). The successfulness of this two-tier planning framework has been analysed in numerous studies (for example, Healey et al., 1985) and is not worth repeating here. However, by the mid-1980s questions were beginning to be asked – predominantly by central government – of both the appropriateness of the planning system to deal with development pressures of the time and of the local government structure operating the planning system. Thornley (1991) provides one of the most authoritative accounts of the political climate for land use planning during the 1980s – under so-called 'Thatcherism' – and details the changes experienced by the system as the Conservative Party in government 'rolled back the frontiers of the state', allowed the market to promote property-led urban regeneration (Turok, 1992; Imrie and Thomas, 1993) and enterprise to flourish (Anderson, 1990; Church, 1986).

One of the most important reforms initiated by the Conservatives during the 1980s which affected the town and country planning framework was the abolition of the county councils in the seven largest metropolitan areas of England. Under the Local Government Act 1985, the metropolitan county councils for London, Birmingham, Liverpool, Manchester, Sheffield, Newcastle and Leeds were abolished, and their statutory powers transferred to the lower-tier authorities: the metropolitan districts and the London boroughs (Flynn et al., 1985). The planning system was also transferred to the new authorities, with a new statutory system introduced for metropolitan planning. To replace the structure plan and district plan in each authority, a new development plan – the unitary development plan – would gradually be introduced comprising the functions of both former plans: strategic and detailed policies. Outside these metropolitan areas, the two-tier structure plan and district plan would remain in operation as the statutory planning system. The new planning arrangements within the metropolitan authorities after 1986 have been subject to assessment by analysts (for example, Thew and Watson, 1988; Roberts et al., 2000) and some commentators have focused more on the resultant lack of strategic planning policy to operate across the former metropolitan county areas (Williams, 1999a; Thomas and Roberts, 2000).

The effects of Thatcherism on the town and country planning system during the 1980s were widespread. The reforms, or deregulation of planning, not only affected the local governmental administrative framework and its duties but also the planning system itself. Forward planning functions and development control powers of local authorities were amended significantly following the passing of a number of Acts of Parliament, white papers and government circulars. In particular, the forward planning duties of urban authorities were removed in certain areas as the government introduced Enterprise Zones (Hedley, 1984), Urban Development Corporations (Anderson, 1990) and Simplified Planning Zones (Allmendinger, 1997), which removed planning restrictions and allowed the market to regenerate derelict urban areas in such cities as Bristol, Cardiff, Sheffield, Liverpool and London Docklands without bureaucratic control (see Imrie and Thomas (1998) for a comprehensive review of the policies and effects of UDCs).

On the development control side of local authorities' work, the reduction in control was almost as marked (Tewdwr-Jones and Harris, 1998). In the mid-1980s the government reduced the status of development plans in local authorities' determination of planning applications. A White Paper, *Lifting the Burden* (HM Government, 1985), was published which relegated development plans – and ultimately the policies within those plans – in favour of other material considerations, the most prominent of which was the encouragement to create employment. Following this paper in the two to three years to 1987, local authorities seemed to be unable to effectively control development in their areas, particularly for large-scale housing initiatives and out-of-town retailing development. This period of time has become known as the 'appeal-led' planning process, as developers often appealed to central government ministers to overturn the unfavourable decisions of local authorities and allow their proposals to go ahead (Rydin, 1993).

The planning system experienced further uncertainty upon the publication of a government Green Paper in 1986, *The Future of Development Plans* (DoE/Welsh Office, 1986). The Secretary of State for the Environment at the time, Nicholas Ridley, issued a consultation paper advocating the abolition of structure plans and their replacement with county planning statements and the introduction of district-wide unitary development plans, as had recently been introduced to the metropolitan areas following the abolition of the metropolitan counties. The amount of criticism which the proposals attracted was widespread, and further disillusioned the planning profession and local authority associations.

By 1987 local authorities were beginning to object to the undermining of local democracy in this respect and harassed the government to return to a local authority-led planning system. Additionally, the Planning Inspectorate – responsible for arranging and determining appeals to the national government ministers – was being placed under increasing pressure as the number of appeals against local authority decisions reached significant levels. Simultaneously the government received a great deal of criticism from Conservative voters in the rural south-east of England and their own Members of Parliament for not acting to control the possible development of new housing settlements in the south-east of England in the countryside. As a consequence of this pressure the government acknowledged the problems operating within the planning system and, as a first step, announced that in future, where a local development plan was up to date and relevant to the development needs of an area, it would be accorded enhanced weight as a decision-making tool within both local authorities and at appeal, central government at the time espousing local choice and the need for communities to determine the scope for future development within their own localities (Waldegrave, 1987).

Although this may have marked a watershed for the Conservatives' policy towards planning, it did not halt additional reforms and proposals to further amend the planning framework. The 1986 Green Paper's proposals were carried through into *The Future of Development Plans* White Paper of January 1989 (HM Government, 1989), which again proposed the abolition of structure plans. But by the winter of the same year, the government's enthusiasm towards radical planning reform was diminishing. The replacement of Nicholas Ridley as Environment Secretary with Chris Patten resulted in a change in direction for Conservative policy towards planning. In the autumn of 1989 Patten announced that the most controversial element of the White Paper's proposals – to abolish structure plans – had been withdrawn, but reiterated that further legislation was required. The 1988–89 period was also notable for the government's embracement of green politics, as the major political parties developed policies for environmental protection (McCormick, 1991; Bomberg, 1996). Environmental issues, that can only be effectively co-ordinated by the state, were seen by the government as the ideal means through which popular support could be accumulated, and recognised that action on green issues could only be secured with the support of local government. The Environmental Protection Act 1990 set the seal on a move towards state concern for green issues, and indirectly had the effect of bolstering the functions of local authorities as guardians of the environment.

The renaissance of planning policy, or at least the bolstering of local planning authorities' functions, had already occurred in the form of withdrawing the White Paper's proposals for structure plan replacement and concern for the environment by the time Margaret Thatcher was deposed as leader of the Conservative Party in the autumn of 1990. Consolidating legislation in England and Wales to replace the 1971 Town and Country Planning Act was introduced through Parliament. The 1971 Act had been severely hampered by many amendments up to 1990, mainly as a consequence of legislation but also as a cause of changing statutory procedures as detailed in White Papers, circulars, and other statutory instruments. Given the plethora of documentation existing, legislation was required to bring together all these different amendments into one set of planning acts. In 1990, therefore, the government legislated for consolidation of the town and country planning statutes, encompassing all the revisions and amendments to the planning system that had occurred in the previous 20 years. Rather than one parliamentary Act, however, the consolidating legislation was divided between: The Town and Country Planning Act 1990, detailing the principal legal requirements on planning policy; the Planning (Conservation Areas and Listed Buildings) Act 1990, which focused on the built heritage; and the Planning (Hazardous Substances) Act 1990, which covers pollution and waste material. The Scottish planning legislation was eventually consolidated under the Town and Country Planning Act 1997. In England and Wales, although Chris Patten and his equivalent within Wales as Secretary of State had stated that further legislation was required, this was not what the government had in mind, and the remainder of the 1989 White Paper's proposals remained on the table for discussion for the time being. Therefore the change in government policy towards the planning system was already occurring in 1989, over one year prior to Mrs Thatcher leaving office, although this had not been enacted in legislative changes. The pace of change and modified policy stance of the government towards the planning framework was more marked, however, following John Major's appointment as Prime Minister and Michael Heseltine's reappointment as Secretary of State for the Environment in November 1990 (the latter was Environment Secretary between 1979 and 1983).

The first principal change occurred in the form of amending the administrative framework of planning. Following the government's decision to review local government strategically, following the decision to abandon the community charge or 'poll tax' and increase greater public sector accountability, Michael Heseltine announced in the autumn of 1990 that a comprehensive review would be undertaken of local government structure and functions in each of the three countries of Britain (Clotworthy and Harris, 1996). The exact reasons why the government announced the reorganisation of local authorities remain a point of speculation, a process that was hotly contested locally (Johnston and Pattie, 1996; Game, 1997) and a government policy decision that has been described as 'against all reasonable expectation, and perhaps against reason itself' (Young, 1994: 83).

The reorganisation of local government would proceed separately in each of the three countries: England, Wales and Scotland. In England, the minister announced the establishment of an independent Local Government Commission to consider local government reform and the associated planning framework in separate regions of the country, while in Wales and Scotland reorganisation would be pursued by the central government ministers themselves and the relevant government departments. Planning as an administrative function of local government would be directly affected by the reform.

Meanwhile, the government announced that the long-promised legislation for the future of the planning system would be tabled for parliamentary time in the 1990–91 session. The resultant statute, the Planning and Compensation Act 1991 that received Royal Assent in July of that year, made widespread reforms to the planning process but had particular effect on the provisions for planning policy. Some elements of the 1989 White Paper relating to development plans were included in the bill. The most important reforms concerned the speeding-up of development plan preparation, to remove the need for central government minister- ial approval for structure plans, to require district authorities to mandatorily prepare district-wide local plans for the whole of their administrative areas, and to increase the weight afforded to development plan policies for decision-making purposes (the so-called 'section 54A' requirement).

Other important measures stepped up or introduced at this time included the issuing of national planning statements by the government in the form of Planning Policy Guidance Notes (PPGs) after 1988 (Tewdwr-Jones, 1994c), and the preparation of Regional Planning Guidance Notes (RPGs) jointly by county coun- cils within each region of England and central government after 1990 (Roberts, 1996). The release of coherent national and regional planning policy documents, associated with the provisions of the 1991 Act, resulted in the establishment of a new framework for the planning system. The then chief planning adviser at the Department of the Environment stated that the planning system would now com- prise a coherent and interlocking framework of planning policy (Wilson, 1990) across the country.

The impact of the provisions of the Planning and Compensation Act 1991 and the effects of the PPG and RPG documents are continually being felt in local authorities and by the private sector across the country, and it is this new planning policy system upon which research for this book is focused.

Following on from this outline of the nature and format of the planning policy process it is necessary to outline the definitions used in the book and to establish the boundaries for the research.

DEFINITIONS AND GEOGRAPHICAL BOUNDARIES

The British town and country planning process is a complex system, since it is a function shared between central government and local government, and occurs at multi-levels of administration in variable forms. The difficulty of assessing these varied relationships in government and planning policy formulation should not be underestimated. Planning research in the field of policy formulation and implemen- tation in England, Scotland and Wales is a challenging activity, not least because of the complex number of agencies and the different levels of elected government responsible for land use planning, and the oft-times uneasy relationship between law and policy. The local levels of government are sometimes awarded legislative powers to act on behalf of central government; in other areas, central government does not impose statutory requirements on local government but rather a broad policy framework and expectation, within which an element of discretion exists. Planning policy formulation in all three countries sits between and across this relationship. The introduction of changes to the framework of planning policy formulation at the national, regional and local levels requires a reassessment of these complex relationships, to explore the nature, scope and significance of national consistency, regional certainty and local discretion within the context of a national (that is, UK) approach. Some distinct terms employed in this book require explanation at the outset.

NATIONAL CONSISTENCY

Although the UK government has a distinct remit in the planning system of England, Scotland and Wales, the UK has never produced a comprehensive national land use or physical plan. Planning primarily occurs at the local level of government through development plan formulation and planning control, but within a policy framework provided nationally. National government ministers are responsible for ensuring national consistency, certainty and co-ordination between different areas of the country. The devices ministers use to implement this consistency remit include issuing national planning policy guidance, selecting and 'calling-in' certain types of planning applications from local authorities where the impact of the developments may be felt nationally or regionally, and being responsible for determining planning appeals against refusal decisions of local authorities. It is intended, therefore, that the national UK government only provides a check and balance system to ensure local government operates consistently across the geographies of Britain (Quinn, 1996, 2000). What are the limits to this national consistency remit? Where does the process of national planning guidance end and national planning policy direction start?

The political structure within England, Scotland and Wales (and the planning system inherent within that) occurs at two directly elected levels: central government and local government. Between these two levels there currently exists a democratic and strategic policy vacuum in the form of regional government. This has been a politically contentious area, with the Labour Party arguing for some form of directly elected regional level of government for the English regions, and the Conservative Party staunchly defending the status quo existence of national government and local government. The Conservatives did recognise the value of regional policy-making by establishing Regional Planning Guidance Notes in 1990 and the Government Regional Offices (the GROs) in 1994 (Mawson and Spencer, 1997). But these offices were not independent of central government but rather the central government's regional arms. There had been some disquiet politically and from business of the need for formal regional government (for example, see Constitution Unit, 1996), but from a planning perspective the need for a regional level of strategic policy-making that translates the national policy objectives into regional contexts, and simultaneously provides the regional framework for local government's policies, has been proven extensively over the years, both by academics and the government (DoE, 1990; Glasson, 1978; Minay, 1992; Roberts, 1996; Wannop and Cherry, 1994). Upon taking office in 1997, the Blair government implemented stronger regional policy-making. This would be achieved through the creation of Regional Development Agencies (Lunch, 1999; Roberts and Lloyd, 2000), enhancing Regional Planning Guidance (Murdoch and Tewdwr-Jones, 1999), and promising the establishment of Regional Chambers and Regional Assemblies at a later date (Harding et al., 1999).

The national consistency label used in this thesis refers to the British planning system. Even taking into account devolution to Scotland and Wales after 1999 and the decentralisation commitment to the English regions, the government still retains a desire to operate the planning policy formulation process as one across Britain, without implementing radical changes to the form and legal basis of the system. The present form of planning at the sub-national level occurs through the National Assembly for Wales, the Scottish Parliament, and the Government Regional Offices implementing national and regional planning policies at the local authority level but within a national or regional context. The establishment of regional planning policies in England in the early 1990s was, in point of fact, nothing more than an extension of national planning policies, but the enhancement awarded to these policies since 1997 potentially creates a new opportunity within the planning polity to enable the government to effectively deal with socio-economic, environmental and political problems unique to and inherent within each region, and to adequately reflect those problems in the policy-making process. This book considers rather whether the formulation and implementation of existing national planning policy across England, Scotland and Wales adequately reflects the planning problems within each area. What opportunities exist in the present political and governmental climate for the planning policy agendas within distinct sub-national areas of Britain to be implemented in the UK government's push for national consistency?

CERTAINTY

Central government's introduction of the plan-led planning system in the Planning and Compensation Act 1991 was based on a desire for more certain conditions for developers and the general public. The quest for certainty in planning policy formulation necessitated, at its simplest level, the production of mandatory district-wide plans by the district level of local government. At the more detailed level, the quest for certainty directly translated into the plan preparation process by the government requesting local authorities to prepare policies within their plans that indicated in more secure and certain language: (a) the spatial areas where development and regeneration was considered desirable or possible; and (b) the spatial areas where the natural and built environment should be protected and conserved from development.

This quest for certainty in planning policy-making found expression through the central government's regional offices, the Welsh Office and the Scottish Office (prior to 1999), increasing their monitoring role of local authorities' development plans more prominently than hitherto. The regional offices were given authority to highlight areas of inconsistency both within plans and between plans and national and regional planning guidance, and policies that lacked certainty in policy expression. In relation to a desire for national consistency, the quest for certainty could potentially mean central government utilising national planning policy to enforce local policies to be in strict conformity to central government's planning agenda, without taking sufficient account of unique local or regional circumstances. Certainty also stemmed from the Conservative government's claim, prior to 1997, for more rule-based policy-making procedures as one of the principal tenets – a rule of law – of New Right ideology. To what extent was central government's quest for certainty in planning policy formulation after 1991, and again after 1997, a practical expression of New Right ideology in the governments of the 1990s? Also, in what ways has this quest for certainty resulted in more standardised, centrally determined planning policy being enforced on the local policy-making level of government?

LOCAL DISCRETION

Planning occurs primarily at the local government level. It is reflected in the formulation of structure plans, local plans and unitary development plans by directly elected councils and the implementation of local policies through the planning control process. An extensive amount of literature has been devoted to scrutiny of the relationship, independence and interdependence between local government and central government (see, for example, Rhodes, 1988, 1992). This book is not concerned with central–local government relations *per se*, but rather with the nature and scope of planning policy tensions between the central state's objectives and local and territorial desires. It seeks to assess the threat to and from central government planning policy. In particular, the work attempts to establish the nature of and possibility for locally and regionally formulated planning agendas to survive the national consistency monitoring of central government, and assesses whether local areas retain an ability to utilise discretion against state centrality within the planning policy formulation process. To what degree are local planning

authorities able to formulate locally derived planning policies within their development plans that are not in strict conformity with the planning objectives of the
national government? To what extent is the national government utilising its
national consistency remit to ensure limitation of local discretion in planning policy
formulation?

This research is devoted to the planning policy relationships between central
government (and its regional offices) and local government in England, Scotland
and Wales. It is recognised that the United Kingdom government operates on
behalf of the people of England, Scotland, Wales and Northern Ireland. However,
in planning administration terms, the land use process operates distinctly in different parts of the UK. Scotland possesses its own planning legislation and policy,
separate to England and Wales, and since 1999 has possessed its own parliament (Allmendinger, 2001b). Within Wales, primary legislation is shared between
England and Wales, even after the creation of the National Assembly for Wales in
1999. National planning policy had been released jointly between the two countries until 1996, but the format was amended after this period with the publication
of separate documents (Powell, 2001; Tewdwr-Jones, 2001c). In Northern Ireland,
the planning system is operated in its entirety by the Department of the Environment Northern Ireland Office and not as a function of local government. With the
establishment of the Northern Ireland Assembly, regional spatial policy matters will
be addressed in due course (McNeill and Gordon, 2001; Shirlow, 2001). Because
of this anomaly, reference to 'national' in discussions of the British government, in
respect of this book, relates to England, Scotland and Wales (that is, Britain)
alone.

The selection of England, Scotland and Wales only also reflects the planning
policy process operated by central government in the latter 1980s and early 1990s
when national planning policy guidance in the form of Planning Policy Guidance
Notes (PPGs) was released jointly by the Department of the Environment and the
Welsh Office, reflecting the government's view that the planning policy process
between the two countries was identical. PPGs were first released in January
1988 at the commencement of the plan-led planning system and remain in place
today as the principal form of national planning policy provided to local authorities
by central government. They have also been used by central government as the
principal source of policy vehicle intended to promote national consistency across
England and Wales. A separate series of Planning Guidance Wales (PGW), more
recently termed Planning Policy Wales (PPW), has been released by the Welsh
Office since 1996 as a replacement for the previous joint-departmental released
PPGs. Part of the research for this book occurred just prior to this change,
although the possibilities for the development of a distinctly Welsh planning policy
were being discussed by central government, local government and planning

professionals at the time (that is, in the period 1993–96), even prior to devolution. Scotland possesses a series of National Planning Policy Guidelines (NPPGs) that are similar to the English PPGs and the Welsh PPW in that they express government policy objectives and provide expectations as to how local government should operate the planning system within Scotland.

SOME NOTES ON RESEARCH METHODOLOGY

The complexity of researching different planning policy relations within a complex structure of central government and local government was a factor borne in mind in devising appropriate stages of empirical research for the work. In particular, the research methodology had to satisfy the stated key themes outlined earlier in this chapter.

The research therefore had, first, to assess the nature and significance of the national government's planning policy impact on local government's planning policy across England, Scotland and Wales. Second, research was also required at the regional level to identify the extent to which regional institutions of the planning polity had been empowered by the post-1997 proposals and whether this was occurring within a nationally controlled set of parameters or whether central government permitted the emergence of regional policy autonomy. Third, assessment also had to occur at the local government level to identify in detailed nature the role and significance of the government's national planning policy, the Planning Policy Guidance Notes, on the formulation of local planning policies, to assess whether and to what extent the tenet of those local policies were undergoing change by the national government's intervention. And fourth, methods had to be devised to assess the extent to which a sub-national policy agenda within Britain could be formulated within the national consistency approach adopted by the Government Regional Offices and their equivalents in Scotland and Wales. These four aspects stemming from the key themes of the book resulted in a three-stage methodology being devised for the research project. The research undertaken for this work therefore comprises three distinct stages.

STAGE ONE

An aggregate survey of local planning authorities (namely, district councils) in England and Wales and analysis of the survey results at an all-England and Wales level, focusing on an aggregate overview of national impact on local processes. This was accompanied by two case study analyses at the sub-national level in England and Wales identifying different dimensions of the national and regional planning policy–local planning policy relationship.

STAGE TWO

An analysis of the position of a district authority of local government, West Dorset District Council, within England and Wales and the extent to which national planning policy guidance impacted upon the formulation of local planning policies, by examining the national planning policy role utilised by the Government Regional Office, the Government Office for the South West, in attempting to achieve consistency and certainty in planning policy formulation. This case study would examine in great detail the nature of the regional office's comments in monitoring West Dorset's local plan, the significance of the comments, and the degree to which West Dorset amended policies within their plan to ensure that the consistency defined by the regional office was achieved. The focus here would be on individual national impact on local processes.

STAGE THREE

An analysis of the position of both Wales and Scotland as sub-national areas within Britain and the extent to which Wales and Scotland warranted distinctive treatment from a national planning policy perspective. This stage would identify the extent to which a national consistency approach across Britain was being undertaken (reflecting the priorities of the UK government) and the extent to which it was considered desirable. This would also point to what work was required under devolution to establish differentiated planning policies from those existing prior to 1999. The focus here would essentially be on sub-national impact on national agendas.

STRUCTURE OF THE BOOK

Following this introductory chapter, the book is structured into three further parts. Part 1 considers the policy and literature associated with theoretical contexts for the analysis of planning policy formulation, particularly the New Right ideology that influenced the Conservative governments after 1979 and the New Labour ideology that has influenced the Labour government since 1997. These assessments are preceded in Chapter 2 by a focus on theoretical perspectives of planning and the institutional aspects of the planning polity within the context of political and governmental relations. The planning policy relations and tensions between central and local government are highlighted in Chapter 5 with a particular focus on the role of central government in providing national consistency in planning law and policy, and in the impact of new planning legislation and guidance on sub-national autonomy and local discretion. Thus Chapter 5 considers the legal and professional components of the planning policy formulation process by assessment of the distinction between consistency and discretion, and between regulation and autonomy.

From this debate, Part 2 considers the research component of the book, by presenting results of a survey of all district and unitary local planning authorities in England and Wales on the significance of the national consistency remit in planning policy formulation. These survey results relate to the questions identified at the close of the preceding section and additionally form the basis of discussion of the three case studies in Chapters 7, 8 and 9. These case studies centre on the nature of local, regional and sub-national discretion (through an examination of regional planning in Chapter 7, West Dorset in Chapter 8, and Wales in Chapter 9) within the national consistency approach of central government, and the research seeks to clarify what national changes in political ideology and statute have meant for both these from a policy and governmental perspective.

Part 3, finally, provides discussion on the form and operation of devolution within Britain and its impacts on planning and the planning polity. This part of the book provides some conclusions to the research, through further discussion of the implications of devolution on the national remit of the UK government within the planning polity and on the results collected and analysed, associated with discussion of more theoretical concerns on New Right and New Labour thinking towards political and governmental planning relations in the 1990s. The book concludes by relating the discussion to the key research themes outlined earlier in this chapter.

POLITICAL IDEOLOGY, POLICY RELATIONS AND THE PLANNING PROCESS

This part of the book is devoted to analysing from a theoretical perspective two interconnected issues. First, the practical and policy nature of planning and its manifestation as a governmental process. This will include debate on searching for an appropriate planning theory context within which to situate the study, and is devoted principally to procedural planning theories that are best placed to assess the micro-political aspect of planning. Second, Part 1 will explore the ideological framework of planning and its manifestation as a political process. This will include an extended debate on the political ideological underpinnings within central government that has shaped and reshaped both the attitudes towards planning as a state activity and the trajectory of the planning system. This second aspect principally discusses libertarian theory and New Right ideology in Chapter 3, and New Labour ideology in Chapter 4, that formed the ideological context for the 1990s and early twenty-first century governments. As such, these theories form the macro-political aspect of planning. These two interconnected theoretical issues are illustrated in Table 2.1 (see p. 26).

Both theoretical elements discussed in this chapter are necessary. This book is devoted to analytically combining discussion of political ideology, multi-level government activity and planning practice. The impact of central government national planning policy on local planning policy formulation since the early 1990s appears to have been considerable, even under the operation of the local-orientated, plan-led planning system. This book attempts to assess whether this process was part of the Major government's New Right ideology and the Blair government's New Labour ideology, and the development of a rule of law in particular (the macro-political theoretical context). But this book is also concerned with assessing the impact of political ideology on the sub-national, regional and local planning systems in the plan-led process, and the degree to which local planning agendas were able to be expressed in policy through the discretion available to local government (the micro-political context).

At the present time, both elements have been the subject of separate theoretical debate. It is hoped that this book will go some way towards making a distinctive contribution by forming links between the two schools of thought and in being the first attempt to analytically combine macro-political and micro-political debates in planning theorising about the planning system in Britain since 1990.

The first part of the section identifies the current theory applicable to the British planning policy process and, from this discussion, considers three theories that might assist or explain 'post-Thatcherite' planning policy relations between central and local government. This literature area is considered to be a more than appropriate context within which to set the research questions, going right to the heart of central government's control over the activities of local planning authorities. It also indirectly illustrates the problem of attempting to identify an appropriate planning theory literature context for the study.

Chapter 5's main focus for this assessment will be on national (i.e. 'macro') changes to planning policy, although it is recognised that this misses the point about how policies are implemented (Marsh and Rhodes, 1992) and the variation in planning practice locally (Healey et al., 1988). The chapter also follows Thornley's (1991, 1993) approach in the analysis of change during the Thatcher years: it concentrates on legislative and policy change rather than policy outcome. This is mainly due to the lack of any clear assessment of policy outcome which, as Marsh and Rhodes (1992) point out, takes from 10–15 years to be fully appreciated.

CHAPTER 2

A THEORETICAL CONTEXT OF PLANNING POLICY

There is a great deal of literature concerning the role, rationale and operation of the town and country planning process in Britain (see, for example, Tewdwr-Jones, 1996a; Cullingworth and Nadin, 2002). Rare within this literature, however, is the lack of specific reference to the form and function of statutory instruments within a wider conceptual discussion of the purpose, justification and form of a planning system (two notable exceptions are Allmendinger (2001a) and Allmendinger and Tewdwr-Jones (2002)). Some commentators have suggested that this academic gap in the literature reflects the gap between the academic and practical sides of the planning process (e.g. Alexander, 1997; Allmendinger and Tewdwr-Jones, 1997a), and the lack of a co-ordinating, all-embracing theory to describe the activities, role and rationale of planning intervention and operation (e.g. Breheny, 1983). What might be equally true to those who identify the gulf between the two elements of planning is the problem of the plethora of theories that have been advanced to explain planning, a point reflected in the work of Taylor (1998) and Allmendinger (2002).

INTRODUCTION

While the multifarious theories provide a helpful framework for the study of the planning process they can all too often provide no assistance in assessing the relationships between the different definitions of planning, different types of planning and the variety of action and operational situations planners (again defined differently) work within and for. While it is possible to accept the viewpoints of Davidoff and Reiner (1962), who suggest that the world is too diverse for a precise theory of how planning operates, it is useful to assess which theories bear some relation to the study area. Therefore, attempting to discuss statutory planning in Britain post-1990 from a theoretical perspective can yield problems, and this is how the subject is now discussed. Initially, however, this section adopts the approaches of Yiftachel (1989) and Poulton (1991a) who distinguish a planning theory between analytical, procedural and urban form frameworks. Yiftachel (1989) suggests that analytical theories are useful in explaining how different political priorities may inhibit the implementation of statutory plans by setting plans and policies within the context of land use planning as a form of state intervention. Procedural theories, on the other hand, are more concerned with the organisational, political and professional limitations that may limit the ability of the state to achieve particular desired ends in the plan-ning system, although they are rarely concerned with outcome itself. Urban form the-ories are generally concerned with the most desirable urban patterns and structures, but are often devoid of political (statutory) and organisational discussion. Poulton (1991a: 230), too, identifies three similar branches of theory but distin-guishes positive theories from theories of planning's aims:

1   Theories of aims, advocating what planning should try to achieve, why, how, and for whose benefit it should do this ('analytical theory').
2   Theories of procedure, covering how the planning process works and propo-sitions about how it should work to be more efficient ('procedural theory').
3   Theories of social criticism, calling to account the function of planning in society ('urban form theory').
4   Positive theories, explaining why planning is the way it is and hence, by impli-cation, how it may or may not be used, or what the outcomes of planning activity are likely to be.

In relation to the nature of the research study, its focus on statutory planning policy in government agencies, and the two theoretical elements illustrated in Table 2.1, the following theoretical discussion is restricted to considering which analytical and procedural planning theories might be of value. These are considered alongside non-planning specific theories in the realm of political science (on the subject of intergovernmental relations and discretion and autonomy between agencies) and recent geographical theorising concerning scales of governance. None of these three sets of theories will provide definitive Holy Grail answers to the big questions

Table 2.1 The micro-political and macro-political theoretical contexts discussed within the book

Type	Manifestation
Micro-political	Debates devoted to the operation of the planning polity; the use of procedural theories to explain how the policy process operates; the degree of certainty, flexibility and discretion available to local government in adopting local policies and the impact caused by higher tiers of government
Macro-political	Debates devoted to the state's ideological context for the planning polity; the use of libertarian theory to explain the government's approach to policy generally; differences, similarities and continuities between governments of different political persuasion towards the state and planning

Source: author

of what planning is, what it is supposed to achieve, for whom, and why. My critics will, no doubt, suggest alternative theories that may have been useful, and no doubt they probably are. But I do believe that the theories discussed below do offer us some assistance in conceptualising the problems of and within the matters discussed as the theme of this book, and that, for me, is sufficient justification.

ANALYTICAL AND PROCEDURAL THEORIES

Analytical theories assist in setting out the prevailing social, economic and environmental contexts within which the state operates planning, and are therefore of use in explaining the juxtaposition of market-led and plan-led regimes characteristic of 1980s and 1990s land use planning in Britain. They can also assist in suggesting how changing political priorities may inhibit the use and/or operation of plans and policies in practice, the difference between means and ends as a political configuration. Analytical theories have been categorised as 'assenting' and 'dissenting' by Low (1991); that is, whether theorists believe states are accommodating or hostile towards capitalism as an underlying form of society. Assenting theory derives principally from the work of Weber and is variously described as 'pluralist' (the state and bureaucracy operating among many interests to achieve policy outcomes) and 'corporatist' (where policies are the product of a limited number of interest groups through negotiations and where the state and bureaucracy are termed 'urban managerialist'). But pluralist and corporatist theories provide little assistance in explaining the nature and operation of plans.

Procedural planning theories have historically provided a better insight into the practical operation of land use plans and policies, although each attempt at procedural planning theorising has often emerged as a response to the increasing complexity of processes that form, shape and determine how the built and natural environment is controlled by the state. Six principal procedural planning theories are relevant to this discussion:

1   'Blueprint' planning, developed between the 1940s and 1960s, viewed the plan as a fixed end-state product, the vision of design and engineered approach, but inevitably failed to address the rapidity of changing socio-economic conditions and could not adequately take account of resource implications.

2   'Rational-comprehensive' planning, primarily associated with the work of Faludi (e.g. Faludi, 1973) and the use of systems analysis (McLoughlin, 1969), was influential during the 1960s and 1970s, and focused on means rather than ends, to ensure a planner 'would present one's choice in a form which could have resulted from a rational planning process, even if this has not actually

been the case' (Faludi, 1973: 38). The theory became increasingly susceptible to attack from urban form theorists ('substantivists' as opposed to 'proce-
duralists') for suggesting that planning decision-making could be rational and
for ignoring the complexity of the processes of physical change.

3   'Incremental' or 'mixed-scanning' planning, reflected in the work of Lindblom
     (1959) and Etzioni (1968), emphasised that decision-making in operation is
     the consequence of continual adjustment, where plans are subject to
     increased flexibility to accommodate changing circumstances and the influ-
     ence of other considerations.

4   'Decision-centred' and 'bounded rationality' planning, a modified form of
     rational-comprehensive planning promoted by Faludi (1987), suggested that
     the role of plans is to facilitate a rational process of decision-making and to
     enable decisions to be made; plans are to operate as a guide rather than a
     blueprint that have to be followed.

5   'Communicative' and 'transactive' planning, initiated from the work in the
     1970s and 1980s of Friedmann (1973, 1987) but more recently developed
     transatlantically by Forester (1989), Fischer and Forester (1993) and Healey
     (1992, 1993, 1997) where plans are viewed as the basis for continual
     debate and argumentation between relevant interest groups rather than
     solely the product of planning professionals and bureaucrats.

6   'Libertarian' planning is associated with New Right ideology and promotes
     the interests of the market in plan content and emphasises the limited nature
     of statutory documents in meeting real world dilemmas (Sorenson and Day,
     1981). Plans, where they do exist, are rather to set the broad rules and
     framework only.

AGENCY AND INDIVIDUAL CHOICE THEORIES

Strategic choice theorists identify four complementary modes to decision-making:
the shaping mode, how to structure the set of decision problems; the designing
mode, the course of action available within the structure shape; the comparing
mode, comparing the implications of pursuing different courses of action via social,
economic and other criteria; and the choosing mode, commitment to actions over
time and reviewing the management of those future actions. Decision-makers are
offered the possibility of switching freely between each of these modes and can
randomly work back to modes previously considered in the light of new insights
and perceptions. The IOR School's later work, *Public Planning: The Inter-Corporate Dimension* (Friend et al., 1974), develops the uncertainty of related decision
fields in their research on Droitwich in the West Midlands. It recognises the degree

to which decision networks and intergovernmental relations may affect the decisions being formulated by individuals in one authority. In this case, it was in relation to how Droitwich planners could expand the town to cater for overspill from Birmingham while being faced with pressure from the county council:

> Opportunities for connective planning arise when people acting in policy systems which operate in particular action spaces are stimulated by their perceptions of decision problems to alleviate and shape networks of decision-makers in order to explore alternatives and from among them select commitments to action.
>
> (Friend *et al.*, 1974: 56)

Thus the links between different agencies, and the ability of actors and decision-makers within the agencies to communicate their viewpoints, become a focus for attention in how decisions are formulated. While this theoretical framework is particularly useful to analyse the operation of the planning polity in Britain, within the context of planning policy relationships between central and local government, it has not been subjected to much praise by planning theorists. Faludi (1987) suggests that the reason for this is the 'planning environment' (to use his 1973 termi-nology) within which land use planning operates in the UK. Planning theorising by British public policy researchers is rare and is often related to the procedures and practice of planning (i.e. putting plans and policies into place), whereas in the United States, one of the principal donors of planning theories, academics are less attracted to practical case studies to test out their theoretical hypotheses. As Faludi (1987: 96) remarks, 'It is its positive yet at the same time realistic attitude to planning which characterises the "IOR School" and which is difficult to transplant into a different context.'

For the most part, British policy researchers have failed to recognise or have failed to accord sufficient weight to the influence of the school of thought on British planning practice, their anthologies of methods and theories of planning being notable for the absence of references to strategic choice (see, for example, Batey and Breheny, 1982; Healey *et al.*, 1982; McDougall, 1983). This lack of attention might be the result of the theory sitting too closely with the criticised rational planning model, although the main proponents of strategic choice have been at pains to state that it is 'rationality-seeking' rather than rational (Friend, 1983). Cooke (1983), identifying a proceduralist-dominant theory, also believes the IOR School does not provide a 'detailed analysis of power relations, conflict generation and resolution, and the nature of dominant coalitions', since it fails to be concerned with the substantivist outcome of planning decisions. Similar arguments have prompted Healey (1979) to suggest that the work leads to academics becoming over-preoccupied with matters other than the improvement of planning and for viewing inter-corporatism or 'intergovernmentalism' as the panacea of planning decision dilemmas. It has also been criticised, perhaps wrongly, with its identification for a quest for certainty in decision situations, although, as Faludi (1987) has remarked, even if certain knowledge exists it hardly mitigates the usefulness of strategic choice to assist our appreciation of the problems of planning practitioners or of a concern for the improvement of day-to-day decision-making.

Faludi (1987) has suggested that the IOR School could have done much more to respond to its critics and in attempting to ally strategic choice with other emerging planning theory literature. One particular school of theory that bears some similarities is the work of 'social learning', 'transactive' or 'humanistic' theorists (e.g. see Friedmann, 1973; Argyris and Schon, 1978; Schon, 1982, 1983; Rein and Schon, 1993). But this has never been achieved. Partly to bridge the gap between the IOR school, the inter-corporatist model and academics' lack of concern with its relationship to British planning practice, Faludi himself sought to utilise the work of the IOR School to develop his 'decision-centred' theory of environmental planning (Faludi, 1986, 1987).

Faludi developed his 'decision-centred' view of planning following an examination of local planning in the Netherlands and in Oxford in the UK (Thomas et al., 1983). During this study, of which Faludi was one of the inceptors, it was found that in many cases plans were not performing as intended when the policies within the plan had been drawn up. There was an immediate tendency to blame these 'failures' on implementation, but it became apparent that some of the departures were the consequence of interpretation of the plan and on its flexibility for meeting changing circumstances (Friend and Jessop, 1969). In other words, the success of the plan in being implemented was not due to the implementers and the circumstances that impinged on the implementation task, but rather on the procedures through which the plan was used and the courses of action needed by decision-makers in assisting them in evaluating choices.

A plan containing policies commits an agency to a given task – for example, in setting out what is permissible and what is not. While this provides a degree of certainty in agency expression it does not necessarily mean that these commitments ('operational decisions', to use Faludi's terminology (1987: 117)) will be implemented. The implementation task will depend on the commitment and power possessed by the agency in each case. For example, a central government department might possess a specific programme of reforms or of policies, but would not expect to implement the programme itself; it could delegate the implementation task of the programme to local government, or other agencies. This concept underlies Faludi's planning doctrine.

Faludi believes that to ameliorate decision dilemmas, analysts should undertake a 'decision analysis'. The decision must be made within its context or planning environment and, reflecting the arguments of substantive theorists (e.g. Scott and Roweis, 1977; Needham, 1982), it has to occur within an assessment of its impact upon social, economic and environmental concerns. This relates to Reade's (1987) arguments, advanced simultaneously to Faludi's, where he suggested that professional planners are uninterested in evaluating the outcome of their decisions or in monitoring the likely effects of their policies. It also resembles Healey *et al.*'s (1988) concern over how policies and decisions vary spatially and locally according to the different circumstances within which planning operates.

Furthermore, Faludi suggests that flexibility is an essential prerequisite of formulating a plan since it can then respond to changing circumstances and take account of any uncertainty surrounding planning decisions. However, Faludi does not mention the scope of flexibility to encompass discretion; that is, as a decision-making tool in itself. He merely advocates theorists recognising changing social, economic and environmental circumstances and how decision-makers must respond, although he identifies the 'superior wisdom' (1987: 126) this places in the statutory plan tools. While plans can provide an indication of a decision, they should be flexible enough to be side-stepped, ignored or changed to respond to new situations; that is, they should never attempt to become blueprints. Faludi uses the analogy here of a personal diary to illustrate the 'nonsense' planners advocate when they argue that plans should be followed at all costs:

> The 'man in the street' would agree that a plan that is not being followed has failed. He would never dream of applying the same criterion to the one plan that he is probably using himself: his personal diary. A calendar has all the attributes of a plan. It helps in taking decisions concerning appointments, birthdays, annual holidays, and the like, chiefly by pointing out overlaps. But nobody says that it is ineffective when appointments are cancelled. Rather, in informing us about our commitments, a calendar helps to define decision situations, and that is all we should expect of plans.
>
> (Faludi, 1987: 127)

The agency and individual choice theories discussed in this section do provide some useful ideological frameworks from procedural planning theory (even if today they are somewhat unpopular) to assist in an analysis of post-Thatcherite planning policy formulation in Britain. Of particular attention is Friend *et al.*'s (1974) inter-corporatist dimension, which takes into account the effects of one agency's decisions on the development of choices in another agency, and correlates with the relationship within the statutory planning process between central government as an initiator of legislation and policy guidance, and local government as the implementers of central government law and statutory plan implementation. Similarly, Faludi's (1987) decision-centred dimension, that emerged from the same school of thought as Friend *et al.*, advocates greater flexibility in statutory plan-making and for the impact of plans and decisions to be comprehensively moni-tored. He is particularly concerned with the operational decisions planning agencies develop, although he fails to recognise how flexibility can be defined according to the different perspectives of each agency. Therefore, while opera-tional decisions might relate to a mandatory task, or the expectation that a decision will be made in a particular way, they can equally mean something that should be seen to be taken account of, not necessarily followed.

INTERGOVERNMENTAL RELATIONS

Rather than focus on planning and decision-making forms, how useful might it be to consider other theories relating to the independence and interdependence of agencies to explain relationships and conflicts within the planning polity, and how much discretion is available to one agency when that agency has to carry out func-tions on behalf of another? Any discussion of agency discretion in the context of the planning policy process leads to consideration of the legal, policy and discre-tionary relationship between central government and local government. Rhodes (1980) has suggested that the relationship between these two levels of govern-ment is essentially ambiguous and confused, and poses considerable problems for academic assessment. Although local government does possess a clearly separate political role from central government, it is perhaps too strong to suggest that the tiers operate in partnership or even equally. Both tiers are autonomous (both are elected separately by the electorate and both are able to raise taxes), but local government is only autonomous in the constraints or regulations laid down by the central state through legislation. Rhodes suggests that if one accepts the argu-ment of autonomous tiers, it is far too simplistic to suggest that local government autonomy has been depleted by successive stages of direct administrative and budgetary pruning and through the reorientation of local government as agents or enablers of central government. To discuss 'central government' and 'local govern-ment' is therefore difficult since both are multidimensional and involve a plethora of government departments, agencies, quangos and institutions, termed by Rhodes as the 'national community of local government' (Rhodes, 1980).

Rhodes also argues that local government has never been fully autonomous since, aside from financial liaisons, both tiers regularly enter into negotiations on a wide variety of substantive policy areas and local authorities are in some instances implementation agencies on behalf of the central state; statutory planning, as state regulation, is an obvious example of this. To focus in on which tier has control, independence or political monopoly therefore both masks the real interrelationships existing and does not assist in any analysis. As Rhodes (1980: 276) states: 'In short, there is a tension between interdependence and the exercise of executive authority and analysis must focus on the interaction between the two. Neither bargaining nor control is the appropriate focus even when the relationship is asymmetric.'

The role of local government to implement national policy is a key reason for its autonomy, and this relationship – described as a 'dual-polity' by Bulpitt (1983) between high politics (national agenda setting) and low politics (policy implementation) – was prevalent in central–local government relations until 1979. Sharpe (1979) also describes the relationship being the two tiers as 'executant': central government is non-executant as a policy-making agency and local government is executant as the policy-implementation agency. The Conservative governments of the 1980s and 1990s, despite their reduction of local authority powers, recognised the functions local authorities perform and, even during a period of local government reorganisation from 1993–95, did not attempt to realign them as mere sub-agencies of the central state. However, central government has changed the role of local government across the years, leading commentators to suggest that local authorities have been 'bypassed' (Pickvance, 1991) or 'circumscribed' (Booth, 1996) by the transference of some of their powers to quangos and central government ministries and by a greater limiting role on their discretionary powers.

In relation to discretion, the existence of part-autonomy means that elements of discretion will exist, thus further enhancing their interdependence and allowing scope for manoeuvring. The real question is how and to what extent is the remaining discretion used? This will vary between government tiers and between different circumstances, but it will be for local authorities to recognise the extent and availability of discretion to ensure that this can be utilised to maximum advantage. Rhodes (1981) points out that variations in the degree of discretion is a product of the goals and relative power of the interaction and the process of exchange between central and local government. Quantifying or assessing the discretionary element of local government autonomy is therefore difficult to achieve, since interaction and exchanges between the two tiers varies politically, spatially and over time. However, discretion might best be considered through a legal perspective of the autonomy of local government in relation to the central state; that is, through 'administrative law'.

The existence of administrative law in Britain has long held a deep interest in academic and legal circles. The nineteenth-century theorist Dicey argued that administrative law did not exist in England (cited in Booth, 1996: 114), stating that individuals and agencies are solely responsible to the law courts for the use of statutory powers. Harlow and Rawlings (1984) view Dicey and others (who consider that the power of the state should be controlled through legal restraints) as 'red light theorists', denying that public administration possesses any discretionary element and insisting that public administrators should rely on the procedural rights associated with rule of law. Adler and Asquith (1981) also discuss the discretion/legal argument by suggesting that the calls for increased legality to mitigate discretion is, in point of fact, a reflection of the crisis with which the legal profession deals with discretionary judgement. Lawyers trained in the tradition of *Gesellschaft* find it difficult to cope with discretion as part of the power wielded by modern governments.

Harlow and Rawlings (1984) also identify 'green light theorists' in administrative law, however, who not only recognise the existence of discretion but who view its existence as a positive feature of modern administration. Davis (1971) believed that the administrative process had to be legalised through administrative rules, rather than a reliance on courts of law, while Jowell (1973) examined the legal means through which discretion might be controlled: 'legalisation', based on the existence of explicit rules for decisions, and 'judicialisation', the subjecting of decisions to courts of law for scrutiny. Both are considered to be legitimate ways through which the legal process could formally integrate discretionary judgement in administration by providing more clarity and accountability. However, both methods are rigid and can become over-legalistic in their application. It is also doubtful whether such a complex process as land use planning could ever be completely determined by rules and regulations since it would be extremely difficult to identify every possible outcome or solution to as yet undistinguished problems. Legalisation of statutory planning discretion would therefore be impractical, since it would fail to provide adequate solutions to the complexity of planning problems.

Another reason why statutory planning discretion should not be subject to complete rule of law was the alienation of successive central government administrations to become directly involved with land use implementation. The planning process has always relied on discretion as part of the central state's overriding duty in land use processes, mainly through agency delegation to local authorities and by introducing a policy (as opposed to legal) presumption in favour of development. This permits local authorities to act flexibly to achieve that policy requirement. The only ways in which local planning authorities' discretion has been limited by central government over the last 50 years, according to Booth (1996), has been through the judgements of the courts, central government call-in applications, the appeals process, and through the issuing of national planning policy. For Booth, the degree to which central government can limit local authorities' discretion is therefore exceptionally limited, and this has caused a great deal of resentment at times on the part of central government towards local government. As Rhodes (1988: 180) remarks, 'The degree of discretion (and capacity for resistance) of the only directly elected territorial institution in the UK has frequently provided a major obstacle for a centre determined on local compliance with central objectives.'

DISCRETION AND AUTONOMY

Booth (1996) argues that discretion is not an opposite term for regulation. Discretion does not in itself lead to unbound flexibility. Certainly it reduces the rigidity of rules and regulations, but it is necessary to have rules to ensure that discretion is not operated in an *ad hoc* or unrestricted manner. Therefore, discretion is an inherent and independent part of regulation; it is the area of judgement left over by a surrounding area of regulation (Dworkin, 1977). Jowell (1973: 187) views discretion in government as the 'room for decisional manoeuvre possessed by the decision-maker', while Ham and Hill (1985: 4) suggest that, 'A public officer has discretion whenever the limits of his power make him free to make a choice among the public courses of action or inaction.' Discretion, therefore, occurs within defined limits, and these defined limits in government activities form the laws and policies. But discretion can have different interpretations.

Bull (1980), cited in Ham and Hill (1984: 149), differentiates between discretion that is the simple interpretation of rules by an organisation, and discretion as the responsibility rested in public officials to make decisions as they think fit. The latter is far more flexible than the former, although to use Bull's case study of social service supplementary benefits in Britain the distinction can usually be attributed between an agency or organisation (possessing discretionary powers conferred by statute) and an individual public officer (possessing duties conferred by the agency and subject to professional or local control). A similar distinction is provided by Page (1985) who classifies 'street-level discretion' (the interpretation of rules and guidelines formulated at a higher level) and 'institutional discretion' (the determination of whether a service should be provided, to whom, how and at what level).

Bull (1980) also identifies between discretion to interpret rules and discretion to depart from rules in particular circumstances. As he remarks:

> My concern is that the failure to distinguish between these different levels and types of activities can contribute to a confusion of issues: the extent to which Parliament should leave scope for agencies and/or officials to exercise discretion in exceptional circumstances; and whether and how checks can be imposed on the inevitable power of officials at the point of delivery to make a judgement about claims by their fellow human beings for that service.
>
> (Bull 1980: 68)

This distinction is important, especially from a local government perspective and in relation to this research, since it can assist us in explaining how the planning polity has operated in Britain since the early 1990s. Three questions come to mind:

1   Did the legislation and policy operating prior to 1991 permit either (a) the local authority discretion in the interpretation of planning laws and policies

conferred by the state, or (b) the individual officer discretion to decide each case on its merits based on professional judgement?

2   Does the plan-led planning system as introduced in 1991, by introducing greater certainty in the process, limit in any way the discretionary powers of the local planning authority, of the individual planning officer, or both?

3   Does the plan-led system, by introducing greater certainty in the process, limit discretionary powers of the authority or officer to either interpret the laws and policies or to depart from the laws and policies to a greater extent than was previously the case?

This raises a further issue: the distinction between professional and administrative discretion. Adler and Asquith (1981: 13) consider professional officers to be the very embodiment of discretionary actors, since they justify their actions and decisions by reference to professional knowledge but are, in themselves, subject to fairly weak forms of accountability and control. The professional's use of discretion is often labelled 'professional judgement' and, particularly in the planning process, has been accorded a high status throughout the planning polity's history. Administrative discretion does not possess any form of enhanced or superior status since it is usually characterised by rigid rules and guidelines and can be more easily controlled. Essentially, administrative discretion is more dependent on 'institutional as against individual freedom of action' (Booth, 1996: 111).

Some of the commentators mentioned above argue that discretion and regulation exist not as autonomous from one another, nor are they necessarily at opposite ends of a scale. However, a related discussion has been advanced by Reade (1987), who claims that the distinction is rather between 'corporatism' (discretionary) and 'pluralism' (regulatory). Corporatism is considered by Reade to be anti-bureaucratic, pragmatic and discretionary, thus permitting the operation of a bargaining or flexible mode essential to the practice of planning polity and moves away from discussion of a rule of law. Winkler (1977), too, promotes a corporatist view of public administration and suggests that pluralist planning is undesirable: 'The most absurd thing any directive State can do is to make a plan and then follow it . . . Flexibility is essential to all planning . . . all rules are restraints; they bind the State as well as the subject' (Winkler 1977: 50).

A related concept has been advanced by Reade (1987, discussing Bailey (1980)) as 'functional theory', the carrying out of key functions in society, and 'trait theory', individuals' possession of unique knowledge and qualities. However, rather than relate these theories to discretionary and regulatory arguments, Reade argues negatively that trait theory describes the practices of professional planners in Britain who, by virtue of their discretionary and professional powers, have never sought any justification for their actions; they merely rely on 'professional judgement', promote technocracy, and can operate politically, possibly against central and regional planning policies (1987: 157).

The commentators discussing the existence of discretion and regulation in public administration can therefore be distinguished between those who view the two as inherent parts of one another and essential for the operation of state activity, and those who recognise the existence of both but who claim that discretion equates to professionalism and, as such, has been deliberately used by professional groups to promote a self-perpetuating role, a role where experts make and take decisions in glorious isolation. Both of these perspectives will prove useful for discussions later in the book.

SCALES OF GOVERNANCE

Another form of theory that has been popular in the last few years relates to scales of governance. Over the last two decades, there has been a renewed interest in theorising and understanding the sub-national territorial level within an increasingly global economy and questions over the future of the nation-state. Initial interest was centred on reinvigorating the theory of agglomeration (Scott, 1983, 1986) and the local outcomes of global processes of restructuring through the localities literature (e.g. Cooke, 1989). Lately, attention has turned towards the 'new regionalism' (Keating, 1997; Lovering, 1997; Amin, 1999) and the rescaling of political processes (Jones and MacLeod, 1999; MacLeod and Goodwin, 1999) in an attempt to establish the autonomous institutional capacities of regions to organise for economic development (Amin and Thrift, 1992, 1995; Scott, 1998; Storper, 1997; Phelps and Tewdwr-Jones, 2000).

The emergence of the sub-national level has occurred partly by changes outside the UK, including the 'hollowing out' of the nation-state (Ohmae, 1996), globalisation (Brenner, 1999), and changes in governance (Stoker, 1990), and to developments within the European Union. Policies towards creating a 'Europe of the Regions' (Jonas and Ward, 1999), together with proposals on spatial planning and the EU Structural Funds (Batchler and Turok, 1997) and inter-territorial cooperation at the regional level through the INTERREG IIC initiative and the European Spatial Development Perspective (European Commission, 1991, 1994, 1999), have all indirectly promoted the regional level. Within the UK, the push for regional governance had emanated from a variety of financial, political, institutional, spatial and governmental factors (see Baker (1998) and Tewdwr-Jones and McNeill (2000) for overviews).

The growing literature on the restructuring of global economies and their impact on the local level points to the importance of institutions and networks and an emphasis on social and institutional factors in regional growth and success (Amin and Thrift, 1995; Cooke and Morgan, 1998; Di Maggio, 1993; MacLeod, 1997). Such networks of institutions can be characterised by high levels of contact, co-operation, information exchange and sharply defined structures of coalition and collective representation (Powell and Di Maggio, 1991) to produce institutional 'thickness' or 'capacity'. The success of a particular region, therefore, is not only dependent on the existence of advantageous physical assets or resources but 'also through the emergence of socially and institutionally mediated forms of selective co-operation between actors' (Raco, 1999: 991). However, as Amin and Thrift point out, 'It should be remembered that institutional thickness is not always a boon. It can produce resistance to change as well as an innovative outlook' (1995: 103).

This outlook obviously depends on the individual characteristics of the region. Di Maggio (1993) classifies networks as either structural (spatially concentrated and resistant to change), strategic (less spatially concentrated and more open to change) or cognitive-aesthetic (not spatially concentrated and fluid). Regions, as understood here, are likely to fall into the first two of these categories as there is undoubtedly an element of spatial concentration by definition, although this does not exclude other forms of institutional networks simultaneously existing. Consequently, it cannot be guaranteed that existing networks will automatically embrace new forms of regional packages despite their general welcome. Of critical importance in the success of new regional planning and governance mechanisms in integrating with existing regional institutions and networks will be the attitude and dispositions of those currently involved in regional planning, economic development and governance.

The future scale of governance and the spatial policy dimension of the state on the one hand (Jones and MacLeod, 1999; MacLeod and Goodwin, 1999), and institutional compatibility and co-ordination on the other (Baker et al., 1999; Roberts and Lloyd, 1999; Murdoch and Tewdwr-Jones, 1999), remain potential problems for theorists. Against the backdrop of fragmented local public and private bodies are issues such as the centralisation of power, the confusion caused by 'institutional congestion' of ad hoc bottom-up arrangements currently in place, and the lack of direct accountability. Such caution may be wise, since the evolving forms of governance have released 'a real tide of imagination and optimism ... to plan the development path of this small nation' (Hague, 1990: 296).

Although the new shift in institutional relations and policy processes has therefore been welcomed by a range of regional actors, there is nevertheless a possibility that the new arrangements for economic and land use regional planning specifically and regional governance generally are embraced as a relative rather than absolute advance. Furthermore, there remains heated debate as to whether the creation of new regional institutions alone are able to generate successful economic strategies for the English regions similar to the regional 'success stories' in other parts of the European Union (cf. Cooke and Morgan, 1993; Hudson *et al.*, 1997; Lovering, 1999) without a deeper consideration of and sensitivity to 'path-dependent regional economic and political geographies' (Jones and MacLeod, 1999). More fundamentally, questions emerge on the scale of this new regional level of governance and its relationship to the existing national and local levels of governance, including whether the regional level is the most appropriate spatial scale to 'solve' wider policy concerns in the country (Jones, 1999).

The ongoing changes to regional planning and governance, meanwhile, have been examined from a number of different perspectives. Of critical importance to the success of evolving forms of land use and economic planning and governance is the attitude and co-operation of existing institutional agencies networks and policy partnerships that evolved during the 1980s and 1990s. As institutional and network theories demonstrate, there are important and powerful existing interests who have the ability to facilitate or thwart the new regional policy initiatives.

CONCLUSIONS

The relation between the above discussion, derived almost entirely from analysis of planning theories, theories of political science, administrative law and social welfare, and political geography, can all be applied equally and differently to an analysis of the British planning polity process. Central government's statutory laws conferred on local authorities require the statutory planning process to be operated in a particular way. While many of these duties are regulatory, there are a number of duties where local authorities possess the discretionary ability to interpret statute.

This is especially true for policy and regulatory functions foisted upon local government by new legislative and policy expectations, and these two elements are the principal two aspects of statutory planning that comprise the bulk of local authorities' planning work. The absence of regulatory frameworks in certain local areas was permitted because parliament had made the preparation of policies a discretionary function of local government. The situation since 1991 has been amended as a consequence of New Right policies and a determination for local government to become more answerable to central government. Local authorities have been required to develop policies to meet the agendas of higher tiers of government; some of this has been dictated by law and central policies, other func-tions have developed through independent discretion. In the period over the last ten years, how has central government utilised its national policy consistency and co-ordination remit over new legislative and policy mechanisms of other levels of government? This is the theme of Chapters 3 and 4.

CHAPTER 3

THE POLITICS OF PLANNING POLICY: the Major era

INTRODUCTION

John Major was elected Leader of the Conservative Party and became Prime Minister in November 1990 immediately upon the resignation of Margaret Thatcher. The Conservatives had said to the first woman prime minister in the UK, 'enough is enough'. Thatcher had been Tory leader for 15 years and Prime Minister for the previous 11 years. As she was driven away in the official car from 10 Downing Street on that cold autumnal morning with tears in her eyes, there was widespread admission in politics, in the media and in society that Britain was now a different place compared to 1979, thanks to her ideologies, her policies, and her style of leadership. To some, she was a figure of hatred; to others, she was the saviour of the British economy. The legacy she provided to her successor was a totally changed economic and social order, a completely overhauled central government and local government, and an upturned town and country planning system.

This chapter will not repeat the contents and analyses of the authoritative works on Thatcherism and urban planning that already exist (see, for example, Thornley, 1991; Brindley et al., 1989; Allmendinger, 1997; Allmendinger and Thomas, 1998). Neither will it review the impacts of Thatcherism or the Thatcher governments on the planning polity and the planning system in a detailed way; this has been covered partly in Chapter 1 and more comprehensively by Thornley (1991). Rather, it will discuss the ideological underpinnings of Thatcherism in order to identify whether elements of this ideology continued to be utilised in government after her resignation. This is necessary because one of the purposes of this book is to assess whether rule of law (one of the ideological tenets of Thatcherism) continued under the government of her successor, John Major, in the 1990s, and – if it did – whether this created a legacy for the incoming Labour government of Tony Blair after 1997 that has been difficult to shake off.

Assessment of rule-of-law ideology is a fundamental issue since this assists in our wider analysis of central government and local government relations and the impact the ideology has had on the planning polity for directions of the town and country planning system since 1990. It may also be useful in explaining whether local, regional and sub-national policy agendas have been formulated successfully in the face of central government employment of a national consistency and co-ordination remit within planning.

The chapter is structured to reflect this assessment. Following a brief introduction to libertarian theory and New Right ideology, that formed the bedrock of
Thatcherite philosophy towards the state and market, the chapter will consider the
political legacy provided to the Major government after 1990 and how this manifested itself under a different leader and different administration, particularly
towards town and country planning.

LIBERTARIAN THEORY AND THE NEW RIGHT

Libertarian theory, also described as 'New Right' ideology, has been advocated in
the planning literature by, among others, Sorenson and Day (1981), Sorenson
(1982), and more recently Pennington (2000, 2002). They propose a normative
structure for planning in the tradition of free markets, a rule of law, and a scepticism towards state intervention. Various commentators and academics proposed
elements of a libertarian theory for land development before this, including Hayek
(1960), Pennance (1967), Siegan (1972), and Walters (1974), and Thornley
(1991) provides a comprehensive account of land and property interests within the
context of this liberal literature. The origin of libertarian theory as a planning
concern emerged from widespread dissatisfaction with three existing theories,
according to Sorenson (1982). First, the failure of 'left critical theory' that, inspired
by Marxist thought, viewed planning and planning systems solely in terms of facilitating existing class structures and therefore failed to provide a signpost for the
future and advocate alternative planning mechanisms. Second, the 'frustrated idealism' of social reformers (such as Robert Owen, Titus Salt and Ebenezer Howard)
who viewed planning as a set of ideas and utopias and urban problems as ways to
generate social reform but who became disappointed as the scale of urban problems escalated and social justice was not able to outpace market development.
Third, and finally, the inadequacy of normative or prescriptive theory which has
sought for 50 years to provide a body of theory that best justifies and guides planning intervention and which was the subject of discussion in Chapter 2. Planning
professionalism has failed to provide sustaining theories, and those which have
emerged have been largely weak.

To counter these theoretical failures, Sorenson advocates a new way of theorising planning in the marketplace based on Whig-Liberal tendencies of a laissez-
faire version of capitalism: market order, rule of law, property rights and defence of
personal liberty. Land use planning is viewed by Sorenson as the product of an
economic rationale to achieve net benefits without compromising a liberal market
order. Examples of this rationale include planning control and zoning, mediation in
land use conflicts, and the preservation of scarce resources. By understanding

these planning activities within an examination of the ways in which the market operates, urban problems might be less compounded, planners would be able to recognise their own role within it and assist in improving conditions. As Sorenson states,

> Reduced consumer choice of alternative living styles, ossified land-use patterns, stifled commercial competition, dull uniformity in design, increased urban blight, higher housing costs, negative redistribution of wealth from poor to rich can all be traced back to a failure to comprehend operation of the dominant market order.
>
> (Sorenson, 1982: 185)

Efficient and economic urban planning is viewed as utopic, but it is desirable to give effect to personal development aims. The only legitimate way this can be achieved in a democratic society, according to Sorenson, is through the private sector. If planning was redrawn as a partnership with the private sector in urban development and regeneration, planning could 'come of age and leave behind its fuzzy idealism' (1982: 185). In a paper the following year, Sorenson (1983) attempts to move the debate towards a market theory of planning while acknowledging the imperfections of a total reliance on the market. He admits that the market would not perfectly allocate resources and that many failures by the market require public planning intervention. But to have no input from the market would require government control and direction, and since public administration is 'impoverished' compared to market mechanisms, this would not permit entrepreneurial flair. Although he does not advocate a definitive set of planning procedures, he does suggest a list of 'principles' or checklist for a libertarian approach to land use intervention:

- to prefer the market for solutions to ameliorate problems;
- to plan only in those locations where the government has a good chance of solving problems in a cost-effective way;
- to apply rule of law: 'Planning laws and regulations should be known publicly, be applied consistently and universally without any retrospectivity, and be debated adequately prior to enactment' (1983: 79);
- to promote diversity and innovation, through performance standards for example;
- to encourage entrepreneurship in small businesses and to aid site assembly;
- to decentralise power to solve problems at the smallest spatial scale possible;
- to establish competing centres of advice for planners to take account of market changes;

- to avoid favouring one interest over another in conflicts;
- to compensate property interests for any adverse planning affects;
- to facilitate access to legal recourse;
- to value individual rights and freedoms as the 'linchpins' of liberalism.

These principles are noteworthy, with hindsight, for it is possible to identify elements of these as justifications for many of the planning changes and policies introduced in Britain by the Conservative governments after 1979. Sir Keith Joseph, a close supporter of Margaret Thatcher and a right-wing ally, had also been influenced by libertarianism in *A Bibliography of Freedom* (Centre for Policy Studies, 1980), which identifies a list of books on New Right thinking drawn principally from the United States and, in the context of planning, which highlight the failures of public-sector-driven urban development and the virtues of decentralised, private sector market solutions to urban policy. Works by Jacobs (1965, 1970) and Banfield (1974) feature prominently in the CPS paper; the former argues for a partnership approach, recognising the benefits and disadvantages of both public and market-led solutions to urban ills, while the latter argues against government intervention in the market. Other commentators highlighted include Siegan (1972) and Walters (1974), and their experiences of American city problems. Siegan, in particular, advocated the removal of zoning classifications in American cities to permit the real estate market 'greater opportunity to satisfy the needs and desires of its consumers' (1972: 247). British thinkers also contributed to the emergence of New Right ideology, including the work of Banham *et al.*'s (1969) 'non-plan' experiment (removing planning regulation and allowing the market to develop in much the same way as development in American cities), and Denman (1980), who associated planning with the post-war requirement for physical reconstruction and, as such, was no longer required since it had served its usefulness. All commentators are linked by their advocating of the input of market forces to land and property development, and for planners to recognise and integrate this role.

Throughout the 1970s, according to Thornley (1991), in both Britain and the United States, a critical debate was developing that questioned the role and value of planning and where alternatives to planning were being trumpeted. The proposals gained political support in the Conservative Party in Britain and, when the Thatcher government was first elected in 1979, provided the political platform upon which to test out many of these principles. The ideological foundation is of importance for this stance, since it formed the political rationale for the general approach of the Conservative governments in the 1980s. As a consequence it provides the macro-political framework within which change to the planning system, and to planning policy formulation in particular, occurred. This framework has to be subject to in-depth scrutiny before undertaking micro-political and practical planning research since one directly impacts on, determines and shapes the other.

The next section goes on to highlight the Thatcher governments approach to planning in the 1980s by utilising some of the theoretical arguments previously discussed to identify the legacy that the Thatcher government provided for the incoming Major government in 1990. This is necessary in order to discuss the components of Thatcherism towards planning and how planning policy was changed to reflect a New Right ideology in favour of the market. A key question in this debate is whether the Conservative governments after 1990 under the premiership of John Major continued this ideological approach or developed an alternative, 'toned down' or 'post-Thatcherite' policy towards planning.

THE THATCHERITE LEGACY

A number of authors over the years have questioned the consistency of Thatcherism (Riddell, 1983; Hirst, 1989; Bulpitt, 1986), but there exists a widespread belief that Margaret Thatcher possessed a coherent set of political ideas or ideologies that guided both her behaviour and her approach towards government. These ideas centred around the economy and government: how government itself should be organised and the style and content of government's policy towards the economy (Thornley, 1993). Various labels have been provided to describe this approach: social market economy and authoritarian populism (Gamble, 1984), free economy strong state (Gamble, 1988), economic liberalism and authoritarianism (Edgar, 1983), neo-liberalism and combative Toryism (Norton and Aughey, 1981), and liberalism and Conservatism (King, 1987). Despite the existence of these various labels, all the authors acknowledge the move apparent in Britain after Thatcher's election in 1979 towards a freer, more competitive, open economy and a more repressive, authoritarian state (Gamble, 1984), representing clear signs of New Right thinking. Studies indicate that this ideological commitment was translated into government policy (Kavanagh and Seldon, 1989; Marsh and Rhodes, 1992; Allmendinger and Tewdwr-Jones, 1997b). The government's economic policy, for example, reflected a liberal strand and was based on monetarist principles designed to reduce inflation, and the subsequent switch to privatisation that aimed to reduce the public sector and deregulate the market (Jackson, 1992; Johnson, 1991). The introduction of trade union legislation, for example, was a combination of liberalism and authoritarianism in an attempt to reduce their influence on the operation of the market and regain control and reassert the government's authority following the 'too cosy' approach taken by the previous Labour government in the 1970s (Marsh, 1991).

Debates over the coherence and influence of Thatcherism as an ideology have also occurred within debates assessing changes to the British town and country planning system. Thornley (1991), for example, identifies three distinct views: continuity, consolidation and free-market. The continuity view considered that much of the ideological rhetoric would be lost or abandoned when the government recognised the problems of policy implementation (Healey, 1983). The consolidation view accepted the reforms of the Thatcher governments but considered these to be a mere continuation of past trends (Griffiths, 1986; Lawless, 1983; Reade, 1987). The free-market view suggested that the Thatcher years amounted to fundamental change in the state and in politics, introducing a greater reliance upon the market, the centralisation of control and the minimising of local discretion (Ambrose, 1986; McAuslan, 1981; Thornley, 1991). This latter view is probably the more representative (Thomas, 1994).

During the reforms to policy in the 1980s, planning was viewed as vulnerable. Claims that the Thatcher governments were causing the 'death of planning' (e.g., Brindley et al., 1989; Imrie and Thomas, 1993) were largely disproved; rather, attempts were made to explain why the government did not achieve as much as was envisaged (Kavanagh and Seldon, 1989; Cloke, 1992; Marsh and Rhodes, 1992). These studies do point to implementation difficulties rather than a lack of consistency of ideology or policy. In pursuing a centralised and enforcing agenda the government chose to ignore, or else failed to recognise, the local conditions considered necessary for effective policy implementation (Marsh and Rhodes, 1992). Allmendinger and Tewdwr-Jones (1997b) identify the lack of clear and consistent policy objectives such as privatisation (Marsh, 1991); unintended consequences of certain policy initiatives such as increasing public expenditure through unemployment benefit by trying to reduce inflation (Savage and Robbins, 1991); and the role of external factors such as the European Union and social and economic restructuring (Bradshaw, 1992). All these combined to mean less was achieved than intended, and the planning system was not immune from this.

Allmendinger and Tewdwr-Jones (1997b) identify the philosophical origins of the Thatcherite approach to urban planning and trace these back to a number of sources stemming from the key concepts of liberalism and authoritarianism, the need to deregulate the market, and the centralisation of decision-making (Thornley, 1991). In practice and in policy implementation this meant an approach based on three broad principles: rule of law, centralisation and market orientation.

The Thatcher governments identified rule of law as a way of minimising local discretion, centralising control and providing the market with greater certainty. The limitation of local discretion was a central factor in calls by Jones (1982), the British Property Federation (1986) and the Royal Institute of Chartered Surveyors (1986), to replace or at least water-down the then town and country planning process in order to aid business interests. The changes enacted within the rule-of-law tenet during the 1980s did not rely on the courts, or were judicially based. Rather, rule of law involved the removal of local administrative discretion and its replacement with central diktat. Local planning considerations and local authorities' planning policies were downgraded in status, as were local authorities' powers in utilising local policies to guide and refuse inappropriate applications for planning permission. Associated with the use of greater central control, greater emphasis was placed by ministers on speedy decision-making within planning, thereby commodifying the system, making it more efficient and accountable (Thompson, 1987; Tewdwr-Jones and Harris, 1998).

The scope and use of the planning system was rolled back to allow enterprise and business to flourish, by removing the burden of planning conditions on approved permissions and withdrawing certain types and scale of development under the Use Classes Order and the General Development Orders (UCO and GDO) requiring planning permission. It was not only a case of bypassing local planning administration; elsewhere local planning discretion and control was removed altogether, through the introduction of simplified planning systems in Enterprise Zones (Hedley, 1984), Urban Development Corporations (UDCs) (Anderson, 1990), and Simplified Planning Zones (Allmendinger, 1997), and this allowed a more flexible planning system to operate pragmatically according to changing conditions.

Related to rule of law was the issue of centralisation. The Thatcher governments considered that too much policy was available to the discretion of local authorities who may be unsympathetic to central government objectives. Although there was no shortage of suggestions from the right wing of politics for central government to control all planning matters itself (see Adam Smith Institute (1983), for example), this was not introduced nationally other than indirectly within the government's parachuted-in initiatives of Enterprise Zones, Urban Development Corporations and Simplified Planning Zones. The planning system was nevertheless reorientated towards the centre in the 1980s through greater use of centralisation policies. Amendments to the GDO and UCO increased central control at the expense of local powers, while UDCs and other simplified planning regimes were centrally designed and implemented initiatives, operating beyond local authority discretion and accountable directly to central government ministers.

The third tenet of the Thatcher government's approach was market orientation. Simplified planning procedures for development control purposes were introduced locally through the release of detailed central government circulars, including Circular 22/80 and Circular 14/85 (Tewdwr-Jones, 1996a). These were complemented in 1986 by a Green Paper titled *The Future of Development Plans* (Department of the Environment/Welsh Office, 1986) aiming to limit the number and role of local development plan policies. Local planning professionals were constantly reminded from central government ministerial speeches, within national policy circulars and the later Planning Policy Guidance Notes (PPGs), that they were a 'burden on business' (DTI, 1985). Thornley (1991: 143) sums up the overall effect of these changes when he states that the intention of central government was: 'to retain the bones of the planning system but give it new shape. This purpose is one which has its primary aim in aiding the market.'

The 1988–9 period was also notable for most of the major political parties embracing 'green politics' (McCormick, 1991; Bomberg, 1996). Environmental issues were suddenly viewed by politicians as an ideal means through which popular support could be accumulated. Perhaps more cynically, it was the result of the European Parliamentary elections at this time that had caused a new way of thinking; the significant increase in the Green Party share of the vote was a complete surprise but also sent warning shots across the bows of the Thatcher governments. Partly in response to these voting patterns, but also in recognition of the need for political action on environmental issues, the Thatcher government and the Prime Minister herself was moved to 'act' on the environment. Greater political interest in global warming, the depletion of the ozone layer and pollution in urban areas necessitated regulative action on the part of the state in order to intervene in the market's absence. Although many welcomed this renewed enthusiasm, there seemed to be a clear dichotomy between an environmental agenda identified by Thatcher (global warming, international commitments from developed countries, and pollution) and an environmental agenda that could be linked to and provide a renaissance to the planning process (direct state involvement). Thatcher appointed Richard Branson, head of the Virgin Group, to a taskforce to deal with environmental matters, dubbed in the press as her 'Minister for Litter'. At a bizarre press call on Parliament Green, Thatcher and Branson picked up the litter from the grass that officials had strewn there deliberately just five minutes beforehand for the benefit of television news cameras and the media.

The Environmental Protection Act 1990 set the seal on a move towards state concern for green issues, and indirectly had the effect of bolstering the functions of local authorities as guardians of the environment. However, a significant proportion of the legislation had emanated from the European Commission and had to be transposed into domestic legislation (Tewdwr-Jones and Williams, 2001), a fact that Thatcher and her government were none too keen to admit too.

By November 1990 and the time of her highly public and politically enforced departure from office, Margaret Thatcher had overseen a massive restructuring of the state generally and of the British planning process. With primacy now given to the market and increased centralised control over state functions, the planning polity had been regeared. Even the mellowing reforms of the late 1980s towards

enhancing local authority planning policies once again and concern over environmental issues had not fundamentally altered the ideological principles upon which
Thatcherism was founded. If anything, as Allmendinger and Tewdwr-Jones point
out:

> The changes after 1988 in the final two years of Thatcher's premiership had not
> caused a thawing out of ideological conviction; they had merely been
> modifications to a continuing political campaign of reorientating the state. In the
> eyes of the Prime Minister herself, the work was not complete.
>
> (Allmendinger and Tewdwr-Jones, 1997b; 104)

A MAJOR CHANGE? IDEOLOGY AND POLICY AFTER 1990

Margaret Thatcher's resignation from office as British Prime Minister in November
1990 marked the end of an era. I recall my reactions vividly upon hearing the news.
I was working in local government at the time and, as news of her resignation
spread around the office, we sat in silence; when someone finally made a remark, it
was a simple statement of disbelief: 'She's gone? . . .' For a leader that had
promised to 'go on, and on, and on', she had not been receptive to the prospect of
leaving office at all, especially at the thought of her witnessing the premiership
being handed over to Michael Heseltine, her arch-enemy, who had challenged her
for leadership of the Conservative Party. In the end, it was not Heseltine who took
the leadership of the Party but John Major, her Chancellor of the Exchequer, who
had been endorsed by Thatcher during his leadership election campaign. A more
different, and possibly unlikely, leader is difficult to imagine. A self-made man and
stockbroker from Brixton in South London, the son of a circus performer, Major had
entered Parliament and central government from local politics, and contrasted
markedly with his predecessor in style of leadership (Major, 1999). Generally
regarded as 'quiet', 'decent', 'nice' and 'hard-working' within his party, he was soon
portrayed in the media and in popular forms of entertainment as rather grey, possessing a Britain-as-a-small-world outlook (he was famously presented as wearing
underpants on the outside of his trousers in Steve Bell's cartoon depictions of him
in the *Guardian*, in contrast to the portrayal of Mrs Thatcher wearing a man's pin-
stripe suit). As Thatcher's anointed successor, Major was quick to realise – in the
words of the lady herself – that there would be 'no turning back' from her policies:
Thatcherism must live on (Seldon, 1997).

The 1979–90 governments had broken with the post-war social democratic
consensus and fundamentally altered the role of government for the better
(Thatcher, 1992). This alteration had significant impacts on town and country
planning and government in Britain but, after 1990, commentators sought to

assess whether the Thatcherite ideology would continue under the leadership of her successor. What would happen to political ideology, and in what direction would planning head after the reforms of the Thatcher years? Opinion was mixed between the experts: some thought that the Thatcher ideology was relaxed (for example, Willets, 1992; Thornley, 1993), while others saw little difference (Rydin, 1993). Within town and country planning, there appeared to be less of a central-isaton agenda and, following the creation of the plan-led planning system from 1989 onwards, more emphasis towards allowing local discretion. That prompted other commentators, meanwhile, to look in detail at some of the changes to and within the planning system and identify a hidden agenda in what appeared to be pro-planning changes. They argue that the effect of these positive planning changes has been to allow central government to dictate local policy through the explosion in centrally formulated policy guidance (MacGregor and Ross, 1995; Tewdwr-Jones, 1994a, 1994b), but the implications of this are far from clear. What can be said is that there has been very little agreement on the direction of 'post-Thatcherite' changes to planning and even less understanding of the longer-term implications.

The whole event of Margaret Thatcher's resignation and John Major's election as Conservative Party leader and Prime Minister had been swift. The political party had demanded change, but there was no indication of exactly what sort of changes in ideology, policy or style of leadership the party or country could expect from Thatcher's successor. Identifying a clear expression of John Major's ideological beliefs or political agenda was quite difficult, both at the end of his premiership and even at the outset (Kavanagh, 1994). Major's first words on opening his first Cabinet meeting as premier, 'Well, who would have thought it?!' (quoted in McIntyre, 1995), illustrates a man perhaps a little unprepared for the task before him. Although he had contributed to the Thatcher years in a number of senior Cabinet positions, including serving as Chancellor and Foreign Secretary, once he was elected as Party Leader he seems to have been continuously dogged by the need to find a 'big idea' (Hogg and Hill, 1995). This may have been related to the fact of attempting to make his mark following in the footsteps of his political heavy-weight predecessor, and not wanting to be seen as her 'stooge'. He possessed a very different style of leadership to Thatcher (Riddell, 1994), but in relation to policy the differences were not so obvious. Kenneth Clarke, Major's Chancellor after 1993, famously endorsed his party leadership campaign in 1990 by com-menting that he was 'Mrs Thatcher with a human face'. This hint at continuity was encouraged by the endorsement of Major's election candidature by the lady herself, and her insistence that not only would Thatcherism live on but that she 'would have her hands on the steering wheel'. With that sort of burden on your shoulder, it is little wonder that Major lacked the convictions to announce a 'big idea', a point he discusses in his autobiography (Major, 1999), although his initiating of the Northern Ireland peace process is significant.

Another reason why a distinctive Major ideology did not emerge is, according to Norton (1990), due to the small and dwindling number of Thatcherites remaining on the backbenches by the time of Thatcher's replacement, while Crewe (1994) points to support for Major in the leadership campaign from a number of Members of Parliament simply because he was not Mrs Thatcher. Obviously, any prospective party leader must try to appeal to a wide spectrum of support, but the Conservative Party at the time clearly demanded a departure from the strident overtures of conviction politics long eschewed by Thatcher. Note, however, that the demand was for a change of style and not necessarily a change in ideology, although some of the Thatcher government policies in 1989–90 based on her ideological convictions were causing concern among party activists (the most evident example of this concern was in relation to party political and public perceptions of the community charge or 'poll tax' that certainly played a contribution to Thatcher's downfall). Campbell (1994) has suggested that the change in leadership did herald the promise of a different ideological approach and that the new government was anxious to portray itself as an administration reuniting all wings of the Conservative Party around a post-Thatcher consensus.

The confusion between Thatcherite style and Thatcherite ideology dogged the Major governments (Allmendinger and Tewdwr-Jones, 1997b). There is little doubt that some of the Thatcherite agenda continued, including proposals to privatise the post office, the railways and the coal industry, a monetarist emphasis on controlling inflation through the money supply, deregulation, and market testing in Whitehall, all of which possessed identifiable Thatcherite stamps. But there was also sniping from the right wing of the Conservative Party over tax rises and Europe. Most tellingly, John Major emphasised an attachment to the European Community while 'True Thatcherites' followed the 'no such thing as Europe' line, leading Major to label the 'Eurosceptics' – as they became known – 'Bastards' in an off-the-record briefing to the press. Four factors help to explain this confusion, according to Allmendinger and Tewdwr-Jones (1997b), and the forces pulling both away from the Thatcher legacy and back towards it:

- *Conciliation rather than confrontation.* Mrs Thatcher was able to utilise a large parliamentary majority to enforce change, a mandate lacking by the Major governments (Marsh and Rhodes, 1992).
- *The loss of common enemies.* When Mrs Thatcher was elected in 1979 she quickly identified her targets for action (the trade unions, for example); John Major's problems and opponents were not as easily identifiable as Thatcher's had been ten years earlier (Kavanagh, 1994).

- *From economic to social.* Although Mrs Thatcher had said, famously, that there was 'no such thing as society', social problems did rise up the political agenda in the late 1980s and required very different responses to the economic issues that the Thatcher governments had sought to tackle in the early 1980s.
- *External pressure.* The European Union and international money markets had began to influence the direction of policy and constrain the scope for unilateral action by the early 1990s (Kavanagh, 1994).

The Major governments did possess pressures, both pulling away from the Thatcher legacy and pushing for continuation. In opinion polls commissioned by national newspapers there was considerable support by the public for the government to pay more attention to the neglected social aspects. At the same time, there was no obvious inclination (aside from the replacement of the community charge) to roll back the main planks of Thatcherism. On the contrary, there was continued public support for most of the policies pursued during the 1980s, especially law and order, union restraint and privatisation (Kavanagh and Seldon, 1994).

All of the above factors clouded the ideological direction of government after 1990, mainly because it was far more difficult to identify major policy differences between the two leading political parties than it had been in the 1980s. In terms of policy Kavanagh and Seldon (1994) conclude that, on the whole, there was a continuation of Thatcherism under John Major, although with the important caveat of the way he put his own stamp on policy approaches. Major insisted after his election that there would be no such thing as 'Majorism'; the prospect of a distinctive ideological approach to government and policy agendas was, therefore, immediately dismissed. In its place, the period 1990 to 1997 witnessed a disparate collection of themes that Major himself espoused towards government. He did suggest in a speech in the June following his election that there lay a prospect of a 'quiet revolution' in government policy (*The Times*, 28 June 1991, quoted in Campbell, 1994: 795), a particularly distinctive phrase used by Edward Heath (Thatcher's predecessor as Conservative Party leader) in 1970. But this did not materialise itself into any grand ideological goal or policy direction, with Major himself recognising that his position had rested on Thatcher both for his election and during his term of office; divorcing himself from that legacy was therefore going to be extremely problematic (Major, 1999). The 'vision thing', the concept Major sought in placing a distinctive stamp on his administration, appeared to be absent. Calls by the premier at party political conferences for 'a classless society' and for 'a nation at ease with itself' seemed to stray from Thatcherite ideology since they display a primary concern for social welfare and community above a primacy for the market. But, for one reason or another, neither phrase produced any distinctive policy approaches divergent to Thatcherism. The Conservative slogans coined by Major, 'Back to Basics' and 'The Feelgood Factor', attracted criticism and were ridiculed in the media.

CONCLUSIONS

This chapter has shown that the libertarian or New Right ideology developed in the 1980s was continuing as a government ideology in the 1990s, albeit in a different way. It is possible to identify significant differences between Margaret Thatcher and John Major in their styles of leadership. What is the case is that the ideological direction provided by Thatcherism was too strong for Major to either resist it influencing government policy or else he was unable to resist the momentum within his own party for the Thatcherite success, and (by implication) ideology, to continue. The differences between Thatcher and Major towards policy and government can essentially be brought down to a complex number of factors that build on Thatcher's style and ideology. These include personality factors; structural, economic and social changes; pan-European pressure; ministerial accountability and electoral (un)popularity. What we witnessed after Margaret Thatcher's departure as Prime Minister was a shift towards centrally dictated policy concerns but the retention of market forces.

The term 'New Right' could be used to signal an attitude or frame of mind. But the actual approach of the two New Right prime ministers between 1979 and 1997 differ and these differences are important. It is all too easy to group Thatcher and Major together and label them under a banner that implies market primacy over state provision. Sensitive analysis of style and ideology of the two administrations indicate not so much an anti-government or public sector ethos, but rather a subtle reorientation of policy-making and government. The subtlety and dynamics of the market/state relationship require a research agenda that recognises the different ideological approaches that inform policy development. John Major may have lacked the 'vision thing' that so characterised his predecessor's term of office, but his government did introduce a redefined Thatcherite style of ideology that attempted a more balanced approach to government and policy-making. The impact that these changes had on the planning polity, and on the town and country planning system in particular, is discussed in Chapter 5.

CHAPTER 4

THE POLITICS OF PLANNING POLICY: the Blair era

INTRODUCTION

'New Labour's' election to the UK government in May 1997 promised the start of a new era in politics. A promise to modernise the institutions of Britain, associated with the objective of fostering social justice and community inclusion with concern for the market, has created a new approach to government. Tony Blair, the Prime Minister, was viewed as the embodiment of vision and change, as the government started to amend 18 years of Conservative policies structurally, constitutionally, and sectorally. From the outset, given the widespread reforms to the Labour Party itself, it was uncertain about how and the extent to which New Labour would be different to its Conservative predecessor.

As far as attitudes towards the British planning system were concerned, New Labour attitudes were remarkably silent on the prospect of reform. For a process that, procedurally, had changed very little in format and style since its statutory inception in the 1940s one would have thought that this institutional process was an obvious candidate for Blairite 'modernisation'. But New Labour possessed very few ideas to amend planning while in political opposition between 1979 and 1997. Initial changes to planning appeared either to be piecemeal or else focus on the regional agenda, and it has only been in the Blair government's second term of office that more deep-rooted changes have been earmarked. These impacts on planning suggest continuation rather than radical overhaul, but this is a topical subject.

This chapter assesses the legacy for New Labour in the fields of planning and environmental policy left by the outgoing New Right Major government, and additionally attempts to identify the political ideological ethos and history of policy development behind changes to planning occurring after 1997. It outlines the major policy amendments announced to date and offers a perspective on the development of the planning polity under a New Labour administration since 1997.

AN OVERVIEW OF NEW LABOUR

The scale of the Labour Party's parliamentary victory in the British General Election on 1 May 1997, and what appeared to be the widespread sense of relief amongst the general public that accompanied it, brought an end to the increasingly shambolic government of John Major. The collapse of the financial markets in 1992,

growing Euroscepticism within the Conservative Party, a weak parliamentary majority and leadership, sleaze, and political in-fighting, had contributed to the party's
unpopularity. The contrast with the reborn, confident, well-organised, and media-
aware Labour Party machinery could not have been greater. Despite varied views
within Labour on both the left and right wings of the party, the country put its confidence in a political party that appeared united under the leadership of Tony Blair
with the offer of a fresh start of new ideas, policies and confidence. Within days of
taking office, New Labour announced that the Bank of England would be made
independent, there would be a ban on landmines, and council house receipts
would be released. Within a few months of election, referenda on devolution for
Scotland and Wales were held, a windfall tax from the recently privatised utility
companies was included in the Chancellor's Budget, there was a promise to
reform the House of Lords, and 'hit squads' for failing schools were established.
Within a year, legislation was introduced to provide a minimum wage and an
independent foods standards agency, a national childcare strategy, and a Freedom
of Information Act. We were, in the new Prime Minister's words, to work towards 'a
new and confident land of opportunity in a new and changing world' (Blair, 1996:
34).

The pace and extent of change within that initial year in office for Labour
seemed to underline the end of an era (Allmendinger and Tewdwr-Jones, 2000a).
For 18 years Britain had witnessed four governments of the New Right, combining
economic liberalism and social authoritarianism. The New Right in British politics
did possess some common ground on political and ideological objectives. Gamble
(1988) sums up these ends as involving a freer, more competitive, open economy
and a more repressive, authoritarian state. What had changed significantly over
that period were the means to achieve those objectives.

Allmendinger and Tewdwr-Jones (2000a) identify three main reasons for this
change. First, the different styles of the New Right leaders (Thatcher and Major)
had naturally placed different emphases on different policy objectives. Second,
given the long period in office, many of the problems that had been identified in the
early 1980s had been tackled in earlier New Right administrations (for example, the
power of the trade unions and state ownership of industry). Finally, we can also
witness policy tensions within the New Right itself. The unique combination of
liberal and authoritarian tenets proved both a strength in uniting the disparate
wings of the Conservative Party and a weakness in formulating detailed policy pre-
scriptions. In the latter 1980s, for example, this was illustrated by tensions
between market-orientated policies and the need to account for an increasingly
environmentally aware electorate. More fundamentally, there were tensions
between the party in government and its traditional rural support over the role of
planning and development, and these tensions had important implications for the

shape and trajectory of town and country planning policy after 1990. These tensions led to shifts in policy that redefined the role of the planning system as being
a tool of rural preservation masquerading in discourses on sustainability and
environmental protection.

As Chapters 1 and 2 indicated, New Labour had inherited a planning system
very different from that existing in 1979. But the Labour Party itself had undergone
something of a radical overhaul over the same period. Among the many changes in
direction witnessed in the 1990s under three Labour leaders – Neil Kinnock, John
Smith and Tony Blair – to make the party more appealing to the electorate, Labour
had abandoned the concept of national ownership in Clause IV of its constitution,
scrapped Keynesian demand management and embraced (the more New Right
ethos of) monetarism, and reversed its hostility towards the European Community
(unlike the Conservative Party, that had torn itself apart over the issue). But, like the
Conservatives, New Labour also possessed inherent tensions in some policy areas.
Robin Cook, Labour's Foreign Secretary between 1997 and 2001, had illustrated
one of these tensions (a primacy of economic growth over environmental protection)
after the 1983 General Election, remarking 'Labour's record on ecological issues is
wretched' (quoted in Anderson and Mann, 1997: 168). Labour was seen traditionally as the party of production and anything that might threaten this was viewed with
suspicion. Trade union interference and other interests in the 1980s blunted
environmental concerns within the party. In order to gain re-election, Labour had to
change and it could no longer afford to be simply the party of production. It had to
appeal to 'Middle England', variously described in the popular media and by Labour
Party media personnel as the 'average man in the street', 'Joe Public', 'Mondeo Man'
and 'Sierra Man', and this was the same constituency that had been so influential in
directing planning policy under John Major in the early 1990s. As a result, with New
Labour balancing its own inherent tensions and those it inherited from others, three
questions were posed by Allmendinger and Tewdwr-Jones (2000a) in their early
review of the trajectory of planning issues after 1997:

- What would be the direction and influence of New Labour upon the environ-
  ment and planning?
- How would the approach differ from the trajectory of planning under the
  Major governments?
- What lessons could be learned for planning from the experience of how it
  was treated by the New Right governments of the 1980s and 1990s?

In assessing these questions, Allmendinger and Tewdwr-Jones (2000a) examined
the development of Labour Party policy towards the environment and planning
during the 1980s and 1990s. They then assessed a number of policies, decisions
and consequences that emerged during Labour's first term in office between 1997

and 2001, their indications and implications. This discussion is repeated here, but with a new section explaining the development of policy after 2001.

New Labour, the Socialist Tradition and the 'Third Way'

By the time of its election in 1997, New Labour had transformed itself from an 'Old Labour' party into 'New Labour', a party that now believed in a 'third way' between market-led policies and state governance, intending to break away from established debates and dualisms (Tiesdell and Allmendinger, 2001). Old Labour had been viewed as politically unelectable but, more fundamentally, also overly concerned with the distribution of wealth, too preoccupied with rights, and too static in policy development. The 'third way', by contrast, required new policies and political approaches that recognised the impact of globalisation and other changes to contemporary social and economic circumstances on governance, and a concern with responsibilities, strong communities, and economic prudence (Driver and Martell, 1998, 2000). As Blair has remarked: 'just as economic and social change were critical to sweeping the Right to power, so they were critical of its undoing. The challenge for the Third Way is to engage fully with the implications of that change' (Blair, 1996: 6–7).

Driver and Martell (2000) suggest that for New Labour this involves:

- promoting wealth creation and social justice;
- promoting the market and community;
- embracing private enterprise, but not in favour of the market necessarily;
- endorsing a role for the state but not a reliance on governments as direct service providers; and
- concentrating on community rather than individuals in society (highlighted in Tiesdell and Allmendinger, 2001).

The third way necessitates a pluralistic way of looking at emerging social and political orientations beyond mere 'left' and 'right' of politics before the latter 1990s (Blundell and Gosschalk, 1997; Giddens, 1998). The practical implications of this approach has been criticised as both confusing and overly concerned with style (see, for example, Jacques and Hall, 1997; Leadbetter, 1998) and lacking a dominant ideological thought or 'big thinker' (Harris, 1998). Giddens (1998) has been most closely associated with the articulation of New Labour's third way (Tiesdell and Allmendinger, 2001).

There has been some sniping from those within New Labour, particularly on the left, who accuse the leadership of being 'crypto Conservative' (Jacques and

Hall, 1997), and there remain widespread accusations concerning image or soundbite politics, the role of 'spin doctors' and opinion polls/forums in policy formulation (Rawnsley, 2000). Part of the reason for this is the difficulty in pinning down the politics and approach of Tony Blair and New Labour in office (Allmendinger and Tewdwr-Jones, 2000a). The problem is that, academically and practically, neither fit in to any convenient category of left or right; some have classified New Labour as pure 'pluralist politics' (Marquand, 1996), others have described it as traditional Christian socialism or 'individualism' (Perryman, 1996), 'revisionism' (Jones, 1997) or 'indistinguishable from Conservatism' (Jacques and Hall, 1997). Tony Blair has attempted to define his approach describing it as 'practical', not theoretical (Blair, 1996: ix) and seeing his mission as returning Labour to its traditional values (1996: xii). This suggests that New Labour do not belong to any established school of thought and therefore trying to fit the party into the old landscape of left and right is both pointless and fruitless. However, this is not to say that we cannot identify distinctive philosophical and political approaches of the government. Three overall themes, identified by Allmendinger and Tewdwr-Jones (2000a), help identify New Labour: their attitude towards the state, society/individuals, and the market.

THE STATE
Blair's state has far more in common with the Gaitskell/Crosland revisionism of the 1950s than the Alternative Economic Strategy of Michael Foot in the early 1980s. But Blair goes further than the benevolent Keynesianism of democratic socialism. The state under New Labour is seen in terms of enabling and enforcing. The concepts of community and individualism are central to the ethical 'social-ism' of Tony Blair. Individuals should be given freedom and opportunity, but also the responsibilities that go with them such as upholding the law and (more distinctively) the need to help each other out: 'Compassion with a hard edge' as he termed it at the 1997 Labour Party conference. The state therefore co-ordinates action only when individuals cannot or will not. The second role of enforcing or social justice comes into play when the responsibilities or rights are infringed. The New Labour view of the state therefore differs from the liberal and authoritarian perspectives of the New Right. The state becomes more than a mere setter and arbiter of rules for a free market to operate within.

SOCIETY/INDIVIDUALS
Blair has said that his brand of socialism could best be described as ethical in that

> individuals are interdependent, that they owe duties to one another as well as
> themselves, that the good society backs up the efforts of the individuals within

it, and that common humanity demands that everyone be given a platform on
which to stand.

(Blair, 1996: 16)

There is almost a symbiotic relationship here. Gone is the 'no such thing as
society, just individuals' line of Margaret Thatcher to be replaced by a more coherent and collective vision of individuals and society – a middle road between the
atomistic New Right view and the collective old socialist view. But another
perspective is the community building role given to the state. The state is to act to
enable community building and wider democratic involvement, thereby decentralising rather than centralising power.

THE ECONOMY

To the liberal tenet of the New Right, the economy or the market was the ends.
Blair tempers this: 'you can combine ambition with compassion, success with
social justice' (Blair, 1996: 107). And further states:

> I reject the rampant *laissez-faire* of those who believe government has no role in
> a productive economy; and I reject too, as out of date and impractical, the re-
> creation or importation of a model of the corporate state popular a generation
> ago.

(Blair, 1996: 109)

Blair considers that the market economy is in the public interest, but it is not the
public interest, only a means of achieving other ends including freedom and
opportunity. As a consequence, Labour has embraced liberalism and, in making the
Bank of England independent, the Chancellor of the Exchequer won plaudits from
the right-wing Adam Smith Institute but less praise from his own party for keeping
– in the first three years of the Labour government – to the Conservative government's spending limits. Although mechanisms of liberalism associated with the
New Right, such as control of inflation through the money supply, have been
present, there are nevertheless some important distinctions between the New
Right and New Labour. While the New Right sought to dismantle barriers to
market mechanisms such as trade union law and price control, New Labour believe
in a positive role for government in aiding the market through provision of an edu-
cated workforce, basic minimum social conditions and a minimum wage.

On the whole, therefore, Tony Blair considers New Labour to be a combination of
fixed and flexible: 'We need neither the politics of the old Left nor the new Right
but a new left-of-centre agenda for the future – one that breaks new ground, that
does not put one set of dogmas in place of another' (Blair, 1996: 31).

Certain themes reveal similarities as well as differences in the approach of New Right and New Labour but, as far as planning is concerned, the two main differences that underlie policy approaches are the community/democracy and the social justice/social inclusion emphases. But how have these manifested themselves in policy?

NEW LABOUR AND ENVIRONMENTAL POLICY PRIOR TO 1997

Labour's approach to the environment since the 1970s could be best described as eclectic (Allmendinger and Tewdwr-Jones, 2000a). It is doubtful whether Labour could ever have been described as the natural party of the environment when in opposition, and it is perhaps more accurate to suggest that it has been dragged towards a greater environmental sensitivity from outside the party by public demands in addition to those small pockets of green pressure groups within the party. The problem for Labour, as with the New Right in the 1980s, lies in the tensions inherent within the party between proponents of economic growth and environmental protection. The trade unions and constituency Labour MPs have traditionally been antagonistic towards the environment and its protection, fearing that it may threaten economic growth. However, given the reorientation of Labour to appeal to 'Middle England', greater regard had to be shown towards conservation and environmental protection issues. Labour has had to 'walk the tightrope between a suspicious and sceptical tradition within the party and the need to maintain the support of a pro-environmental protection constituency outwith it' (Allmendinger and Tewdwr-Jones, 2000a: 1388).

Labour's historical perspective could be summed up by one of its most influential thinkers, Tony Crosland, who in 1971 denounced the 'elitist, protectionist and anti-growth view of the environment by those who want to kick down the ladder behind them' (cited in Anderson and Mann, 1997: 166). This genre of thinking dominated party policy until the early 1980s. Following this period, with the establishment of groups such as the Socialist Environmental Resources Association and experimental policies of several local authorities, including South Yorkshire and Greater London, environmental policies began to infuse Labour thinking.

In 1986, in a move designed to exploit the public's growing interest in green issues, the party published its first statement on the environment, including proposals for the establishment of a Ministry of Environmental Protection. The then Labour leader, Neil Kinnock, also appointed David Clark to the newly created Shadow Cabinet post of Minister of Environmental Protection. Although this marked a watershed for Labour policy towards environmental matters, it did not appear to last very long. Following trade union disquiet and the loss of the 1987 General Election, Kinnock dropped the Shadow Cabinet post.

The late 1980s witnessed changes at the international and national levels with regards to the need for action on environmental protection. The publication of the Brundtland Commission's report on the environment, Margaret Thatcher's environmental-conversion speech to the Royal Society, and the electoral support for the Green Party in the European elections fuelled a debate in the UK in the years 1988–9. The Conservatives, partly fearful of electoral unpopularity within their own party if they were not seen to be embracing environmental matters, suffered a poor standing in the 1989 European elections against the Green Party, the latter winning 15 per cent of the vote. The unexpected success of the Green Party was a major turning point for Conservative ideology towards green issues, but it was also a significant event for all major political parties, demonstrating the emergence of environmental matters as mainstream items on the political landscape for the first time.

In response to the changed circumstances, Kinnock appointed Jack Cunningham to a reinstated shadow environmental post and this was followed a year later by the publication of the *An Earthly Chance* report which demonstrated how far environmental concerns had affected Labour as the natural party of production. The report proposed using the tax system to encourage change, thereby embracing the market rather than relying on pure intervention and regulation as a means of working towards sustainability. Weary of the problems and tensions within the party, its authors argued that Labour should:

> overcome our traditional image as a "producing" party, apparently giving priority to jobs and pay packets rather than to environmental concerns. We need to recognise that some of our decisions will be unwelcome – at least in the short term – to some of our closest supporters.
>
> (quoted in Anderson and Mann, 1997: 170)

Following the advance of environmental matters onto the political stage in the late 1980s, the early 1990s – by contrast – were dominated by economic recession which replaced green issues on the high political agenda of all main political parties in the run up to the 1992 General Election. The Rio Earth Summit did raise the issue again, however, leading to the publication of Labour's *In Trust For Tomorrow* (ITFT) report setting out their thinking on environmental matters. ITFT contained many proposals, including establishing stronger rural planning controls, environmental employment programmes, a moratorium on new road building, light rapid transit systems for cities, and targets for renewable energy and carbon dioxide emissions. This led Jonathon Porritt, the then Green Party leader and later the Prime Minister's adviser on sustainable development, to describe it as 'genuinely radical stuff '. However, when Tony Blair became leader of Labour in 1994 he seemed ambivalent to environmental concerns and ITFT. In his first Shadow Cabinet reshuffle in the same year, he transferred its main author, Chris Smith, into shadowing the Department for National Heritage, and demoted the shadow environmental protection portfolio to outside the Cabinet while giving the pro-nuclear power MP Jack Cunningham responsibility for energy.

The Blair opposition period of 1994–7 witnessed the ascendancy of the 'spin-doctor' in party politics (Rawnsley, 2000), an attempt by the political party to construct and frame news stories concerning New Labour's political image, renaissance and its manifesto, and influence the media, in the run up to the all-important 1997 General Election. A series of major speeches by Blair and Gordon Brown, Shadow Chancellor of the Exchequer, began at this time with the intention of courting big business and industry to Labour's policies, dubbed the 'prawn cocktail offensive'. Weary of the need to prove itself worthy of managing the economy, shadow ministers began to downplay ITFT's significance on Labour thinking, having calculated it would potentially alienate business. This led to criticism in the media which, in turn, resulted in backtracking by the political leadership.

In a speech to the Royal Society in February 1996, Tony Blair publicly backed ITFT. Calling for a balance between economic growth and environmental concerns, he went on to claim that ITFT:

> was a very important document, for it helped demolish two myths. It argued that environmental protection and social justice could be achieved together, and it stated that high environmental standards could improve rather than damage our competitiveness.

> (Blair, 1996: 227)

Later that year the shadow environmental spokesman was again upgraded to Cabinet status and following some continued criticism of Blair's green credentials, the 1997 election manifesto, 'New Labour: Because Britain Deserves Better', included proposals for an environmental task force, a review of road building and the promotion of energy conservation (Anderson and Mann, 1997: 172).

NEW LABOUR AND PLANNING POLICY PRIOR TO 1997

If the environment had not figured strongly in New Labour thinking in opposition, then planning was its Cinderella (Allmendinger and Tewdwr-Jones, 2000a). Labour's proposals for the town and country planning system prior to the 1997 election were a distant and poor relative to the radical approach towards environmental concerns of ITFT. Like the environment, planning to Labour Party members and party strategists had been associated with either countryside dwellers or a middle-class mechanism to thwart jobs, housing and development. Nevertheless, some themes emerge strongly.

Despite Labour's historic ambivalence towards environmental matters prior to 1997, environmental policy does now influence – although does not dictate – planning policy. Some proposals from 1997, particularly those found in ITFT, were welcomed by environmental campaigners, where concepts of sustainability and sustainable development formed a 'planning ideology' for policy development. But this appeared to extend, rather than amend, the Major government's approach to planning issues, emphasising the balancing act approach expected of policy- and decision-makers in assessing development proposals.

Urban regeneration featured highly and consistently throughout the pre-1997 documents. Criticisms of the property-led New Right approach, as well as of the competitive aspects of the Single Regeneration Budget and City Challenge, were widespread although alternatives to these approaches were not highlighted at the time. Planning would seek a more holistic approach to cities building on and encouraging cultural capital in addition to physical and economic regeneration. The former Labour Shadow Planning Minister, Keith Vaz, who had property interests and later became Europe Minister and a source of investigation into parliamentary propriety when in office, saw town centre managers as the key to helping small towns compete with out-of-town retail developments. It is noteworthy that, throughout this period, there was a tension between the pro-out-of-town Vaz and others in the Shadow Cabinet, particularly the Shadow Environment Secretary Frank Dobson, who opposed further out-of-town development. Vaz dubbed Labour the party of the city centre but simultaneously criticised the then Conservative Environment Secretary John Gummer for restricting further out-of-town development. At this time there was no promise of radical rethinking of urban policy, although the later establishment of the Urban Task Force in 1998 was to herald the promise of change.

Keith Vaz paid close attention to the processes of planning and, in terms not dissimilar to those of the early 1980s Conservative secretaries of state, chastised planners for being too slow and overtly bureaucratic but, again, simultaneously claimed he wanted planners to become the 'superstars' of local government. Speedy and efficient planning policy- and decision-making seemed to be the principal hallmarks of the general attitude towards planning at the time, an issue that had long preoccupied the Conservative ministers in the 1990s and their concern of planning acting as a barrier to economic growth (Tewdwr-Jones and Harris, 1998). Limited third party rights of appeal and general commitments to 'democratise planning' further were proposed (Crow, 1996b), but these were not considered threatening enough to raise serious criticism from property interests.

Indeed, despite a General Election manifesto suggestion in 1997 towards introducing limited third party appeals in planning cases where decisions were taken by local authorities against their own policies contained in development plans (an even weaker proposal from that originally put forward by the Labour Party), the prospect of new legislation introducing such an initiative was quietly abandoned by the Labour government once in office.

Similar to the Major administration, Labour had been dogged by matters concerning facilitating regional economic development while safeguarding and making a commitment towards environmental protection. John Prescott, the Deputy Leader of Labour, in particular, was more than interested in extending the potential of the UK regions to compete for inward investment projects. Taking the successful policies of the Welsh Development Agency and Scottish Enterprise to develop a collaborative governmental approach in attracting foreign direct investment to Wales and Scotland, respectively, through state-provided subsidies and funding, Prescott became interested in establishing similar structures and institutions to enable the English regions to compete on a similar basis for inward investment as Wales and Scotland (Tewdwr-Jones and Phelps, 2000). The perceived unfair playing-field with regard to employment generation was not only related to foreign investment, however. As Member of Parliament for Hull in the East Riding of Yorkshire, Prescott was agitated at the loss of employment and industry from his English constituency to Wales where firms were being attracted by a government agency offering high financial incentives.

Labour's commitment towards employment-creating endeavours and in establishing more democratic structures regionally was viewed as the necessary framework to enable the UK regions and businesses to compete economically in Europe and in the global economy. This would be achieved later by the creation of Regional Development Agencies in England (DETR, 1997) and the possibility of Regional Chambers and elected assemblies (Harding et al., 1999; Roberts and Lloyd, 2000; Webb and Collis, 2000). This approach undoubtedly led the development of Labour policy towards economic development, even though the impact on planning was essentially one of structures and processes, rather than policy reorientation, and there is little in the policy documents that identifies this approach as town and country planning. Nevertheless, there has been concern expressed already regarding the links and compatibility between regional economic strategies and regional planning (Baker et al., 1999; Murdoch and Tewdwr-Jones, 1999; Roberts and Lloyd, 1999).

The manifesto commitments towards the creation of a Scottish Parliament and a Welsh Assembly (Scottish Office, 1997; Welsh Office, 1997), were as much a sign of Labour's enthusiasm to create the appropriate structures for regional economic competitiveness in Europe as a need to democratise the regions with elected government. Scotland, in being promised the prospect of primary legislative powers, would be able to amend the planning system to suit its requirements; Wales, possessing policy-making and secondary legislative powers only, may nevertheless be able to amend planning policy quite distinctly compared to that operating in England. But these issues were not highlighted prominently prior to the 1997 election. Similarly, proposals to create a Mayor for London and elected assembly (DETR, 1998i), together with the new Northern Ireland governance structures emerging from the Northern Ireland peace talks, would also impact upon the planning polity.

New Labour in Office and Changes to the Planning Polity

With government spending pegged at Conservative limits for three years, it was perhaps inevitable that commentators would claim that the new government was a little slow in 'getting moving' on planning and environmental matters (Lock, 1998). The first noticeable move brought about by Labour on day one of the new government in May 1997 nevertheless seemed to indicate that changes to planning and environment were about to be set in place. Tony Blair appointed John Prescott, his party deputy leader, as the new Deputy Prime Minister and as 'Secretary of State for the Environment, Transport and the Regions' to head a combined superministry. On the one hand, the change indicated government priority towards proposed regional policy but also suggested plans to co-ordinate land use planning, environmental policy and transport planning into a sustainable whole. The superministry would also reflect the government's (especially Prescott's) eagerness to foster institutional capacity building on a more formal basis as part of the national and regional planning framework. Within a few months of taking office, a plethora of changes concerning the planning polity framework of town and country planning were announced, including manifesto plans to introduce Regional Development Agencies, a strategic authority and mayor for London, a consultation paper on integrated transport, referenda for a Scottish Parliament and Welsh Assembly, a consultation paper on 'modernising planning' and regional planning guidance, and a sequential test for new housing sites emphasising 'brownfield sites'. Proposals to amend the land use planning system, including the formulation of planning policies and implementation of development control, were absent from the early period in office, although possible changes were mooted in 1998. It would take until Labour's second election victory in 2001 for more radical proposals to be released discussing amendments to the statutory land use planning.

Five years on from their initial election victory it is now possible to gauge reaction, intention and the trajectory of change brought about by the New Labour government. A complete and comprehensive review of New Labour policies and legislative changes after 1997 is impossible within the confines of one chapter of a book, and so the following discussion should be viewed as an overview of the principal changes as they impact upon or change the town and country planning system.

THE IMPLICATIONS FOR THE PLANNING POLITY OF CONSTITUTIONAL REFORM

The electorate's support for devolution in Scotland and Wales in September 1997, together with proposals for an elected mayor for London, set about New Labour's commitment to constitutional reform, enhanced democratic representation, and what might be termed a strategic renaissance at the regional level. The planning functions within Scotland and Wales, and within London and Northern Ireland, have been directly affected by the creation of a Scottish Parliament, a National Assembly for Wales, a democratically elected mayor and elected Greater London Assembly, and a Northern Ireland Assembly. Extended debate on the form and function of the planning system after 1999 in these areas was notably absent from the government consultation papers when they were first released (see, for example, DETR, 1998b; Scottish Office, 1997; Welsh Office, 1997). In particular, the planning relationships between the new agencies and the local planning authorities, and the relationship and separation of national (i.e. Scottish/Welsh/Northern Irish) planning policy from National (UK) planning policy, were unclear (Alden, 2001a; Upton, 2001).

SCOTLAND

Scotland's Parliament would be able to devise and implement its own planning legislation and its own planning policy to set a strategic vision within which the Scottish unitary local authorities can work (Scottish Office, 1997), thereby marking the complete independence of Scottish planning from that of the rest of the UK (Tewdwr-Jones and Lloyd, 1997). This had already commenced to some extent as a consequence of historical legislative and policy separation (Hayton, 1996; Rowan-Robinson, 1997), but the establishment of Home Rule gave the Scots the opportunity to carve out distinctiveness from the rest of the UK that was previously impossible to implement (Tewdwr-Jones, 2001b), an issue which is still regarded as only partially achievable (Allmendinger, 2001b, 2001c) (see Chapter 11).

WALES

The situation in Wales is less certain since the National Assembly for Wales would possess secondary legislative and policy powers, and would rely on Westminster for primary legislation (such as town and country planning) (Welsh Office, 1997). Any new or revised parliamentary legislation relating to planning would therefore apply to both England and Wales, although the drafting and issuing of Planning Policy Guidance to interpret the legislation (that is, the non-statutory component) could vary enormously between the two countries, should a Welsh Assembly determine that the policy responses required in Wales need to be fundamentally 'separate' from the previous national (i.e. English) model (Powell, 2001; Tewdwr-Jones, 2001c). Wales had not been so favourable towards the issue of Home Rule as the Scots, which partly explains the distinction between the Scottish and the Welsh proposals (Tewdwr-Jones and Lloyd, 1997), although some pressure exists within Wales for carving out distinctiveness to a greater degree than hitherto (Tewdwr-Jones, 1997b, 1998b; see Chapter 10).

NORTHERN IRELAND

Devolution for Northern Ireland was bound up indecorously with the progress of the Northern Ireland peace talks in the mid- to late 1990s. The town and country planning system there was always operated on different lines compared to elsewhere in the UK (Shirlow, 2001). Planning as a function of government has been the preserve of the Department of the Environment (Northern Ireland) rather than local authorities. One of the reasons for this was concern over whether the planning system, by promoting and regulating new housing sites, would be used politically by local councils to allocate land on sectarian grounds alone (Neill et al., 1995). The main responsibilities of the Department for Regional Development in Northern Ireland would eventually include:

- strategic planning
- the city vision process
- transportation strategy
- transport policy and support
- ports and airports policy
- roads and water policy
- provision and maintenance of roads
- provision and maintenance of water and sewerage services

Planning strategically and regionally would be the levels over which Northern Ireland would have responsibility for and the proposals, when announced, related to establishing what has been termed a regional development strategy or regional framework for spatial policy (DRDNI, 2000; Berry et al., 2001; McNeill and Gordon, 2001), the use of the term 'regional' deliberately chosen to avoid potential political associations with the use of the alternative word 'national' (Shirlow, 2001).

LONDON

The proposals for London reflected the loss of strategic policy- and decision-making powers within a London-wide authority in 1986 upon the abolition of the Greater London Council and the six metropolitan county councils by the Thatcher government (Flynn *et al.*, 1985). The vacuum caused by the removal of a strategic authority for London was noteworthy and the Labour government wished to rein-state an authority as part of its devolution plans but additionally give Londoners the opportunity to elect a mayor for the first time in the UK for their capital city (DETR, 1998i), a process that is common practice in other major world cities (for example, New York and Barcelona; see McNeill, 2001). Labour believed that planning for Greater London would require a London-wide strategy of one form or another, and this eventually found form in the shape of the 'Spatial Development Strategy', or 'London Plan' as it is more commonly known (see Mayor of London, 2001).

The purpose of the London Plan will be to:

- form the strategic plan setting out an integrated social, economic and environmental framework for the future development of London in the context of the wider South East region and Europe;
- look forward over a 15–20 year period;
- integrate the physical and geographic dimensions of the Mayor's other strategies, including broad locations for change, providing a framework for land use management and development;
- set out proposals for implementing and funding the strategy;
- be the London-wide context within which individual boroughs will set their local planning policies through their Unitary Development Plans;
- be London's response to European guidance on spatial planning (the European Spatial Development Perspective); and
- set the policy framework for the Mayor's involvement in individual major planning decisions in London.

When the draft London Plan is published in 2002, it will provide a detailed formal planning document to be subject to a statutory three-month consultation period. The responses to this consultation (and, in turn, the Mayor's views on the responses) will be considered by a government-appointed panel who will hold an Examination in Public on the draft London Plan. This examination will test the strategy for robustness, effectiveness and consistency with other strategies and government policy, and the panel will decide which issues to investigate and who it will wish to hear on them (Edwards, 2000).

UK PLANNING

With devolution forming a core strategy of the Blair government's proposals, the planning polity has been directly affected. This has led to suggestions that the national planning framework within the UK is becoming fragmented, with a concentration on strategy and spatial policy-making within each of the four countries, in London, and in the English regions, a prospect welcome in some quarters but perhaps not in all. 'National' planning policy will be drafted and implemented differently within the four countries of the UK more thoroughly than hitherto. It is perfectly correct to assert that national policy was heading in this direction in any case, given procedural changes to the planning policy process over the last ten years or so. Scotland had implemented a separate series of National Planning Policy Guidelines (NPPGs) from those Planning Policy Guidance Notes (PPGs) issued by the Department of the Environment for England (Hayton, 1996). The Welsh Office had gone its own way in 1995 following the ideological aversion of the then Secretary of State, John Redwood, against a national planning framework and his refusal to release joint-national policy statements with England between 1993 and 1995 (Tewdwr-Jones, 1997b). Although this ideological position rested upon a belief that policy should be formulated and determined locally without the heavy-hand of central government, the implication of this policy vacuum indirectly resulted in the further fragmentation of national planning policy in Britain. When William Hague, Redwood's replacement as Welsh Secretary, was appointed in 1995 he immediately sanctioned the release of national planning policy guidance to keep pace with that for England, but additionally took the opportunity to issue guidance in a very different format from that for the rest of the country (one document was issued rather than the 25 separate policy documents issued within England).

The fragmentation of planning policy in England, Scotland and Wales had therefore already occurred some two years before Labour had placed the devolution issue (or separation of the policy-making function) before the people of Scotland and Wales and, later, Northern Ireland and London. By devising separate planning policy systems in the three countries prior to 1997, the Conservatives did leave New Labour with a useful legacy to build upon in the creation of distinctive 'English', 'Welsh' and 'Scottish' planning policy based on a realistic identification of the underlying socio-cultural, political, economic and environmental differences within the three countries. The concern now emanating from some quarters is over the lack of an effective national spatial planning framework for the whole of the UK, an issue that is being championed by the Royal Town Planning Institute (see Shaw, 1999; Upton, 2001; Wong, 2001).

THE IMPLICATIONS FOR PLANNING OF EUROPEAN INTEGRATION

As the mid- to late 1990s witnessed the spatial fragmentation of national planning policy in the UK, the European Commission appeared to be heading in the opposite direction. For the last 20 years, the UK has possessed a unique planning system in Europe that rested on strong central government direction (Quinn, 1996; 2000). Other Member States within the EU have lacked this central co-ordinating role, and the European Commission has been particularly eager over the last few years to extend its remit in the field of spatial planning and to fill a vacuum at the Member State level with regard to planning and land use (Alden *et al.*, 2001); the EC possesses no legal mandate over planning matters and has therefore relied on voluntary co-operation on the part of Member States on the issue of spatial planning (Williams, 1996). Local authorities' links to the European Commission, to EU regions and local areas, and to EC funding have been evident for over ten years (Bishop *et al.*, 2000). Recent research has indicated that the national and regional planning policy levels in Britain, however, have neglected the European dimension markedly (Tewdwr-Jones *et al.*, 2000; Tewdwr-Jones and Williams, 2001), possibly as a consequence of the Thatcher and Major governments' attitude towards the European Union. Labour has been committed to enhancing the European dimension of British planning (DETR, 1998h) and this will mark out the government's approach distinctively from its predecessor, although the scale of this change has yet to be realised in practice and could well result in a very different type of planning process in the UK in future from that operating in the 1990s (Tewdwr-Jones, 1999c, 2001a).

On a pan-European scale, the emergence of the European Spatial Development Perspective (ESDP) (CSD, 1999) has been the European planning ministers' attempt to set a framework for the integration of the separate national planning policies of each of the Member States (Faludi, 2000, 2001; R.H. Williams, 2000), a move that was always going to cause problems for the central government in the UK. There were three reasons for this difficulty. First, the political context within which this debate was proceeding in Britain was uncertain, given the ideological position of the Major government towards Europe. Second, Britain – unlike some of her European partners – already possessed a form of national spatial planning perspective in the guise of Planning Policy Guidance notes in England, National Planning Policy Guidelines in Scotland, and Planning Guidance Wales that, combined, formed the national (albeit non-statutory) position on planning and land use (note the narrow remit). Third, the push by New Labour upon gaining office in May 1997 for constitutional reform at the regional level (inclusive of Scotland and Wales) necessitated a simultaneous debate on both the nature and scope of both national and regional planning policy guidance within Britain. Co-ordinating a national spatial development perspective for the whole of the UK in an era of devolution within the country would, therefore, become more problematic (Alden, 2001a; Tewdwr-Jones, 2001a).

As we enter into a period where European interest in spatial planning is increasing with the publication of both the framework documents, the ESDP and

'Europe 2000+' (both of which identify very different administrative boundaries for regional planning across Europe but not on Member State lines; Martin, 1992), the fragmentation of national and regional planning policy within the UK is an even greater prospect. Labour's Planning Minister, Richard Caborn, signed up the UK to the ESDP in June 1997, just a few weeks after taking office, and thereby consolidated government policy towards European planning issues overnight. This will result in an enhanced role for European spatial planning matters in policy agenda-setting simultaneous to a constitutional reform commitment towards regional planning in Scotland, Wales, Northern Ireland and the English regions. The government will need to ensure that the Scottish Parliament, the Welsh Assembly and the Northern Ireland Assembly are permitted to establish their own strategic planning visions, but to what extent the Labour government will continue with a commitment to provide a national planning perspective that is all-inclusive and consistent with any enhanced European Union spatial planning remit remains to be seen (Tewdwr-Jones and Williams, 2001). There seems a likelihood that, by adopting the European Spatial Development Perspective and enhancing the regional planning level in England and separate planning policy for Scotland, Wales, Northern Ireland and London, a national UK planning policy will gradually be watered down.

The prospect is one in which the government will move from a position of ensuring strong central government planning policy guidance and local authority co-ordinated regional planning guidance, to a new process of participating in a European-formulated planning perspective together with stronger strategic spatial planning policies devised by democratic assemblies at the sub-national (UK) level. Regional planning policy in the UK, it seems, may never be the same again.

REGIONAL DEVELOPMENT AGENCIES AND THE REGIONAL RENAISSANCE

The driving force behind changes at the regional level in England has undoubtedly been the Deputy Prime Minister, who wanted to replicate the institutional framework for inward investment success of both the Scottish and Welsh Development Agencies (Tewdwr-Jones and Phelps, 2000; Jones, 2001; MacKinnon and Phelps, 2001). In the consultation paper on setting up RDAs published in 1997, *Building Partnerships for Prosperity* (DETR, 1997), the idea was to establish nine new regional development agencies plus one for London, based on the administrative areas covered by the present government offices for the regions (Roberts and Lloyd, 2000; Webb and Collis, 2000). Termed 'agencies for change' by the Deputy Prime Minister, he set out their task as developing and implementing regional economic strategies in partnership with regional interests such as local authorities, training and enterprise councils, industry, business and voluntary groups (*Hansard*, 3 Dec. 1997, col. 357). The RDAs appeared to dovetail into the proposed Regional Assemblies (White, 2000), although their appointed boards are initially accountable only to the Secretary of State with input from Regional Planning Conferences and the proposed Regional Chambers (Harding et al., 1999; Jones, 2001). Powers are derived from the subsuming of regional responsibilities of the Rural Development Commission and English Partnerships, so that the RDAs are awarded a regional, a rural and an urban policy remit (Deas and Ward, 2000), but they presently possess no formal statutory planning powers.

The RDA proposals were criticised for being too weak (House of Commons Environment, Transport and Regions Select Committee, 1998), causing confusion (Walker, 1998), being another unaccountable quango (Yeo, Hansard, 14 Jan. 1998, col. 443), lacking a social agenda (Lloyd, 1999), failing to link in adequately to regional planning (Baker et al., 1999; Murdoch and Tewdwr-Jones, 1999; Roberts and Lloyd, 1999), and being too urban-orientated (Rural Development Commission, 1997). Whichever of these perspectives one takes, there has been confusion concerning their powers and relationship to other bodies.

Originally, it was intended for the RDAs to possess more powers than they actually ended up with, including some limited planning responsibilities. Concern was expressed at the time about an unelected body assuming planning control (Local Government Association, 1999), since the legislation establishing the agencies gave the Secretary of State the authority to transfer wide-ranging planning powers from local authorities to the RDAs, including development control functions. The then Planning Minister, Richard Caborn, justified the transferral of the powers on the grounds that the agencies should be working in partnership with local authorities, but this caused consternation among some, including the British Urban Regeneration Association (Planning, 3 April 1998).

A second area of concern related to the relationship between the RDAs and other public bodies. It was proposed that the RDAs would work within the context of the regional offices of the DETR (later to become DTLR after 2001), together with the Regional Assemblies and Regional Planning Conferences, and an enhanced role for the development of Regional Planning Guidance (DETR, 1998g). Given the lack of a statutory relationship between the RDAs and these other bodies, commentators were unclear as to how the RDAs would ensure co-ordination and collaboration on strategic planning for regional economic development (Baker et al., 1999; Murdoch and Tewdwr-Jones, 1999; Roberts and Lloyd, 1999). John Prescott, the Deputy Prime Minister, made it clear that RDAs would vary from region to region and that their powers may also change over time (Hansard, 3 Dec. 1998, col. 359). This uncertainty between different agencies of governance ensuring compatibility and collaborative or partnership working seems to have been avoided in Wales and in Scotland where regional economic agencies had worked alongside planning agencies for two decades (Tewdwr-Jones and

Phelps, 2000), and more recently under devolution. Simultaneous to the democratisation of strategic policy-making through the creation of a Welsh Assembly, the government had awarded significantly enhanced powers to the Welsh Development Agency to act as a 'one-stop-shop' for inward investment. This change, which must be seen as a reaction against the enhanced powers awarded to the English regions, clearly demonstrates a determination on central government's part for the Welsh Assembly's role to be clouded in the bidding for regional inward investment projects by the WDA, prompting questions on the relationship between the agency and the democratic assembly (Lovering, 1999).

While RDAs appear to fill a much-needed gap in the strategic policy make-up of England and could co-ordinate the currently fragmented and wasteful duplication of individual local authorities attracting inward investment, they seem to lack accountability and focus (Harding et al., 1999) and have been accused of containing an overt political side in the membership of their boards, some of whom are prominent Labour Party figures (Jones, 2001). The creation of the RDAs has resulted in a plethora of local bodies and regional quangos that occupy a crowded institutionalised space in the regional policy framework, one that seems to have been added to incrementally without strategic debate concerning whether an overhaul or institutional thinning-out is necessary. The number of formal and informal forums that now exist in the regions to co-ordinate strategic policy delivery, each of which possesses a diverse range of representative 'stakeholding' organisations, suggests a greater need for co-ordination. With this thought in mind it was no surprise when central government decided to take on more responsibility for regional co-ordination through the establishment of a Regional Intelligence Unit within the Cabinet Office (Cabinet Office, 2000), a move which could be regarded as a potential threat to circumvent the decentralisation powers recently awarded to the regions.

There has also been concern about the co-ordination across England, Scotland, Wales and Northern Ireland and their economic agencies. The enhanced powers awarded to these different agencies all suggest the possibility of greater inter-regional competition, especially for inward investment purposes, following a number of recent very large regional economic development projects that have been criticised for generating wasteful bidding-up of total incentives packages between sub-national territories (Phelps and Tewdwr-Jones, 2000, 2001). Rather than create a level playing field for the bidding of economic investment projects, the devolution and decentralisation powers may in point of fact create greater competition. Any intervention to control that competition could well result in accusations of central government interference.

MODERNISING PLANNING

Within Labour's first year in office, *Modernising Planning*, a ministerial statement, was issued in January 1998 and discussed the government's views on the current planning system in England; it also contained some suggestions for small-scale improvement. Proposals debated within the statement include calling for the:

*   integration of a greater European dimension into UK planning;
*   more prescriptive central government planning policy on large-scale planning applications and infrastructure projects;
*   speeding-up of public inquiry procedures;
*   greater use of Special Development Orders and parliamentary procedures centrally;
*   widening the 'inclusiveness' stakeholders participating in the preparation of Regional Planning Guidance;
*   speeding-up development plan preparation;
*   use of fiscal incentives to steer development.

The statement represented more of a shopping list without any coherence other than a broad concern with speed and efficiency (echoing the New Right campaigns) and both the centralisation and devolution of policy guidance (Tewdwr-Jones, 1998a).

As a statement that concentrated on the need for greater efficiency in planning procedures, *Modernising Planning* proposed adding a further category to the planning statistics monitoring system introduced under the Conservatives: a new 'improvers' category was intended to give recognition and encouragement to those local planning authorities that had shown a significant and sustained improvement in their development control performance. Once again, the emphasis was clearly on the quantity of decisions and not their quality (Tewdwr-Jones and Harris, 1998), a matter first developed by Conservative ministers in the early 1990s.

In many ways the statement sealed the Labour government's rather passive inheritance of the New Right's planning policy legacy, and although welcomed at the time (Tewdwr-Jones, 1998a; Hull, 2000) there was also some disappointment at the lack of anything radically new or different from a government that had been elected simply because it was different. There was nothing contained in the statement to suggest that there would be a 'big bang' for post-Conservative planning, nor – perhaps surprisingly – suggestions towards creating a role for planning in fostering the government's major push on social exclusion: planning's role was simply to aid the market (Allmendinger and Tewdwr-Jones, 2000a). The RTPI's response to the document seemed to be confused about what was happening. The president at the time, Tony Struthers, commented, 'I am delighted that the

Government recognises the need for strategic decisions to be taken in a regional framework' (RTPI, 1998). The possibility of the government creating a more commodified, reduced and fiscally led planning system on similar lines to that proposed under the Conservatives did not seem to warrant comment.

A year later, in 1999, the government released an updated version of *Modernising Planning* setting out progress on the modest proposals they had put forward a year previously (DETR, 1999). The statement indicated progress on such matters as development plans and development control, but now also included statements on sustainable development, transport, housing, economic competitiveness, and other policy sectors. Some of these had stemmed from the original statement, but many had also emerged quite independently during the previous 15 months. The most controversial aspect of the January 1998 statement, the introduction of fiscal measures within planning, was passed over quickly within the updated document with a mere two-word reference: 'Under consideration'. This indicated that the government going through a period when political accusations over future taxation plans were being debated more widely. Furthermore, the use of the planning system to promote economic growth, or rather to inhibit economic competitiveness, was also an emerging debate.

The government's apparent ambivalent, even sceptical, view of planning and their lack of urgency or vision for reform to the process was to prove almost fatal in 1998. The debate over new household projections and development in England had been a row brewing under the Conservative administration from the late 1980s (Baker and Wong, 1997). When a number of structure planning authorities began to react against central government's projections, a strange amalgam of interests emerged that simultaneously attacked Labour's policy on planning for housing and precipitated a wider debate on whether the government was overtly urban-minded by failing to adequately ensure protection of rural and countryside interests.

PLANNING FOR THE COMMUNITIES OF THE FUTURE

There can be little doubt that the Labour government were not prepared for the extent of the rural revolt over new household provision in England. At the same time, they could not have predicted the extent of their parliamentary success in the traditionally Conservative-supporting rural areas in the General Election of 1997 that provided the party with a new constituency of shire Members of Parliament. Prior to the 1997 election, the Labour Opposition were deriding the Conservative government's attempts to grapple with the issue of a projected demand for 4.4 million new households in England by 2016, pointing to a clear shortfall if 'brownfield' sites were depended upon. Nick Raynsford, later Labour's Planning and Housing Minister, remarked:

It's a recipe for disaster. There is a serious mismatch between where the brownfield sites are and where the housing demand is. At the rate we are going, we will be one million houses short by 2016 and the Government's *laissez-faire* policies are doing nothing to help.

(Nick Raynsford, Shadow Housing Minister, reported in *Planning*, 13 January 1997: 2)

The message seemed to be that Labour in power would seek a balanced approach between undeveloped ('greenfield') and developed ('brownfield') land and accept the projected figures formulated under the Conservative government (Allmendinger and Tewdwr-Jones, 2000a). After the election, the Labour government seemed to be following this line, illustrated by the Deputy Prime Minister making a number of decisions on structure plan allocations. In August 1997 he released green-belt land for housing development in the West Midlands. In December of the same year he ordered West Sussex County Council to increase their housing land allocations within the structure plan. In January 1998 he made no objection to the release of large amounts of green-belt land for housing development outside both Newcastle upon Tyne and Stevenage.

By this time, events had already started to go against this policy ethos. Pressure was mounting from the rural protectionist lobby, and disgruntled local authorities, bitterly opposed to the prospect of having to find additional housing land in the face of local electoral opposition, began objecting to the scale of development proposed for their areas (Murdoch and Tewdwr-Jones, 1999; Murdoch and Norton, 2001). Furthermore, a more general rural backlash appeared to be growing against what the political opposition termed 'anti-rural' measures, including high increases on fuel duty, a backbench parliamentary bill to ban fox hunting, the government's 'right to roam' in the countryside legislation, and further restrictions on beef farmers following the BSE crisis. An umbrella group, Countryside Alliance, organised a march of 200,000 people on London during 1997 (repeated in 1998) in protest against these perceived countryside threats. The Alliance possessed disparate countryside interests, with many farmers joining the demonstration, coupled with the pro-fox hunting lobby, but it also contained a clear anti-government planning lobby eager to voice their concerns about future housing development.

The government responded to this by promising the creation of a rural ministry (duly delivered in the shape of the Department of Environment, Fisheries and Rural Affairs (DEFRA) from 2001), and increased public expenditure on rural public transport and village schools once Gordon Brown, the Chancellor, had broken free from the previous Conservative public spending limits. In planning, with the government eager to prove that it was not an urban or metropolitan-biased political party (as it was being accused by the rural demonstrators), the protests led to a complete reassessment of the proposed 4.4 million new household projections. The government released a consultation paper, *Planning for the Communities of the Future*, in February 1998 (DETR, 1998f), in an attempt to placate the country-side lobby. Although a great deal of the paper was devoted to justifying the figures and explaining the changing demographics of the UK more generally and the requirement for more housing land, among the suggestions proposed was a sequential test, similar to the planning approach for the assessment of retail appli-cations (DoE, 1996), that required developers to demonstrate that all brownfield sites had been exhausted before putting forward applications to develop greenfield sites. The government was calling for the abandonment of the so-called 'predict and provide' approach to housing allocations (Baker and Wong, 1997) and to replace the scheme with an 'assess and cascade' approach.

The overall suggestion put forward by the government was that, in future, housing growth forecasts would merely be a guide and decisions on county housing provision would be made in the light of other considerations such as the availability of supply. In addition, with evidence of some parallels to the Conservat-ive government's 'local choice' ethos of 1989, greater responsibility would be handed over to local planning authorities through revamped and enhanced Regional Planning Guidance (see also DETR, 1998f). This would allow the deter-mination of housing supply figures to be made locally and, more cynically, to free central government ministers of the development dilemma in much the same way as that proposed by Chris Patten when Secretary of State in the late 1980s (Booth, 1996; Tewdwr-Jones, 1996b). A target of 60 per cent of new housing to be developed on brownfield sites was set to be implemented by 2006, but this figure was to prove problematic. The government simultaneously announced the establishment of an Urban Task Force, chaired by the architect and Labour peer Richard Rogers (Lord Rogers of Riverside). The Task Force revised the figure to 50 per cent, thereby echoing the previous administration's target (Urban Task Force, 1999), but the government was committed to its 60 per cent figure. Finally, the possibility of a greenfield development tax was floated in an attempt to place pressure on the house-building industry to direct development to urban areas (similar to the 'fiscal measures' suggested in the *Modernising Planning* statement).

A further problematic issue for the government in 1999 was the South East Regional Planning Guidance Examination in Public, chaired by Professor Stephen Crow, who had the unenviable task of recommending to the minister the release of further greenfield housing land in the pressurised south-east of England against vociferous countryside, environmental and public opinion. The Crow Report found that south-east England (excluding London) needed 1.1 million new homes by 2016, some 62 per cent more than those proposed by the local authorities (Crow, 1999). SERPLAN, the South East Regional Planning Conference that represents local authorities in south-east England, insisted to the government that no more than 33,400 homes could be built annually without serious damage to the region's environment, quality of life and infrastructure. It stated that planning policy had to focus on a more sustainable development policy. John Prescott, however, insisted that authorities had to meet a target of 43,000 new homes a year, effectively a mid-figure between SERPLAN's low-end target and the Crow Report's high-end projection of 55,000 homes a year.

Prescott unveiled a green paper for housing in the spring of 2000, labelled *Quality and Choice: A Home for All* (DETR, 2000b). In addition to a number of structural changes to the housing market and specific measures for key-sector workers in London, building on proposals put forward in the *Planning for the Communities of the Future* consultation paper, the paper set the previously advocated targets for house-building: 60 per cent of new housing development on brownfield sites and the remaining 40 per cent on greenfield sites. In December 2000 Nick Raynsford, the Housing Minister, released a housing policy statement, *The Way Forward for Housing* (DETR, 2000d) and announced that the government had cut its target to 39,000 new homes a year in south-east England following further discussion with SERPLAN.

It is interesting to note, in passing, that the target for brownfield housing development, the sequential test and the greenfield development tax were all ideas originally envisaged by the Conservatives prior to May 1997. More generally, these changes demonstrate three important points (Allmendinger and Tewdwr-Jones, 2000a). First, it is indicative of how far the Labour Party has developed when the party that was proud to be associated with house-building in the post-war period seems to be reducing expectations of new building. Second, Labour's electoral constituency now clearly extends beyond the urban to the rural, a fact that was picked-up rather late in the day by the government, especially with regard to fox-hunting, the future of farming, the implications of both the BSE crisis and, in 2001, the foot-and-mouth epidemic, and John Prescott's proposals for reducing car journeys.

A NEW DEAL FOR TRANSPORT AND TRANSPORT 2010

Transport was a policy area the Labour government was committed to tackling. Underinvestment in public transport during the previous 18 years had not assisted ongoing problems of congestion, increasing traffic emissions affecting the environment, the poor performance nationally of a privatised railway, and rising levels of traffic and car journeys, all of which are politically contentious issues (Vigar, 2002). The government's response emerged in 1998 in the form of the integrated transport White Paper *A New Deal for Transport* (HM Government, 1998). Among the proposals put forward within this paper, were:

- proposals for local authorities to prepare Local Transport Plans;
- improved provisions for pedestrians and cyclists;
- a priority to public transport;
- establishing pilot charging schemes to fund local transport improvements;
- the introduction of Bus Quality Partnerships and additional support for rural bus services;
- the establishment of a Strategic Rail Authority and ensuring improvements to the privatised railway as in the customers' interests;
- the introduction of a national public transport information system;
- the establishment of a Commission for Integrated Transport to oversee links between land use planning and transport and different modes of transport, and with policies for education, health and economic growth;
- to reduce the need to travel.

At the time of the paper's publication, the press and media – and for that matter the rural vote – concentrated on the last of these points, particularly how it would affect such constituents as countryside dwellers, parents taking their children on the 'school run' for safety reasons, and the costs on car owners. A consortium of road hauliers, road users' organisations, the Countryside Alliance, and others, sought to defeat the government's proposals and to attack John Prescott personally as the minister responsible for the planned policies. The media, only too eager at times to report bad news stories and crises, highlighted the fact that Prescott had use of two official ministerial Jaguar cars in his role as Deputy Prime Minister and Environment and Transport Secretary, and it was only a matter of time before the tabloid press coined a memorable new nickname for Prescott: 'Two Jags'. Embarrassment followed embarrassment: at the Labour Party conference in 1999, Prescott and his wife were filmed by television news crews being chauffeured in his ministerial car a mere 400 metres between their hotel and the conference centre (so as to avoid disturbing Mrs Prescott's hair, according to Labour Party media officials later), prompting anti-government transport campaigners to question whether the minister himself was committed to one of his key policies – reducing the need to travel.

Prescott, who additionally had to justify the government's proposals to privatise air-traffic control and explain the government's position in relation to the ailing railway network, was permanently bruised by the media coverage of transport policies. Prior to the 2001 General Election, Prescott witnessed the removal of most of his transport responsibilities when his deputy, Gus MacDonald, was given responsibility for fronting government policy statements. Prescott retained his role as Deputy Prime Minister after the 2001 election but played no further part in transport policy matters.

Another government transport plan, *Transport 2010: The Ten Year Plan for Transport*, had been published in July 2000 (DETR, 2000e). This sets out the Government's strategy for modernising the transport network to provide an integrated system and covers all modes of transport. It is intended to provide a long-term programme of new investment to deliver the priorities identified in the Integrated Transport White Paper, and aims to commit £180 billion of public and private expenditure over the next ten years. The Local Transport Plans are intended to deliver this commitment. These plans set out a comprehensive integrated transport strategy with consideration of land use planning and reflect environmental, economic and social considerations, and the promotion of social inclusion. Among the programmes intended to be covered for investment are major public transport and road schemes costing over £5 million (for example, integrated improvements to town centre transport systems, new bus corridors, and light rail schemes); integrated transport schemes (for example, measures to improve bus services, and schemes to promote cycling, walking and road safety); and local road maintenance and bridge-strengthening schemes.

BEST VALUE IN PLANNING

As part of the Labour government's commitment to modernise local government, a consultation document was released in July 1998 entitled *Modernising Local Government: In Touch With the People* (DETR, 1998a). At the heart of this paper was a proposal to introduce the concept of 'best value' in the Local Government Act 1999. Best value is intended to concentrate local authorities' minds on service delivery and quality. It was proposed that local authorities would possess a duty to deliver services to clear standards – covering both cost and quality – by the most effective, economic and efficient means available. In carrying out this duty, local authorities would be accountable to local people and have a responsibility to central government in its role as representative of the broader national interest. Local authorities would set the performance standards for all the services for which they are responsible. Under best value local people will be clear about the standards of services which they can expect to receive, and be better able to hold their councils to account for their record in meeting them.

Best value is also intended to help authorities address cross-cutting issues facing citizens and communities, such as community safety or sustainable development, which may be beyond the reach of a single service or service provider. These issues can only be tackled successfully with co-operation between partners and a shared understanding of the outcomes that need to be achieved. The community leadership role proposed for local councils gives them an opportunity to shape the agenda across the board, so that efforts are focused and combined effectively. The government has been of the opinion that one of the most significant causes of failure to achieve a best value service is the lack of consideration of how resources are used in relation to common objectives. Best value is intended to support improved performance measurement when local authority services need to be integrated with those delivered by other public or private agencies and service providers. Planning, and the development control service in particular, would be directly affected by this change (see Thomas and Lo Piccolo, 2000, for an early assessment in relation to race issues within planning).

PLANNING: DELIVERING A FUNDAMENTAL CHANGE

There had been very little about the planning system in the Labour Party's manifesto in 2001 but it was clear by the summer of that year that a changed agenda was evident in government. In 1998, the McKinsey Institute had published a report arguing for the planning system to be deregulated (McKinsey Global Institute, 1998), and highlighted the fact that local authorities were inefficient in delivering planning for business and economic growth in words not too dissimilar from those of Conservative ministers in the mid-1980s. The appointment of Lord Falconer as the new planning minister in June 2001 suggested that the Prime Minister himself had recognised that a problem existed and entrusted changing planning to his friend and colleague.

The government has announced that it intends to reform the town and country planning system by 2002–3 and, with this target in mind, released a Green Paper for consultation in December 2001, entitled *Planning: Delivering a Fundamental Change* (DTLR, 2001b), setting out its proposals. The principal changes outlined include:

- the abolition of structure plans, local plans and unitary development plans;
- the introduction of Local Development Frameworks that contain core policies and more detailed action plans for smaller areas of change, and a Statement of Community Involvement;
- Action Plans would comprise area master plans, neighbourhood or village plans, design statements, and site development briefs;
- enhanced links between local authorities' Community Strategies (already being prepared under the Local Government Act 2000) and land use planning;
- the replacement of Regional Planning Guidance with Regional Spatial Strategies that would be statutory documents, and sub-regional strategies where necessary;
- focusing national planning policy on issues of national and regional interest;
- allowing local authorities to charge for aspects of the pre-application development control service;

- encouraging masterplanning for specific sites;
- increasing community involvement;
- introducing delivery contracts between local planning authorities and developers for large development proposals;
- establishing stronger enforcement powers;
- introducing new Business Planning Zones where planning is deregulated.

The implications for national, regional and local planning policy formulation and implementation will be addressed in Chapter 5. It is worth noting here, however, that these proposals amount to a radical rethink of the town and country planning system. Of particular interest is the abolition of structure plans (and, by implication, most of the planning policy functions over development plan formulation) and restricting national planning policy to issues of national and regional importance. The planning paper, in addition to responding to business interests with deregulation of the system for certain areas (mirroring the Enterprise and Simplified Planning Zone concept introduced by the Conservatives in the 1980s), also expects planning to perform a stronger role in community problems and policy-making, and this is certainly a marked and welcome contrast to the operation of the system over most of the last 30 years. Two separate consultation documents were also released simultaneously, dealing with national infrastructure projects (DTLR, 2001a) and planning gain (DTLR, 2001c). Scotland is already processing its own reform of planning (see Scottish Executive, 2001), and the National Assembly for Wales released its own Green Paper in early 2002.

CONCLUSIONS

Like the Conservatives before them, New Labour have – at times – possessed an ambivalent if not suspicious attitude towards planning. This derives from the government's emphasis on economic growth and its perception (rightly or wrongly) that planning inhibits this. The limited agenda that existed for planning prior to 1 May 1997 concerned providing a far more strategic role for planning through constitutional change, and it is interesting to note that many of the proposed changes during Labour's first parliament of 1997–2001 (household growth projections and an integrated transport strategy, for example) were either by-products of wider changes or thrust upon the government by events.

Similar patterns of reaction can be viewed between Labour and the Conservatives over a desire to transfer planning policy responsibilities – and thus the onus of decision-making – from central government to local district councils. This occurred in the latter 1980s (dubbed 'local choice') and is mirrored by the transfer of responsibility from central government to the regional level in the latter 1990s.

This reaction, that does not necessarily democratise the regions directly but rather provides for more transparency in existing processes, could be termed 'regional choice'. In both cases, the government is attempting to shed a degree of responsibility for taking planning decisions that could potentially alienate a supporting faction of its political party. Ironically, the conflict of interests that Labour is having to contend with in the latter 1990s are the same as those that caused problems for the Conservatives a decade earlier: the development industry and the shire residents, although this latter group has now been strengthened through the concomitant support of the environmental lobby.

Other changes have been driven by all-too-familiar concerns: an overt concern with procedures, speed and efficiency, to the detriment of concern for planning outcomes. Although Labour has now lost its anti-environmental label, to a degree, there still remains a gulf between the rhetoric of environmental protection and planning policy formulation that by its very nature has to reconcile economic development, regional inward investment, commercial and retailing venture, with sustainability agendas. Constitutional reform and regional planning agendas may not be the panacea the government is suggesting, since this level of governance will similarly face difficult choices and face pressures between vested interest groups. Such a regional renaissance will also contribute towards a gradual withering-away of national policy co-ordination and its replacement with fragmentation and regional competition, a process not helped by the most recent proposals to reform national planning policy (DTLR, 2001b) and the divorce of planning, transport and environmental policy-making between three separate central government departments in June 2002. Planning is now housed within the 'Office of the Deputy Prime Minister'. So much for policy integration and coordination.

CHAPTER 5

NATIONAL, REGIONAL AND LOCAL PLANNING POLICY RELATIONSHIPS

INTRODUCTION

Chapters 3 and 4 considered the planning polity from a political ideological and government policy perspective. This chapter, by comparison, assesses the relationships between government tiers from a purely planning policy perspective. It focuses on the relationship between central government planning policy and policy formulated at other tiers.

The provision of national planning guidance from central government to local authorities and property developers to shape urban land use policy and practice has been a feature of the planning system in Britain since the 1940s. This guidance, however, has not been released in any consistent form and has occasionally been subject to criticism by commentators. While the original post-war role of national planning advice was to provide strategic direction (Switzer, 1984), central government has modified its planning remit and has recently utilised its land use obligation to set parameters on detailed planning control and policy matters at the local level. The nature of central government intervention in local land use matters has therefore changed over time. The current form of national advice in England, Scotland and Wales is contained within the series of national planning policy guidance notes: Planning Policy Guidance in England (PPGs); National Planning Policy Guidelines in Scotland (NPPGs); and Planning Policy Wales (PPW). This chapter considers the role and significance of national planning policy in planning practice at the local district authority level of policy-making and determination, particularly in relation to the introduction of recent planning legislation.

The rationale for undertaking this approach is a belief that as the nature of central government involvement in the planning process has changed over time to reflect current concerns (such as the local environmental agenda), so too has the methods employed by the central state to secure consistency, certainty and continuity in planning policy execution. The chapter is structured to reflect these arguments. Following an introduction to central government's role in providing national planning direction, an assessment is made of the changes to statutory planning since 1990. Issues relating to the reorientation of statutory planning between the Major and Blair governments leads us to consider more theoretical questions – in particular, whether the flexible or discretionary nature of planning practice in Britain has been fundamentally shifted as a result of the governments' quest for certainty. Since certainty formed the underlying tenet to statutory changes to the planning system after 1990 and found policy expression through national planning guidance, British planning could now be situated at the juncture of an unhappy ideological conflict between the discretionary nature of British planning (enshrined in professionalism and reflected in each-case-on-its-merits planning control) and the more certain, less pragmatic forms of statutory planning (follow-the-plan planning control operated after 1992). Greater regulatory controls exercised by central government over local government functions during the 1990s through legislation and national guidance documents have resulted in uncertainty within the planning profession. National guidance has formed a linchpin in bringing about this conflict.

The chapter therefore considers the two opposing ideological components of the statutory planning policy process now existing. Particular attention will be paid to assessing whether central government planning legislation and guidance has enhanced or ameliorated the distinction between the prescribed ('this is what should be done', reflecting rule of law ideology) and the pragmatic ('this is what could be done'). The chapter goes on to suggest that the increase in central government guidance to local planning authorities, coupled with the legislative requirements of the Planning and Compensation Act 1991, has led to an ideological conflict in the operation of statutory planning that involves issues related to administrative law, professionalism, and flexibility and certainty. Finally, the chapter will be drawn towards some conclusions about the extent and direction of change and what factors, if any, have influenced this. The discussion ends by utilising the theoretical arguments to address practical planning policy issues.

CENTRAL GOVERNMENT'S ROLE IN PROVIDING CONSISTENCY AND DIRECTION

The British land use planning process has changed very little since its statutory inception in the 1940s. Planning is primarily restricted to considering land use issues through the management and co-ordination of policy at various levels of administration by a variety of agencies and actors. Implicit to the operation of the land use planning system is a national co-ordinating level, where the social, economic and environmental needs of spatial areas can be addressed in an integrated way. Although this suggests that planning can only be operated effectively when land use issues are considered strategically (Bruton and Nicholson, 1985; Rowan-Robinson et al., 1987; Breheny, 1991), the provision of a national element of strategic co-ordination by the central state is an essential ingredient in physical development. As Diamond (1979) has remarked, strategic planning sets out a frame of reference for the organisation of planning at the lower tiers of administration. The planning process is managed and implemented by national and local tiers of government and is hierarchical in policy framework (Tewdwr-Jones, 1994a). Although there has never been a national physical plan in England, Scotland and Wales, central government has always provided a clear approach in determining and promoting planning policy to be operated across the various spatial areas. Rather than developing a statutory national physical plan, the government has preferred to rely on a system of discretion rather than prescription, a process where central government sets down the legal framework and broad policy for local government to interpret.

When Britain was in the throes of the Second World War and the country was concerned about how it should commence rebuilding itself, physically, economically and socially, central government was charged with taking a lead in providing strong national direction and co-ordination. Indeed, it was during this period that planning was formally given a role in bringing about physical change, a response to the recognition of starting anew and that those changes could only be co-ordinated by the state. One of the first pieces of planning-related legislation that emerged in Britain to secure this national planning lead was the Minister of Town and Country Planning Act 1943. Under the provisions of this Act, a central government minister was charged with overall responsibility for development, environmental protection and physical rebuilding, and these essentially became the core building blocks upon which statutory land use planning was based. The minister was charged with the duty of 'securing consistency and continuity in the framing and execution of a national policy with respect to the use and development of land throughout England and Wales' (Section 1). The role of central government in overseeing a national policy approach to physical planning, and to ensure that national policy was implemented by government planning agencies, was therefore placed at the heart of the emerging statutory planning legislation. Whether the framers of this statute intended to extend this duty to detailed local planning matters at this time, in addition to strategic direction, however, is difficult to determine.

The duty on the part of central government for land use planning has been fulfilled by successive planning ministers over the last 60 years. Different ministers, and governments of different political persuasions, have utilised this obligation to define the role of the planning system by a variety of methods, including direct intervention in local planning issues, providing national policy advice and passing planning-related legislation. Although Section 1 of the 1943 Act was repealed in 1970 (when the office of Secretary of State for the Environment was created), the duty of central government in planning has not changed drastically since the postwar period. However, the interpretation of the duty has modified according to how interventionist planning ministers have been when in office. In 1958 Enoch Powell, as planning minister, was questioned on the role of the minister's duty as set out in the 1943 Act, and provided a characteristically terse answer by stating: 'You must regard those words as a piece of flotsam left on the beach by the receding tide of post-war optimism' (quoted in Switzer, 1984: 74).

The exact role of central government in planning has therefore been modified; following the rebuilding of the British economy in the 1950s, there was no need for a minister of the crown to frame national policy on planning since local government agencies (charged with implementing land use planning at the local scale) could co-ordinate and develop future physical land use change by negotiating with developers and the public without the necessity of involving heavy central state intervention. However, as the British economy has ebbed and flowed in the period since, central government has retained its overriding duty to intervene in the land use planning system to achieve both economic recovery and to reflect party political mandates, but not consistently. This explains why there has never been a consistent form of policy documentation to reflect central government's planning agenda.

The various devices utilised by central government ministers to amend or change planning practice have included the introduction of planning-related legislation, the issuing of policy advice (particularly in government White Papers, departmental circulars and guidance notes), providing planning decisions (through central government call-in applications and the appeals process), and through ministerial speeches. This chapter considers one form of central government's legitimate remit in land use planning: the role of national planning policy guidance notes, as amended by recent legislation. The principal form of central government planning advice in England and Wales at the present time is the series of Planning Policy Guidance Notes (PPGs). This chapter considers the role of PPGs in the British planning process within the context of the distinction between strategic national direction in policy formulation and detailed local planning policy preparation. Although discussion will be restricted to the 1980s and 1990s, the present form of central government planning policy will be analysed in the context of the changing role of national planning strategies and the changing nature of central government's planning mandate. Particular attention will be devoted to assessing the relationship between central government planning policy and locally prepared development plans under the current principal legislation, the 1990 Town and Country Planning Act as amended by the 1991 Planning and Compensation Act.

NATIONAL PLANNING POLICY AS A FUNCTION OF CENTRAL GOVERNMENT

Central government national planning statements in England, Scotland and Wales currently manifest themselves in circulars, and other types of statements peculiar to each country. Within England there are Planning Policy Guidance Notes (PPGs), Minerals Planning Guidance Notes (MPGs), and Development Control Policy Notes (DCPNs). Ministerial speeches and statements may also be regarded as material considerations on certain occasions, particularly where they are accompanied by a departmental press release.

In Scotland, a series of separate National Planning Guidelines (NPGs) – additional to Scottish Office circulars – have been used to form national strategic direction in land use matters since 1974. Their origin stems from a select committee on land resource use in Scotland (House of Commons Select Committee on Scottish Affairs, 1972; referred to by Rowan-Robinson *et al.* (1987: 371)), and they have been widely applauded for their strategic direction and coverage (Lyddon, 1985; Rowan-Robinson and Lloyd, 1991; Raemakers *et al.*, 1995; Lloyd, 1996). Although they have been modified over the last 20 years, from 1991 onwards they have been referred to in Scotland as National Planning Policy Guidelines which Hayton (1996) has suggested is a retrogressive move towards the English and Welsh PPG model. A series of Planning Advice Notes (PANs) supplements the NPPGs.

In Wales, central government planning guidance has been released jointly with the Department of the Environment-formulated English guidance, although there have been some exceptions, notably Circular 30/86 on housing for senior management (Welsh Office, 1986) and Circular 53/88 on the Welsh language (Welsh Office, 1988b). For the most part, circulars and Planning Policy Guidance Notes have been released under the names of both the Secretaries of State for the Environment and for Wales. However, following the appointment of John Redwood as Welsh Secretary in 1993, no further planning guidance was released in Wales until 1996, when all existing PPGs were replaced by just two documents: Planning Guidance Wales *Planning Policy* and *Unitary Development Plans* (Welsh Office, 1996a, 1996b) (see Chapter 9 for further discussion). After 1999, the documents were renamed *Planning Policy Wales* and are supplemented by a series of Technical Advice Notes (TANs) focusing on more detailed issues.

Central government has possessed an overriding duty to secure consistency and continuity in the planning policy process since 1943 and has utilised circulars and planning policy guidance to reflect changing political and administrative needs. These changes have dictated the form and extent of central government intervention in local planning policy concerns over the last 50 years. Given the timescale involved, and as a reflection of political realities, this section reviews central government's planning role in and over the activities of local government in three phases: 1968 to 1987, when circulars were used to provide guidance on the two-tier structure and local plan system; 1988 to 1991, the first period of Planning Policy Guidance Notes; and 1992 to 2002, the period that marked the introduction of the plan-led Planning and Compensation Act 1991 and the statutory recognition of the environmental agenda and its subsequent integration into the second period of Planning Policy Guidance Notes. The period since 1997 has seen the situation amended slightly by devolution and decentralisation across Britain, and the revision of some existing documents.

1968 TO 1987

Until 1988, central government planning statements were released in England and Wales through a series of departmental circulars, concentrating on a mixture of policy, procedural and legal issues. During the 1970s and 1980s, central government utilised circulars to inform local authorities of the appropriate contents of structure and local plans and in the use of statutory plans for development control purposes.

Both Circular 55/77 *Memorandum on Structure and Local Plans* (DoE, 1977) and Circular LP1/78 *The Form and Content of Local Plans* (DoE, 1978) were issued as clear guidance to local planning authorities in their detailed operation of planning policy, and further warns that if the circulars are not followed central government would have the right to overturn refusals and conditions for planning permission on appeal. Healey (1983) suggests that the general tone is directive rather than advisory and sets down an element of firmness on local planning authority procedures. While this was recognised as a potential threat to the autonomy of local government, Healey believes that the firmness by central government was undermined by two factors. First, central government guidance had also stated that the planning legislation was to permit a 'flexible approach to cater for differing local needs, circumstances and resources' (DoE, 1978: para. 3). If local authorities followed this guidance, flexibility permitted an alternative line to be taken against central government guidance if local circumstances justified it. Second, if local authorities did act against the advice of central government, there was some uncertainty as to whether the government would intervene in local policy-making. Although Healey states that the formal powers of central government intervention are treated as a last resort (DoE, 1977: para. 3.23), intervention in local plans was increasing in the late 1970s and early 1980s.

Following the election of the Conservative government in 1979, civil servants started to draft the legislation that subsequently became the Local Government, Planning and Land Act 1980. Immediately, the government released a White Paper entitled *Central Government Controls Over Local Authorities* (HM Government,

1979) that emphasised their commitment to reducing central government control over local planning matters to permit local authorities more 'local discretion and autonomy' and 'better value for money' (ibid., para. 11). The White Paper proposed curbing central controls over certain areas and revising administratively more complex areas of the legislation. The principal proposals were to repeal:

1   Power to require preparation or amendment of development plan schemes and to prescribe their contents and procedures.
2   Specification of content of local plans by direction.
3   Prescription of availability for inspectors of local plans other than at a local office.
4   Prescription of content of public participation-statement.
5   The requirement that the adoption of a local plan must be delayed until the structure plan is approved (ibid., paras. 8–9).

Healey (1983) remarks that the proposals mark a retreat from the earlier increase in central government concern with content and a reduction in interference in local authority discretion, although McAuslan (1981) states that this 'bonfire of controls' constituted quite the opposite of an increase in local discretion and autonomy. If anything, the proposals of the White Paper and the subsequent legislation amended central government intervention in local planning, as ministers became preoccupied with speeding-up plan-making and releasing a greater amount of land for development. Healey (1983) suggests that it seems likely that ministers would have wished to abolish structure and local plans altogether but were persuaded by civil servants to retain them with regard for the need for 'consistency and continuity' in planning policy.

The 1980 Act weakened the position of structure plans in the planning system since district councils could adopt their local plans with or without the approval of county councils. While this may have expedited cumbersome administrative procedures, the weakening of the strategic policy-making element also weakened central government's position since the neat, concise 'top-down' nature of planning policy was interrupted. Following the enactment of the legislation, it became apparent that if central government was going to retain a strategic interest in securing consistency and continuity in planning policy, and if structure plans were now rather weak planning tools, greater attention would have to be focused by central government on monitoring the content of local planning documents. This monitoring exercise was actually concerned with ensuring that local plans adequately reflected the interests of property developers, were up to date and responsive to the market, operated efficiently, and contained policies that were solely related to land use. Healey concisely provides an overview of the position in the early to mid-1980s:

> Central government, at both political and administrative level, thus commonly portrays local authorities in the planning field as 'inefficient'. No doubt they sometimes are. However, this position ignores the possibility that local authorities may have different political priorities from those of central government when using the tool of a local plan.
>
> (Healey, 1983: 80)

In the mid-1980s a committee of inquiry appointed by the Nuffield Foundation to consider the land use planning process in Britain highlighted 'a need for concise and consistent statements of national policy where national issues are at stake in questions of land use and development' (Nuffield Foundation, 1986: 160–1). The inquiry highlighted the fact that England and Wales did not possess consistent strategic national planning statements, other than in departmental circulars, and the committee was particularly impressed by the series of NPGs produced in Scotland. The aim of national planning statements in England and Wales would be:

- to identify and to define the kinds of development which may raise national issues relevant to land use planning;
- to set out the national aspects of land use which should be taken into account by local planning authorities in their development plans;
- to suggest where there may be a need for interim development control policies in relation to national issues;
- to explain the criteria which form the basis for directions requiring certain planning applications to be notified to the Secretary of State.

The committee called for a clear distinction to be made between the issuing of national policy, as opposed to national guidance. Examples of national statements might involve covering such issues as energy installations, defence installations, transport infrastructure, major manufacturing plant and large new settlements.

The British government also recognised the value of national planning direction in land use planning. In a 1986 Green Paper, *The Future of Development Plans*, the government gave a commitment to continue releasing departmental circulars and ministerial statements 'as an important influence on the formulation of proposals in development plans' (DoE/Welsh Office, 1986: 13). It is interesting to note here a different perception of the role of national planning direction between the government and the Nuffield committee's recommendations. Nuffield (1986) called for strategic direction on planning issues affecting national interests and for the government to state its planning policy objectives clearly, possibly in the spirit of the continuity and consistency remit inherent in the 1943 Minister of Town and Country Planning Act. But the government was more concerned with a monitoring role for national policy advice, where government planning objectives filtered down the government policy hierarchy to the local level. At this time, the government firmly identified a role for national advice in detailed procedural and local policy issues. Academic commentators, too, also called for national strategic planning direction in England and Wales. Bruton and Nicholson (1985), reflecting Diamond's (1979) suggestions, advocated a hierarchy of levels of planning policy 'where the level above constrains the planning of the level below and conversely is itself constrained by the level above' (p. 25), while Rowan-Robinson *et al.* (1987) also recommended the extension of the Scottish model of national planning guidelines to England and Wales.

1988 TO 1991

In January 1988, in response to the calls for national planning statements and as an acknowledgement of the need for national strategic direction in land use planning, the government issued the first in a series of Planning Policy Guidance Notes (PPGs) for England and Wales; Scotland would retain its separate NPG series. The aim of the PPGs would be to 'provide guidance on general and specific aspects of planning policy' and were 'intended to provide concise and practical guidance on planning policies, in clearer and more accessible form than in Departmental circulars, in the earlier series of Development Control Policy Notes (DCPNs) and in other statements' (DoE/Welsh Office, 1988). Nine documents were originally released covering the following issues: General Policy and Principles; Green Belts; Land for Housing; Industrial and Commercial Development and Small Firms; Simplified Planning Zones; Major Retail Development; Rural Enterprise and Development; Telecommunications, and Strategic Guidance for the South East. No justification was made why these topics were selected rather than any other planning matters and no indication was given over what timescale they would apply or be reviewed. The first three documents in a separate 'Minerals Planning Guidance' series were also published at this time. The government stated that these documents would in future provide the principal national policy advice; circulars, although retained, would focus on legislative and procedural matters.

In the White Paper *The Future of Development Plans*, published in January 1989 (HM Government, 1989), the government stated that the first PPG documents had been 'generally welcomed' and would be 'extended to cover other policy matters from time to time' (para. 2.3) (see Table 5.1). From this period, the government viewed the PPG series as a vital component of the planning framework, a strategic system of policy documentation that extended across national, regional, county and local levels. Each of these policy levels, according to the then chief planning adviser at the Department of the Environment, was 'intended to interlock as far as possible to make up a coherent whole' (Wilson, 1990: 85). In addition to the national dimension, the government also advocated the establishment of a Regional Planning Guidance (RPG) series of publications. The purpose of RPGs would be to interpret national planning guidance to provide the framework for the preparation of local authorities' development plans at the local spatial scale. Although RPGs would be released under the name of the Secretary of State for the Environment, they would be prepared jointly by local authorities in each of the regions and would be the subject of monitoring by each of the Department of the Environment/Welsh Office regional offices (see Table 5.2).

The strategic function of national planning advice has therefore been recognised as part of the overriding duty on the part of central government planning ministers. But in addition to providing national strategic direction, PPGs and RPGs could also be useful in providing guidance on local policy concerns to

Table 5.1 National planning policy in England

PPG1	General Policy and Principles (1997)
PPG2	Green Belts (1995)
PPG3	Housing (2000)
PPG4	Industrial and Commercial Development and Small Firms (1992)
PPG5	Simplified Planning Zones (1992)
PPG6	Town Centres and Retail Development (1996)
PPG7	The Countryside – Environmental Quality and Economic and Social Development (1997)
PPG8	Telecommunications (2001)
PPG9	Nature Conservation (1994)
PPG10	Planning and Waste Management (1997)
PPG11	Regional Planning (2000)
PPG12	Development Plans (1999)
PPG13	Transport (1994)
PPG14	Development on Unstable Land (1990)
PPG15	Planning and the Historic Environment (1994)
PPG16	Archaeology and Planning (1990)
PPG17	Sport and Recreation (1991)
PPG18	Enforcing Planning Control (1991)
PPG19	Outdoor Advertisement Control (1992)
PPG20	Coastal Planning (1992)
PPG21	Tourism (1992)
PPG22	Renewable Energy (1993)
PPG23	Planning and Pollution Control (1994)
PPG24	Planning and Noise (1994)
PPG25	Development and Flood Risk (2001)

Source: Department for Transport Local Government and the Regions.
These documents may be downloaded from http://www.planning.odpm.gov.uk/ppg/index.htm

Table 5.2 Regional planning policy in England

RPG1	Northern Region (2001)
RPG3	London (1996)
RPG3A	London–Strategic Views (1991)
RPG3B/9B	Thames (1997)
RPG6	Regional Planning Guidance for East Anglia to 2016 (2000)
RPG8	Regional Planning Guidance for the East Midlands (2002)
RPG9	Regional Planning Guidance for the South East (2001)
RPG10	Regional Planning Guidance for the South West (2001)
RPG11	Regional Planning Guidance for the West Midlands (1998)
RPG12	Regional Planning Guidance for Yorkshire and The Humber (2001)
RPG13	Regional Planning Guidance for the North West (1996)

Documents published since 2000 are replacement drafts to existing notes. All other notes are subject to revision.
These documents may be downloaded from http://www.planning.odpm.gov.uk/rpg/index.htm

achieve a convenient way of monitoring the planning system across various spatial scales and thereby ensure that a high degree of uniformity would be achieved in planning practice across local authority decision-making (Tewdwr-Jones, 1994c). National planning direction can therefore be effective to achieve both strategic overview and local consistency, since it can be used to react to land use problems and to reflect changing political priorities between different governments and ministers, without the necessity to instigate long and complex legislative changes. For example, the 1971 Town and Country Planning Act was implemented over a 20-year period by five separate Conservative and Labour governments, but was supplemented by a series of departmental circulars reflecting policy changes. The role of national planning guidance in England and Wales has thus been described as 'achieving important shifts in planning policy with the least possible fuss' (Nott and Morgan, 1984: 623). The documents offer policy advice in relation to land use planning on different aspects of planning in general terms to a variety of audiences. They are neither statutory nor legally binding on the people or agencies who use them, nor should their wording normally be subject to intense scrutiny by the courts. However, PPGs can take on the form of influential policy directives since their contents affect all planning functions (policy formulation and implementation) operating at every level of planning administration. They are 'the muscle, or sinew, that holds together the skeleton of the planning system' (Chapman, 1995).

Scotland revised its series of national policy statements from 1991 onwards when the NPGs were replaced with National Planning Policy Guidelines (NPPGs). There are currently 19 in the series (see Table 5.3).

Table 5.3 National planning policy in Scotland

NPPG1	The Planning System (2000)
NPPG2	Business and Industry (1993)
NPPG3	Land for Housing (1996)
NPPG4	Land for Mineral Working (1994)
NPPG5	Archaeology and Planning (1994)
NPPG6	Renewable Energy Developments (2000)
NPPG7	Planning and Flooding (1995)
NPPG8	Town Centres and Retailing (1998)
NPPG9	The Provision of Roadside Facilities on Motorways and Other Trunk Roads in Scotland (1996)
NPPG10	Planning and Waste Management (1996)
NPPG11	Sport, Physical Recreation and Open Space (1996)
NPPG12	Skiing Developments (1997)
NPPG13	Coastal Planning (1997)
NPPG14	Natural Heritage (1998)
NPPG15	Rural Development (1999)
NPPG16	Opencast Coal and Related Minerals (2001)
NPPG17	Transport and Planning (1999)
NPPG18	Planning and the Historic Environment (1999)
NPPG19	Radio Telecommunications (2001)

Source: Scottish Executive.

These documents may be downloaded from http://www.scotland.gov.uk/planning

A series of Planning Advice Notes supplements the documents.

1992 TO 2002

In the 14 years since 1988, the government has issued a further 28 PPGs including revising 14 existing documents (see Table 5.1). The vast majority of these revisions reflected the environmental agenda and the government's commitment to the concept of sustainability as outlined in the Environmental Protection Act 1990 and the *This Common Inheritance* paper (HM Government, 1990).

Wales decided to go its own way in 1995 with the preparation of Planning Guidance Wales, consolidating the policy statements across 24 policy guidance notes into just two documents: one covering development plan preparation and the other dealing with policy issues. A separate series of Technical Advice Notes supplemented the two documents. This has meant that where the government has changed its policy on certain substantive disciplines, it has been necessary to revise the whole document rather than focus in on a key policy statement. Devolution to Wales in 1999 resulted in another change with the publication of a replacement policy note, Planning Policy Wales, issued in 1999 and, at the time of writing, the National Assembly for Wales is about to publish a third revision. After 2002 it is proposed to issue Supplemental Policy Statements on certain relevant topics where a policy change is advocated, rather than release a complete revision to Planning Policy Wales (see Table 5.4).

As the product of Conservative governments between 1988 and 1997, the PPGs reflect dominant party political ideology. When Labour was voted to office in 1997, a complete revision of all 22 PPGs was possible. This has not occurred, although certain statements have been revised – including those for housing, transport, and development plans. Three new PPGs have been introduced into the series, however: PPG10 'Planning and Waste Management', PPG11 'Regional Planning', and PPG25 'Development and Flood Risk'.

The current PPG series is viewed, en bloc, as the national planning policy framework in England. The use of these documents in planning practice has rarely been assessed by researchers. Professional officers' attitudes towards central state planning guidance has, however, been generally positive (Insight Social Research, 1989; DoE, 1995; Tewdwr-Jones, 1997c), although certain documents and certain statements within some PPGs have attracted criticism (e.g. House of Commons Welsh Affairs Committee, 1993). PPGs do feature prominently in the planning decision-making processes at a local level (Tewdwr-Jones, 1994b), thus reflecting the extent of influence national statements can have at the local spatial scale.

The government commissioned a research project to consider the effectiveness of Planning Policy Guidance Notes in 1994. The project, undertaken by Land Use Consultants, assessed local planning authorities' attitudes towards the procedural effectiveness of the PPG series as a tool for disseminating policy guidance. They reported in the following year (DoE, 1995), and the overall conclusions of the research found that:

- PPGs had assisted greatly in ensuring a more consistent approach to the formulation of development plan policies and the determination of planning applications and appeals;
- the approach of the documents closely reflect the government's planning policy priorities as they are set out in PPGs;

Table 5.4 National planning policy in Wales

Planning Guidance Wales: Planning Policy (2002)
Planning Guidance Wales: Unitary Development Plans (1996)
Minerals Planning Policy Wales (2000)

These documents may be downloaded from http://www.wales.gov.uk/subiplanning/
A series of Technical Advice Notes supplements the documents.

- PPGs are a remarkably effective means of disseminating national planning policy priorities;
- PPGs have yet to make clear how the planning system can help to secure the objectives of sustainable development;
- there is scope to increase the operational effectiveness of the PPG series.

While the results of this research provide an invaluable assessment of the planning policy process in operation, it is unfortunate that, as a government-sponsored project, no attention was paid to the merit of the PPG series against any other form of national strategic direction. The research was solely concerned with the use of the documents in practice. Since this results in a gap in the literature and assessment, this chapter goes on to provide a brief review of the merit of the PPG series before discussing some detailed research questions.

Although there is no legal duty on the part of local authorities to follow the guidance contained within the documents, the government does possess a policy requirement for local authorities to take national planning advice into account when undertaking policy and decision-making duties. As the first national document, PPG1 'General Policy and Principles', makes clear,

> where such statements indicate the weight that should be given to relevant
> considerations, decision-makers must have proper regard to them. If decision-
> makers elect not to follow relevant statements of the Government's planning
> policy they must give clear and convincing reasons.
>
> (DoE/Welsh Office, 1992b, para. 21)

Central government policy requirement is consequently clear: local planning authorities must follow the statements within PPGs in carrying out their planning duties. If they wish to depart from established government policies they will have to demonstrate comprehensively the locally justified grounds for departure. As a result of this requirement, planning practitioners seem uncertain of the exact status of PPGs in the planning system. For example, on what occasions can local circumstances outweigh national policy? It has been illustrated in research that local planners accept PPGs as statements of government policy, and welcome informed guidance on a variety of substantive areas associated with town and country planning (Insight Social Research, 1989). However, there still appears to be too much room for debate and interpretation of their legal standing. Particular concern has been raised on the cumbersome wording of some of the more recent PPGs (see for example the Welsh Affairs Committee Report and their consideration of 'the personal needs of the applicant', House of Commons Welsh Affairs Committee, 1993, para. 24).

According to the then head of the development plans and policies division of the Department of the Environment, the release of too many PPGs to guide decision-makers would cause 'policy gridlock' (Wakeford, 1993), adding that the ministerial bottom-line for the number of PPGs would be a maximum of 22 (we are already at 25). The nature of topics covered by PPGs during the last ten years has varied between detailed development control policies and more general strategic issues such as transport and retailing. Some topics have been addressed in great detail, however, including those PPGs for telecommunications, archaeology, sport, and noise. It is interesting to note that there are no plans at the present time to release guidance on other matters, despite the changing requirements of developers and the necessary policy response from local planning authorities over time. The government has never provided any justification why particular topics have been covered by PPGs and why other issues do not warrant guidance. Local planning authorities are requesting more guidance on a broad range of topics and these have included disabled access, urban design, urban policy, and economic development. The government is, however, resisting these calls.

On translating PPGs into local plan policies, because of the uncertainty existing over the combination of broad and detailed policies within PPGs, local planning authorities do not know whether to slavishly adhere to the wording of PPGs or merely follow the broad policy. Paragraph 21 of PPG1 stipulates that the government expects PPGs to be followed unless there are very strong grounds to the contrary, and this is resulting in local planning officers considering PPGs' sentiments to be practically mandatory. There is also a belief within practice that if a topic or policy issue is included in a development plan which has not received attention by any current PPG, that policy would be frowned upon by central government (see the judgement in the British law courts in *Regina* v. *Worthing Borough Council* (1983) by MANN J on Secretary of State guidance where he declared that, 'In my judgement it is quite unreal to suppose a local planning authority would do otherwise than accept the opinion as decisive', transcript quoted in *The Times*, 22 November 1983). The weight afforded to government policy statements in development control determination and at appeal is often understated, but has been comprehensively researched over the years (Davies *et al.*, 1986; Tewdwr-Jones, 1994b). Even under the plan-led system, PPGs can frequently override the contents of local development plans as material considerations.

The Welsh Office and its successor the National Assembly for Wales, the regional offices of the Department of the Environment (now ODPM), and the Scottish Office and its successor the Scottish Executive, have all been taking an increasing role in the monitoring of all development plans produced by local authorities since the implementation of the Planning and Compensation Act 1991 (DoE, 1992b). The planning officers within these regional offices scrutinise all plans to ensure consistency with national and regional policies by comparing the plan contents with an administrative checklist of the key policy requirements of each PPG. Where a local planning authority has included a policy which is adverse to this checklist, or has failed to consider a key policy issue, it is the duty of the officer to inform the local planning authority in the government department's response of the policy inconsistencies or conflict. Local planning authorities, wishing to avoid lengthy policy battles with central government over the most contentious issues, are replicating central government policy in their plans with statements that are easily interpretative for any given situation, and are leaving the interpretation task to development control officers or supplementary planning guidance (Jones, 1996).

RECONSTITUTING PLANNING 1: THE 1991 PLANNING AND COMPENSATION ACT

In the late 1980s, central government had introduced a hierarchical policy framework but had additionally committed itself to introduce further planning legislative changes. The Planning and Compensation Act 1991 reinforced the role of the development plan, and thus local authority planning policy following the so-called appeal-led or market approach of the 1980s (Thornley, 1993). The importance of the statutory plan in the town and country planning system of England, Scotland and Wales brought a renewed vigour to development plan policy-making with the requirement for all district authorities to mandatorily prepare development plans and for decision-makers to base their decisions in accordance with the provisions of the plan, unless other planning considerations indicated otherwise. The move towards a plan-led system was already underway by the late 1980s, prior to the introduction of the 1991 Act, but the statutory change heralded the promise of greater local choice and discretion. The plan-led process did not, however, intend to completely remove the requirement for central government's overriding duty in the planning process and there was an acknowledgement that national planning guidance would still be required in setting out broad strategic direction (for example, see the comments made by Sir George Young, the British government's planning minister to the House of Commons upon Parliament's debate of the Planning and Compensation Bill, *Hansard*, cols. 501 and 502, 16 May 1991).

The plan-led approach, legitimised by the 1991 Act, is found within Section 26 of the statute. The clause, which became Section 54A of the Town and Country Planning Act 1990, reads:

Where in making any determination under the planning Acts regard is to be had to the development plan, the determination shall be made in accordance with the plan unless material considerations indicate otherwise.

Following a gestation period where the British courts determined the meaning of the clause for planning decision-makers (for comprehensive accounts, see Purdue, 1994; Herbert-Young, 1995; MacGregor and Ross, 1995; Gatenby and Williams, 1992, 1996), it is now widely accepted that Section 54A has introduced a presumption in favour of development proposals that are in conformity with the plan. The statute does not, however, create a presumption against development which is contrary to the plan's policies. This is an entirely different matter.

The policy interpretation of Section 54A was set out within central government PPG1 'General Policy and Principles' of March 1992. PPG1 both interprets the statute and provides policy requirements. So although the note discusses the statutory tests that have been established, it also reiterates the government's interpretation of the statutory clauses and provides the political context. Thus, where an applicant proposes a development that is clearly in conflict with the development plan, he or she would need to produce convincing reasons to demonstrate why the plan should not prevail. PPG1 also states that there is a presumption in favour of development and, as such, the plan can be overruled if there are other material considerations that indicate otherwise. Such other material considerations include the relevance of policies, the age of the policies, and whether the proposed development would cause demonstrable harm to interests of acknowledged importance. The presumption in favour of development is an interest of acknowledged importance which indicates that a local planning authority would have to establish clearly why the objectives of the development plan would be materially affected if development was allowed to proceed.

A further material consideration which could indicate otherwise against the provisions of the local development plan is the extent to which plan policies are consistent with national and regional objectives. PPG1 states categorically that, 'if the development plan is to carry full weight it needs to be up to date and consistent with national and regional policies as well as relevant to the proposal in question' (DoE/Welsh Office, 1992b).

The increased weight afforded to the development plan and local authority decision-making is therefore not autonomous for the lower tier of government as we might at first conclude. Local policies have to be consistent with national and regional policies, and where there is inconsistency developers may use this as grounds to outweigh the provisions of the local development plan. 'National and regional policies' in this context seems to refer to contents of the Planning and Regional Planning Guidance Notes (and their Scottish and Welsh equivalents), although there is scope to suggest that the term could equally apply to national macro-economic policies, regional industrial policies, or sectoral policies for land development. It has never been clearly stated that relevant national and regional policies are solely contained within land use planning documents. However, since draft PPGs are today subject to detailed comments by all central government departments, not solely the Department of the Environment, PPGs should embody all policy views of the government relating to planning, the environment and economic development.

This results in a planning system which is heavily determined, from a policy point of view, on the priorities of central government and creates uncertainty for local authorities wishing to take an alternative policy line to the content of national policy documents. It also raises legitimate questions on whether in fact it creates a plan-led planning system at all, since plans and policies may over time be regarded as out-of-date, irrelevant to the development demands of an area, or inconsistent with central government's planning policies. Such nuances that have accompanied the legal and policy requirements of the 1991 Act lead us to question the extent of this increase in centralised planning policy-making and whether local planning authorities view this as greater intervention. It is this aspect of the plan-led regime that prompted the development of the research for this book in the first place. Questions arise on whether increasing centralisation has emerged by greater use of the government's own Planning Policy Guidance Notes – the national policy statements – and the increased monitoring of local authorities' planning policies by the regional offices of the Department of the Environment and within Scotland and Wales to ensure conformity of local policies to the policies contained within PPGs. PPG1 (DoE/Welsh Office, 1992b, para. 21), makes clear that if local authorities formulate policies that are inconsistent with national guidance, and if they then attempt to base their planning decisions on those local policies, the Secretaries of State could not guarantee that the local development plan would be afforded increased weight as a decision-making tool in the spirit of Section 54A. In fact, judging from the policy requirements stated earlier and the judgements of the British courts, the likelihood of local policies outweighing national policies seems extremely unrealistic. The local plan-led label afforded to the new planning system therefore needs to be described as plan-led, providing there is consistency with central government policies. As Thornley (1996: 198) has remarked, 'the local autonomy that has been awarded local authorities through the "local choice" approach and the greater importance of development plans has to be regarded as circumscribed'.

RECONSTITUTING PLANNING 2: DELIVERING A FUNDAMENTAL CHANGE

The publication of the Green Paper on the future of the planning system in December 2001 signals further changes to the formulation and issuing of national planning policy statements in England over the next few years (see Chapters 10 and 11 for discussion about reforms to planning in Wales and Scotland respectively). As Chapter 4 discussed, the consultation document, *Planning: Delivering a Fundamental Change* (DTLR, 2001b) proposed the abolition of structure plans, local plans and unitary development plans and advocated the preparation of Local Development Frameworks. At the regional tier, it is proposed for Regional Spatial Strategies to replace Regional Planning Guidance, and for Sub-Regional Strategies to be prepared where there is concern about strategic issues in the absence of structure plans.

Changes to the national level of planning policy are also advocated. The government has suggested that national planning policies should, in future, only focus on issues of national and regional importance, simplifying the guidance to remove all non-policy issues, and to concentrate on major sectoral topics. In the month following the Green Paper's publication, the government also released two other consultation documents focusing on planning gain (DTLR, 2001c) and, important for this discussion, national infrastructure statements (DTLR, 2001a). This follows widespread criticism within Parliament and external interests on the inquiry into the proposed fifth terminal at Heathrow Airport, a quasi-legal event that lasted seven years and cost millions of pounds. The government has been concerned about the length of time taken for these inquiries into major developments and the finances involved. It has proposed that such major developments in future could be initiated via Parliamentary legislation.

It seems that, if implemented, the government's proposals on amending the national level of planning policy will make this level of the planning polity more similar to the proposals of academics and the Nuffield Foundation in the mid-1980s. Whether this would result in the government and government regional offices taking less interest in monitoring policies of local planning authorities is a mute point. The consultation documents make it clear that national and regional policy statements should nevertheless be taken into account in plan preparation and are material considerations in development control. The national consistency remit is therefore retained in any proposed legislation enacted in 2002/3.

NATIONAL CONSISTENCY, LOCAL DISCRETION

The planning process in the UK, unlike much of Western Europe, is considered to be discretionary as opposed to regulatory. That is to say, the existence of legislation supported by government advice and a plethora of case law have formed the basis of policy- and decision-making capacities. Planning is operated within the context of administrative powers and administrative flexibility which, in turn, has provided a great deal of administrative discretion. Planning authorities have not been dictated to by central government or the courts in following a clear plan or programme; rather, they have been informed of the relevant material considerations that they must take into account in forming policies or decisions (see Purdue, 1989; Layfield, 1990; Tewdwr-Jones, 1993). Governments throughout the last 50 years have consistently held the view that it is impossible to predict all future scenarios and actions in advance through a grand plan or blueprint. Policies and plans, where they do exist, can provide an indication of what decisions should be made, but under the British legal system there is nothing to stop a policy-maker from ignoring those policies in favour of other more material circumstances. Such other material considerations might include the views of third parties, environmental protection, or economic need. Indeed, successive British governments have provided guidance to developers and local planning authorities on what they have considered to be the most material issues to take into account when forming or implementing policies, assisted by law judgements that have determined the definition of material considerations. In addition to reflecting the policy priorities of the government of the day, the most material considerations can therefore indicate changing social, economic or environmental considerations within a particular spatial scale.

Discretionary planning systems are therefore praised for their ability to react to situations, for being flexible and being devoid of rigid, unadaptable rules. Discretion is concerned with processes, 'about who decides and with what degrees of freedom, about the way in which the system legitimates the power to act' (Booth, 1996: 132). However, the problem with discretionary planning systems is that they are not particularly accountable. Since there is no legal requirement for decisions to follow policies axiomatically, each case is determined on its merits. It is extremely problematical for non-policy or decision-makers to identify how decisions are likely to be made, a scenario labelled 'para-planning' by Booth (1996): policy that is implicit in the accumulation of individual decisions but is not evident in formal policy documents. The discretion that is available is usually entrusted to local politicians or professional planners, but exacerbates uncertainty among users groups.

Regulatory planning systems have developed primarily in those countries where written constitutions and administrative law exist. Planning has a clear role in defining rights and limits to rights of individual property owners. Certainty is guaranteed since a blueprint is produced in advance of decisions. A complete statement of what is permissible and what is not is used as a basis for policy formulation and implementation; there are no other more material considerations that could deviate from the stated decision route. The decisions or policies that are made under this regulatory process are therefore far more administrative in their operation, relying less on political judgement and, particularly, less on individuals' discretion. The plan becomes a master plan, taking on more significance as the sole material consideration, with a greater sense of importance being placed on certainty, knowing what is going to be acceptable and having the certainty of receiving a positive decision if technical considerations are fully met. Under both discretionary and regulatory planning systems, it is the expression of the factors to be taken into account when formulating policies or making decisions that warrants attention. Discretionary systems possess policies that permit flexibility and do not display a rigidness through such phrases as 'normally', 'may', 'ought to', and 'will consider'. Regulatory processes are far more positive in their syntax: 'will/will not', 'should/should not', and 'can/cannot'. Essentially, discretionary systems are political in their operation, while regulatory are administrative.

In Britain it has been the discretionary or flexible nature of planning that has been a feature of development planning and control since its statutory inception in 1947. No planning permission would be guaranteed in the control of development and no forward planning policies would automatically be implemented, despite their prominence in a development plan. This was the legal position up until 1991; local authorities were encouraged to prepare development plans for their areas but there was no mandatory legal requirement for their existence nor was there any certainty that once prepared the policies in the plans would be followed in planning control. Each case was decided on its merits, taking the existence of local and national planning policies as two considerations among many. During the 1980s under the Thatcher governments and the orientation of the planning system to meet market demands, local authorities were viewed as possessing too much freedom to intervene in market concerns. Clearly, if the market was allowed to flourish the conditions had to be created where the role of local authorities in prohibiting or restricting market development was severely curtailed. Rather than central government introducing legislation that removed local authority planning powers and allowed the market to operate in a free economy, a move called for by several commentators at the time (see, for example, Jones, 1982), the government reduced local planning authority powers to allow the market to take the lead but within an agenda set out by central government. This had the effect of returning the power to choose to the grassroots (that is, non-state) level and creating the conditions under which the market could flourish, in accordance with New Right ideology, but with increased control from the centre (Booth, 1996). Indeed, despite the threat of abolition, the operation of the statutory planning process had survived almost in the same format at the end of Margaret Thatcher's premiership compared to the period of her accession in 1979. The changes had been in the control and emphasis in direction of planning, rather than with its position to contribute to social, economic and environmental change.

By the late 1980s, as Chris Patten's 'local choice' concept filtered through national planning policy guidance to local authorities (see Chapter 3), greater authority was returned to local democratic processes and thus there was a significantly reduced reliance on centralised decision-making. This was legislatively introduced in the Planning and Compensation Act 1991 that had the effect of introducing the mandatory requirement for local authority-wide local plans and enhanced the status of the development plan as a decision-making tool. Booth (1996) has suggested that the change of heart emerged for three reasons: pressure from the rural Conservative-supporting shires against large settlement proposals; pressure from the house-building industry itself to use development plans to mediate in future housing development, particularly in the south-east of England; and, perhaps more significantly, as a means to control indirectly the discretionary powers of local planning authorities against oppositional standpoints from developers and the public. Essentially, this latter point encompasses the local choice concept, but Booth is advocating that in addition to using the statutory process to return planning decisions to the locality, local choice could also be used deliberately by central government to monitor local authorities' decisions against a national norm and ensure that greater accountability was introduced for local authorities' actions. The discretionary nature of the statutory planning process, the praised component of British land use planning, was therefore directly threatened by this greater monitoring and accountability role. Through local authorities being required to produce up-to-date policies in development plans, the development industry and local people were ensured greater 'certainty of outcome' (Booth, 1996: 90) while the house-building industry was provided with less uncertainty and delay. With local authorities then being required to follow the policies in the plan in determining planning applications for development, an element of rule of law was being introduced that mitigated against discretionary judgement.

For the first time since 1947, central government was strongly advocating the statutory development plan's policies as the basis for a clear certain statement of local authorities' future decisions. The plan-led process introduced by the 1991 Act requires local authorities to include all relevant policies in the plan for development control purposes. Exactly what level of detail should be included in the policies within these neo-blueprint documents, and how flexible they can be, is a matter for the law courts. But what is clear in the Act's inception is an attempt to generate greater certainty and prescription through legislative as opposed to policy driven requirement, a concept alien to the discretionary British land use process. The planning process, and local authorities' discretion, has always been susceptible to guidance from central government on particular substantive areas of the built and natural environment. In the 1980s in particular, through the release of circulars and Planning Policy Guidance Notes, the centre imposed a political view on how local policies should be formulated and decisions made (Davies *et al.*, 1986; Thornley, 1993; Tewdwr-Jones, 1994a, 1994b). But the Planning and Compensation Act 1991 introduced a legal change, rather than through policy advice, that enhanced local choice on the one hand and increased the centre's monitoring role of local planning authorities' actions on the other. Any local discretion that remained following the implementation of the new statutory requirements was now going to be subject to greater regulatory scrutiny from the centre.

FLEXIBILITY AND THE PLANNING PROCESS

The need for flexibility and responsiveness in the British land use planning process has been stressed by commentators throughout the last 30 years (e.g. Keeble, 1969; Brindley *et al.*, 1989; Thornley, 1993). Although flexibility and responsiveness provide discretion for local authorities to meet local needs and enable developers to stimulate the local economy, there is a concomitant problem. Flexibility also permits an uncontrolled role for local authorities to formulate policies and implement decisions that could be adverse to central government's planning policies. In the absence of statutory local plans for most of the country before 1991, it was extremely difficult for central government's planning agenda to be interpreted at the local level in policy formulation, and given that local authorities in Labour Party hands were ideologically opposed to Conservative Party philosophy towards planning and the market, the centre acknowledged that local authorities could refuse the market development rights directly through the discretion that was available. This, in turn, fostered the appeal-led approach so characteristic of the 1980s as dissatisfied developers appealed against the refusal decisions of the local authorities directly to the Secretaries of State.

The introduction of the 1991 Act did not reintroduce a form of state regulation on the part of local government, it merely attempted to foster greater certainty for the development industry in localities where local authorities had hindered the market. Local authorities, too, welcomed the new provision. Following the uncertain period for statutory planning throughout the 1980s, the plan-led process had legitimised the role of statutory development plans and planning control once again. The sigh of relief with which the Planning and Compensation Act 1991 was met emanated not only from developers, eager to participate at the outset in local plan policy formulation, but also from local authority professional planning officers who welcomed the certainty which would now accompany their activities and the support that would be provided to them through the appeals process.

However, the plan-led clause of the legislation does not introduce as much secure certainty as was first claimed. The statutory development plan has been made the first consideration among many for planning controllers to look to. Unlike in a regulatory system, the plan has not become the sole consideration, or a blueprint for all decision-makers to follow. Its status has been enhanced, but not at the expense of other considerations that are retained as part of the broader picture. Booth (1996: 100) has labelled the clause 'enigmatic'; this has been interpreted by central government as a presumption in favour of policies within the plan. It does not prohibit the existence of other material considerations nor does it remove the influence that other material considerations might have in the determination process. The statutory amendment, therefore, is a policy not a legal change, and given its position as a policy statement can quite easily revert back to its pre-1991 position. The simple fact remains that other material considerations, depending on the circumstances, could still outweigh the policies of the local plan (MacGregor and Ross, 1995; Purdue, 1994; Tewdwr-Jones, 1994a). One other more material consideration that could outweigh the plan is national planning policy guidance issued by central government in the form of circulars and Planning Policy Guidance Notes.

PART 2

PLANNING POLICY CONFLICTS IN GOVERNMENT RELATIONS

Part 2 considers the form and function of the planning polity in practice. It discusses empirical research conducted over an eight-year period at all levels of planning policy-making within Britain. The intention here was to assess how different scales of government, and their planning policy functions, affect other government tiers and planning policies. As has been indicated in Part 1, town and country planning is a process stretched across various government levels and government tiers, both formally and informally, forming a complete mosaic of planning in Britain at the commencement of the twenty-first century. Changes to the UK level of planning will impact upon local levels of government; devolution and decentralisation within Britain will affect local planning policies and provide a link to the emergence of national and sub-national policy agendas. All these changes point to immense restructuring occurring within the governmental and institutional framework of planning.

This section of the book addresses policy relationships and conflicts within the planning polity of Britain. Chapter 6 discusses research findings that sought to assess how central government impacts upon local planning policy-making, how the UK government employs its national planning policy remit to ensure consistency across various geographical and political scales. Chapter 7, by comparison, considers how the regional level of planning policy has been enhanced over the last ten years by presentation of research findings that sought to question the adequacy of regional planning policy mechanisms in England, Scotland and Wales in a decentralised Britain. Chapter 8 considers the planning polity at the local level of government by assessing, through detailed research, how the policies, plans and proposals of one district local authority in south-west England has been affected by central government national planning policy and the scrutiny of a Government Regional Office.

Chapter 9 takes a slightly different approach, by considering national relationships within Britain. This chapter considers, through research analysis, to what extent the parameters of the planning system were constructed similarly across England and Wales in the run-up to devolution in 1999, and whether there was scope for national and local policies in Wales to be different from those being formulated in England. This is an important issue to address since it could mask the ongoing political, social, economic and environmental desires within different national and sub-national areas of countries to respond in definitive ways to their own problems through their policy-making abilities, and whether a UK government national consistency remit potentially undermined that desire.

CHAPTER 6

NATIONAL CONSISTENCY IN THE PLANNING POLICY PROCESS

INTRODUCTION

The research discussed in this chapter was founded on one principal hypothesis. Namely, that the direct and indirect roles of central government through the use of its national Planning Policy Guidance Notes had increased significantly since the introduction of the plan-led planning system. As has already been noted in Chapter 5, the dearth of evidence of an investigative nature in this area necessitated a large-scale empirical piece of quantitative research that attempted to assess the national position across England and Wales. The research took the form of a survey of all district planning authorities in England and Wales and focused on the formulation and implementation of planning policies under the new planning regime. A request was made for each survey questionnaire form to be completed by a senior member of staff within the planning department who had direct knowledge of both the forward planning (policy formulation) and the development control (policy implementation) functions. In the majority of cases, therefore, the surveys were completed by chief or senior planning officers. The survey was directed to all 401 district authorities in England and Wales: 296 English non-metropolitan districts, 37 Welsh districts, and 68 London and metropolitan boroughs. A survey of a single, coherent data group eradicated any sampling bias. Under the Town and Country Planning Act 1990, non-metropolitan districts in England and Wales are required to prepare district-wide local plans that focus on detailed land use policies and allocations. The London and metropolitan boroughs prepare unitary development plans, part II of which is identical to a non-metropolitan local plan. From April 1996, following completion of this particular research project, local government in Wales, in Scotland and in certain areas in England underwent reorganisation with the result that the planning policy framework in these areas has also been amended. The reorganised authorities are now required to prepare unitary development plans similar to those of metropolitan areas. See Harris and Tewdwr-Jones (1995) and Clotworthy and Harris (1996) for further discussion.

Questionnaires were posted to each local authority in October 1993, with a second mail-out occurring in the following month. The research questionnaire was collected by stamped addressed envelope between October 1993 and January

1994 from each responding local authority planning department. Completed returns represented the professional opinion of the responding officers rather than the formal opinion of the district authority. The questionnaire itself was divided up into three parts, each section relating to a distinct policy area: the development plan, implementing the plan, and central government planning policy. Questions corresponding to each of these themes sought to assess whether local planning authorities:

1   accepted central government's remit to discuss/question local planning policies;
2   identified an increasing role on the part of central government towards local plan/unitary development plan preparation;
3   believed that central government's querying of local policy topics showed a tendency to focus on particular substantive areas;
4   requested further national planning guidance from central government on policy topics not presently covered by the series;
5   considered the plan-led planning system to have increased the planning powers of local authorities and thus the concept of local choice.

The research results are presented under the following headings: the adequacy of national planning policy; the significance of national planning policy; perceptions to the national approach to planning; and national consistency, national guidance and local discretion. Finally, general conclusions are drawn from the research at the end of the chapter.

THE ADEQUACY OF NATIONAL PLANNING POLICY

Local planning authority officers, when asked for their views of Planning Policy Guidance Notes and the guidance contained within them, were generally very favourable towards the documents (Table 6.1). The research question requested respondents to comment on the role of all the documents, not specifically in relation to particular PPGs. Of respondents, 66 per cent were either fairly or very satisfied with the guidance, indicating a healthy role for central government policy in the planning policy process. Reasons advanced by those respondents who possessed a negative view of PPGs remarked that the PPGs were unsuccessful since 'they mean all things to all people', were at times confusing and lacked clarity, and bore an unnecessary amount of detail that local authorities felt obliged to follow.

The generally positive view towards PPGs can best be explained by a comparison with the policy guidance previously released by the government in the form of circulars and Development Control Policy Notes. These documents were not particularly accessible and, compared to the PPGs, certainly do not display concise guidance on particular topics. In the present pressure on local planning authorities to produce development plans and determine planning applications within government-stipulated timescales, the availability of accessible reference documents on planning matters is obviously welcome. This might explain the positive view of respondents.

Criticism of the existence of national planning policy statements which occasionally appear to outweigh local policies, and criticism of the clarity and wording of the documents, reflects their role as guidance statements for both the public and private sector sides of planning. Consequently, as was discussed in Chapter 3, it is sometimes possible to quote the same PPG statement to justify opposing views at the same planning appeal. These criticisms cannot be readily answered and could apply just as much to any form of national policy statement. The government will at least find satisfaction that the existence of PPGs appears to find favour with respondents representing two-thirds of local planning authorities in England and Wales.

In terms of the content of PPGs, local planning authority respondents were again satisfied with the degree of detail included within the documents. As Table 6.2 illustrates, almost two-thirds of officers considered PPGs to possess about the right detail of policy guidance, compared to one in five who thought there was insufficient detail, and one in ten who considered PPGs to be overly detailed. Respondents expressed a view that since many local authorities are preparing statutory district-wide local plans for the first time they are consequently reliant on the documents as a source of guidance and information for their plans' contents. If this viewpoint is to be accepted, officers with no previous experience of plan formulation are more likely to request as much guidance and detail as they can possibly receive.

Table 6.1 Satisfaction with national planning policy

Satisfaction with national policy	District authorities	
	No.	%
Very satisfied	3	1
Fairly satisfied	206	65
Not very satisfied	89	28
Not at all satisfied	10	3
No response	9	3
Total	317	100

Source: Tewdwr-Jones (1997c)

Table 6.2 Adequacy of national planning policy

Level of detail	District authorities	
	No.	%
National policy is too detailed	32	10
National policy is sufficiently detailed	198	63
National policy is insufficiently detailed	67	21
No response	20	6

Source: Tewdwr-Jones (1997c)

When questioned on the role of PPGs in England and Wales, local authorities presented quite a varied set of views on the priorities of national planning statements (Table 6.3). Respondents were requested to rank five statements in order of their perceived priority. The statements originated from government statements contained in previous policy documents (for example, Circular 1/88 that explained the role of PPGs when they were first introduced) and from the views expressed by advocates of national strategic planning documents, most notably the Nuffield Foundation's recommendations (see Chapter 5). The statement that attracted the most agreement for the role of PPGs was that relating to the need to provide concise statements at the national level on land use matters: 19 per cent of respondents ranked this statement first above the others. Other statements that found general agreement among the local authorities was the requirement for PPGs to promote guidance on general aspects of policy, to guide the formulation of development plan policies, and to guide development control decision-making. There is a policy requirement for PPGs to be interpreted in the formulation of local plan policies for local spatial areas, so its high ranking in the responses should not cause any surprise. However, respondents also ranked the PPGs' role in development control quite highly and it is interesting to note that national policy guidance should be regarded as a principal part of determining local-based planning applications. Does this reflect a recognition on the part of respondents that PPGs are useful in providing the strategic framework for local authorities' detailed interpretation?

The research questioned whether the respondents believed that there were any further planning topics not currently covered by PPGs but on which they would like to see future guidance (Table 6.4). This was primarily to ascertain whether there was scope to release further national planning documents. Two-thirds of respondents did not believe there to be any planning topics that required further national advice from central government other than those already existing. Therefore, although the role of the documents is widely accepted in the planning process and local planning authorities are content with guidance that advises on

Table 6.3 Perceptions towards the priorities of national planning policy

Role of national planning policy	Rank											Mean
	5		4		3		2		1			
	No.	%	No.	%	No.	%	No.	%	No.	%		
To explain the role of local authorities in dealing with issues that are of more than local importance	167	53	60	10	35	11	32	8	16	5		4.07
To guide development control decisions	47	15	87	28	93	30	56	18	22	7		3.27
To guide the formulation of development plan policies	16	5	22	7	82	26	101	32	85	27		2.29
To provide concise statements at the national level on planning matters	19	6	51	16	51	16	63	20	123	19		2.28
To promote guidance on general aspects of policy	38	12	63	20	51	16	79	25	79	25		2.68

Source: Tewdwr-Jones (1997c)

Table 6.4 The scope for further national planning policy

Scope for further national policy	District authorities	
	No.	%
More national policy should be released	89	28
No further national policy should be released	209	66
No response	19	6
Total	317	100

Source: Tewdwr-Jones (1997c)

detailed plan formulation and plan implementation issues, professional officers believe the national framework to be essentially complete.

For those respondents who considered there to be a need for further national guidance (a significant 28 per cent), the most mentioned topics highlighted were those in relation to disabled access, sustainable development, affordable housing, and urban design. A handful of respondents requested guidance on each of the following: the impact of European Union policies, urban regeneration, and protected areas. Since not every local authority had begun preparing local plans at the time of research, the need for further guidance is understandable. This actually might be understated; the open-ended nature of the research question might be the cause of these figures, and a series of prompts or coded options could have proved more useful and provided greater insight.

THE SIGNIFICANCE OF NATIONAL PLANNING POLICY

The research then went on to assess the influences of PPGs on local plan policy preparation, highlighting the extent to which central government was objecting or intervening in the plan preparation process. At the time of questioning in the autumn of 1993, not every district authority in England and Wales had started preparing its district-wide local plan and these authorities were consequently unable to respond to this particular part of the research. Nevertheless, for those authorities that had successfully progressed their local plan preparation beyond draft stages, the research confirmed the belief that Department of the Environment and Welsh Office regional offices were intervening in the local plan preparation process to either object to or point out those particular policies that did not conform to the central government's own Planning Policy Guidance. Of those district planning departments that had undertaken consultation with central government offices, 67 per cent had received some form of intervention from the regional offices. When questioned on the significance of central government intervention on local authority planning policy formulation (Table 6.5), 39 per cent stated that such intervention was not very or not at all significant, whereas 27 per cent considered it to be very or fairly significant. Respondents were therefore content with the Department of the Environment/Welsh Office's role in planning policy formulation. As a consequence, although the direct and indirect role of central government's PPGs may have increased under the plan-led regime, this has not resulted in dissatisfaction among local authorities, thus confirming the research results of the Department of the Environment's (1995) project. There was also concern from respondents that the word 'intervention' was rather too strong with some respondents, stressing that the comments received from central government were advisory and should not be taken as direction. A considerable number of respondents also noted that central government intervention, although documenting discrepancies between local policies and national policies, also made detailed comments on the wording and semantics of development plans, frequently objecting on 'presumption against' and 'presumption in favour' type of policies. One district authority recorded over a hundred detailed comments on the policies within its draft local plan related to the wording of policies rather than detailed policy content, but this was not considered to be significant in altering the tenet of local policies.

Table 6.6 illustrates the extent of central government intervention in the drafting of local planning policies by subject area, with each topic almost conforming to a subject area for which the government has released its own advisory planning policy guidance.

Of particular interest is the high number of district authorities recording central government intervention in five key policy areas: housing, development control, town centres and retail development, industrial development, and environmental protection. If greater assessment is undertaken of these policy subjects, it is possible to consider why the regional offices intervened in these areas more so than in others.

Table 6.5 The significance of central government planning policy intervention in local planning policy formulation

Significance	District authorities	
	No.	%
Very significant	16	5
Fairly significant	70	22
Not very significant	108	34
Not at all significant	16	5
No response	107	34
Total	317	100

Source: Tewdwr-Jones (1997c)

Table 6.6 Extent of central government intervention in local planning policy formulation

Subject area	District authorities	
	No.	%
Housing	149	47
Development control policies	136	43
Town centres and retail development	114	36
Industrial development	111	35
Environmental protection	105	33
The countryside and rural economy	101	32
Transport and highway issues	101	32
Urban conservation and heritage	88	28
Sport, leisure, tourism and recreation	79	25
Green belts	73	23
Design issues and aesthetics	67	21
Archaeology	51	16
Minerals working	41	13
Telecommunications	35	11
Waste disposal	32	10
Energy generation and renewable energy	25	8
Coastal planning	13	4

Source: Tewdwr-Jones (1997c)

In the housing category, the issue of affordable housing has been an area of policy contention as local planning authorities attempt to include policies within their plans that meet social need. While the legal status of affordable housing in the land use planning process remains uncertain, central government has proved reluctant to accept local authorities' policies. This has led to greater intervention on this particular housing issue, a specific subject highlighted by the respondents. In relation to development control, the research results indicated policy contentions on the issue of planning gain, supplementary planning guidance, and 'presumption against' matters.

This subject could also include policies related to any other substantive area, since most policies within development plans are used as development control policies. Central government comments in relation to town centres and retail development can best be explained by the change in national policy upon the publication of revised PPG6 in July 1993 (DoE/Welsh Office, 1993). This guidance note moved away from encouraging out-of-town retailing to encouraging town centre developments. Local authorities, having already drafted policies to meet the prior PPG6 requirement, therefore found themselves out of line with current government thinking. Given the timing of the research, it is more than likely that this was the factor causing the high number of central government queries. Finally, in relation to environmental protection, the issue that was causing concern among local authorities at this time was that in relation to securing sustainable development. Although central government had embraced the concept of sustainability in 1990 (through the Environmental Protection Act 1990 and the *This Common Inheritance* White Paper (HM Government, 1990)), there remains a great deal of uncertainty over how sustainability can be implemented through the land use planning process. With little guidance emanating from central government at the time, local authorities attempted to co-ordinate the environmental agenda themselves; as the local plan preparation process progressed, the drafting stages were used by both central and local government as opportunities for dialogue on the sustainable policy agenda. Again, this would explain the relatively high number of interventions within this substantive subject area.

The extent of central government intervention in local planning policy formulation can therefore be explained quite readily, through a combination of questioning the legal remit for particular local policies and changes in central government national policy. This indicates a role for central government in the planning process that was originally defined through the early legislation. The government is utilising the contents of PPGs (the current form of national planning guidance) to secure consistency and continuity in the framing of planning policies, reflecting a more strategic role than was initially indicated through the higher executive intervening in detailed local policy matters.

PERCEPTIONS TO THE NATIONAL APPROACH TO PLANNING

The research then questioned professional officers' views of the current national approach to planning, enshrined within the plan-led system introduced by Section 54A under the provisions of the Planning and Compensation Act 1991. Table 6.7 indicates the responses to the question: 'Section 54A of the 1990 Act introduced

Table 6.7 Perceptions of the impact of the plan-led system for local planning decisions

Impact of the plan-led system	District authorities	
	No.	%
A clearer framework for decisions	266	84
Less clear framework for decisions	10	3
No difference for decisions	35	11
No response	6	2
Total	317	100

Source: Tewdwr-Jones (1997c)

a plan-led development control system. Do you think this will result in a clearer framework for planning decisions?' A high 84 per cent considered that the 'plan-led' system would provide a clearer framework for development control decisions, indicating a renewed commitment on the part of professionals to planning policy and an enthusiasm for a process that was perceived to hand some authority back to local government. Only 11 per cent of respondents thought Section 54A would make no difference to decision-making processes. Although it was early in the application of the new statutory clauses, there was a clear expectation on the part of local authority planners in the autumn of 1993 that the 'plan-led' system would provide a boost to local decision-making.

The questionnaire then probed in more detail respondents' perceptions of the plan-led system (Table 6.8). Six statements were outlined and officers were requested to agree or disagree with each. The statements that attracted the most agreement among the respondents were those related to the lengthening of plan preparation time and the renaissance of local decision-making powers. In all, 89 per cent thought that the plan-led system would lengthen public inquiries and Examinations in Public since more attention would be focused on the content of planning policies rather than developers attempting to play down agreed statutory policies later at the development control stage.

Some 74 per cent agreed with the view that Section 54A would result in a strengthening of local decision-making, thus confirming the view that the new system was pro-local planning. Only 52 per cent of respondents, however, considered that the plan-led system would result in greater intervention by central government in the local planning process. This was despite the admission by the Department of the Environment and the Welsh Office that plans were undergoing greater scrutiny to ensure conformity with national and regional planning guidance and the majority of respondents, indicating a high level of central government inter-

Table 6.8 Detailed perceptions of the plan-led system

Statement: 'The plan-led system will result in . . .'	District authorities			
	Agree		Disagree	
	No.	%	No.	%
A strengthening of local decision-making	235	74	82	26
Greater intervention from government	165	52	152	48
A greater role for lawyers	193	61	124	39
Less planning appeals	197	62	120	38
Lengthier local plan inquiries	282	89	35	11
Greater public accountability	206	65	111	35

Source: Tewdwr-Jones (1997c)

vention in plan preparation. There thus appears to be a conflicting view here, and certainly a degree of uncertainty, between respondents who recognise a role for central government in providing broad planning direction and respondents who notice an increasingly interventionist role on the part of the Department of the Environment and the Welsh Office. The distinction can perhaps best be explained by the degree of central government intervention considered necessary and acceptable by local planning authorities.

Central government's strategic role in the hierarchy of planning policy is pivotal, but its role in the detailed day-to-day policy-making process is perhaps giving rise to concern. It might even be the case that professional officers do not consider PPGs to possess a role in altering the details of local policies, merely in providing the broad strategic overview, which actually disproves the research hypothesis.

When asked if they believed whether current central government guidance adequately explained the provisions and implications of Section 54A for local planning authorities, this answer reflected a greater degree of conflicting views (Table 6.9). Of respondents, 37 per cent thought that current national advice adequately explained Section 54A, but 44 per cent thought it was inadequately explained, calling for more guidance on the operation of the plan-led system. This question was also put at an early period in the new process and it will only become significant when local authorities rely on their new development plans for development control processes. It also explains the relatively large number of non-responses recorded for this question.

NATIONAL CONSISTENCY, NATIONAL GUIDANCE AND LOCAL DISCRETION

Finally, and in the light of the uncertainty about the role of PPGs in relation to the adopted and up-to-date local development plan, the research sought to assess

Table 6.9 Adequacy of central government's explanation of the plan-led system

Adequacy	District authorities	
	No.	%
Government adequately explains system	117	37
Government inadequately explains system	139	44
No opinion	51	16
No response	10	3
Total	317	100

Source: Tewdwr-Jones (1997c)

professional officers' perceptions on which of the documents would have greater weight for decision-making purposes if there was a conflict between national and local policies (Table 6.10). This was a somewhat unfair question to ask. After all, the weight to be attached to policies (or any material consideration) is a matter for the decision-maker alone and will, in any case, be dependent on the circumstances of each case. The question was included, however, to ascertain whether the expectations of the plan-led clause in local authorities would suffer if a conflict between national and local interests arose. In the event of conflict between an up-to-date development plan and a recently released PPG, 57 per cent of respondents believed the local plan would receive greater weight; 30 per cent thought the national document would have priority. It will be interesting to assess through planning appeal research data whether this majority verdict has been upheld in practice.

CONCLUSIONS

The role of a national co-ordinating level of planning policy in England and Wales in providing national consistency has been widely accepted by land use professionals. Although the nature of central government's legitimate remit in the planning system has undergone significant amendments over the last 50 years, it is still possible to identify a need for the central state to secure consistency and continuity in planning policy formulation. As different political mandates have influenced this central role in land use processes, the state has modified its remit away from providing national strategic direction and more towards monitoring detailed local state policy and procedural functions.

The research discussed in this chapter sought to assess whether the direct and indirect role of the national Planning Policy Guidance Notes has increased significantly since the introduction of the plan-led system. It has been shown that

Table 6.10 Perceptions of policy priority in the event of conflict between national and local planning policies

Priority policy document	District authorities	
	No.	%
The local plan	181	57
National planning policy	95	30
No response	41	13
Total	317	100

Source: Tewdwr-Jones (1997c)

while central government has been intervening in detailed local planning policy-making more extensively than hitherto by utilising the contents of PPGs, this role has been generally accepted by professional officers practising in local planning authorities. Respondents indicated that there is a role for central government to provide strong national strategic direction in the land use planning process, and that local authorities accept both PPGs as central government's current form of national direction and the content of the documents. While the role of PPGs has increased over the last six years following the introduction of a new legislative framework, this has been accepted as a necessary part of plan formulation by practitioners who do not consider this role to be either significant *per se* or cause significant alteration to the tenet of local authority policies. Some respondents expressed dissatisfaction with central government in carrying out this monitoring role. However, the majority of authorities recognised the strategic role PPGs were providing, especially in relation to implementing a sustainability agenda. There is great optimism for the plan-led process introduced by the Planning and Compensation Act 1991 and a belief that Section 54A strengthens local decision-making powers, despite the admission that central government's intervention has increased. This displays a confidence among professionals of the security attached to up-to-date development plans for development control purposes but within a framework set strategically by central government through Planning Policy Guidance Notes. In this sense, although the research hypothesis has been proven and there is an increasing use of PPGs in the planning process, planners seem content with the scope of that guidance.

Central government's role in the land use planning process has not altered significantly since the 1943 Minister of Town and Country Planning Act first introduced a duty on the part of ministers to secure consistency and continuity in the framing and execution of a national policy for land use and development. Although the instruments central government has used to achieve this consistency and continuity role have changed over the last 50 years, and have been inconsistent in their prominence, the overriding duty can still be identified. Planning Policy Guidance Notes are the present form of national policy for land use and development. Although some commentators, including the author, have previously expressed concern at the increased use of the documents to intervene in detailed local planning matters (see Tewdwr-Jones, 1994c), there is generally a degree of acceptance among professionals across England and Wales for an executive remit that perhaps makes this concern not as significant as was previously thought. The introduction of any new planning system will yield uncertainty and a requirement for central government to provide strategic direction. The use of PPGs in providing direction and monitoring in the plan-led process, although far from perfect, forms an important part of the operation of land use planning in England and Wales.

CHAPTER 7

REGIONAL CERTAINTY AND COMPATIBILITY IN THE PLANNING POLICY PROCESS[1]

INTRODUCTION

This chapter considers the position, format, role and status of regional planning in Britain in the latter 1990s. Since 1997, constitutional change in the United Kingdom has affected the regional level of policy-making. In addition to proposals to establish an enhanced form of regional planning and policy-making, the government has announced a plethora of policies with regard to economic development, housing, the environment, transport, and the new mechanisms established to co-ordinate and adopt these policies at the regional level, a move that has been described as incremental regional planning (Murdoch and Tewdwr-Jones, 1999). The lack of an overall policy approach to this 'new regionalism' (Amin, 1999; Keating, 1997; cf. Lovering, 1999), and the rescaling of political processes (Jones and MacLeod, 1999; MacLeod and Goodwin, 1999), highlights the unfocused way in which the policies have been thought through to date, and the potential this breeds for incompatibility between each of the policy areas and new regional agencies seems to be too apparent (Allmendinger and Tewdwr-Jones, 2000b). One of the purposes of this regional renaissance is the attempt to establish the autonomous institutional capacities of regions to organise for economic development (Amin and Thrift, 1992, 1995; Phelps and Tewdwr-Jones, 2000; Scott, 1998; Storper, 1997).

The concern over creating certainty in the regions and compatibility between institutions of government rests on the motivations and remit of each of the regional players themselves. The Regional Development Agencies, created in 1999, possess a clear agenda, namely to foster economic rejuvenation. The other policy initiatives, however, are vested with either local planning authorities or regional assemblies or groupings. Furthermore, proposals in the fields of housing, transport and the environment appear to be potentially at odds with the interests of economic development. The government has sought to address this concern by suggesting that the new regional planning framework will be sustainable, but seems to be a convenient way of indicating there are conflicting interests that regions are going to have to reconcile themselves (Cowell and Murdoch, 1999;

---

1 Some of the material in this chapter has been developed in partnership with Jonathon Murdoch and Philip Allmendinger and I am grateful to them both for the development of ideas and approaches to the subject of regional planning.

Murdoch and Tewdwr-Jones, 1999). The key question is, to what extent will the new mechanisms permit a sustainable and co-ordinated approach to regional policy-making? With the lack of formal regional government, at least for the present time, where will the degrees of power lie in the potential struggles that could emerge between the multifarious agencies of governance at the regional level on the one hand and between central government as initiators of the regional renaissance and local government as the implementation level?

This chapter attempts to consider these questions by explaining the evolving form of regional policy-making in England and reviewing the emerging new spatial planning processes that the government has established since 1997. Following an introduction to the nature of regional planning and government in the 1980s and 1990s, and New Labour's policies for the region, the chapter then reviews regional planning. This involves assessment of policy synchronisation, policy expectation, and sectoral deliveries. The chapter concludes by assessing the implications for regional governance and planning of these policies, and identifies both the compatible and irreconcilable functions that regions are now expected to co-ordinate. This discussion is centred within debate concerning the relationships between central government and the new regional spaces.

GOVERNMENT AND THE REGION WITHIN THE UK

The regional tier of government in the UK has traditionally been the weakest of all tiers. The British state has been characterised as a unitary state bound together by a tradition of parliamentary sovereignty. Parliament is at the centre of law-making in the UK and also determines what the government shall be. Government itself is usually run by a single decision-making body: the Prime Minister in liaison with the Cabinet. Cabinet government, with collective responsibility, permits a further concentration of power especially as it is serviced by a unitary civil service. Therefore, within the UK, any political devolution of power has long been resisted.

Administrative devolution has been permitted, however, for this can usually be achieved with little loss of sovereignty and power by the central state. Thus, local government has grown up within the unitary state in order that certain state services and functions might be better administered locally. A welcome side-effect for the central state is that local delivery of services and functions can act to insulate the central state from local pressures and demands. These come to be focused on the local state. Some degree of regional administration has also been permitted: in the administration of the utilities, planning, the health and education services, and so forth. Again, these functions can be undertaken on a regional basis while the power remains at the centre.

The exception to this unitary dominance has been demands for political devolution to the nations of Ireland, Scotland and Wales. Over the last two hundred
years or so these demands have gone through cycles of intensity and have had dif-
ferential effects on the polity of the UK. Thus the struggle for home rule in Ireland
led to the (southern) Irish state becoming established in the first half of the twentieth century, while some degree of devolution to the Northern Ireland has been in
evidence over the last twenty or thirty years (for instance, Northern Ireland possesses its own Secretary of State and recently has acquired its own Assembly). In
Scotland and Wales, the various pressures for political autonomy have largely been
resisted so that until recently these countries were merely served by administrative
regional governments (both possessing Secretaries of State and government
departments in the form of the Scottish Office and Welsh Office). This situation
has recently and fundamentally changed with the creation of Parliament of Scotland in Edinburgh and a National Assembly for Wales in Cardiff, following legislation introduced by the New Labour government in its first year of office (see
Scottish Office, 1997; Welsh Office, 1997). Political devolution is therefore
becoming more apparent in the UK, and is also beginning to affect England too.
The pressure for devolution in the various countries that form the UK has led to a
more developed tier of regional government (Bradbury and Mawson, 1997). This,
in turn, is impacting upon the spatial planning processes existing within the countries (Alden and Offord, 1996; Roberts, 1996). The regional tier of planning is
usually the neglected tier since attention – and to a degree power and autonomy –
is devoted to both the national and local levels of policy-making and decision-
making. In particular, the main debates tend to focus on the degree of local versus
central direction in the system (see, for example, Tewdwr-Jones, 1997b; Ying Ho,
1997). Despite this, or perhaps even because of it, the New Labour government's
proposals for enhanced regional policy-making have been couched in terms of the
new regional level reconciling the planning differences between the national and
local levels of governance.

THE REGIONAL STATE AND PLANNING UNDER THE CONSERVATIVES

The issue of political autonomy for, or devolution to, Ireland, Scotland and Wales
has rumbled through British politics for many years. During the twentieth century
the 'Irish problem' has remained an almost continuous feature of UK politics, while
Scottish and Welsh devolution emerged particularly strongly in the 1970s and
1990s. During the 1970s, James Callaghan's Labour government committed itself
to referenda in Scotland and Wales on the issue of devolution but stacked the

odds against success by stipulating that two-thirds of those voting must come out in favour for the legislation to be passed. In the event, a simple majority was all that could be mustered in Scotland while in Wales devolution was even less well supported (only 20 per cent of those voting, a mere 12 per cent of the total electorate, voted in favour). It seemed, therefore, that regional government on mainland Britain was to remain on the political back-burner.

With the election of the Thatcher government in 1979, the danger arose that the regionalist cause would be pushed off the political agenda completely. During the 1980s the Conservatives set about dismantling many of the regional institutions that they had inherited from the previous Labour government, especially those linked to economic management such as Regional Economic Planning Councils (see Morgan and Alden, 1974). It was expected that both political and administrative regional institutions would decline further as the Thatcher governments pushed forward their reform programmes. However, during this period new pressures began to emerge which led to a reassertion of the regionalist agenda. Moreover, these new pressures were not just confined to the Celtic periphery but came to bear upon England as well (Wannop, 1995; Murdoch and Tewdwr-Jones, 1999).

Most of England appears to lack the call for a strong regionalist agenda with autonomous governing structures (Harvie, 1991). Traditionally there have been few strong regional cultures which provided the necessary political support for regionalisation (although there are exceptions, of course, such as the North-East). People have generally identified with either their local communities or the nation (John and Whitehead, 1997). Moreover, the present structure of a strong central government would seem to block any movement to enhance regional government. The shire or county councils have been responsible for many of the traditional functions allocated to regional authorities in other European states since 1888, including transportation and strategic planning. In addition, some English counties (such as Hampshire and Kent) are larger than regions in other states (John and Whitehead, 1997). A further problem rests on the difficulty of defining clearly what actually constitutes an English region: Scotland and Wales possess regional territories that coincide with previous national territories, whereas in England the regional boundaries have been created by central government agencies responsible for agriculture, transport, and planning. The shift towards a system of governance from government (Stoker, 2000) has exacerbated the complexity of this situation. As John and Whitehead state:

> The administration of England has been organised into a plethora of institutions of overlapping boundaries, whether those of the government departments or of the quasi-autonomous governmental bodies (quangos) ... English central government is organised primarily by function not territory, with each central

> government department and quango choosing whatever pattern of
> decentralisation it finds most appropriate for its purposes. The implication is that
> there is no natural administrative logic to regional decentralisation of central
> functions to regional bodies.
>
> (John and Whitehead, 1997: 8)

Therefore, a move towards establishing regional government would have to 'create new boundaries about which there would be endemic disagreement, or inherit existing boundaries which might fatally damage a democratic regional project by their incoherence' (John and Whitehead, 1997: 8). Despite these problems and uncertainties, the regional tier of government in England has gradually emerged more prominently over the last twenty years or so. There are now many administrative and governmental bodies operating on a regional basis, and the establishment of a strengthened regional tier of institutions has emerged more prominently since the 1980s. Mawson (1998) suggests the following reasons for this emerging agenda:

1   Fragmentation of the public sector arising from privatisation, the establishment of quangos and the market orientation of public services, reflecting the move towards governance (Stoker and Mossberger, 1995; Rhodes, 1997).

2   A support structure for business and economic development and the promotion of institutional capacity building for regional economic development and inward investment (Amin and Thrift, 1992, 1995; Phelps and Tewdwr-Jones, 2000), which was widely seen as inadequate in comparison to that of other European countries and of Scotland, Wales and Northern Ireland (Harding et al., 1996).

3   Responding to the need to manage the implementation of European Structural Fund programmes by central government officials at the regional level and to Single Programming Documents and other strategies for financial grant bidding purposes (Batchler and Turok, 1997; Tewdwr-Jones and Williams, 2001).

4   Political concerns about the increasing number of 'undemocratic' agencies (quangos) existing between local and national government (Morgan and Roberts, 1994).

Allmendinger and Tewdwr-Jones (2000b) have also identified other factors that have provided a renaissance for the region, and these include the 'hollowing out' of the nation-state (Ohmae, 1996), globalisation (Brenner, 1999), changes within the European Union towards the region (Keating, 1997; Jonas and Ward, 1999), and the establishment of transnational spatial planning programmes at the regional level (Tewdwr-Jones et al., 2000). Within the UK, the push for regional governance has also emanated from a variety of financial, political, institutional, spatial, and governmental factors (see Baker (1998) and Tewdwr-Jones and McNeill (2000) for overviews).

In the light of these concerns, policy-makers and political activists came to view the regional level as having the potential to play a pivotal co-ordinating role such that national policies could be tailored to local circumstances by networks of regional and local stakeholders. It was against this background that the Conservatives, under John Major, made a commitment in the 1992 election manifesto to the introduction of integrated regional offices in the English regions, known as the 'Government Offices for the Regions' (Mawson and Spencer, 1997). These regional offices were to be a rationalisation and simplification of the complex regional networks related to economic and urban policy. In April 1994, the Major government launched a new network of ten Government Offices for the Regions. Regional civil servants in the Departments of Employment, Environment, Transport and Industry were made accountable to one Regional Director who was to be responsible for all staff and expenditure. A set of overall objectives were established for the GORs. These were:

- to achieve operational requirements of departments;
- to contribute local views to the formation of government policy;
- to promote a coherent approach to competitiveness, sustainable economic development and regeneration;
- to develop local partnerships between local interests to secure these objectives (see Mawson and Spencer 1997: 76).

CENTRAL GOVERNMENT IN THE REGIONS: THE MONITORING ROLE

Central government offices in the regions were originally set up in the 1970s as a more effective way of administration in the regions. Regional government offices are similar in concept to branch plants in that they embody the major departments of the government on a much smaller scale than that of the headquarters. Until recently, the functions of the regional offices operated as separate entities. This system continued until the creation of integrated regional offices in 1994, established in order to unite the various departments to provide a more comprehensive and accessible service, a one-stop shop for customers (Mawson, 1997a). At the same time, the Single Regeneration Budget was set up by the government to allow spending levels to be set locally in the light of local needs, rather than calculated in London. This would permit local people to be given more influence over spending priorities.

Regional government functions are co-ordinated by the integrated regional offices in England: South West, South East, London, Eastern, East Midlands, West Midlands, North West, Yorkshire and Humberside, North East, and Merseyside. The change in 1994 was expected to provide the catalyst for creating new opportunities to forge partnerships and to create prosperity by building on local strengths. Each of the integrated regional offices undertakes government functions in the regions related to the functions of the Department of the Environment, the Department of Transport (merged and renamed after May 1997), the Department of Trade and Industry, and the Department of Employment.

The main areas of work the government offices deal with are in relation to Secretary of State call-ins, planning appeals, general planning functions, and – relevant to this research – development plan monitoring. Each of the regional offices, as their primary aim when scrutinising development plans, must ensure that the role of development plans at the local level meets the government's expectations set nationally. The overall aim for development plans, in the eyes of the regional offices, is:

> to reconcile the regeneration and competitiveness objectives for an area with
> the protection of the local environment in a way that supports the national
> policies for sustainable development.

> (author's interview, 1997)

Since this objective forms the overall national political rationale for the planning service across Britain, local planning authorities' development plans are viewed as crucial in indicating the type of development that will or will not be permitted in an area and forms a strategy of certainty for developers and communities. To achieve this overall objective, each of the regional offices is charged with ensuring that the contents of development plans are consistent with national planning policy guidance and to make representations on behalf of the Secretary of State for Transport and the Environment to the local planning authority whenever and wherever a plan or policy is considered to be unacceptable.

Copies of development plans are received directly from local planning authorities and distributed to each section of the government office. The scrutiny of local plans by the regional offices requires thorough co-ordination between the constituent parts of each department, the aim being to speak with one voice. Since national planning policies are agreed across all government departments, all potential interests have to be co-ordinated. The government officer charged with scrutinising a particular local plan works to a 'Local Plan Procedure Checklist', a standard list of duties common to all government regional offices (outlined in Table 7.1)

The government offices' checklist is followed strictly upon receiving the local plan documentation. This involves checking that the local planning authority has

Table 7.1 Local plan procedure checklist used by government regional offices

Stage	Procedure
1	Check all documents are received and correct
2	Acknowledge letter to local planning authority
3	Inform all departments of the regional office
4	Inform Planning Inspectorate Agency
5	Inform Ministry of Agriculture Fisheries and Food (now DEFRA)
6	Consult other government departments
7	Consult newspaper advertisements of plan draft/deposit
8	Update regional office records
9	Check plan's contents against all national guidance
10	Identify all inconsistencies and problems
11	Notify local authority through written representation
12	Update officer's personal diary (includes noting dates of comments, co-ordinating all comments from other government departments, sending copy of plan to library, and updating of computing records)

Source: Author; interview carried out with officials of the Government Office for the South-West, May 1994

followed the requirements set out in the statutory planning regulations, the Town and Country Planning (Development Plan) Regulations 1991, with regard to plan publicity and ensuring that the local planning authority has obtained a certificate of conformity with the structure plan. A copy of the plan is then sent to the other directorates within each government regional office and an administration team co-ordinates the government office's responses to the policies contained within the local plans.

The initial scrutiny of local plans is carried out by administration staff within the development plans team of each government office. The administrative staff have access to a DTLR local plan policy checklist which outlines what core national policies should be contained within the local plan. This list is usually not for public consumption, but a copy of the list dating from 1994 was reproduced in a DoE research project, *The Effectiveness of Planning Policy Guidance Notes* (DoE, 1995). The checklist contains key policy statements that have to be included within each local plan, and mirrors the key national policy statements to be found within the Planning Policy Guidance Notes. These key statements include, for example in relation to historic buildings and conservation areas, the need for local plans to contain policies which preserve or enhance areas of townscape, conservation areas and archaeologically important sites. The checklist also requires the built environment section of a local plan to include policies on issues such as traffic management and road improvements.

In addition to making sure that a local plan contains the relevant policies for the area, the administrative staff of the government regional office also highlight any policy areas where the local plan is not in conformity with national planning policy guidance. The case officer within the government regional office is required to scrutinise the local plan against the contents of the government's own national planning policies, as set out in the Planning Policy Guidance Notes (PPGs). Feedback from the other departments of the government regional office is also collected at this stage. The local plan is then given to the professional planning staff who ensure that the plan reflects both national planning policies guidance and local opportunities and strategies.

To many commentators this decision to establish these regional institutions was seen as a radical departure from the anti-regional stance taken by the Thatcher governments in the 1980s (Mawson, 1997b). However, it soon became clear that this institutional innovation was well in keeping with the traditional line of administrative devolution which has been practised by the British state for much of the post-war period. Complaints began to emerge that the GORs were simply not fulfilling expectations of greater regional autonomy in policy-making. Most criticism was directed at the relationship between the GORs and central government. As Evans and Harding (Evans and Harding, 1997: 23) state:

> GORs are unlikely to act as regional advocates, not least because Senior Regional Directors report to the Secretaries of State of their four constituent departments. Whitehall also decides on the disbursement of key funds ... In the event of a clash of interest, it is difficult to see how territorial concerns will prevail over central departmental priorities.

The GORs were also viewed as having little influence over centrally formulated policies. The policy process was simply too well-established to incorporate GORs at an early stage, thus policies emerged with little evidence of a regional input (Mawson and Spencer, 1997). Furthermore, the Regional Directors were criticised for failing to include local stakeholders (business people, local authority representatives, and so on) in the establishment of regional strategic priorities. This led on to further complaints that the Directors were acting like viceroys for central government in the regions: powerful and unaccountable bureaucrats following a centrally imposed agenda.

The emergence of the GORs can therefore be seen as a limited exercise in regional administrative devolution, able to perhaps deal with European regional initiatives but lacking a real ability to promote and co-ordinate regional policy (John and Whitehead, 1997). Despite these criticisms, however, some commentators do believe that the GORs represent a significant step towards some degree of regional government. Hogwood (1996), for instance, has argued that these offices potentially represent 'a greater degree of practical coordination of activities and alignment of regional boundaries than was actually achieved under the substantially more ambitious economic planner emphasis of the 1960s'. The GORs may have proved to have been a useful tier for the establishment of stronger regional policy-making if things had remained the same in the mid-1990s, but the winds of change were blowing already. The election of the Labour government in 1997 heralded a new commitment to establish even more substantial decentralisation of power to the regions.

REGIONAL PLANNING IN THE 1980S AND 1990S

The regional level has traditionally been the weakest tier of planning in the UK, especially in England (Wannop, 1995). While local planning authorities have been co-operating at a regional level for many years, it is only over the last decade or so that central government has given any real encouragement to regional planning. Baker (1998: 154) states that 'the period from the late 1970s through to the early 1990s can be identified as almost totally barren in terms of regional and even strategic (sub-regional) planning policy in the UK'. By the late 1980s, however, there were increasing concerns in the south-east of England about the spread of new housing development and its impact on the environment, leading to pressure for some strengthening of strategic planning. The 1986 Green Paper, The Future of Development Plans, highlighted the progress that had been made in certain regions, such as East Anglia and the West Midlands, in producing regional strategies to guide the strategic policies of local authorities (DoE/Welsh Office, 1986). The consultation paper proposed that the Secretary of State should begin to issue guidance to the regional planning forums so that the regions could be more explicitly linked into a national structure (Tewdwr-Jones, 1996b). Neither the Department of the Environment nor the Welsh Office at the time wished to see the regional planning system develop into a more effective and institutionalised form of regional planning (Alden and Offord, 1996; Roberts, 1996).

Towards the late 1980s a more coherent system of Regional Planning Guidance (RPG) began to emerge. The 1989 White Paper *The Future of Development Plans* (HM Government, 1989) encouraged consortia of local authorities to prepare regional guidance, and PPG15, produced in 1990, stated that 'the aim should be to have guidance in place for most regions during the early 1990s' (quoted in Baker 1998). Under the consortia arrangements, conferences of local planning authorities were required to produce advice to the Secretary of State in the form of draft guidance. The Secretary of State would then take this into account when publishing Regional Planning Guidance (initially regional guidance was published as part of the PPG series but a separate RPG series was established in 1989).

The plan-led system introduced by the Planning and Compensation Act 1991 emphasised that the primary function of regional guidance was to provide the necessary framework for the preparation of structure plans or part one of unitary development plans. PPG12 of 1992 covered the preparation, content timing and progress of regional planning guidance and made the following points:

- regional guidance will normally cover those issues that are of regional importance or that need to be considered on a wider basis than structure plans;
- regional planning guidance will be limited to matters relevant to development plans;
- topics covered depend on circumstances in each region;
- guidance will suggest a development framework for a period of 20 years;
- it will cover priorities for environment, transport, economic development, agriculture, minerals, waste and infrastructure (DoE, 1992b; Murdoch and Tewdwr-Jones, 1999).

Regional Planning Guidance has now been produced for all regions of England. The Standing Conferences within each region have responsibility for the future revision of regional guidance and, in the latter 1990s, have been revised under Labour's proposals to enhance regional planning policy (DETR, 1998g). Baker (1998) remarks that its status and importance has grown since the early 1990s, and various reasons are credited for this, including institutional innovations elsewhere in government such as the establishment of the GORs. These offices have resulted in a desire for greater co-ordination between regional actors, and this prompted the need for a regional planning presence. The main impetus for regional planning was a recognition that many policy concerns can only be adequately addressed at a wider scale than that of existing development plans:

> The quest for sustainable development patterns, the role of green belts; the
> impact of large out-of-town employment and retail centres; the relationship
> between metropolitan areas and their hinterlands and meeting future housing
> needs all involve planning policy considerations which cross existing
> administrative boundaries. These can only be addressed by an effective regional
> planning framework ...
>
> (Baker, 1998: 165)

After Labour's election in 1997, the desire for stronger regional planning continued. Following the establishment of Regional Development Agencies and the devolved bodies in Scotland and Wales, the issue of enhancing regional planning was discussed. In 1998, the government published a consultation paper entitled

The Future of Regional Planning Guidance (DETR, 1998g). The paper states that 'the interests of the English regions have been neglected in recent years and this government intends to reverse that neglect'. It proposes that there are two ways of achieving this: one is via the regional economic strategies; the other is by improving the arrangements for co-ordination of land use, transport and economic development planning at the regional level.

Criticisms have been made of the current regional guidance system, and these have been taken on board. The document identifies that:

- RPG lacks regional focus and spends too much time reiterating national policies;
- RPG lacks targets which can be monitored and reviewed;
- the system is too narrow and land use orientated;
- RPG lacks sufficient environmental objectives and appraisal;
- it takes too long to produce;
- it does not command commitment from regional stakeholders;
- the process of producing it is insufficiently transparent.

The consultation paper sets out to address these issues. For instance, it proposes that the regional planning conference should have more responsibility for actually producing the guidance so that it can better reflect regional rather than national priorities. The conference should also work closely with regional stakeholders for better representation and put forward the proposal that the guidance be subject to an Examination in Public hearing in order to make the issues more transparent. These changes were enacted in 1999 and have been welcomed by planning professionals, developers and environmentalists. The proposals contained within the December 2001 Green Paper on the future of planning go a degree further, with the possible replacement of Regional Planning Guidance with Regional Spatial Strategies that are meant to be similar to regional plans (DTLR, 2001b; see Chapter 4).

REGIONAL PLANNING IN WALES
The situation in Wales is slightly more complicated. Wales possesses no formal regional planning policy and, as a consequence of devolution, the National Assembly has concentrated its efforts at the national agenda. Local government reorganisation in 1996 had abolished formal strategic policy-making when the eight counties and 37 districts were replaced by 22 all-purpose unitary authorities (Harris and Tewdwr-Jones, 1995). Following the passing of the Local Government (Wales) Act 1994, the Welsh Office recognised that strategic planning was nevertheless necessary and encouraged local authorities to voluntary co-operate to address issues of a strategic nature with the aim of producing part one of their

unitary development plans. In the latter 1990s, regional groupings of local authorities have been established for this purpose, although they vary in format and title. Three groupings existed covering the whole of Wales:

•   South East Wales Strategic Planning Group, that prepared Strategic Planning Guidance for South East Wales in January 2000 (SEWSPG, 2000);
•   North Wales Planning Group, that prepared Regional Planning Guides for North Wales (that remain in draft at the time of writing; NWPG, 2000);
•   Mid and West Wales Strategic Planning Group, that prepared the Mid and West Wales Strategic Planning Statement in 1999 (MWWSPG, 2000), and has since been superseded by Regional Planning Guidance (South West Wales) for certain authorities, prepared by the South West Wales Strategic Planning Group in 2000 (SWWSPG, 2000).

Despite the lack of a central co-ordinating role on the part of central government, the unitary authorities have progressed statements to an advance level and the Mid and West Wales Strategic Planning Statement was even subject to an informal Examination in Public in January 1999. While these statements have been first and foremost useful for the preparation of strategic policies for unitary development plans, there has been a recognition of their value as regional statements, especially in co-ordinating the strategies and policies of other organisations and institutions that are themselves organised on a regional basis. The Assembly, for example, possesses Regional Committees and the Welsh Development Agency is structured regionally within Wales.

REGIONAL PLANNING IN SCOTLAND

The regional planning tier in Scotland does not exist in any meaningful way. Scotland's local authorities had been required to prepare regional plans (equivalent to structure plans) in the 1960s and 1970s but the Thatcher governments had reorientated the system to an English and Welsh model in the 1980s (Hayton, 1996). Local government reorganisation in 1996 in Scotland had, similar to Wales, created unitary local authorities, but the planning system to be operated by this new structure was different to that implemented in Wales. Rather than prepare unitary development plans, local planning authorities were required to prepare local plans and structure plans. Structure plans would have to be prepared by amalgamations of local authorities across traditional local government boundaries, such as that covering Glasgow and the Clyde Valley (see Goodstadt, 2001, for a review of the experience).

The Scottish Office had released a future of land use planning consultation document in January 1999, prior to the establishment of the Scottish Parliament and Scottish Executive, and this had considered – amongst other things – the potential for regional planning statements (Scottish Office, 1999). This was put forward in parallel to suggestions to revisit the necessity for structure plans and whether to release more locationally specific national planning policy. In its response to the consultations, the Scottish Executive determined that a sub-national level of planning policy was not desirable at the present time but would review the situation within a few years. Allmendinger and Barker (2001), in their review of the desirability of regional planning in a post-devolved Scotland, note that an enhanced regional policy tier is not necessarily wanted – by the planning profession at least. This may have signalled the proposals that were to be released by the Scottish Executive in the summer of 2001.

In June 2001 the Executive released the *Review of Strategic Planning* consultation document (Scottish Executive, 2001). As part of the proposals contained within this document, it is suggested that the four principal cities – Glasgow, Edinburgh, Dundee and Aberdeen – should be covered by two tiers of development plan, one strategic and one local. The upper tier, to be known as the 'Strategic Development Plan', will provide a city-region coverage, but planning outside these urban areas will comprise a single tier of development plan with spatially specific revised 'National Planning Policy Statements'.

New Labour and the Push for Regionalism

The Labour Party had adopted a strongly regionalist agenda in the early 1990s. Electoral success by Scottish nationalists in Labour's heartlands in the late 1980s led to a hardening of Labour's commitment to Scottish devolution and, as the 1992 General Election approached, this caused a reconsideration of the party's attitude to the English regions. As Labour came to adopt a policy of Scottish devolution, many English Labour Members of Parliament, especially those with constituencies in the north of England, became concerned about untoward effects, primarily in terms of economic growth, for their English constituencies. Thus they urged some move towards an English form of regional government. In 1991 the Party published a consultation paper entitled *Devolution and Democracy*, which outlined the case for English regionalism (Labour Party, 1991). The reasons cited included the democratic deficit at the regional level, the need for more effective and accountable regional structures, and the economic development imperative of regional agencies.

Regionalist thinking continued as the party once again settled into opposition following Labour's election defeat in 1992. The Party published another consultation document in 1995 entitled *A Choice for England* (Labour Party, 1995). This argued the case for making GORs, quangos and other agencies more open and accountable to the regions and local authorities, through the creation of indirectly elected regional chambers comprising a relatively small number of nominated councillors. In 1996, Labour launched the second key component of its proposals for the English regions in the form of a report from its Regional Policy Commission that advocated the establishment of regional economic development agencies working under the control of regional chambers (Regional Policy Commission, 1996).

As the 1997 election approached, the concerned English MPs managed to pressure Tony Blair into promising the speedy introduction of the regional economic development agencies, formally referred to as Regional Development Agencies (Mawson, 1998); in return, they pledged support for Scottish (and Welsh) devolution (Murdoch and Tewdwr-Jones, 1999). Upon taking office in May 1997, Labour moved swiftly to establish the RDAs. An issues paper was published in the summer of the same year stating that each region would gain its own RDA based on existing GOR boundaries. Upon establishment, the RDAs would promote: economic development and urban regeneration; business efficiency, investment and competitiveness; employment, skills and educational development; and sustainable development (DETR, 1997).

The RDAs would be managed by boards which would be appointed by the Secretary of State, although it was stressed that the minister would have to take heed to regional issues, problems and personnel in making these appointments. Discussion of the proposed regional chambers had receded by this time and were postponed until Labour's second term of office. The boards were to be made up of six people from business, three from local councils and the remainder from the unions, voluntary sector and other interest groups (see Jones, 2001, for a review of board membership). Initially the boards would be expected to draw up an economic plan which should address the development needs of the region and investigate ways of levering finance out of the private sector so that regional development funds could be established.

The discussion paper was followed by a White Paper in December 1997 entitled *Building Partnerships for Prosperity* (HM Government, 1997). The White Paper proposed nine RDA regions. The new development agencies would 'promote sustainable development and social and physical regeneration and ... coordinate the work of regional and local partners in areas such as training, investment, regeneration and business support'. The RDAs were to take over some functions of the GORs and certain quangos, and would engage in the drafting of a research regional economic plan, administering regeneration functions of English Partnerships and the Rural Development Commission, administering European Structural Funds, co-ordinate inward investment, reclaim and prepare factory sites, market the region as a business location, and contribute to policies and programmes on transport, land use, environment, further and higher education, crime prevention, health and tourism. The government also made it clear that RDAs would not be taking powers away from local government. As a consequence, although the possibility was raised by the planning minister during the parliamentary scrutiny of the RDA bill in 1998, town and country planning was excluded from the RDA remit and remained under local authority control. It was stressed that this function would still be operated by democratically accountable bodies which, in the absence of the regional chambers, indicated local government. Nevertheless, in formulating their strategies the RDAs would have to take account of local and strategic planning policies, in addition to Regional Planning Guidance.

It is clear that the establishment of the RDAs was a significant new chapter in the ongoing march towards stronger regional government in the UK. Together with devolution to Scotland and Wales they might be seen to mark the emergence of a substantially enhanced regional tier. However, unlike in Scotland or Wales, where a degree of coherence and co-ordination can be discerned in the relationships between the various agencies operating at regional and local scales, the arrangements in England are still characterised by a fragmentation of functions amongst the various agencies. Moreover, the relationships between RDAs and other regional actors seem rather ambiguous; for instance, it is still far from clear even now how the relationships between regional planning mechanisms and the regional economic strategies will prevail in practice (Baker *et al.*, 1999; Roberts and Lloyd, 1999). More seriously, it has been argued that the RDAs are now pale imitations of those originally envisaged by the Regional Policy Commission and John Prescott, the Deputy Prime Minister. According to Peter Hetherington, writing in the *Guardian* in November 1998:

> The RDAs were originally meant to be all-singing and dancing. The English regions would acquire a layer of government to match the power and wealth of the long established Welsh Development Agency and its opposite number north of the border, Scottish Enterprise. But rival ministers and mandarins decided that RDAs in the Prescott mould with powers drawn from several departments – notably development grants from industry, known as selective regional assistance, and the work of Training and Enterprise Councils (TECs) – represented one step too far. So they rebelled ... the RDAs ... have been cut down to size.

In the absence of local popular support for these regional bodies, the establishment of elected and democratic regional chambers slipped down the government's list of priorities in its first parliament between 1997 and 2001. This once more raises the problem that the RDAs may be viewed too much like central government

quangos until the democratic level is established, an issue not assisted by accusations of cronyism in the appointments to RDA boards of Labour Party supporters
(Jones, 2001). For Hetherington (1998), writing perceptively four years ago, RDAs

> seem destined to become agents of central government, delivering a range of
> functions from re-developing land to building factories, rather than strong
> regional power bases capable of competing with Scotland and Wales, let alone
> Continental counterparts in an emerging Europe of Regions.

For the present time, until regional chambers are implemented in the 2001–5
parliament, RDAs are loosely linked to other regional actors but appear strongly
linked to central government. This raises the difficulty of the RDAs sitting within the
crucible of complex future policy relationships between regional planning strategies, local authorities' development plans, and national planning policy of central
government.

THE ADEQUACY AND EFFECTIVENESS OF CURRENT REGIONAL PLANNING

The limited piece of research, discussed below, was undertaken by Philip Allmendinger and myself in 1999, assisted by Liz Cordy. Parts of it were published in
2000 (see Allmendinger and Tewdwr-Jones, 2000b). The research sought to
ascertain the attitudes of key stakeholders in a variety of existing public and semi-
public bodies in England, Scotland and Wales towards the emerging institutional
forms of regional planning and governance. Although regional planning only exists
in an institutional sense within England, it was decided to broaden the research to
consider the adequacy and desire for regional planning within Scotland and Wales
too since devolution. The overall aim of the research was to gauge perspectives on
the proposed arrangements, and to ascertain likely responses of existing institutional networks with a view to assessing both the perceived horizontal relationships
between the new regional level and other agencies of governance and the perceived vertical relationships between the new regional level and other scales of
governance within each of the three countries. This was illustrated with particular
reference to spatial planning and economic development.

The research sought to gauge the attitude of respondents towards the existing institutional arrangements for regional governance and planning. The first question sought to ascertain whether respondents felt that current arrangements for
regional planning were adequate. The answer was an overwhelming 'no', with variations between the three nations (see Table 7.2). Though the headline figure for
adequacy of current arrangements shows general dissatisfaction amongst the

Table 7.2 The adequacy of existing regional planning arrangements

	Adequate		Inadequate		Don't know		Total	
	No.	%	No.	%	No.	%	No.	%
England	26	33	52	65	2	3	80	100
Wales	3	18	14	82	0	0	17	100
Scotland	4	19	17	81	0	0	21	100
Total	33	28	83	70	2	2	118	100

Question: Do you feel that current arrangements for regional planning in your area are adequate?
Source: Allmendinger and Tewdwr-Jones (2000b)
Note: Percentages may not add up to 100 due to rounding

respondents, it is interesting to note that this proportion was much lower in England than in either Wales or Scotland. Respondents were asked to develop their reasons for this. Although there was greater satisfaction with arrangements in England there were some strong opinions from those dissatisfied with the arrangements. These included, as stated in responses on the questionnaire returns:

- current imbalances of power between smaller and larger local authorities;
- a lack of resources and staff;
- restrictive timescales to progress regional policy/procedural arrangements.

In addition, a small minority felt that there was some confusion over the role of RDAs and regional assemblies. In Wales general dissatisfaction with current arrangements emanated from the feeling that there was no formal regional (that is, sub-national) planning mechanism, while in Scotland there were a variety of reasons for a lack of satisfaction. A minority of respondents felt that joint structure plan arrangements were unsatisfactory because of competition between different authorities and their conflicting priorities, which were not adequately resolved either locally or nationally. It was considered that this could be achieved by a more effective national planning framework. Some authorities also felt that such a framework need not cover the whole of Scotland but could focus on different regions within it – for example, the central belt.

In contrast to the general dissatisfaction with regional planning arrangements there was broad contentment with current regional planning guidance in England and Scotland, though this was less clear in Wales. In all, 45 per cent of respondents in England and 52 per cent of those in Scotland felt that current arrangements were either very effective or effective (Table 7.3). In Wales, however, the figure was only 18 per cent. And while 1 per cent of respondents in England and no respondents in Scotland considered existing regional planning arrangements to be ineffective, the figure for Wales was 29 per cent. This should not, however, be

Table 7.3 The effectiveness of existing regional planning guidance

	Effective		Marginally effective		Ineffective		Don't know		Total	
	No.	%	No.	%	No.	%	No.	%	No.	%
England	36	45	42	52	1	1	1	1	80	100
Wales	3	18	9	53	5	29	0	0	17	100
Scotland	11	52	10	48	0	0	0	0	21	100
Total	50	42	61	52	6	5	1	1	118	100

Question: How effective are existing forms of regional planning guidance?

Source: Allmendinger and Tewdwr-Jones (2000b)

Note: Percentages may not add up to 100 due to rounding

seen necessarily as an endorsement of existing arrangements in England and Scotland: 52 per cent and 48 per cent of respondents respectively considered existing regional planning guidance to be 'marginally effective'. This led many respondents to comment on how existing arrangements could be improved. In England, there was broad support for a greater integration of planning arrangements between public and quasi-public bodies, and that regional planning guidance could help ensure this. Furthermore, the relationship between regional planning guidance and the objectives of structure, local and unitary development plans was felt to be an area where effectiveness could be improved. Notwithstanding this, a number of respondents considered that although these matters should improve the effectiveness of guidance, the new arrangements for regional planning and governance through regional assemblies and RDAs would provide help in achieving them. In Scotland, the view again pointed towards either a national plan or a stronger strategic vision.

The sentiments of English respondents concerning the need to integrate disparate public and quasi-public bodies' planning and investment decisions was also prominent. Also of equal importance was the desire to tie in public investment decisions to a strategic plan. While being the most dissatisfied with existing regional planning arrangements (mainly because of the lack of them), the Welsh respondents were also the least forthcoming about how this could be addressed. Possible alternatives mentioned included the need to clarify and enhance the status of planning guidance in Wales through the transfer of responsibility in the preparation of guidance to either the Welsh Assembly or the Welsh Development Agency. It is, perhaps, significant here that the WDA should be viewed as a principal alternative actor in the provision of regional planning mechanisms, despite both the prominence of the relatively new National Assembly and the WDA's lack of statutory powers over the provision of spatial planning policy.

Devolution to the Scottish Parliament, Welsh Assembly and the English regional assemblies and development agencies raises the possibility of improving regional planning. However, in England only 22.7 per cent of respondents felt that RDAs would lead to a more integrated approach to regional policy through the strategic overview provided and their emphasis on planning, transport and economic development strategies (see Table 7.4). One area identified by respondents that the RDAs could improve was in raising the profile of regions generally and providing a stronger voice for regional matters. Other views raised included the possibility of RDAs improving democratic accountability in regional planning matters, although as quangos it is uncertain what respondents had in mind by referring to this.

The majority of respondents did not consider that RDAs would actually improve regional planning and guidance. A variety of reasons were offered in

Table 7.4 Optimism expressed towards new devolved institutions* in strengthening regional policy formulation (*for England, via the creation of Regional Development Agencies; for Wales, via the creation of the National Assembly; for Scotland, via the creation of the Scottish Parliament)

	Likely improvement		Likely to be no improvement		Don't know		Total	
	No.	%	No.	%	No.	%	No.	%
England	50	63	23	29	7	9	80	100
Wales	8	47	5	29	4	24	17	100
Scotland	16	75	4	20	1	5	21	100
Total	74	63	32	27	12	10	118	100

Question: Do you think the Regional Development Agencies/National Assembly for Wales/Scottish Parliament will improve the mechanisms for regional policy formulation?

Source: Allmendinger and Tewdwr-Jones (2000b)

Note: Percentages may not add up to 100 due to rounding

support of this, including the feeling that RDAs will be likely to follow their own agendas. A more common view expressed in responses was that economic development and spatial planning are too distinct to be integrated, even through the strategies of RDAs. Other respondents criticised RDAs' lack of accountability, their commercial – rather than public – orientation, and their lack of funding.

The feeling from Scottish-based respondents was more positive towards the ability of the Scottish Parliament to improve regional planning and policy guidance. In all, 75 per cent of respondents felt the Parliament would improve the situation while only 20 per cent felt that it would not. This more positive perspective can be partly explained by the low perception of the current situation. Although there were a variety of reasons for the feeling of improvement, the predominant optimistic attitude was that the Scottish Parliament would avoid the current dominance of parochial politics, focus more on strategic matters and integrate land use planning and economic matters. On the less enthusiastic side, a minority opinion thought that the Scottish Parliament would centralise regional policy guidance which would lead to a loss rather than enhancement of accountability. Similar to the English situation highlighted above there was also a general feeling that the Scottish Parliament would help raise the profile of regional planning generally in Scotland.

Of the Welsh respondents, 47 per cent considered that the Welsh Assembly would improve current regional planning arrangements, not only in terms of providing more of a regional focus through its elected members but also by making the Welsh Development Agency more accountable. However, there was a large minority who felt that the Welsh Development Agency would resist this, given its tradition of centralist and autonomous working. Furthermore, it was considered that tying the Welsh Development Agency more closely in with the Welsh Assembly would not guarantee that spatial planning and economic development became more integrated.

The idea of making new regional planning arrangements more accountable through the various forms of regional governance was also explored (see Table 7.5). In England, 94 per cent of respondents felt that RDAs should be accountable to elected regional assemblies, while 94 per cent of respondents in Wales felt that the WDA should be accountable to the Welsh Assembly. The situation in Scotland is slightly different in that the Scottish Executive is accountable to the Scottish Parliament; the Scottish dimension was therefore excluded from this question. Here the question referred to accountability to the wider public and 76 per cent of respondents felt that current public involvement amounts to little more than tokenism. In England the corresponding figure was 78 per cent while in Wales it was 75 per cent.

Apart from the ongoing changes to regional planning and governance the

Table 7.5 Perceptions towards the scope for increased accountability of regional economic development institutions in England and Wales to democratically elected regional assemblies/government

	Enhanced accountability		Reduced accountability		Don't know		Total	
	No.	%	No.	%	No.	%	No.	%
England	75	94	3	4	2	3	80	100
Wales	16	94	0	0	1	6	17	100
Total	91	94	3	3	3	3	97	100

Question: **England:** Do you think the creation of the Regional Development Agencies will enhance or reduce accountability in the English regions?
Wales: Do you think the Welsh Development Agency's accountability will be enhanced or reduced under the National Assembly for Wales?
Source: Allmendinger and Tewdwr-Jones (2000b)
Note: Percentages may not add up to 100 due to rounding

respondents were also asked to identify ways in which they thought the preparation of regional planning policy could be improved. The majority of English respondents (53 per cent) made no response to this question, although 29 per cent
stressed the need for greater accountability even though it was recognised that
public interest in regional planning matters was generally very low. Suggestions of
how to increase accountability included the greater involvement of local elected
members and local planning officers, and the possible use of citizen's panels for
the mediation of conflicts. Similar to England, respondents in Wales also stressed
the need for greater public consultation and involvement. The form of greater consultation discussed included the possibility of elected regional assemblies both in
England (supported by 86 per cent of respondents) and Wales (supported by 61
per cent of respondents). If such assemblies would be created, 92 per cent of
English respondents and 85 per cent of Welsh respondents would support the
transfer of regional policy formulation to these institutions.

The advantages of such regional assemblies specified by respondents would
be in the greater accountability they would provide to the preparation of guidance
including a 'sense of ownership', and greater legitimacy for the guidance itself. In
addition, a number of respondents also mentioned the role of assemblies in providing policy cohesion. Nevertheless, there was also some feeling in Wales that
assemblies would add a further layer of bureaucracy, be of little or no benefit to
regional planning (24 per cent of respondents) and could provide confusion in the
mind of the public with regard to local authority responsibilities.

Another possible outcome of evolving forms of regional governance is the
fragmentation of national (that is, state) strategic policy formulation and co-
ordination through the emergence of a variety of new actors and mechanisms. The
government has announced the publication of a joint 'concordat' between England,
Scotland and Wales that covers a number of issues, including relations with the
European Union and inward investment bidding (HM Government, 1999), intended
to stop the development of divergent processes on specific policies in each of the
three countries. There was no clear view from the respondents as to whether they
thought this would actually occur in practice (see Table 7.6). Generally, almost the
same percentage of English and Welsh respondents were of the opinion that
fragmentation would or would not occur as a result of devolution and decentralisation. However, in Scotland, a higher proportion of respondents (57 per cent)
thought national strategic policy fragmentation would occur; some of these respondents remarked that they viewed devolution as the path towards this goal.

Respondents were also asked whether state policy fragmentation would be
an issue to be concerned about. In contrast to the results of the previous question,
if such a fragmentation were to occur then only in England (64 per cent) was it
considered to be an issue of concern, while in Scotland and Wales only a minority

Table 7.6 The scope for further fragmentation of the present national approach to strategic policy formulation

	Agree		Disagree		Don't know		Total	
	No.	%	No.	%	No.	%	No.	%
England	38	48	42	52	0	0	80	100
Wales	8	47	9	53	0	0	17	100
Scotland	12	57	6	29	3	14	21	100
Total	58	49	57	48	3	3	118	100

Question: In the light of the creation of the National Assembly for Wales, the Scottish Parliament, the Regional Development Agencies and regional assemblies, do you think there is a danger that the UK government's approach to national strategic policy co-ordination will be fragmented further?

Source: Allmendinger and Tewdwr-Jones (2000b)

Note: Percentages may not add up to 100 due to rounding

(24 per cent and 25 per cent respectively) were concerned. In Scotland additional questions were asked regarding the possibility of a divergence in legislation from England and Wales, 43 per cent considering that this would occur, the most common reason being the ability of the Scottish Parliament to be an expression of existing differences. Only a minority felt that there would be no change because of the continued dominance of Westminster; one respondent felt there would be a convergence of policy.

Respondents were also of the opinion that further national policy was desirable, and this seems rather puzzling in the context of the award of an enhanced regional governance tier, which is intended to assist in the decentralisation of policy-making from national government rather than bolster the activities of the UK government. The reason for this view could be an overwhelming feeling of uncertainty over the new powers awarded to the regional tier; at worse, it might even suggest an inability to define solutions and policies at this new regional level without central guidance which would only circumvent the principle of decentralisation. Finally, other respondents called for what could be termed greater integration of policy areas, including land use, transport and economic development.

Although there was a mixed feeling towards the possibility of a more fragmented national approach to policy formulation the survey sought to explore how any fragmentation could be avoided. Although there were a number of respondents who felt that fragmentation was not necessarily something to be avoided (particularly in Scotland), government generally (be it Westminster, Edinburgh or Cardiff) was perceived as the foil to such a trajectory. Respondents stated that this could be achieved through co-ordinated and clear central guidance. In the event that this was insufficient some local authority respondents suggested a strengthening of the reserve powers of the relevant Secretary of State, although this would address sub-national rather than national fragmentation. The possibility of a supra-national body to ensure greater policy co-ordination was also raised, even though the EU would in part provide such a role.

CONCLUSIONS

The expectations being placed on the new form of regional planning post-1998 are startling. In addition to being subject to environmental assessment and a form of sustainability appraisal, draft regional planning statements are also expected to provide the regional planning framework for issues of more than local importance, act as a basis for local authorities' development plans, develop an integrated transport and land use strategy for each region, support the regional economic strategies of the Regional Development Agencies, and assist bids for European Union financial programmes in line with the government's commitments towards emerging forms of European spatial planning. In addition to these requirements, regional policy also has to take into account national planning policies of central government and the decisions of the Secretary of State. This uneasy combination of policy compatibility and conflict between and within agencies of regional governance responsible for the planning process could lead to tensions in practice. The key questions that emerge are which governmental level of the state will now shoulder the responsibility of resolving the same political conflicts that have always been apparent in the planning system, and will practice meet the rhetoric?

The government's commitments to enhance regional planning in England since 1997 rest on more regional choice in the policy-making apparatus, by extending the range of organisations and bodies in the formulation stages of the guidance in each region and requiring that individual notes meet the needs of specific regions. These organisations, dubbed by the consultation paper as stakeholders, include not only the local authorities and Government Offices for the Regions, but additionally other governmental and non-governmental bodies such as businesses and quangos, all of which are expected to claim ownership of the strategy for policy-making purposes. This move to enhance the regional level while the government still retains overall planning policy agenda-setting at the national level could give rise to conflict. To what extent enhanced regional planning policy will sit comfortably with the state's desire to provide a national planning policy framework that the other tiers of governance are expected to conform to, remains a perplexing question. It strikes to the very heart of the government's dilemmas of decentralising power from the centre to the regions to provide regional choice while retaining authority across the entire state. But in addition to the vertical uncertainty that an enhanced middle-level of policy-making will encourage between the national and local policy agendas, relations across organisations in each region and across sectors will also generate horizontal uncertainty.

The proposals for Regional Spatial Strategies illustrate the greater degree of expectations being placed upon the planning system at this new level, almost as if it is a panacea to resolve regulatory disputes arising at the national and local levels. The broader remit of regional planning sectorally, together with an extension to the number and range of stakeholders expected to participate in the policy-making process, suggests the likelihood of enhanced conflict and dispute rather than its amelioration. The recently introduced RPG Examination in Public (EIP) has increased the public's appetite for participation in strategic policy-making processes (as the South-East EIP demonstrated in 1999), and so there does seem to be a likelihood for the broader ownership of RPGs and the necessity to ensure compatibility between RDAs' strategies and planning tools to actually slow down the planning preparation process, if only to satisfy the stakeholders' demands. The public, the environmentalists, the local authorities, the GORs, and the RDAs, will all expect the RPG and Regional Spatial Strategies to deliver on the complex inter-linked web of sectoral topics contained within regional policy: housing develop-ment, strategic employment sites, protection of the countryside, trunk road development, retailing centre, minerals extraction, and waste disposal.

The difficulty of reconciling these issues in the eyes of more organisations who shall now be afforded an opportunity to participate in the drafting of policies should not be underestimated. And that does not even contemplate the possibility of intergovernmental conflict between national planning policy priorities and indi-vidual regional preferences. Once in place, the government could well be faced with a further dilemma: how to democratise the regions both through planning pol-icies and opportunities for stakeholder participation while speeding-up and making more relevant the strategic planning process of each region.

Regionalism is a growing trend in the UK, not just in the Celtic periphery but in England too. The institutional innovations introduced during the 1990s – among them GORs, RDAs and enhanced regional planning forums – all point to greater regional autonomy. And yet it remains unclear how all these new bodies can act independently of central government. In the absence of separately elected forums in the regions, a reliance will be placed on central government to provide both the policy parameters and set expenditure controls. The government's commitment to support the creation of regional assemblies where there is a clear call for them will provide the democratic mandate the regions require to assert themselves more prominently. However, the creation of these assemblies for most of the English regions appears some years away. The case for regional planning illustrates the tensions and co-ordination apparent between the existing powers exercised by Whitehall and the new decentralised autonomy proposed for the regions. If regions can go their own way in responding to national policies then divergent develop-ment trajectories between regions may emerge. However, the fragmentation amongst the regional organisations of governance in England suggests the con-comitant development of conflicting objectives both sectorally and institutionally. In relation to housing for example, if certain regions promote a more protectionist stance against new developments this will likely generate support from the country-side lobby but alienation from the Regional Development Agencies (Cowell and Murdoch, 1999). The degree of compatibility between the regional stakeholders is therefore a matter of concern; should conflicts arise, which organisation or institu-tion will intervene to mediate, and what position will central government take up in attempts to resolve these sorts of dilemmas? Perhaps one outcome could be greater central involvement, and the establishment of the Regional Intelligence Unit within the Cabinet Office already hints at a greater co-ordinating role over the activities of the regions (Cabinet Office, 2000).

The recent sectoral pressures in the regions that have led to the establishment of new institutions – Regional Development Agencies for economic development, enhanced Regional Planning Guidance and Spatial Strategies for housing
development – are bound to be mirrored by calls for stronger regional policies in
order to 'tie the economic agenda to the physical planning, housing and environmental agendas, in the most difficult piece of "joined up" thinking yet' (Crookston,
1998: 215). It seems apparent that further rationalisation and simplification at the
regional tier of governance will be required, together with the creation of stronger
regional policies, if regional choice is to make any difference. Whether this could
be achieved without some degree of democratic input at the regional level is no
doubt an issue that will continue to occupy the government.

CHAPTER 8

LOCAL DISCRETION IN THE PLANNING POLICY PROCESS

INTRODUCTION

Chapter 6 presented aggregate data showing that there is generally a degree of acceptance among planning professionals within local planning authorities across England and Wales for national planning policy guidance in planning policy formulation. The research discussed in Chapter 6 indicated that the use of the government's Planning Policy Guidance Notes in providing direction and monitoring in planning policy formulation under the plan-led process forms an important part of the operation of land use planning in England, Scotland and Wales. This has occurred while local planning authorities have been required to produce a district-wide local plan if local policies are to benefit from the increased weight afforded to local plan policies in determining development control decisions.

Not all local planning authorities have previous experience of local plan preparation. The mandatory requirement for local plan preparation enshrined within the Planning and Compensation Act 1991 has led to uncertainty within some local authorities who have had to draft plans in a period of legal and policy transition, and many of these producing plans for the first time. In the period since the implementation of the 1991 Act, local planning authorities – uncertain over the status of the plan-led system – have sought to produce local plans that contain a comprehensive set of policies and cover every conceivable aspect of development, and this has resulted in the preparation of more lengthy plans than in the past. Other organisations outside central government and local government (for example, developers, community groups and environmentalists) have recognised the increased weight afforded to local plan policies to achieve certainty, and have also used the local plan preparation process as a means to put forward their own ideals and policy visions during the various stages of plan policy formulation.

The delay in producing local plans under the new planning regime has been noteworthy, but the resultant lengthier plan preparation process and more comprehensive local plans covering a larger number of topics run counter to national planning guidance from central government, guidance that has stated continuously that local plans should be put in place quickly (DoE, 1992b; DTLR, 2001b). The increase in the number of objections being made to local planning authorities has also emanated from the Department of the Environment's regional offices, the

Scottish Office (now Scottish Executive) and the Welsh Office (now Welsh Assembly). The government regional offices have been making a significantly high number of objections to local plans, partly to ensure that plans are slimmer and swifter (Royal Town Planning Institute, 1997), but also to ensure that central government's national planning policy guidance is adhered to by local planning authorities at all times during plan formulation.

Following on from the analysis of the aggregate survey data in Chapter 6, a district council was selected to consider the matters raised by the questionnaire survey on a localised, more in-depth basis. The selection of West Dorset District Council, a local authority in the south-west of England, was made in recognition of the importance of local specificity for theoretical and practical understanding. The choice of West Dorset originated from a breakdown of the questionnaire aggregate data. A decision was made to select a district council whose respondent had expressed strong views within the completed questionnaire on the degree and significance of central government intervention in the preparation of its local plan. West Dorset's questionnaire recorded a significant number of interventions by the region's government office, the Government Office for the South West (GOSW), in its monitoring of both the West Dorset Local Plan deposit version and pre-inquiry changes.

A detailed examination of the nature of the policy differences and conflicts between the national planning policy guidance and West Dorset's local plan would enable an assessment of the degree to which central government's quest for consistency and certainty was resulting in local policies floundering in the face of high levels of interventions. Such an intensive research investigation on the policy formulation functions of one individual local authority would enable a thorough assessment to be made of planning policy relationships and conflicts, and is considered to be the most appropriate vehicle to investigate the issue of national influence over local policy. The focus for the intensive case study examination is solely related to the number of central government interventions made in the drafting stages of that local authority's local plan, as evidenced in the results of the questionnaire survey. The research restricts its focus to the role of central government in local plan formulation, and does not consider the wider influence of other organisations (such as developers, community groups, environmentalists and members of the public) on the process.

An analysis of the position of West Dorset sought to assess the extent to which national planning policy guidance impacted upon the formulation of local planning policies, by examining the national planning policy role utilised by the Government Office for the South West in attempting to achieve consistency and certainty in planning policy formulation. This case study examines in great detail the nature of the government regional office's comments in monitoring West Dorset's local plan, the significance of the comments, and the degree to which West Dorset amended policies within their plan to ensure that the consistency defined by the GOSW was achieved. The focus here would be on individual national impact on local processes, and the degree of discretion that remained during local planning policy formulation.

THE FORM AND NATURE OF GOVERNMENT OFFICE PLANNING POLICY SCRUTINY

In conversation with Department of the Environment civil servants at the government regional offices, central government have been making record levels of objections to local plan policies since the introduction of the plan-led planning system in the Planning and Compensation Act 1991. Indeed, this view is confirmed in the results of the aggregate research survey, presented in Chapter 6, in which respondents recorded high levels of interventions from central government in their comments on local planning authorities' policies. The high number of objections is in part due to drafted local plan policies not being in conformity with national planning policy guidance, as utilised by the government regional offices.

The main guidance advanced by central government to local planning authorities on the preparation of district-wide local plans has been found in PPG12 *Development Plans* (revised in 1999 over its predecessor released in February 1992; DoE, 1992b; DETR, 1999), and in the Department of the Environment publication *Development Plans: A Good Practice Guide* (DoE, 1992a). Chapter 5 briefly mentioned these documents in putting forward a nationally consistent planning system, but this section discusses the form and nature of local plan preparation, as set out by central government, as a prelude to a discussion on West Dorset's experience of planning relations with the Government Office for the South West. This discussion considers format, content and expression, and detail.

FORMAT

Guidance on the format of local plans centres on their structure, layout and design. In particular, PPG12 and the *Good Practice Guide* provide advice to local authorities on the presentation of introductory chapters, policies and the overall presentation of the document. While many of these areas are left to the discretion of the local planning authority, it is clear that the DTLR (now ODPM) is eager to ensure some level of consistency in the format of local plans and clarity of objectives across the country. The government has always insisted that plans should be clear, concise and easily understood by all those who use the documents, but consistency in presentation and format could only further standardise local plans. The *Good Practice Guide* suggests that good presentation and a clear strategy is paramount in enabling the reader to form a clear and certain picture of what is acceptable and unacceptable development in each local planning authority area. The principal purpose of a clear local plan strategy is to establish certain local planning objectives and long-term intentions, provide a robust framework for the development of local planning policies, and ensure performance criteria are established for quality and evaluative purposes.

CONTENT AND EXPRESSION

The government has decided to take a hands-off approach in informing local planning authorities on the detailed content of local plans. Very little policy guidance is advanced within PPGs that explicitly requires local plans to address certain topics. Despite the lack of this explicit guidance, local planning authorities do generally follow the broad and often vague nature of the contents of Planning Policy Guidance Notes. PPG12, for example, merely suggests that a wide range of issues should be addressed in a local plan, but that this will depend on local circumstances and the preferences of individual local planning authorities. Nevertheless, local planning policy formulation must have regard to economic, environmental and social considerations. The government prefers local planning authorities using criteria-based policies which clearly set out the circumstances in which planning permission will or will not be granted, thereby emphasising the much sought-after certainty inherent within the plan-led planning system.

The government is also concerned at the possibility of local planning authorities misinterpreting the plan-led system and misusing the purposes of the local plan, by including aspects of planning, environmental and development matters that are *ultra vires*. This might include, for example, local planning authorities attempting to place a burden of proof on developers in demonstrating the merits of their proposal, or incorporating policies within local plans that are beyond land use planning boundaries. In order to achieve some element of consistency and certainty in planning policy formulation, the expressions contained within local plan policies are also matters of concern to central government. Policies should not be vague or ambiguous, but provide clear statements on local preferences; they must also conform with national planning policy guidance, unless there are local circumstances that justify a departure. No information is given on what is meant by local circumstances, and the degree of any local departure from a national policy position is not elaborated on further. Finally, for the purposes of implementing a plan-led system, local plans must contain policies and proposals that are clearly capable of being implemented.

DETAIL

Determining the level of detail appropriate for local plan policy formulation is also a matter left to the discretion of individual local planning authorities. This does not seem particularly surprising, since only local policy-makers can determine how to meet local planning problems and concerns. It is important for development control decisions to be based on policies contained within the local plan (the embodiment of a plan-led planning system). Nevertheless, the plan should not attempt to cover every possible *ad hoc* planning scenario. PPG12 calls for local plans to be clear and concise: 'The Secretary of State is very much against over elaborate plan-making. Plans should be clear, succinct and easily understood by all who need to know about the planning policies and proposals in the area' (DoE, 1992b: para. 5.3).

Following this overview of the nature and scope of government regional offices' planning functions, especially in local plan monitoring, attention will now be focused on the planning role of the Government Office for the South West in monitoring local planning authorities in the region.

THE ROLE OF THE GOVERNMENT OFFICE FOR THE SOUTH WEST IN MONITORING LOCAL PLAN POLICIES

The case study local planning authority, West Dorset District Council, is located in the County of Dorset in south-west England. The responsibility for monitoring and scrutinising local plans and comparing their contents with national planning policy guidance rests with the government regional office, the Government Office for the South West (GOSW). The government office is one of ten regional government offices in England that undertakes intervention in local plan policy formulation on behalf of the Secretary of State for the Environment. The National Assembly for Wales acts as another government office in performing a similar duty on behalf of the Secretary of State for Wales and the Welsh Cabinet (see Chapter 9). This section focuses on GOSW and briefly outlines how and in what ways the regional office has utilised national planning policy guidance in monitoring local plan policies in the South-West.

GOSW is principally based in Bristol, with satellite offices in Exeter and Plymouth, and comprises the central government departments for the environment, transport, education, employment, and trade and industry, and oversees the implementation of government policy to the counties of Avon, Cornwall, Devon, Dorset, Gloucestershire, Somerset and Wiltshire. Within these seven counties are 46 district and unitary local planning authorities, of which West Dorset is an example of the former. GOSW involvement in the preparation of development plans is undertaken by the Development Planning and Implementation Team within the Directorate of Environment and Transport. According to the annual plan of GOSW, the regional planning objective is to:

> guide the development, use and reclamation of land in a way which gives appropriate weight to economic, environmental and social factors to ensure propriety and timeliness in decision making.

> (GOSW, 1997: 4)

Within this objective, GOSW monitors the work of local planning authorities in the region in the light of national planning policy issued by the Secretary of State for the Environment. The significance of the level of intervention from GOSW in local plan policy formulation varies, depending on the nature of the plan (for example, whether it's a draft or deposit plan), and the degree of significance of the non-conformity between the local plan and national planning policy statements. A consultation draft local plan will usually attract intense scrutiny by GOSW since it forms a new or revised strategy for a local area, or else because a local planning authority has had little prior experience of plan preparation. At this consultation draft stage, GOSW sometimes makes a large number of comments or objections to the contents of the local plan, as was witnessed by West Dorset in 1993.

The Head of the Development Planning and Implementation Team at GOSW, in conversation with the author in 1995, remarked that central government comments can be 'significant' at this point of local plan preparation to enable issues to be addressed at an early stage in the plan process cycle and thereby contribute to reducing the time taken up for the whole plan preparation process. Furthermore, although GOSW is charged with ensuring consistency in local plan preparation across the South-West region, the objections or comments provided by team members to individual local planning authorities are purely advisory, and local planning authorities can exercise discretion in determining whether or not to take the comments into account in preparing a subsequent version of the plan. However, should a local planning authority decide not to follow the advice provided by GOSW on a particular policy or proposal, and decision-makers 'elect not to follow relevant statements of the Government's planning policy they must give clear and convincing reasons' (DoE/Welsh Office, 1992b: para. 21).

When the government regional office submits its comments and objections on the contents of the local plan to a local planning authority, it does so with a brief covering letter. This letter possesses two standard paragraphs that are worth highlighting at this stage:

> I am writing to convey the Secretary of State's objections to policies which appear to conflict with national policies.
>
> In some respects these objections are not made because the Secretary of State necessarily opposes the objectives of the plan's policies but because of the way the policy is expressed which would be likely to cause difficulties in the determination of planning cases.

The government office, as a central government department, therefore appears sensitive to the accusation of interference in the political preferences of local planning authorities, and stresses the technical nature of that intervention where it does occur. However, the distinction between policy advice and technical advice could on occasions be slight.

Beyond the draft stage of local plan preparation, at the deposit and modifications stages, administrative staff will highlight the policy and proposal areas where GOSW concerns have not been met since the publication of the local planning authority's consultation draft plan. These concerns might arise if the local planning authority has not persuaded the government office of the particular local circumstances to otherwise justify a departure from the contents of national planning policy guidance. The weight attached to the government office's comments at this stage therefore increases and the comments themselves become formal objections. Discussions still occur at this stage between the local planning authority and the government office, but if there remain irreconcilable differences between the two planning levels, the Secretary of State for the Environment may use his powers of intervention to issue a direction to modify or call-in all or part of the local plan for his determination.

Alternatively, rather than call-in part or all of a plan, the Secretary of State may be prepared to let a contentious area go forward to the local plan inquiry. The government regional offices do not appear at local plan inquiries, however, to discuss contentious policy differences with local planning authorities since, in the words of the Head of the Development Planning Team at Government Office for the South West, 'the source of the objections is conflict with published national policies with which the Inspector will be fully conversant'. Both a call-in direction and an unresolved policy contention between the government office and a local planning authority rarely occur, but both are a significant rule of power that can be used as a threat against local planning authorities attempting to deviate from a national policy norm. By utilising this threat, GOSW and the other regional offices can ensure consistency and certainty is achieved in local plan policy formulation across Britain, through standardising plans and policies, and reducing local discretion to challenge a national planning policy agenda.

The next section turns attention to one local planning authority's experience of the Government Office for the South West's monitoring and scrutinising role in local plan preparation, West Dorset District Council, and the use of national planning policy guidance to intervene in local plan policy formulation.

WEST DORSET'S LOCAL PLANS: RESEARCH CONTEXT

West Dorset had produced its draft local plan in 1992. After that time, the district council went on to prepare its local plan deposit version, published in June 1994. When West Dorset had responded to the research questionnaire, discussed in Chapter 6, the comments they had received from the government regional office had been logged, noted and evaluated, and formed a focal point for amendments and clarification prior to a local plan inquiry. When the case study research was undertaken in early 1996, the district council had also published pre-inquiry changes to the local plan and had also received further comments and objections from the Government Office for the South West. The existence of two sets of local plan documents for West Dorset enabled the collection of extra material in the form of two stages of comments between the Government Office for the South West and West Dorset's responses. Together with the local plans themselves, these documents provided a rich seam of detailed planning policy information. The timing context for this research is illustrated in Table 8.1.

The research analysis involved a number of stages. First, all comments and objections from the Government Office for the South West were compared against the contents of West Dorset's deposit local plan (stages one and two of Table 8.1). This involved noting the number of comments and objections in relation to each policy area of the local plan and the nature of those comments. West Dorset's deposit plan was segregated into nine policy topics: settlement, housing, employ-ment, shopping and commerce, conservation and environment, tourism, recreation, community and utility services, and transportation. The government regional office's comments related to both specific policies of the plan and to the accompanying text. Both types of comments were recorded. Once all the comments or objections had been noted at stage two of the research, the total number for each policy area was highlighted, and these were then analysed further in an attempt to categorise the nature of the comments. This categorisation process initially related to the three areas previously highlighted: format, content and expression, and detail. However, following some preliminary analysis, it was determined that this classification was too simplistic, and a more detailed categorisation was necessary. The revised cate-gorisation selected classified the comments and objections from the Government Office for the South West into 13 areas, as highlighted in Table 8.2.

These 13 categories, selected as the most occurring comments and objec-tions advanced by the Government Office for the South West, cover all comments made in reply to West Dorset's deposit local plan. The 13 categories are self-

Table 8.1 Timing of West Dorset Local Plan (WDLP) research

Stage	Local plan stage and date	Date of research analysis
1	WDLP Deposit Draft	March–May 1996
2	Comments/objections from GOSW	March–May 1996
3	WDLP Pre-Inquiry Changes	Jan.–March 1998
4	Comments/objections from GOSW	Jan.–March 1998

Source: Author, derived from information supplied by West Dorset District Council

Table 8.2 Categorisation of comments and objections from Government Office to the South West to West Dorset deposit plan

Key	Category
Appropriateness	Appropriateness of policy or text
Certainty	The need for certainty with flexibility
Clarity	Clarity of plan or policy
Implementation	Implementation issues
Local issues	Lack of justified local circumstances
National policy	Consistency with national policy guidance
Non-land use	Non-land use planning issue
Plan consistency	Consistency between different sections of the plan
Policy aims	Uncertainty with aims of policy
Policy status	Uncertainty with status of policy
Policy–text	Confusion between policy and text
Regional policy	Consistency with regional planning guidance
Strategic policy	Repetition of strategic structure plan policy

Source: Author

explanatory in the nature of the problem they summarise but will be explained further during the more detailed assessment of policy differences in the next section. Concentrating on these 13 categories would allow for the discussion of problem areas between central government and the local planning authority in more detail, and would enable an assessment of the nature of government office intervention in local plan preparation, its use of national planning policy guidance in advancing comments and objections to the local level, and the significance of these comments and objections in forcing or coercing West Dorset to amend or delete its local planning policies. Although the 13 categories cover all nine policy chapters of the local plan, it would prove impossible to present the research findings of every single comment in any great depth, due to length constraints. The number of comments and objections relating to all nine chapters and 13 categories are therefore summarised later, together with examples used from different policy chapters of the local plan as illustrations in the following pages.

Following completion of stages one and two of this research, attention was focused on stages three and four. This involved scrutiny of the pre-inquiry local plan changes produced by West Dorset District Council in reply to the Government Office for the South West's comments and objections, and a second set of comments and objections made by GOSW to the pre-inquiry changes. This would enable an assessment of the extent to which the government regional office, employing national planning policy guidance in its comments, enforced directly or indirectly a change to the content or wording of West Dorset's local plan policies, and chart that process over a 12-month period between June 1994 and June

1995. The second set of GOSW comments and objections were classified into the 13 categories utilised in stages 1 and 2 to enable ease of comparison.

Analysis of the results of all stages of this research are presented in the following section. Aggregate and detailed findings are classified into the 13 categories, but additionally indicative examples are provided of these categories from West Dorset's local plan.

NATIONAL PLANNING POLICY OBJECTIONS TO LOCAL POLICY

As depicted in Table 8.3, the total number of objections recorded by West Dorset District Council from the Government Office for the South West to the deposit version of its local plan was exceptionally high. Out of a total of 174 objections, 139 were directly related to policies within the plan and a further 35 related to the accompanying text. Despite the comments made by GOSW officials regarding the general number of objections made to local plans as the plan preparation process occurs (a higher number at the draft rather than deposit stage, but added weight to comments made at the deposit stage and thereafter), it is noteworthy that GOSW still made over 170 objections to a deposit plan, after having scrutinised West Dorset's draft plan in early 1993. Since this research does not include scrutiny of West Dorset's draft plan or GOSW's objections at this stage, we can only speculate on the reasons why such a high number of GOSW objections remained.

Possible reasons include a less thorough scrutiny at the draft stage by GOSW, scrutiny undertaken by a different GOSW official between the two stages, or refusal on the part of West Dorset to amend its draft plan to take into account GOSW objections. GOSW's intervention in West Dorset's local plan policy formulation is notable in certain key policy chapters, including conservation and the environment, and transportation, which recorded the two highest levels of objections and the greatest proportion made against policies, rather than text. It is difficult to read anything more into these figures at this stage – for example, the differences between minor wording objections and major policy differences – since the degree of significance of the objections cannot be assessed.

When the GOSW objections are broken down into the 13 categories (see Table 8.4), the figures reveal a large number of categories where high objections were recorded. These are discussed separate, categories being presented in the order of highest to lowest number of objections, together with indicative examples.

CERTAINTY WITH FLEXIBILITY
The most contentious area related to a desire for certainty with flexibility, representing over 30 per cent of all objections. This category undoubtedly reflects the push

Table 8.3 Total number of objections made by GOSW to West Dorset's deposit plan

Plan chapter	Number of objections recorded		
	Policies	Text	Total
Settlement	4	5	9
Housing	8	9	17
Employment	10	5	15
Shopping and commerce	15	1	16
Conservation and environment	33	8	41
Tourism	16	1	17
Recreation	13	2	15
Community and utility services	11	0	11
Transportation	29	4	33
Total	139	35	174

Source: Author, derived from GOSW comments to West Dorset's deposit plan

by central government for the local plan to provide more certain conditions for developers and communities in providing a framework for planning control decisions locally and is in the spirit of the plan-led planning system introduced by the Planning and Compensation Act 1991.

Nevertheless, the category is certainty with flexibility, and the government regional office has stressed the non-binding role of the local plan on local planning authorities to provide, first, local discretion to determine each planning case on its own merits, and, second, a flexible framework to take account of local social, economic and environmental changes in the plan period. The distinction between a local plan policy providing a certain statement on local development pressures and restraints, and one acting as a flexible tool to accommodate sudden political changes is a difficult balancing act for any local planning authority to contend with.

The highest number of objections relating to certainty with flexibility was that for conservation and the environment, where West Dorset's planning policy formulators had drafted protection policies against development in environmentally sensitive locations. The certainty with flexibility objection from GOSW comprised, in all 53 cases of objection to the deposit plan, a standardised statement:

Government Office for the South West
To provide certainty and flexibility, policies should set out the criteria which will be used to decide planning applications. Such criteria should include any circumstances where exceptions would be made to the general policy. 'Normally' should not be included as it serves only to make a policy unclear, contrary to PPG12 para.7.11.

Table 8.4 Categories of objections made by GOSW to West Dorset's deposit plan by chapter

	1	2	3	4	5	6	7	8	9	10	11	12	13
Settlement	0	5	3	0	1	2	0	0	0	0	2	0	0
Housing	0	5	3	1	3	4	2	0	0	0	11	0	0
Employment	0	7	3	0	0	1	3	2	0	0	5	1	0
Shopping and commerce	0	5	2	2	0	5	0	1	0	2	0	0	0
Conservation and environment	2	17	18	15	1	14	7	4	8	4	7	5	2
Tourism	1	7	3	0	1	2	1	1	1	0	0	0	0
Recreation	0	3	3	1	2	1	2	1	1	1	0	0	0
Community and utility services	3	2	1	0	0	0	1	3	0	1	0	0	0
Transportation	2	2	4	0	0	3	10	9	0	1	2	0	0

Key:

1	Appropriateness	8	Plan consistency
2	Certainty	9	Policy aims
3	Clarity	10	Policy status
4	Implementation	11	Policy–text issues
5	Local issues	12	Regional policy
6	National policy	13	Strategic policy
7	Non-land use issue		

Source: West Dorset District Council planning department

A planning system that had for 44 years emphasised flexibility in policy wording had, through the introduction of the plan-led system, created a new requirement: certainty within that flexibility. Therefore, policies that had previously contained semantic caveats, such as the use of the words 'normally', 'may', 'ought to', and 'will consider' (see Chapter 5), were now frowned upon by central government. Developers and communities required a stronger line from local planning authorities; they needed to be certain what the authority would do, according to the development under consideration, and the location of that proposed development. Catch-all statements would not provide the certainty aimed for under the plan-led system. The type of policies within West Dorset's local plan reflect this change in priorities, and the following illustrative policy statements, taken directly from WDDC's local plan, reflect the non-certain statements that were objected to by the Government Office for the South West:

> *West Dorset District Council*
> Policy L8 Historic Parks and Gardens
> Development that would destroy or seriously affect the enjoyment, the historic character or setting of historic parks and gardens identified by English Heritage in their register of 'Historic Parks and Gardens' will not normally be permitted.
>
> Policy L10 Protection of Statutory Nature Reserves and SSSIs
> Development that may destroy or adversely affect a statutory or formally proposed nature reserve or Site of Special Scientific Interest, either directly or indirectly, will not normally be permitted.
>
> Policy CD7 Development In and Adjoining Conservation Areas
> Development that is likely to have an adverse effect on the character or setting of a conservation area will not normally be permitted. Any development that is allowed must preserve or enhance the character of the conservation area.

In all cases relating to certainty with flexibility objections, WDDC amended the policies at the pre-inquiry changes plan to provide more positive statements by deleting the word 'normally'. The criteria called for by the government office, however, was not followed in several cases by WDDC. The Government Office for the South West prefers criteria-based policies within local plans, since this provides a certain and clear framework for developers and communities. But the inclusion of criteria would only reintroduce an element of local flexibility in the certain policy framework, by indicating the circumstances under which exceptions to the policy might be permitted. The inclusion of policy criteria is a government regional office requirement, and is not a policy requirement outlined in any national planning policy statement. Local planning authorities such as West Dorset that decide not to include criteria-based local policies within their local plans as a matter of choice would therefore seem to be on a sure footing by not following the government office's position on this matter. This permits local discretion in planning policy formulation but could also contribute towards a weak certain local policy statement to be used in planning control and, more importantly, planning appeal cases.

CLARITY

Clarity of policy expression caused Government Office for the South West intervention in West Dorset's deposit plan on 40 separate occasions. While most policy chapters of the plan led to three of four clarity comments by GOSW, it was the conservation and environment chapter that once again received the highest number of objections, with almost a half of all clarity comments devoted to the conservation and environment policies. Clarity in policy expression is an essential component of the provision of certainty in local plan statements. Problems are caused for local planning authorities when policies are vague, ambiguous and simply badly phrased. The local planning authority, developers and members of the public could all possess very different opinions on policy meaning where there is a lack of clarity. Providing local certainty in the spirit of the plan-led planning system has necessitated the government regional offices intervening more often to make comments on the syntax of local policy statements.

West Dorset's difficulties with clarity of policies show little regard for interpretation and implementation, rather than a desire to retain more flexibility in local decision-making processes. The following West Dorset policy examples indicate syntax and meaning problems in their deposit plan:

> *West Dorset District Council*
> Policy E8 Agricultural Diversification
> In considering proposals for the use of agricultural land for any form of development not associated with agriculture, the district council will seek to ensure a satisfactory balance between the agricultural, environmental and economic implications.

Policy E8 was objected to by GOSW because of the inclusion of the phrase 'will seek to ensure a satisfactory balance'. GOSW requested that the policy be amended through the deletion of the phrase in the interests of clarity. West Dorset District Council at the pre-inquiry changes redrafted the policy to provide a more unambiguous statement in the plan.

Other policies possessed similar ambiguous statements, all of which were objected to by GOSW for lack of clarity. These included: 'a substantial increase in traffic' and 'will be resisted' (from Policy E10 Employment at St George's Road Dorchester); 'may be permitted in exceptional circumstances' (from Policy SC2 Out of Centre Stores); 'suitable for a variety of uses' (from Policy SC7 Charles Street

Dorchester); and 'will be resisted' (from Policy CD11 Demolition within a Conservation Area). For the most part, the rewording of these policies and the deletion of the problematic unclear statements made sense, since they could be subject to differing opinions by users of the planning system. On the other hand, the tightening-up of statements within policies could lead to less discretion becoming available to local planning authorities as a means of negotiation with developers and the public. And this is certainly evident in some of GOSW's objections in relation to clarity.

Policy E8, highlighted above, was objected to by GOSW and redrafted to provide a more robust policy statement. But at the pre-inquiry plan changes, GOSW again objected to the policy with the following objection:

Government Office for the South West
It would be better if it reflected the advice in PPG7 (para.2.6) about protecting the best and versatile agricultural land.

Policy E8 was not viewed as being inconsistent with national PPG7 at the initial period of consultation (in fact, PPG7 was not mentioned at all), nor at the pre-inquiry changes. Rather, GOSW simply did not approve of the local planning authority's use of semantics. The use of the phrase 'It would be better' prompts the question, for whom? This is an example of the government regional office objecting in a very detailed and pedantic manner to a local plan policy. While the government regional office provides advice rather than direction in its comments to local planning authorities, and the latter are under no obligation to follow such advice, there is a danger that local planning authorities will replicate national planning policy simply to avoid difficulties between the two levels of government. In the case of Policy E8, West Dorset District Council redrafted the policy for a second time by following exactly the contents of paragraph 2.6 of national Planning Policy Guidance Note 7.

The differences over Policy E8, described above, also impact upon the more conceptual discussion of local discretion in planning policy formulation. Here we have a separately elected arm of the state advising another on the appropriateness of policy wording and causing an amendment to that policy. Local plan policy statements are political expressions made by the independently elected local authorities. One can accept the role of a good practice agency to ensure clarity in expression, but quite another when the government office recommendations result in change to the meaning of policy statements. In the other problematic policy statements highlighted above, all policies were amended following GOSW objection with exception to one, Policy SC2. This was not amended to delete the unclear statement and went forward to the local plan inquiry and the inspector's ultimate determination as a contentious matter between the district council and the government office.

INCONSISTENCY WITH NATIONAL PLANNING POLICY

Table 8.4 indicates that the Government Office for the South West made 32 objections to West Dorset's local plan on the grounds of inconsistency with the government's national planning policy guidance. PPG1 *General Policy and Principles* requires local planning policies to be consistent with national and regional planning policies if local plans are to benefit from the enhanced weight afforded to local policies by the provisions of the 'plan-led' planning system. PPG1 states that,

> if the development plan is to carry full weight it needs to be up to date and consistent with national and regional policies as well as relevant to the proposal in question.
>
> (PPG1, DoE/Welsh Office, 1992b)

This is not a legal requirement, merely a policy expectation, but it does carry significant weight within local planning authorities. Between one and five objections relating to this category were made by GOSW to West Dorset's deposit plan policy chapters; one chapter, conservation and environment, received 14 objections, comprising almost 50 per cent of national–local policy inconsistency objections to the plan as whole.

Examples of inconsistency between national planning policy statements and the policies contained in West Dorset's local plan relate to specific sentences. These include:

SETTLEMENT
West Dorset District Council
Policy SP4 General Criteria for the Change of Use or Adaptation of Rural Buildings
Government Office for the South West
Inconsistent with PPG7, paragraph 2.15, to include reference to the form, bulk and general design in keeping with the building's surroundings.

SHOPPING AND COMMERCE
West Dorset District Council
Policy SC1 Shops and Services
Government Office for the South West
Inconsistent with PPG13, paragraph 3.10, to take into account the accessibility of local convenience shopping.
West Dorset District Council
Paragraphs 6.12–6.15 on location of shops and commercial developments
Government Office for the South West
Inconsistency with PPG6, paragraph B10, to include criteria based policies and certainty for developers.

West Dorset District Council

Policy SC2 Out of Centre Stores

Government Office for the South West

Inconsistent with PPG6, paragraph 31, and PPG13, paragraph 3.10, to account for the availability of a choice of transport mode.

CONSERVATION AND ENVIRONMENT

West Dorset District Council

Policy L10 Protection of Statutory Nature Reserves and SSSIs

Government Office for the South West

Policy L10 is more restrictive than PPG9, paragraph 27.

West Dorset District Council

Policy CD8 Development Affecting Listed Buildings

Government Office for the South West

Inconsistent with PPG15, paragraph 2.18, to cover change of use of listed buildings.

West Dorset District Council

Policy CD10 Demolition of Listed Buildings

Government Office for the South West

Policy CD10 is more restrictive than PPG15, paragraph 3.17.

West Dorset District Council

Policy CD17 Areas of Archaeological Sensitivity

Government Office for the South West

Inconsistent with PPG16, paragraph 21, to request, rather than expect, an archaeological study to be carried out by the developer.

The objections raised in this category fall into two types: matters omitted from the local policies but which national planning policy guidance requires local planning authorities to include in development plans, and local policies that conform broadly to national planning policies but which go beyond the phraseology of PPGs, usually taking a much stronger, or regulatory, policy line.

The former could sometimes be errors of policy formulation on the part of West Dorset, or they might be determined local political decisions not to follow the national planning policy statements' sentiments strictly. Inspection of what happened at the pre-inquiry stages in West Dorset indicate that they were generally matters that had been excluded when the local plan was drafted. Policies SP4, SC1 and SC2, together with paragraphs 6.12–6.15 of the deposit plan, were all redrafted prior to the local plan inquiry to conform to the advice put forward by GOSW in order to ensure consistency between national and local policies. In addition, one of the national planning policy statements utilised by the government office to illustrate inconsistency, PPG13 *Transport*, had been issued in March

1994, just three months prior to the publication of the West Dorset deposit plan, and local planners had not managed to integrate the policies within the document in sufficient time. This explains the inconsistency between national and local policy for Policies SC1, SC2, and CD8, the latter policy being inconsistent with PPG15 *Planning and the Historic Environment* (that was released after the publication of West Dorset's local plan).

The second type of inconsistency possesses a much stronger local political configuration. Policies L10, CD10 and CD17 were all objected to by GOSW since they were regarded as being more restrictive than the guidance contained in the PPGs. All three policies relate to environmental protection or conservation, and aim to protect sensitive landscapes. However, they take a much stronger restrictive policy line than that advocated in national policies. In many ways, these local policies do provide for a great deal of certainty in local areas, by clearly indicating where development will not be permitted, or the criteria by which planning permission will be given. They fell foul of the government office because the relevant national planning policies indicate more flexibility in statements of certainty. In this regard, they conform to a rule of law over environmentally sensitive locations in West Dorset but are inconsistent with national policies that emphasise discretion. As a consequence, GOSW could be accused of double standards by objecting to some local policies because they do not provide sufficient certainty, but then objecting to other local policies where – in the opinion of the government office – they emphasise too much certainty.

Environmental protection policies are some of the most contentious policy subjects locally and nationally since they affect the 'familiar and cherished local scene'. But they are also localised judgements on the built and natural environmental features that are important locally. While national planning policies can therefore set a broad framework, it is very difficult to accept national planning policy overriding locally formulated landscape policies.

In this latter type of objection, West Dorset District Council redrafted Policies L10 and CD17 to conform to the wording of national planning policy guidance and thereby watered-down the restriction of their own local environmental and conservation policy statements in the face of opposition from central government. Policy CD10 relating to the demolition of listed buildings was not amended by West Dorset, and despite continued opposition from the government office, went to the local plan inquiry as a contentious policy area. The chances of this local policy difference surviving the local plan inquiry would be a matter for West Dorset's planners and advocates, and the inspector presiding at the inquiry. West Dorset's policy-formulators would have to provide a good local case. As was previously remarked, the government office relies on the opinions of the presiding inspector to implement national government policy. How impartial this makes the independent inspector in mediating between government office and local planning authority policy disputes is an interesting point.

POLICY–TEXT ISSUES

Policy–text issues caused objections from GOSW on 27 occasions. 'Policy–text' is defined here as matters that West Dorset had included in the local plan's accompanying text but which the government office believed should have been included in the actual policies, or vice versa. This is a legitimate area of concern for the government office in its monitoring of local planning policy formulation. The local plan is a statutory document, and to ensure that plans are used correctly in the plan-led system users must be able to consult the policies within plans to identify the development and environmental issues of concern to each local area. It is, however, a legally contentious area identifying whether the whole local plan, or merely the policies rather than the accompanying text of the plan, possesses enhanced status under the provisions of the 1991 Act.

The government regional offices have interpreted the statute as giving enhanced status only to the policies within local plans, and have therefore been at pains to ensure that the relevant statements local planning authorities use to inform planning control decisions are included within the wording of actual policies. However, this policy position cannot be found in any national planning policy statement, and the government offices are taking a risk in pursuing this line without written support. This is an interesting and unusual example of central government, possessing a direct influence over planning policy formulation at the local level but without justifying their position through any published national planning policy guidance.

The policy–text problem in West Dorset identified by GOSW occurred to a relatively significant degree in the housing chapter of the local plan (on 11 occasions). The following examples from the housing chapter indicate the nature of the problem identified:

HOUSING

West Dorset District Council Para.4.3, Deposit Plan
Permission will not normally be granted for the change of use or other development involving the loss of housing accommodation in primarily residential areas, although exceptions will be considered ...
Government Office for the South West
PPG12 para.7.12 states that policies and proposals should be readily distinguished from the rest of the text. Paragraph 4.3 appears to contain land use policies which should be set out as formal policies of the plan.
West Dorset District Council Para.4.4, Deposit Plan

> Where permission is required for the erection of an extension to a dwelling all
> applications will be considered on their merits having due regard to the
> relationship with neighbouring properties.
> *Government Office for the South West*
> Replication of previous statement, as for paragraph 4.3 above.
> *West Dorset District Council* Para.4.18, Deposit Plan
> If a dwelling is derelict or in practical terms is no longer in existence or the
> residential use has been abandoned, permission for a new dwelling will not
> normally be allowed.
> *Government Office for the South West*
> Replication of previous statement, as for paragraph 4.3 above.

It is interesting to note that the government office has used a standard paragraph
once again to object to different statements within the local plan. In fact on this
occasion, the government office was embarrassed to discover that a complete
replication of the paragraph 4.3 objection had been used on all other objections
in the housing chapter of the plan, including reference to paragraph 4.3 rather
than paragraph 4.4, 4.18, etc. But West Dorset accepted the objections in the
spirit intended. The district council's reaction to these objections was to amend
the text of the plan and integrate all statements into policies at the pre-inquiry
changes.

NON-LAND USE ISSUES

As Table 8.4 indicates, 'non-land use issues' objections were made by GOSW on
26 occasions, where the government office determined that the issue referred to in
a local plan policy was outside the definition of the statutory planning system, or
beyond the scope of local plans. This is also a contentious area, since the scope of
the planning system is large, and local planning authorities may wish to use the
system to co-ordinate broader socio-economic and environmental change. The
British government, however, along with the courts, have narrowed the meaning of
planning to refer to land use issues alone (that is, matters relating to the use,
control and development of land), and not to the reasons, management or users of
changing land use and development. This has caused problems for local planning
authorities over the last 50 years who, eager to implement policies to ameliorate
identifiable local problems, have attempted to use planning to achieve non-land
use issues, especially in relation to the provision of affordable housing to secure
development for a particular user of the land (low income groups).

West Dorset's problems in this objection category occur in nearly all policy
chapters of the local plan, but are notable in the environment and conservation and
transportation policies, and are illustrated in the following examples:

CONSERVATION AND ENVIRONMENT

West Dorset District Council
Policy L3 Heritage Coast Management
Government Office for the South West
PPG12 para.5.6 advises that non land use policies should not be included in local plans. Policy L3 is a management statement rather than a policy concerned with the use and development of land. It should be deleted as a policy, although it could usefully be included in the reasoned justification.
West Dorset District Council
Policy L6 Forestry Commission Forests
Government Office for the South West
Replication of previous statement, as for Policy L3 above.
West Dorset District Council
Policy CD2 Tree Planting
Government Office for the South West
Encouraging applicants to manage and provide trees, and the intention to make Tree Preservation Orders, are non-land use matters which should not form part of the policy (PPG12 para.5.6). However, the plan could set out the policy or policies which will apply to trees covered by TPOs.

TRANSPORTATION

West Dorset District Council
Policy TR15 Cyclists and Pedestrians
Government Office for the South West
This is a general management statement rather than a land use policy and should be deleted (PPG12 para.5.6). However, the plan should include specific policies or proposals for the improvement of cyclist and pedestrian safety (PPG12 para.5.27) and should show how this matter will be taken into account in deciding planning applications.
West Dorset District Council
Policy TR16 Provision for People With Disabilities
Government Office for the South West
This is a general management statement rather than a land use policy and should be deleted (PPG12 para.5.6). The local plan should include specific policies or proposals for access for the disabled, and should show how this matter will be taken into account in deciding planning applications.

The examples illustrated here combine pure management issues that are beyond the scope of the planning system, and planning matters that are not strictly land use concerns but which could be included in the plan's accompanying text. The distinction between land use and non-land use in the latter type can often be blurred, and it is interesting to note the government office's liberal use of para-graph 5.6 of Planning Policy Guidance Note 12 to justify its objections in this cat-egory. In the above examples, Policies L3, L6 and CD2 were all redrafted substantially and found favour with GOSW in the comments to the pre-inquiry changes. Policies TR15 and TR16, however, remained problematic areas. West Dorset redrafted rather than deleted the policies, and the government office con-tinued to object on the grounds that they were not specific policies merely state-ments of intent. The precise rationale for this objection seems to be based on the requirement for clear and certain local policy statements related to specific pro-posals. The amended policies were simply too flexible in their syntax to appear acceptable to GOSW. Nevertheless, these policies were two further examples of national–local policy contentions progressing forward to the local plan inquiry for the inspector's determination.

CONSISTENCY IN THE PLAN

This category of objection centres on a lack of consistency between different sec-tions of the local plan. This might arise when different chapters of the local plan have been formulated by different planning officers, and insufficient attention provided to harmonisation and integration. But it can also arise as a consequence of another problem. Policies within the plan should be in general conformity; 'general' is an important word here since clearly some parts of the plan are bound to be pulling against other policies. For example, a policy to promote economic development and the designation of employment sites might appear to conflict with a policy elsewhere in the local plan to safeguard the environment against obtrusive developments.

The statutory planning system in England, Scotland and Wales recognises the importance of retaining policies that pull in opposite directions in order to provide certainty with flexibility, and for local planning authorities to determine each case on the merits of all relevant policies of the local plan and other material con-siderations. In some ways, this is a problematic area in relation to the provision of certainty in plan policy formulation. Certainty requires a clear and unambiguous statement of local planning choices, but taking this to its logical conclusion one would expect the local plan to specify in some detail where development would be built, what sort of development would be allowed, and the criteria to be taken into account by decision-makers. Local plans should provide these elements within their policies but will nevertheless include other considerations that could cancel out statements making particular intentions. From this perspective, the enhanced status of policies provided by the plan-led system to provide certainty cannot exist to the same extent as when there are no policies pulling in different directions, a fact recognised by some planning lawyers recently.

The government office's objections to the lack of consistency within the local plan seem to be, therefore, only partial, and relate to detail rather than generality. Examples from West Dorset's deposit plan in this category include policies within the employment, conservation and environment, community and utility services, and transportation chapters.

EMPLOYMENT

West Dorset District Council
Paragraph 5.11(i) Criteria for employment development on specific site
Government Office for the South West
This paragraph refers to an `area of search' shown on the proposals map. The proposals map inset for Dorchester does not appear to include such notation.
West Dorset District Council
Policy E5 Employment Uses in the Countryside
Government Office for the South West
The requirement is inconsistent with local plan policy SP4, criterion (i) of which states that planning permission will not normally be given to conversion proposals which involve substantial rebuilding.

CONSERVATION AND ENVIRONMENT

West Dorset District Council
Paragraph 7.82 Under Policy CD11, it states that criteria for determining proposals within a conservation area are set out in Policy CD10
Government Office for the South West
If the criteria set out in Policy CD10 are to be used to decide applications covered by CD11, these should be re-stated in that policy or the policy should contain a clear cross-reference to Policy CD10.

The examples provided above illustrate the type of objections made by the government office. A considerable number of the objections in this category related to inconsistency between policy statements and the local plans proposals map, and these are clear basic errors on the part of West Dorset's plan policy formulators. Other types of objection relate to policy specifics, and are of a nature discussed previously, assuming that different chapters of the plan were produced by different individuals. There were no differences between national planning policies and local planning policies here, nor can there be any political significance attached to the government office's objections. This is one category of objection where the intervention relates to providing a cohesive and integrated local planning document that could be used by the local planning authority.

IMPLEMENTATION

Implementation objections numbered 19, and the vast majority of these were to be found in the conservation and environment chapter of the local plan. Implementation problems made by the government regional office relate to policies that were deemed to be difficult to implement in local decision settings, either because of the syntax used within the policies or as a consequence of issues that could not be achieved by local planning authorities. The following examples illustrate the nature of objections:

CONSERVATION AND ENVIRONMENT

West Dorset District Council
Policy L13 Coastal Defence
Government Office for the South West
The policy as drafted does not provide objective criteria against which planning applications can be decided, as advised by PPG12, para.1.1. The policy should be redrafted to set out the circumstances in which planning permission will or will not be granted.
West Dorset District Council
Policy CD10 Demolition of Listed Buildings
Government Office for the South West
The policy as drafted does not provide objective criteria against which planning applications can be decided, as advised by PPG12, para.1.1. Sub-paragraphs (i)–(iv) set out general considerations rather than criteria. The policy should be redrafted to set out the circumstances in which planning permission will or will not be granted.

The objections relate primarily to clear criteria by which applications for planning permission can be judged by local planning authorities. This is beneficial to the authorities themselves in providing clear statements for local elected members to follow, but it is also beneficial to developers and members of the public to provide them with local certainty and a benchmark upon which to judge the decisions of local planners. All objections made by GOSW to West Dorset along these lines were redrafted as requested at the pre-inquiry changes.

POLICY AIMS

Government Office for the South West objected on ten occasions to policies within West Dorset's local plan for their aims, usually as a consequence of the local planning authority attempting to make achievements that were outside the scope of the local plan policies specifically and the land use planning system generally. The conservation and environment chapter of the plan was again the most problematic, comprising eight out of the ten objections. The following two examples illustrate the type of objections made:

CONSERVATION AND ENVIRONMENT

West Dorset District Council
Policy L10 Protection of Statutory Nature Reserves and SSSIs
Government Office for the South West
Separate policies should be set out for sites of international and national importance for nature conservation.
West Dorset District Council
Policy CD7 Development In and Adjoining Conservation Areas
Government Office for the South West
The local plan should not attempt to extend statutory duties which prevail within conservation areas to proposals outside conservation areas. The second sentence of the policy should be deleted.

The latter example is interesting, since the local policy attempts to make a case for greater local environmental protection than that advised within national planning policy guidance. From the author's personal planning experience, this policy could have been implemented if it had been split into two: one for development within the conservation area, and another for development adjoining the conservation area. This would have provided two decision-making contexts for the local planning authority and would probably not have been objected to by GOSW since they would not be inconsistent with the national planning policy guidance provided by PPG15 *Planning and the Historic Environment* of 1994. In the event, West Dorset District Council deleted the policy completely, and GOSW did not see fit to advise the authority to formulate two distinct policies as described. This is even more puzzling given that that was actually the principle behind the approach recommended by GOSW in their objections and comments to West Dorset's Policy L10. The government office in this case could therefore be accused of ensuring only partial consistency in local planning policy formulation, and an element of inconsistency between comments on different sections of the local plan. The inconsistency can be categorised into those issues central government believes should be subject of clear policies (internationally and nationally protected nature conservation sites), and those issues the local planning authority believes should be included within the local plan (locally protected conservation areas). In the case of Policy L10, this was divided into two separate policies as recommended by GOSW at the pre-inquiry changes.

STATUS OF POLICY

Policy status issues were highlighted by GOSW on nine occasions in their objections to the deposit plan. The nature of the objections centred on uncertainty on the part of the government office towards the use of supplementary planning guidance (SPG), either stated within specific policies or mentioned as references in the accompanying text. Supplementary planning guidance, such as development briefs and design guides, is a convenient way in which to elaborate certain proposals in more detail than that permitted in local plans. The government, as stated in PPG12, recognises the valuable role supplementary planning guidance performs in providing advice to local planning authorities and developers, but is concerned at the possibility of functions being delegated to guidance that should otherwise be included within the statutory plan. Government offices are also eager to ensure that supplementary planning guidance does not usurp the local plan in relation to specific projects or decision scenarios.

The objections to West Dorset's plan primarily occur in the conservation and environment and shopping and commerce chapters, although isolated examples also exist in the recreation, community and transportation chapters. The example set out below suggests that West Dorset, in this and other cases, was attempting to include policies in the local plan relating to particular projects by simply referring to the existence of supplementary planning guidance and how decisions would be made in accordance with those documents, rather than clear criteria set out in the plan itself.

SHOPPING AND COMMERCE

West Dorset District Council
Policy SC6 Shopping and Commercial Development Associated With
Development at Herrison and Poundbury
Sites will be set aside for shops and commercial development at Herrison and
Poundbury, commensurate with the scale of development and in accordance
with the development briefs for these areas.
Government Office for the South West
Supplementary planning guidance, such as development briefs, does not have
the same status as development plan policies although it may be a material
consideration (PPG12, paras. 3.18 and 3.19). The local plan should not require
compliance with, or attempt to delegate decisions to, supplementary guidance.
Any matters contained in such guidance and which are likely to provide the
basis for deciding planning applications or conditions, should be set out as
policies of the local plan.

This policy does not provide the certainty that local plans should aim for, although it does raise questions relating to the role and use of supplementary planning guidance in the plan-led system. Supplementary guidance does not possess any enhanced status similar to development plans for development control purposes, but they can be a material consideration provided that they are in conformity with the local plan, they have been subject to a council resolution of adoption, and have been subject to public consultation. The worry for the government offices is that local planning authorities, having progressed supplementary planning guidance in conformity with government policy on SPG, will attempt to place matters in the briefs that are either beyond the scope of the land use planning system or else inconsistent with the contents of national planning policy guidance. Only local plan policies have to be in conformity with national and regional policies, and this potentially provides a great deal of discretion available to local planning authorities to progress their own local agendas. To what extent decisions based on the contents of supplementary planning guidance alone can be relied upon is a contentious area, and certainly one relating to individual cases.

The government has attempted to close this loophole by not giving any significant weight to supplementary guidance for development control purposes, and by ensuring that the guidance is in conformity with the local plan (which, in turn, should be consistent with national and regional policies). But there is scope for certain matters to lie outside the statutory plan, to be beyond the reaches of government regional offices, and to be not in conformity with national planning policy guidance. To date, very little research has been undertaken since the introduction of the plan-led system to identify whether certain local planning authorities have attempted to take this approach, as a means of avoiding detailed scrutiny of policies by central government.

LOCAL CIRCUMSTANCES

Central government insists through the policy guidance contained in both PPG1 and PPG12 that local plans have to be consistent with national and regional planning policies:

> Since the commencement of section 54A, the Secretaries of State have been examining development plans carefully to identify whether there appear to be conflicts with national or regional policy guidance. They will continue to do so and will normally draw the attention of local authorities to those conflicts which do not appear to be justified by local circumstances.
>
> (DoE/Welsh Office, 1992b: para. 29)

Central government policy requirement is consequently clear: local planning authorities must follow the statements within PPGs in carrying out their planning duties. If they wish to depart from established government policies they will have to demonstrate comprehensively the locally justified grounds for departure. These local circumstances are not defined by central government, since the onus is on the local planning authority to show that local circumstances are sufficiently important to override the national policies. One might think that local planning authorities, as councils elected independently of central government, may wish to attempt to formulate their own policy solutions to local planning problems and utilise this policy caveat often to justify the particular local circumstances that local planning policies seek to deal with. However, this is actually quite a rare occurrence. In West Dorset's local plan, for example, the Government Office for the South West only identified eight local circumstances within all the policies that were at variance with national planning policies, and objected to each of the eight!

No one local plan chapter dominates this category of objection, and examples can be found in the settlement, housing, conservation and environment, tourism and recreation chapters, some of which are indicated below:

SETTLEMENT

West Dorset District Council
Paragraph 3.22 on the importance of encouraging diversification of the rural economy: 'In exceptional circumstances, such as the need to conserve a listed building, conversion to residential use may be permitted, provided that the conversion is necessary for the long term conservation and maintenance of the building and that the proposal fully respects its character.

Government Office for the South West
This paragraph suggests that the council's policy will be to discriminate against residential conversions in rural areas and in favour of those uses which encourage the diversification of the rural economy. Such an approach is inconsistent with PPG12 paras.7.5 and 7.11. The policy should be redrafted to set out clearly and unambiguously the council's policy for conversions. This should be accompanied by a reasoned justification which sets out the local circumstances which warrant discrimination for or against particular uses.

HOUSING

West Dorset District Council
Policy H7 Local Needs Within Defined Development Boundaries

Government Office for the South West
The local plan provides no evidence to support the inclusion of policy H7. PPG3 para.38 states that authorities may reasonably seek to negotiate for an element of affordable housing to meet local needs. The reasoned justification should be redrafted to provide evidence of the type and scale of local need for affordable housing and should also indicate what is meant by 'local' and 'affordable' in the local context.

CONSERVATION AND ENVIRONMENT

West Dorset District Council
Policy L9 Green Corridors
Government Office for the South West
The policy should be redrafted to set out the local circumstances in which
planning permission would or would not be permitted and the circumstances in
which landscaping and particular types of layout would be required.

TOURISM

West Dorset District Council
Policy T3 Holiday Accommodation in Rural Areas
Government Office for the South West
Criterion (i) of the policy is inconsistent with PPG7 para.2.15 which states that
there should generally be no reason for preventing the re-use or adaption of rural
buildings for new uses provided their form, bulk and general design are in keeping
with their surroundings. PPG7 para.D5 states that it may be appropriate to apply
strict controls over residential conversions in the open countryside. However, the
local plan provides no local justification for departing from national guidance or for
seeking to apply strict locational control over holiday accommodation. The policy
should be redrafted to accord with national planning policy or the reasoned
justification redrafted to set out the relevant local circumstances.

These four examples relate essentially to planning controls over residential use in
the countryside. In relation to the settlement, housing and tourism examples, the
policies go further than the advice contained within national planning policy guidance. The government office seems to be accepting a case for local departures
from national policy but will only consider these where there is clear local evidence
– for example, in relation to local needs. If West Dorset had completed a local
housing needs survey and then based their policies on the outcome of this survey,
local circumstances could have been advanced to meet a locally defined planning
problem. In the event, paragraph 3.22 was deleted in its entirety, as was Policy L9.
Policy T3 was redrafted to accord with national planning policy guidance, and
Policy H7 was amended to conform to PPG3, but the district council stated that a
local housing needs survey was being simultaneously implemented by the housing
department, and the results of this would inform subsequent stages of the local
plan.

Here we have a clear case of the local planning authority back-tracking and
replacing the locally formulated planning policies with statements drafted at the
national level. It also indicates an unwillingness on the part of the district council to
enter into protracted negotiations with the government office to justify its locally

based approach. This is somewhat regrettable, and if this approach was adopted across most local planning authorities in the south-west of England, the resultant local plans would be standardised regional statements, devoid of spatially specific policies or else devoid of local problems. This approach by the government office to implement national planning policies at the local level suggests an inability, or even unwillingness on the part of central government, to even recognise the existence of particular sub-regional planning problems that can be addressed locally.

APPROPRIATENESS OF POLICY

The appropriateness of policy category considers cases where the government office objected to either policy or text issues within West Dorset's local plan. Eight objections were logged in total, and the vast majority of these were located in the conservation and environment and community and utility services chapters. The following examples illustrate the nature of the problem identified by GOSW:

> CONSERVATION AND ENVIRONMENT
>
> *West Dorset District Council*
> Policy L4 Land of Local Importance
> *Government Office for the South West*
> The policy is more restrictive than that applied in green belts, although the identified areas are not so designated. The policy should be redrafted so as to reflect the local importance of the areas designated.
> *West Dorset District Council*
> Policy CD4 Conservation Areas
> *Government Office for the South West*
> This is unnecessary given that the plan goes on to set out the policies that will be applied in conservation areas (CD5–7). The policy should be deleted.

Policy L4 was redrafted at the pre-inquiry changes to conform to national planning policy guidance and became less restrictive; the policy was rewritten as a general countryside protection policy. Policy CD4 was deleted completely since the council considered that other conservation policies within the local plan covered the subject matter adequately. In these cases, it is of concern that a government official sitting in a room 100 miles from the authority should decide indirectly the level of policy restrictiveness suitable for local environmental protection policies; it is even more worrying that the district authority itself should not want to make a particular local case for the formulation of a more restrictive local policy solution. This is especially true with regard to environmental and landscape policies, since these matters – perhaps to a greater degree than any other policy subject – are uniquely localised issues.

INCONSISTENCY WITH REGIONAL PLANNING POLICY

This category was highlighted by the government office on six occasions in the plan, five of which were in the conservation and environment chapters. As discussed above, local planning policies are required to be consistent with national and regional planning policies. Regional Planning Guidance Notes are generally broad statements on the planning issues within particular regions, although they possess a very narrow focus on spatial planning matters. They are, to all intents and purposes, regional replications of national planning policy guidance. The Regional Planning Guidance Note for the South West is RPG10, originally released in 1994. In each of the objections made by GOSW inconsistency with the RPG was raised, but only along with other objections on the same policies, most notably for inconsistency with national planning policy. For example, West Dorset's local plan Policy L11 (Protection of Sites of Nature Conservation and SSSIs) was objected to for the following reason:

> *Government Office for the South West*
> This policy appears to apply equal protection to locally important sites as that afforded to sites of national importance. This is inconsistent with RPG10 para.4.17 which states that the greatest weight should be given to protecting internationally and nationally important sites.

However, this objection could equally have been justified by GOSW by reference to national Planning Policy Guidance Note 9 'Nature Conservation' which makes the identical statement, and there is nothing within RPG10 which is unique to the South-West in relation to this subject from the general guidance contained in PPG9. A similar objection was made to West Dorset Policy CD16 (Areas of Archaeological Significance) and the need to differentiate between sites of national and local importance, and was made with reference to both PPG16 *Archaeology and Planning* and RPG paragraph 4.23.

REPETITION OF STRATEGIC PLANNING POLICY

The final objection category is that relating to local plan policies replicating strategic planning policies of the structure plan. This research has not concerned itself with the planning policy formulation duties of county councils or structure plans. However, local plan policies have to be in general conformity with the strategic policies set out in the structure plan by the county council. In West Dorset's case, this required adherence to Dorset County Council's structure plan. The objections raised by GOSW related either to statements of a strategic nature that were more suited for a structure plan rather than a local plan, or rather specific policies from Dorset's structure plan that were replicated in West Dorset's local plan. Only two objections were made and both occurred in the conservation and environment chapter.

Both objections relate to two policies concerning landscape protection: Policy L1 (Areas of Outstanding Natural Beauty) and Policy L2 (Heritage Coast Protection). In both cases, Areas of Outstanding Natural Beauty and Heritage Coasts are designated strategically and are catered for by structure plan policies. The government office objected to unnecessary replication of strategic policies without a more detailed set of criteria by which West Dorset would assess applications within these areas for planning permission. As GOSW highlighted:

> *Government Office for the South West*
> The policies appear to be unnecessary repetition of policy C5 of the Dorset Structure Plan. The local plan should develop structure plan policies and give them local definition and detail.

However, at the pre-inquiry changes to West Dorset local plan, the district council refused to amend the policies to provide the objective criteria required, despite continued objections from GOSW. Both unamended policies were put forward to the local plan inquiry as a matter of contention between GOSW and West Dorset District Council. It is somewhat ironic to note that the district council should obstinately refuse to amend its policies in this less-contentious and more definitive policy area, but be quite prepared to alter its policies – including the tenet of certain policies – to suit central government in other policy sectors.

CONCLUSIONS

This chapter has provided a detailed assessment of the impact of national planning policy guidance on local planning policy formulation through an examination of the Government Office for the South West's use of national policies in its monitoring of West Dorset District Council's deposit local plan. The case study research has also presented the first in-depth policy analysis of planning relations between central government and local government under the plan-led planning system since the introduction of the Planning and Compensation Act 1991.

The general aim of the research, to assess the relationship between tiers of government and the planning polity in policy formulation, has been discussed by drawing on detailed examples from the policy contents of West Dorset's local plan and through assessment of the nature, scope and impact of GOSW's policy objections. The government office utilised its national consistency remit to ensure that a local strategy of certainty was formulated through detailed comments on every aspect of the contents of the local plan. While these comments are regarded by central government as advisory, and that local planning authorities are under no obligation to follow the advice given, the West Dorset research has shown that – if applied more generally – local planning authorities are amending the contents of their local policies to meet the advice provided by central government. In some cases, this advice has been justified, particularly in relation to the semantics of particular policies, the appropriateness of policies, the scope of the land use planning system, and replication of policies published elsewhere. However, a great deal of the advice provided by the government office also related to local political statements, and a requirement to water-down policies regarded by GOSW as overtly restrictive and for certain statements to replicate the policy statements contained within national planning policy guidance. From this perspective, the government office was insistent that local certainty had to be provided – but additionally with flexibility.

The certainty and clarity of definitive local policy statements found favour with the government office, but it also objected if those policies became too certain and too definitive when based on locally defined criteria and not on the contents of national planning policies. There is some concern here that the government office displayed inconsistency in their comments on different parts of the local plan. On certain matters, certainty with flexibility was encouraged, but on others the flexibility seemed only available if it had been predetermined (or even circumscribed) by the contents of national policies, which hardly displays any confidence on localised planning agendas in the spirit of the plan-led system.

On occasions when the local planning authority had sought to provide a policy at variance with national planning policy, the government office objected for the local authority's failure to provide the clear locally justified grounds of departure. Local circumstances are not defined for local planning authorities by central government and there is some concern here that by not providing clear statements of what criteria would be acceptable to the government offices to permit localised exceptions to national policy agendas, the government might be accused of double standards. When the government office objected to local circumstance policies, the district council duly backed down in the face of national opposition, and did not feel inclined to push the issue further to ensure that the local matter saw off national policy encroachment. This was especially the case in conservation and environment policies in West Dorset intended to protect local landscape features. Localised statements that either went beyond the policy position outlined in national planning statements, or else were not thoroughly justified according to the local circumstances, were all amended, following GOSW objections, to read as replications of the contents of PPGs.

The government office's use of national planning policy guidance to ensure that localised agendas were amended, and thereby refuse localised non-standard exceptions to the overarching national rule, has therefore been illustrated and proves one of the aims of the book. More interestingly, if other local planning authorities in the south-west of England have had similar experience to West Dorset in their reactions to GOSW policy objections, the local plans within the region would start to read as very general, bland and standardised statements, with a limited spatial dimension. This can hardly be said to be in the spirit of a locally and locality-led planning system.

The research results in West Dorset have also confirmed the results of the aggregate survey data, presented in Chapter 6. West Dorset indirectly accepted the role of national planning policy guidance in being prepared in virtually all inconsistency situations to amend their local plan policies. The reasons for this lack of political will to object could be varied. West Dorset may have had little prior experience of local plan preparation, and could have relied on national planning policy guidance and the objections and comments provided by GOSW to act as sources of information. Indeed, a recent survey undertaken for the Royal Town Planning Institute has indicated that 81.1 per cent of respondent plan professionals regard central government as their main source of thinking about planning (Royal Town Planning Institute, 1997). Alternatively, West Dorset's planners may have decided, as a political choice, not to contend national objections for fear of not being able to see locally variant policies being supported for development control purposes. A third possible reason is one relating to the competence of West Dorset District Council itself, whose policy officers may have simply lacked experience in plan preparation and produced a bad local plan that required the government office to make more interventions than usual. As such, the degree of significance to be attached to West Dorset as one representing more generally experienced situations across the country must be borne in mind.

By taking each of the government office's objections, and then assessing West Dorset's reaction to those comments, the research has indicated that the national consistency remit has greatly influenced the local agenda, and removed to a degree the local discretion that would otherwise have been available.

The next chapter, Chapter 9, considers the use of national planning policy guidance in the light of setting sub-national agendas, and the degree to which the national consistency remit militated against the formulation of sub-national spatially specific policies at variance with the national planning agenda.

NATIONAL AGENDAS AND PLANNING POLICY
VARIATION: Wales vs. England

INTRODUCTION

Chapters 6, 7 and 8 presented research findings to indicate that the national consistency remit pursued by central government, through the national Planning Policy Guidance Notes, could mitigate against regional and local discretion in planning policy formulation, through the detailed intervention by government regional offices in monitoring draft and deposit local plans and requiring consistency between national and local policies. The focus for these chapters was, predominantly, assessing national impact on local policy-making to the detriment of local planning policy agendas.

This chapter sets out the empirical results of a further case study analysis. The research assesses, first, the position of Wales as a sub-national area within England and Wales and, second, the extent to which Wales warranted distinctive treatment from a national planning policy guidance perspective prior to devolution in 1999. This two-stage assessment would identify the extent to which a national consistency approach across England and Wales was being undertaken and the extent to which it was considered desirable. The origin of this focus rests on the fact that the government's primary legislation, both before and since devolution, applies to England and Wales, and the fact that Planning Policy Guidance Notes had been released jointly during the 1980s and early 1990s between the Department of the Environment and the Welsh Office. After 1996, the Welsh Office released national planning policy guidance for Wales, separate to that for England. This followed criticism by national and local politicians of the lack of a distinctly Welsh dimension to the jointly released national policy guidance (House of Commons Welsh Affairs Committee, 1993). Since 1996, national planning policy in Wales has been released separately to that in England. The key question is: to what extent is it distinctive?

After 1996 Wales retained identical legal provisions to those for England, but the government permitted the development of a separate sub-national policy system compared to that previously developed for England and Wales jointly. The development of the research methodology utilised for this chapter therefore sought to identify, through an analysis of the new (post-1996) policy approach, the extent to which a distinct sub-national area within England and Wales would be able to formulate separate sub-national planning policies, as called for by the politicians, against a legislative national consistency remit employed to cover England and Wales as a whole. Such an in-depth analysis would provide an indication of whether planning problems, unique to Wales as a particular sub-national locale of England and Wales, could be addressed through the formulation of policies by the Welsh Office and Welsh local government as exceptions to national (England and Wales) policies in central government's quest for overarching consistency across England and Wales. The focus of the research presented in Chapter 9 is therefore on sub-national impact on national planning agendas.

To what extent did the national consistency remit enjoyed by central government in England and Wales ensure the adoption of a national planning policy approach that militated against the development of a Welsh sub-national alternative planning policy agenda prior to 1999?

The form the detailed case study research took initially related to a detailed comparison between national planning statements between the different government departments. This sought to analyse the policy content of all jointly released English and Welsh national planning policy guidance published prior to 1993 and the English-only released national planning policy guidance released between 1993 and 1996, and compare the contents with the newly released Welsh national planning policy guidance documents. This would identify those policies considered by the government to be sufficiently important as overarching English and Welsh planning statements, and thereby illustrate the government's determination to continue with its national consistency remit across England and Wales to the detriment of sub-national planning policy agendas, and those policies that were at variance with the joint English and Welsh, or English only, approach, thereby illustrating central government's weakening of its overarching national consistency remit by permitting a strategic sub-national (Welsh) approach. The research assesses the situation prior to devolution in 1999; see Chapter 10 for the structure and nature of the planning polity in Wales as it has emerged in the last few years under the National Assembly for Wales. Before going on to outline the analysis of the results, it is necessary to discuss the particular circumstances of Wales's position in the planning system, through a brief discussion of the development of the Welsh Office and the promotion of a distinctive Welsh planning agenda. This will provide a firm context upon which an analysis of the current position can then take place.

NATIONAL CONSISTENCY AND SUB-NATIONAL AUTONOMY: PLANNING IN WALES

Land use planning in Wales is poised between a distinctive socio-political forma-tion and the centralised legal and bureaucratic apparatus of the British state. This chapter focuses on the implications of this juxtaposition for the planning system in Wales by examining the structure and operation of the Welsh planning system at both a national and local level. The principal research area assessed is the extent to which the Welsh Office in its administration of the land use planning system reflected regional and, to some extent unique, political realities or reinforced wider policy- and decision-making intervention originating in England.

WALES' LEGISLATIVE AND ADMINISTRATIVE PLANNING STRUCTURE

Similar legal and administrative planning arrangements exist in England and Wales. From a purely land use planning perspective, Wales shares a common system to that east of Offa's Dyke. Constitutionally, as part of the United Kingdom, 'Welsh' planning has an identical legal approach, but from a policy perspective differences in the implementation of the legislation are possible. Until the introduction of the 1991 Planning and Compensation Act one of the main things that distinguished Welsh planning was the lack of mandatory prepared district development plans; local plan coverage was sparse throughout the country. This has now been addressed, albeit very slowly, through a requirement in the 1991 Act enforcing dis-trict authorities in Wales to prepare district-wide local plans. The 1991 Act also introduced Section 54A to the 1990 Act, further strengthening the status of devel-opment plans for development control purposes; this clause applies equally to England as it does to Wales, and Scotland has an identical provision. Other statu-tory planning requirements identical to England have included the requirement for county councils to approve structure plans (now replaced by unitary development plans, and the content of the use classes and general permitted development orders. Indeed, overall there are far more similarities than differences between planning legislation west and east of Offa's Dyke. However, the statutory planning process is arguably more distinctive, particularly at the national all-Wales level (Tewdwr-Jones, 1997b, 1998b). There are several reasons for this that relate to the good relations that have existed between agencies of government in Wales, the strategic planning guidance exercise that has been developed since 1990, and underlying these two initiatives the particular socio-political characteristics existing in the country. In assessing each of these distinctive arrangements in more detail it is possible to examine the issues of 'territorial nationalism' (Tewdwr-Jones, 1997b) to illustrate the distinctive features of the land use planning system in Wales by ref-erence to political and cultural aspects of administrative implementation.

The reorganisation of local government in Wales in 1974 introduced a two-tier system of eight counties and 37 districts. All of these authorities existed autonomously and had specific powers. The planning framework that was operated by this structure of local government was the 1971 Town and Country Planning Act, subsequently consolidated by the Town and Country Planning Act 1990. The land use planning system in Wales comprised legislation and central government Planning Policy Guidance and circulars at the all-Wales level, structure plans providing key strategic direction at the county council level, and local plans providing detailed local policies at the district council level from which the development control process is operated. Although minor changes occurred to this broad framework, the administrative structure of the planning process in Wales remained broadly unchanged for a 20-year period until the implementation of the 1994 Local Government (Wales) Act that completely modified the local government structure and, in turn, the planning system operated by it.

The 1994 Act created a completely new form of local government structure in Wales with the abolition of the eight counties and 37 districts and their replacement with 22 all-purpose unitary authorities (Harris and Tewdwr-Jones, 1995). In England, local government reorganisation underwent a restructuring only for certain areas, with the retention of the status quo for most counties but implementation of unitary local government in certain provincial cities (Clotworthy and Harris, 1996). The principal reason for this difference was the decision by the government to progress local government reorganisation separately in each of the three countries of Britain. Scotland and Wales were dealt with by the respective Secretaries of State, while in England the Department of the Environment established an independent Local Government Commission to consider the scope for reorganisation in different areas. Although the reorganisation in Wales marked a true separation from the Department of the Environment's proposals, the nature of local government in Wales has developed characteristically separate to England. As the Council for Welsh Districts state:

> Wales is different. It has a distinctive cultural, linguistic and political environment. The distinctive circumstances of Wales make clear the case for a vibrant system of local government that can respond to local needs and differences.
>
> (Council of Welsh Districts, 1991, para. 10.1)

Hambleton and Mills (1993) also highlight a number of structural and administrative differences in local government in Wales compared with the English picture, portraying the government framework prior to 1994 as a 'picture of stability and consensus' (p. 46). Boyne et al. (1991) maintain that central government through the Welsh Office has been prominent in transforming relations between central and local government by fostering, with a key but relatively small number of local authorities, a system of 'good government'. They conclude that the distinctive characteristics of Wales effectively amounts to a separate Welsh local government system.

The contents of the Local Government (Wales) Act 1994 were essentially derived from the Welsh Office's White Paper *Local Government in Wales: A Charter for the Future*, published on 1 March 1993 (Welsh Office, 1993b). The Act introduced 22 unitary authorities to replace the existing 45 councils from 1 April 1996, with shadow political elections occurring one year previously. The Welsh Office's reasoning for restructuring local government in Wales was contained in two often-quoted key paragraphs within the White Paper:

> The Government believes that the present system of local government in Wales is not widely understood, nor does it sufficiently reflect people's identification with their own communities and loyalties.
>
> Moreover, a two-tier system of counties and districts contain [*sic*] within it a potential for friction between authorities – and for duplication of administration – which reduces the ability of the system to deliver services economically, efficiently and effectively. And there is little public understanding of the responsibilities of each tier, a situation which undermines the direct accountability to local people upon which good local government should be based.
>
> (Welsh Office, 1993b: paras. 1.2, 1.3)

The principal issues for the land use planning system in Wales caused by the reorganisation process relate to three areas, and each of these effectively introduces a very different planning approach to that operating in England. The immediate concern for analysts was how the Welsh Office planning policy guidance would be expressed and delivered to the new unitary authorities (Harris and Tewdwr-Jones, 1995). How would the planning process operate in a unitary, as opposed to two-tier, local government structure? And what effect would reorganisation have on the future delivery of strategic planning policy? In addition to these procedural questions, other theoretical issues were raised: for example, to what extent would the revised planning polity truly reflect those distinctive social-political and cultural territorial differences?, and would the new planning map alter, reduce or reinforce the system of perceived good government in Wales?

THE EMERGENCE OF WELSH TERRITORIAL PLANNING

Following the establishment of the Welsh Office as a separate government department in 1964, an attempt was made to create a distinctive planning policy framework that looked at the future social and economic development needs of Wales. The Welsh Office blueprint, *Wales: The Way Ahead*, published in 1967, sought to provide a clear regional economic plan for Wales that local authorities could work to in progressing their development policies for local areas (HM Government, 1967). The debates surrounding the economic development and future of Wales were facilitated at this time by a parallel political discourse that began emerging as a powerful influence on public and political perceptions of how the nation would develop. The election in 1966 of a member of the Welsh Nationalist Party, Plaid Cymru, to the House of Commons signalled the importance within both the communities and in political circles of debate surrounding the future growth of Wales. Arguments corresponding to the future planning of Wales were thus indecorously bound up in social and political dialogue. The political programme espoused by Plaid Cymru, focused on the principle of decentralising political authority and the preservation of Welsh culture, together with issues relating to future economic growth, created a distinct agenda for the people and government of Wales. Although Plaid Cymru, as a pressure group, may have initially attempted to influence future Welsh Office thinking and policies on the economic growth of Wales, once their manifesto gained stronger public support across the country, the policies of the Welsh Office following *Wales: The Way Ahead* were subsumed under a wider debate initiated by Welsh nationalists. Plaid Cymru's agenda there-fore developed into a stronger political force across Wales.

As the Welsh Office's planning agenda began to be determined by the nationalists' lead, who in turn created the discourse and support among wider sec-tions of Welsh society, the pressure placed on central government to formulate appropriate policy responses was not met. This led to a perception within Welsh political circles and the wider public that the issues under discussion were failing to be addressed in any official or systematic way. Thus, as the Welsh Office was criticised for not setting the broad planning agenda (that is, those contentious policy areas brought forward by the nationalists), a statutory policy vacuum began to develop at an all-Wales level. This lack of national planning only began to be addressed in 1988 with the release of central government Planning Policy Guid-ance Notes (PPGs), 21 years after the publication of *Wales: The Way Ahead*. In the intervening years, the lack of an effective all-Wales tier of planning policy precipitated strong territorial political mobilisation to counteract the perceived intrusive extension of metropolitan (and English or non-Welsh) institutions and pol-icies. This political force, termed 'opposition planning' by Clavel (1983), parallels the 'official planning' of the planning polity operated by the Welsh Office, and created the conditions for a divergent range of planning issues to be debated within Welsh political communities and wider social networks. These issues were predominantly centred on housing, the Welsh language, and economic develop-ment – core areas of official planning around which territorial opposition emerged. Although the planning agenda was led by agencies other than the Welsh Office throughout the 1970s, this induced a regional consensus in the country (Rees and Lambert, 1979) where the views of the Welsh Office, the local authorities and elements of the nationalist agenda (promoted in a political sense by Plaid Cymru) were debated to ensure that the interests of Wales and the future prosperity of the country were paramount.

The Welsh Office did not completely retreat in agenda setting for planning and development in Wales. Through a variety of government agencies such as the Welsh Development Agency, the Land Authority for Wales and the Development Board for Rural Wales, in addition to central government initiatives (for example, urban policies and funding from the Inner Urban Areas Act 1978 and the Valleys Programme 1988), the Welsh Office created the conditions for the renewal of both urban and rural areas. The difference was that these policies were often implemented outside the official land use planning system, although there can be no doubt that structure plans of the county councils were viewed by central government as a strategic co-ordinating level for the plethora of initiatives in place. Land use planning issues that existed outside these areas were not comprehensively dealt with, and it is in this arena that 'opposition planning' fostered.

An example of the way the Welsh Office's land use planning procedures were counteracted by the opposition during this time is in the proposals for new towns in Newtown-Caersws in Mid-Wales and Llantrisant in Glamorgan. Although proposals for a third town, at Cwmbran near the English–Welsh border, did succeed and the town itself was designated and built, the two other designations were abandoned following a concerted campaign against a policy that was viewed as reflecting British, as opposed to Welsh, interests (Edwards and Thomas, 1974). This abandonment reflects the failure on the part of the Welsh Office systematically to enforce a Welsh element to the wider institutional or state planning system.

The Welsh Office's position on the provision of an overview planning policy for Wales, to update and replace the 1967 *Wales: The Way Ahead*, was one of consistently rejecting the need for broad strategic policies and a reliance instead on strengthening existing structure plans as a means through which changing social and economic circumstances could be co-ordinated. They were also used to co-ordinate an informal partnership and joint collaboration between the Welsh Office and local government. Even in 1978 the then Secretary of State for Wales continued to reject the principle of all-Wales planning guidance:

> My preference in the field of economic planning is not the imposition of a grandiose all-Wales plan from on high, but rather to approach the needs of Wales area by area and to collate the proposals drawn from the experience of those nearest to the problem. This is what democracy is about.
>
> (John Morris MP, Welsh Office press note, 16 February 1978)

An ideological debate developed in opposition political circles relating to the most salient issues for central government intervention. The official policy vacuum that existed throughout this time created on the one hand an informal national planning response, and on the other a broad consensus among Welsh public organisations for the development of 'good government'. The underlying conditions that created this regional and territorial nationalism to respond on planning matters in Wales were the Welsh language, a Welsh nationalist tradition, and, perhaps more distinctly, a Welsh cultural homogeneity.

Wales, as a country, illustrated two distinctive phenomena in the planning polity: the interaction of national centrality and local policy-making. The Welsh Office, as a central government department, reflected the policies of the British government as they could be applied to Wales and reinforced the institutional characteristics associated with land use planning. From this perspective, the Welsh Office consequently operated as a regional office for the government. However, the Welsh Office also operated for Wales as the national government office for Wales, ensuring that the interests of Wales, Welsh businesses, the Welsh environment and the Welsh public were paramount in future economic, environmental and social decisions. The Welsh Office was thus juxtaposed between operating within an institutional framework widely recognised as British, while protecting territorial and cultural concerns that were acutely Welsh. Given this contraposition, at frequent intervals in the planning history of Wales particular forces and groups in society possessing defined political viewpoints against a British institution have felt isolated from policy-making arenas, antagonistic towards central government politicians and officials, and independent from laws and policies that may have originated outside of Wales. The land use planning system is located at the centre of this disunion and provides an example of the difficulty of fostering separate planning policy agendas while implementing common legal frameworks.

ATTEMPTS AT DEVELOPING A WELSH PLANNING AGENDA

As discussed earlier in the book, during the 1980s, as the land use planning system in Britain became market-orientated and embraced Thatcherite political ideology to the detriment of state planning controls (Thornley, 1993), the very purpose of planning was questioned. The state's role in co-ordinating a planning system was debated, and attempts were made by the Conservative governments in the mid-1980s to weaken the development plan process (for example, through *The Future of Development Plans* White Paper, HM Government, 1989). As the professional debate ensued over what role planning should take in facilitating future development requirements of the market, other contemporary commentators advocated a stronger planning or institutional top-down policy framework (Bruton and Nicholson, 1985). This would involve setting planning policies in a hierarchy from national to local, with each level of policy conforming to the proceeding level. The committee of inquiry appointed by the Nuffield Foundation also recommended a strengthening of the national level of planning policy in order to provide some strategic co-ordination at the regional, county and district tiers of government (Nuffield Foundation, 1986).

In 1988, in recognition of the need for a national level of planning policy, the government introduced the first in a series of Planning Policy Guidance Notes (PPGs) for England and Wales as a whole. The first eight documents, dealing with such substantive issues as development control, housing, industrial development, retailing and the countryside, were released under joint authorship between the Department of the Environment and the Welsh Office. The documents dealt with detailed land use planning issues rather than acting as broad statements of national policy. The Nuffield Inquiry's recommendations therefore cannot be viewed as the intellectual foundation for the introduction of PPGs (Tewdwr-Jones, 1994c). Over the past ten years the provision of national planning guidance to shape local policy and procedures in England and Wales has been one of the most important planning trends introduced by the government and has taken on some degree of significance with the introduction of the pro-planning or plan-led system in the Planning and Compensation Act 1991. The influence of the PPGs is considerable, not only in the drafting of strategic and local planning policies but also in the co-ordination of regional planning guidance and the development control process (Tewdwr-Jones, 1994a, 1994b). However, the exact role of national policy guide-lines remains uncertain since, as was discussed in chapters 6 and 8, they can often appear as mandatory rather than advisory, and this has political con-sequences for the means through which central government in Wales (in other words, the Welsh Office prior to 1999) implemented national planning policies.

The Welsh Office did not attempt to implement a radically different policy approach to the planning system in Wales from that operating by the Department of the Environment in England. Both central government departments released cir-culars and Planning Policy Guidance Notes under joint-authorship over a long period of time, thus reflecting the government's view of the planning system being essentially identical in both countries. Central government's planning policy was and is delivered through a mixture of circulars that focus on legislative changes, and PPGs that deal with policy issues that are of direct relevance to the formula-tion and implementation of development plans. Occasionally, however, some circu-lars and PPGs have been issued separately in Wales from the policy documents in England, either on topics that have a distinct Welsh flavour or because legal and administrative systems in the two countries are, in these instances, separate.

Until 1995, the Welsh Office introduced very few separate planning policy statements distinctive from the Department of the Environment, although these are worth mentioning briefly. These documents were additional to the plethora of circulars and Planning Policy Guidance Notes issued jointly by the two departments.

Circular 61/81, *Historic Buildings and Conservation Areas*, was released separately in Wales to reflect the distinct historical and administrative arrangements in the principality (Welsh Office, 1981). Circular 30/86, *Housing for Senior Management* (1986), was introduced as part of the Welsh Office's drive to stimulate local economies and inward investment in Wales. In particular, the then Welsh Secretary was of the opinion that the lack of an adequate pool of housing attractive to and suitable for senior managers and senior technical staff was a possible disincentive to business people who might otherwise be prepared to invest and develop in Wales. The circular outlined the policy request for each local planning authority in Wales to allow for the designation of additional development sites for new houses or low-density groups of houses to allow for the encouragement of commerce and industry 'in and adjoining towns and villages (as well as in proposals for new settlements)' (Welsh Office, 1986: para. 1). Circular 53/88 *The Welsh Language – Development Plans and Planning Control* (Welsh Office, 1988b) outlined how the Welsh language should be treated as a material consideration in planning policy formulation and implementation, and is particularly relevant as a distinctive policy approach. The latter two circulars reflect what has probably been the most distinctive policy difference between land use planning in Wales compared to that for England, and although welcomed by relevant Welsh organisations are limited compared to the plethora of other guidance that has been jointly released. Indeed, concern has been expressed about the adequacy of some of the policy (Tewdwr-Jones, 1998b). Circular 30/86 has since been withdrawn; Circular 53/88 was replaced by a new Technical Advice Note (TAN20) in 2000; see Chapter 10.

Finally, the Welsh Office did introduce three separate Planning Policy Guidance Notes: PPG3, *Land for Housing* (Welsh Office, 1992b); PPG12, *Development Plans and Strategic Planning Guidance in Wales* (Welsh Office, 1992a); and PPG16, *Planning and Archaeology* (Welsh Office, 1990). PPG3 was released to reflect the role of the quangos Tai-Cymru/Housing for Wales and the Land Authority for Wales in the promotion and development of housing provision in the country. PPG12 was introduced in reflection of the lack of Regional Planning Guidance for Wales as it existed in England and the role of the distinctive organisations in Wales as statutory consultees in development plan preparation. PPG16 was introduced in recognition of the existence of separate historic monuments and conservation quangos in Wales and their role in the planning system. The emphasis, therefore, was on the institutional differences between Wales and England, rather than policy differences.

What is clear in this evidence and in almost all of the central government circulars and Planning Policy Guidance Notes issued jointly with the Department of
the Environment (some 17 PPGs) was the lack of a distinctly Welsh policy dimension, and it is questionable why so many other policy topics were not considered
suitable to warrant the issuing of separate policy guidance appropriate for a
Welsh audience. In addition to the policy guidance on the countryside and the
rural economy, other substantive planning issues covered by these common policies included industrial development, retailing, telecommunications, recreation,
coastal planning, tourism, renewable energy, and mineral extraction, and were
some of the more politically sensitive issues within the planning system operated
in Wales. This question is located within a wider debate, precipitated by critics of
the state, on the role the planning system should take in Wales and whether the
core planning areas of concern were addressed adequately by a Welsh – as
opposed to English – central government department. It led the political opposition to label the Welsh Office dormant in the face of Department of the Environment initiatives and to question the extent to which the Welsh Office was
sufficiently interventionist in planning issues in the country. This emphasises the
distinct and difficult role for the Welsh Office at the time between operating as a
centralised bureaucratic agency of the British state while attempting to implement
and co-ordinate planning policy that reflects distinctive socio-political traditions. It
also reinforces a belief that central government during the 1970s through to the
1990s has still been largely ineffective in defining clear planning policy statements (that is, in 'official planning'), thereby causing the development of an alternative planning agenda organised within new territorial coalitions such as rural
areas (through 'opposition planning').

The provision of central government planning guidance, therefore, has been
more noticeably debated in Wales than in England, since the planning issues
addressed in the documents have often been closely identified with a state political
agenda. In the 1980s and early 1990s, the political role of the Welsh Office in relation to planning was one of centrality with the Department of the Environment. On
occasions, separate planning agendas emerged, causing political embroilments
throughout the national and local political circles on such issues as rural housing,
windfarms, opencast mining, economic development and retailing; but these
debates were initiated through reactionary politics. Although Peter Walker, the
Secretary of State for Wales between 1987 and 1990, was widely applauded for
his interventionist role in facilitating an urban programme for the valleys (Welsh
Office, 1988a), the methods employed by the Welsh Office to progress and
encourage economic change and urban renewal were outside the land use planning system, and relied on a combination of central government grants, government agencies (such as the Welsh Development Agency and the Land Authority

for Wales), private sector investment, and political co-operation across government agencies. The role of the official planning process to co-ordinate development in Wales, and of the Welsh Office in providing a national planning policy framework, was not apparent. Although it is possible to suggest that the Welsh Office failed in this respect, it might also have been a deliberate move on the department's part to recognise the diverse and varied nature of planning for different areas within Wales. A system of all-Wales guidance may not, therefore, have been appropriate. An alternative system to all-Wales policy advice could have focused on distinct spatial localities, such as urban, rural and valley areas. Whether the Welsh Office, in its determination to strengthen strategic policies through county councils' struc-ture plans, was indicating a spatial approach to planning through the 1970s and 1980s, is difficult to assess. Certainly, with the benefit of hindsight, there are grounds to label the spatial approach inadequate.

The uncertainty over the Welsh Office's land use planning agenda was exac-erbated further in 1993 by the appointment of John Redwood as Secretary of State. A change in Welsh Office policy caused principally by personal political ideology on the part of the minister resulted in no further Planning Policy Guidance Notes being released in Wales. Following the publication of a PPG on retailing and town centres jointly by the Department of the Environment and the Welsh Office in July 1993 (DoE/Welsh Office, 1993), the minister refused to sanction the release of any further planning documents. Many joint-department PPGs remained in draft format at the time and were scheduled for release over the following two years. But the withdrawal of the Welsh Office from the Planning Policy Guidance exercise resulted in Wales (and Welsh local authority planners) undergoing a period of disil-lusionment and the creation of a policy vacuum that was more devastating for plan-ning's role in Wales than at any time in the 1970s or 1980s. Indeed, the Welsh Office, that had never particularly believed in promoting an independent planning policy approach in Wales, now found itself slipping behind on those planning policy issues initiated across the border in England. Between 1993 and 1995, five PPGs were released by the Department of the Environment that normally would have applied equally to Wales. The five documents covered Nature Conservation, Transport, Planning and the Historic Environment, Planning and Pollution Control, and Planning and Noise. The refusal on the part of the Welsh Office to release the PPG on transport resulted in a separate policy approach between the Welsh Secretary and the Environment Secretary in England on controlling transport in urban areas, protecting the environment, and encouraging more investment in public transport, some of the more rational areas for the planning system's inter-vention in the 1990s. However, this separatist policy movement was not acted upon by opposition planners to promote an alternative planning agenda for Wales, distinct from that of England. Professional opinion was more concerned with the lack of the same planning guidance, in terms of quantity and detail, as that existing for English local planning authorities (Tompsett, 1994).

Throughout John Redwood's period as Welsh Secretary, the Welsh Office was left in a planning time warp as policies and decisions in England kept apace with the new planning framework, leaving the development industry and local planners in Wales without a comprehensive national planning framework. The exact reasons why Redwood refused to release the 'missing PPGs', as they became known (Tewdwr-Jones, 1997b), have never been critically assessed. The refusal was based on an ideological conviction against the imposition of higher-tier guidance on the activities of lower-level state functions, and a belief that the guidance that was being released was unnecessarily detailed and cumbersome, ironically reflecting the same areas of complaint as political opposition groups in rural authorities of Wales. This fuelled a political row between central government and local government, and also between professional planning officers and the political members they served. Planners felt uncomfortable without official planning guidance, since it presented the possibility of a weakening of local authorities' policies against opportunistic developers. Local politicians, on the other hand, whilst condemning the Welsh Office's failure to act on the planning agenda, recognised an opportunity to implement a more discretionary planning system that could cater for local community needs and foster greater territorial politics independent of central government control. The Secretary of State and the local politicians were at opposite ends of the political spectrum in ideological terms, but believed in the concept of 'local choice', with decisions to be taken at the lowest possible political level. In the rural areas of Wales this conflict has further allowed the planning system to be used by opposition groups to implement non-planning decisions to the benefit of territorial nationalism and a precipitation of local capacity in planning that would otherwise have been dealt with by a strong central government department. The territorial nationalism was not mobilised in any political sense. Most of the rural authorities are run by independent political representatives lacking strategic direction and who are spatially fragmented, a common feature of local state politics (Saunders, 1984). The nationalist configuration did, however, possess some powerful ideas.

The position of the Welsh Office in the planning system during this period of time therefore evolved further. Combined with the requirements of the pro-planning legislation contained in the 1991 Planning and Compensation Act, the Welsh Office fostered a degree of harmony among planning professionals with a stable policy framework and a local authority-led development control process. The national planning guidance in place has been welcomed by the professionals who feel they have the necessary policy parameters to implement a local planning system for communities. But the local politicians have not been so easily convinced.

WELSH LOCAL PLANNING: INTRA-REGIONAL DIFFERENCES

OPERATING PLANNING POLICY PROCESSES

The first structure plan to be approved in Wales was for Gwynedd in July 1977, with the last being approved in 1983 and thereby completing structure plan coverage in Wales. Welsh structure planning has been characterised by a similar process to that of England and Scotland: ongoing replacement and modification. At the more detailed level, complete coverage of Wales by local plans was required by 1996 (Roderick, 1994), but this has been much slower and was never achieved prior to local government reorganisation at that time. This was mainly the consequence of a move towards the production of district-wide plans. In some areas, such as the more rural authorities where no form of statutory local plan may have previously existed, this led to administrative uncertainty and delay in the planning system. The Welsh Office had estimated in 1993 that all but one of the 37 districts would achieve district-wide local plan coverage by 1996, with most authorities adopting their plans well in advance (in evidence to the House of Commons Welsh Affairs Committee, 1993). Although over half the population of Wales was covered by adopted local plans at this time, only three districts had achieved district-wide coverage: Rhondda, Swansea and Wrexham Maelor. Some other authorities possessed local plans covering only minor parts of their administrative areas, whereas six authorities had yet to start preparing local plans: Carmarthen, Ceredigion, Glyndwr, Montgomeryshire, Preseli-Pembrokeshire and South Pembrokeshire. For these authorities, centred in the rural areas of Wales, their only statutory policies were contained in the relevant structure plans. With the enhanced status afforded to development plan policies under the terms of Section 54A of the Planning and Compensation Act 1991, it was imperative for all district authorities to progress statutory local plan coverage as soon as possible to provide a firm basis for development control decisions.

The Welsh Office attempted to deal with the time delay problems by producing advice that stressed the advantage of rapid and attractive plan production and the need for plans to concentrate more upon land use issues (Welsh Office, 1992a, 1993a). While this began to have an impact it is paradoxical that the implementation of Section 54A of the 1991 Planning and Compensation Act and the lack of all-Wales national planning guidance between 1993 and 1995 may have lengthened the time taken for local plan inquiries, thereby undermining the Welsh Office's attempts to speed up plan production. The increased status afforded to local plans means that developers, and others with an interest in land use, are now more interested in influencing the content of the plans to ensure that policies that favour their interests are adequately reflected. The problems with local plan uncertainty in Wales may also reflect a wider view in some local planning authorities, from both officers and members, that the statutory, institutional or 'official' planning system may be irrelevant in addressing the problems facing these communities, especially if these are ones of social and cultural erosion or economic decline. This has undoubtedly resulted in a reliance in some areas of Wales on non-statutory plans and supplementary planning guidance, but also in the view – even since devolution in 1999 – that Wales requires a completely different approach. Local planning authorities have placed non-land use planning policies (as defined by planning law and central government) outside the statutory plan but within supplementary documentation and then used these documents to facilitate community needs. Such topics addressed by supplementary plans have included social housing (White and Tewdwr-Jones, 1995).

PLANNING NON-CONFORMITY AND THE EMERGENCE OF 'IRRESPONSIBLE PLANNING'

To complement the new statutory development plan provisions enacted in the 1991 Act, the Welsh Office decided that some form of quality assessment guidance for the implementation of planning policies would be worth while and released its *Development Control – A Guide to Good Practice* document in the summer of 1993. The aims of the booklet were to assist local authorities in improving their development control procedures and increasing the quality in public sector service delivery (Welsh Office, 1993a). The guide, produced as part of the Citizen's Charter initiative, a forerunner of Best Value, related to the standard of service expected out of development control sections by emphasising the right every citizen has in expecting efficiency in the local development control service. In addition to providing advice on quality and efficiency in Welsh authorities' work, the booklet also attempted to respond to the parliamentary Welsh Affairs Committee's recommendations in its report on the planning system within the country concerning bad procedures and malpractice within Welsh rural authorities, in their report *Rural Housing* (House of Commons Welsh Affairs Committee, 1993).

The report highlighted the actions of planning committee councillors to base decisions upon the personal circumstances of the applicant, commenting that, 'Many of the most disturbing aspects of the evidence we have received have related to the conduct of members of planning committees' (House of Commons Welsh Affairs Committee, 1993: para. 56). The report quotes the evidence of the Director of Planning at Ceredigion District Council in which he remarked that the planning system in the locality had

> become personalised to the extent that the circumstances of the applicant are frequently considered to be more important than the planning merits of the application.

> (ibid.)

The development control issue relates directly to the provision of national planning policy guidance in Wales. A political leader of Ceredigion District Council, an area of Mid-Wales where a strong opposition planning element exists, complained in evidence of the imposition of English policies at the Welsh local level:

> The Secretary of State has gone so far to say that the local communities and local people should decide where and what sort of development to take place in their areas. We are guided by the policy guidance note.
>
> (ibid.: para. 23)

The member then went on to justify the local authority taking an opposing view to national guidance, preferring instead to rely on local knowledge provided by the area ward representative in determining individual planning applications. The uncertainty over the application of non-spatially specific Welsh planning guidance at the community level has also been raised by members of the planning profession. The Director of Planning of Montgomeryshire District Council, in commenting on the role of PPGs in Welsh planning, stated that although the guidance contained an increasing 'Welsh flavour', 'the basic policy in relation to developing the countryside is still very much a national [British] one' (ibid.: para. 26). Cloke (1996) has also highlighted the problems of decision-makers in rural Wales in applying Planning Policy Guidance Notes 3 (Housing) and 7 (The Countryside). Cloke was an adviser to the Welsh Affairs Committee for their rural housing study, and has suggested that there exists a political reaction against the imposition of such 'Anglocentric' guidance, labelling the planning activity within these areas as 'irresponsible':

> it is hard to escape the general conclusion that the degree to which statutory planning provisions, or legally significant planning policy guidance, are adhered to by local planning authorities depends on local political agendas and localised constructions of 'what it is possible to get away with'.
>
> (Cloke, 1996: 300)

The amount of criticism put forward at the parliamentary committee hearings of central government guidance failing to reflect the particular characteristics of Welsh rural communities and the Welsh countryside was so strong it led the committee to recommend to the Welsh Office the amendment of national policies:

> Although we recognise that many of the calls for increasing Welshness to the guidance are, in effect, calls for greater relaxation of controls over developments in the countryside, it is also true that guidance which reflects the settlement patterns of the home counties is unlikely to be equally applicable to rural Wales.
>
> (House of Commons Welsh Affairs Committee, 1993: para. 26)

The politicisation of land use planning, as identified by the Welsh select committee, also occurred as a result of the actions and decisions of the elected members
of certain authorities. As a direct consequence of the imposed rigidity of national
policy – and ultimately decision-parameters – some local politicians in the 1980s and
1990s became frustrated with their inability to apply local interpretation of national
guidance in local circumstances. The professional officers conformed to the policy
planning constraints, but the elected members were reluctant to follow imposed
central government guidance. This reluctance to conform, in turn, resulted in occasions when the local members rejected professional advice, played-down central
government planning policies, and thereby contributed to reports of misrepresenting
the purpose of the land use planning system (Tewdwr-Jones, 1995). An unfortunate
aspect of this localised opposition to the planning system is an anti-incomer dimension, a perception that first had its roots in second-home purchasing from the 1960s
but now forming a core political concern on the part of nationalist groups worried
about cultural and linguistic preservation (Gallent and Tewdwr-Jones, 2000b, 2001).
Although this is part of a political reaction, it is especially difficult for a planning officer
to deal with. The professional has to recognise and manage politicians' requests to
implement an anti-institutional decision-making process against the imposition of
central government policies for everyone in the authority's area. It is one thing for
local politicians deliberately to ignore established government planning policies for
the benefit of everyone in the authority's area, but quite another matter when the
opposition is enacted only when it benefits people born in the locality.

Cloke (1996) recognises the parallels here between the local political config-
urations of the Welsh rural authorities and the Lees Report of maladministration in
the operation of the development control function of North Cornwall District
Council, a local authority in the rural south-west of England (DoE, 1993). Many
issues highlighted by the Members of Parliament in Wales are similar to the contents of the North Cornwall report.

Authorities in both the Welsh heartland of West, Mid- and North Wales and
North Cornwall reflect to some extent the same socio-political characteristics.
These authorities are politically independent, are centred on remote rural areas,
and possess broadly similar social and economic conditions, such as rural depriva-
tion and lack of affordable local housing. Additional to these societal problems is a
cultural phenomenon. In rural Wales, the erosion of Welsh identity and the threat to
the Welsh language is compounded by a supposed 'threat' from non-local people
migrating into the area and eroding both the low supply of housing stock and the
distinctive cultural circumstances either as first-home or second-home owners
(Gallent and Tewdwr-Jones, 2000b), although this latter point does not seem to be
particularly apparent today as it was in the 1970s and 1980s. It remains, nevertheless, and entrenched political perception.

The political representatives of both regions have been attempting to take decisions that meet the needs and problems of the communities they serve while territorially conserving the cultural nuances that are identified as distinctive from the rest of the country. While it is questionable whether this forms the basis of a rural local state (Cloke and Little, 1990), planners in these areas are faced with the problem of local politicians refusing to enact central policies institutionalised and backed by a legal system. The decision-makers view with great suspicion the imposition of outside policies or guidance that have not been formulated at the local level. They also do not believe that policy solutions addressed by anyone other than local people can truly reflect the problems being experienced or create sets of conditions that are appropriate for their own constituencies. Local government and local political representatives are viewed as the best actors to respond to local needs (Jones and Stewart, 1983). In the place of national policies, they develop a local capacity for non-official planning that, while not politically strong, responds to powerful and passionate beliefs held by the wider community.

A great deal of evidence exists, therefore, to assert a sub-national planning agenda within Wales pushing against the imposition of a national consistency policy approach. Shortly after the publication of the Welsh Affairs Committee report, the Welsh Office did adopt a separate planning policy system in Wales by abandoning its joint national policy statement approach with the Department of the Environment for England. But to what extent did the new Welsh system actually promote a separate planning policy agenda to that for England? It is that question that forms the rationale for the empirical research discussed in the next section.

PLANNING GUIDANCE FOR WALES OR WELSH PLANNING POLICY?

John Redwood was succeeded as Welsh Secretary by William Hague in July 1995. Immediately following his appointment, two new draft Planning Policy Guidance Notes were released for public consultation. The two documents, *Unitary Development Plans* and *Planning Policy* (Welsh Office, 1995a, 1995b), incorporated the 'missing PPGs', but the contents and format of the two drafts were radically different to the joint English/Welsh planning guidance previously released. The principal change in the two draft documents compared to their former and English counterparts centred on the number of PPGs that would in future provide the Welsh national planning policy agenda. The Welsh Office replaced all the existing PPGs – some 17 documents – together with a number of circulars and other government statements with the two revised PPGs.

Unitary Development Plans concentrated on preparing UDPs in the reformed unitary local government system in Wales after April 1996. The guidance went further, however, and included detailed guidance on plan procedures within the national parks and on transitionary arrangements between the old and new planning systems. The second document, *Planning Guidance Wales: Planning Policy* was far more interesting, and reduced the advice in the existing 17 PPGs to 200 paragraphs of guidance. The format, contents and even wording of this PPG were extremely different to past Department of the Environment government planning statements. It became apparent that the Welsh Office accepted the need for change in its planning policy guidance, as highlighted by the parliamentary Welsh Affairs Committee in 1993, with the emphasis on developing policy separately from that in England.

The PPG provided definitive statements that concentrate on strategic issues in recognition, most probably, of the lack of a co-ordinating strategic planning agency in Wales once the county councils were abolished in spring 1996. Some agencies in Wales criticised the government for the brevity of the guidance, but failed to appreciate what the Welsh Office was attempting to achieve. For once, the government was attempting to restrict its policy guidance to national and strategic issues at an all-Wales level, a broad framework that permitted individual local authorities and developers a greater amount of discretion to determine local issues. The general role of national planning policy was not amended, however, and local authorities were still required to take account of Welsh Office guidance in preparing development plans and in determining planning applications. But the interpretation of PPGs, where local authorities have the ability to formulate policies and take decisions that are broadly in conformity with the Secretary of State's advice, was left for the local authorities themselves to determine, espousing the concept of 'local choice' that the former Welsh Secretary John Redwood supported.

On the whole, the revised PPGs when released in final format in 1996 did begin to reflect the particular nuances of Welsh social, economic and environmental concerns. But several important questions remained unanswered. Given the change in nature of the PPGs to cover issues of more strategic concern, Welsh local authorities may well feel as though they are entering another policy vacuum, in much the same way as the uncertainty of the 1970s and early 1980s. The former PPGs dealt with many issues in great detail, to the extent that practically all planning matters were covered by the guidance. Local authorities only had to interpret and adapt national policies to suit their own circumstances. The strategic PPGs after 1996 left local authorities with a greater interpretative and policy formulation role, and this may not have been welcome in some quarters. More fundamentally, did the contents of Planning Guidance Wales actually illustrate a separate planning policy agenda for Wales, compared to the previous joint English and Welsh model, or was it merely the format that changed?

PLANNING POLICY DIFFERENCES BETWEEN ENGLAND AND WALES

The form the detailed research took related to a detailed comparison between national planning statements between the different government departments in the period 1993–9: the Department of the Environment's Planning Policy Guidance Notes, and the Welsh Office's Planning Guidance Wales. The aim of this approach was to identify those policies considered by the government sufficiently important as overarching English and Welsh planning statements, and thereby illustrate the government's determination to continue with its national consistency remit across England and Wales to the detriment of sub-national planning policy agendas, and those policies that were at variance with the joint English and Welsh, or English only, approach, thereby illustrating central government's weakening of its overarching national consistency remit by permitting a strategic sub-national (Welsh) approach. It would also illustrate the degree to which Planning Guidance Wales did conform to the distinctive policy called for by the Welsh Affairs Committee in 1993.

The empirical results are discussed in relation to 13 key policy sectors: design; transport and infrastructure; housing; conservation of the natural and built environment; the coast; green belts; economic development; control of outdoor advertisements; tourism, sport and recreation; energy; waste treatment and disposal; land reclamation, unstable land, contaminated land and flood risk; and pollution. The format of the results tabulated as Tables 9.1–9.13 depicts the section of Planning Guidance Wales devoted to that particular topic, together with the relevant English PPG equivalent. Beneath this data, national policy statements from the Department of the Environment's own documentation are listed, together with the relevant equivalent paragraph (if any) in the Welsh version. The DoE's national planning policy statements within each Planning Policy Guidance Note, as they existed at the time, are listed in *The Effectiveness of Planning Policy Guidance Notes* report, published by the Department of the Environment in 1995 (DoE, 1995).

The difficulties of comparing one set of policies with another was appreciated. In particular, there was concern over how to compare policy with policy to identify similarity either in wording, or meaning, or structure of sentence. The approach adopted identifies similarity in the tenet of the policy statements, rather than exact replication. This follows central government advice within PPG1, *General Policy and Principles* to the effect that the semantics of statements within PPGs should not be subject to intense scrutiny (DoE/Welsh Office, 1992b). However, where significant variation occurred in the tenet of two similar policies in separate documents, this was noted.

DESIGN

Comparison between the design policy content of PPG and PGW reveals a slight difference in the amount of policy advice (see Table 9.1). PGW contained just three paragraphs devoted to the subject of design, although the DoE's checklist of national policy statements reveals that they were concerned with just two statements. The impact on surrounding sensitive areas of new development was contained within the Welsh version, but there was no statement that encouraged local authorities to consider good design standards. This could be significant for two reasons. First, there was no duty for Welsh local planning authorities to include a policy in their development plans that promoted good design, unlike their English counterparts; second, without that local policy it would be more difficult for planning controllers to negotiate or even reject development proposals that did not meet the good design requirements of individual local authorities or spatial areas. This could, in turn, have had implications for local authorities' positions in planning appeals.

One hopes that local planning authorities in Wales would, nevertheless, have adopted good design practice in assessing applications for planning permission, and might even have included design policies in their development plans. The difference with English guidance is the very fact that local authorities were not advised to include such a policy. Invariably this may not have mattered, and perhaps what is of more significance is the fact that the Department of the Environment regarded it to be so significant an issue as to inform English local authorities of this requirement explicitly. The more conceptual questions that arise are: Is it necessary for central government to make such a statement, or is it rather first and foremost a local matter? To what extent is it necessary for central government to inform local authorities of particular policy areas in order to ensure that the subject is addressed locally? What would be the impact of Welsh local authorities not explicitly including a policy in their development plans in the context of their enhanced positions provided by Section 54A of the Planning and Compensation Act 1991?

TRANSPORT AND INFRASTRUCTURE

The next topic covers two principal policy areas: transport and telecommunications. As Table 9.2 indicates, PGW devoted 29 paragraphs of guidance to the subject and the DoE identified eight national policy statements. These statements, that included urban development promotion to reduce car trips, to limit car parking, the promotion of public transport, and telecommunications developments, were all repeated in the Welsh document. They may therefore have been classified as overarching national policy statements to apply across England and Wales. No sub-national policy agenda at variance with these statements would be

Table 9.1 Comparison of national planning policies between Planning Policy Guidance Notes for England and Planning Guidance Wales: Design

Paras.	Planning Guidance Wales	Planning Policy Guidance for England
38–40	Design	PPG1
	National policy statements made within Planning Policy Guidance for England and similar statements identified in Planning Guidance Wales	
	To encourage good design standards (n/s)	
	To consider the impact of proposed development on surrounding buildings and landscape in areas designated by virtue of the sensitivity of the environment (paras. 38/39)	

Source: English and Welsh national planning policy guidance notes
Note: n/s refers to 'no statement'

Table 9.2 Comparison of national planning policies between Planning Policy Guidance Notes for England and Planning Guidance Wales: Transport and Infrastructure

Paras.	Planning Guidance Wales	Planning Policy Guidance for England
51–5	Transport	PPG13
56–60	Public transport	PPG13
61–70	Siting of development	PPG13
71	Strategic roads	PPG13
72	Utilities	PPG8
73–9	Telecommunications	PPG8

National policy statements made within Planning Policy Guidance for England and similar statements identified in Planning Guidance Wales

To promote development within urban areas, at locations highly accessible by means other than the private car (para. 61)

To encourage the location of major generators of travel demand in existing centres which are highly accessible by means other than the private car (para. 63)

To strengthen existing local centres – in both urban and rural areas – which offer a range of everyday community, shopping and employment opportunities, and aim to protect and enhance their viability and vitality (para. 63)

To maintain and improve choice for people to walk, cycle or use public transport rather than drive between homes and facilities which they need to visit regularly (paras. 63/65)

To limit parking provision for developments and other on or off-street parking provision to discourage reliance on the car for work and other journeys where there are effective alternatives (para. 66)

To cater for telecommunications development by taking account of strategic requirements of networks (para. 73)

To develop policies for the location of telecommunications developments (para. 75)

To provide flexible criteria based guidelines for telecommunications development where sites other than those identified in the development plan are proposed (para. 76)

permitted since they have formed a central plank of government policy. Government policy in this respect refers to non-planning subjects, towards sustainability (in public transport promotion) and market deregulation and competitiveness (towards telecommunication developments). Both these general policy areas were covered by government White Papers at the time: HM Government (1990, 1994 respectively), and can be viewed as general policy underlying changes to planning policy formulation.

Since national planning policy statements emerged following general government policy developments towards certain specific sectors, one may surmise that these national planning statements do conform to overarching statements to be applied uniformly across England and Wales. The key questions are: Should the statements contained within Planning Guidance be regarded as national policy statements released by central government, or are they merely central government national position statements that local authorities must follow in developing local policies? What and how much discretion do local authorities possess to deviate from this national planning policy line?

HOUSING

Housing policies between Wales and England were practically identical, and all four national policy statements were evident in both sets of documents (Table 9.3). The first statement, however, did display a slight variation in Wales where the future housing provision figures were released by the Welsh Office on a unitary authority by unitary authority basis. In England, housing figures have been calculated on a regional basis and then broken down into county figures. These county figures, in turn, were translated into detailed local plan housing site allocations at the district council level. This approach, described as the 'predict and provide' model, has caused a great deal of consternation locally and one that has recently caused the Department of the Environment, Transport and the Regions to explore ways of introducing more local transparency and consultation in the housing projection figures in England (DETR, 1998f).

Although PPG3 *Planning for Housing in Wales*, and its English counterpart both devoted several paragraphs to affordable housing, the government had not at the time of the research adopted a national policy statement to cover this subject. While this may seem unusual, it was a transitory time for the subject of the planning–affordable housing relationship, since it has long been deemed to be a non-land use issue (Gallent and Tewdwr-Jones, 2000a; Tewdwr-Jones and Gallent, 2000). It is only relatively recently that the British courts of law have determined that the issue of affordable housing can be a material consideration in planning, and the development of planning policy – from the judgements of legal cases – is being progressed slowly.

Table 9.3 Comparison of national planning policies between Planning Policy Guidance Notes for England and Planning Guidance Wales: Housing

Paras.	Planning Guidance Wales	Planning Policy Guidance for England
80–8	Housing	PPG3
89–91	Affordable housing	PPG3
National policy statements made within Planning Policy Guidance for England and similar statements identified in Planning Guidance Wales		
To show the overall scale of housing provision broken down into districts (para. 80) To translate structure plan policies into detailed development control policies and map based housing land allocations (para. 81) To set out criteria against which applications will be considered, for sites not individually identified (para. 83) To make full and effective use of existing urban areas when selecting sites. Development potential of derelict, under-used and waste land should be identified. Open space should be protected (para. 81)		

Source: English and Welsh national planning policy guidance notes

Environmental conservation is a policy area that has been covered by both English and Welsh planning policy guidance, even if the Welsh version took the same policy position as the English equivalents, albeit in fewer statements (see Table 9.4). One national policy statement was absent from Planning Guidance Wales: the need to balance-up protection of the landscape and natural habitats with the encouragement of rural enterprise and development. This catch-all policy may have appeared to the Welsh Office to be too sensitive for a predominantly rural Welsh audience in its requirement to consider rural economic development alongside countryside protection. The Welsh statements, in comparison, gave significant weight to the protection of agricultural land and countryside development. A separate statement in Planning Guidance Wales did, however, call for local authorities to consider the need for diversification of the rural economy (see Table 9.7).

THE COAST

Planning Guidance Wales's statements on coastal planning caused controversy in professional circles when the draft guidance note was released in July 1995, mainly as a result of just one paragraph being devoted to the subject. The previous English and Welsh joint statement on coastal planning comprised a complete guidance note (PPG20 of September 1992). Although the Welsh Office did make it clear in 1995 that the policy content of PGW was identical to the previous guidance, it did not completely satisfy the demands of coastal protection groups and environmentalists who claimed that three-quarters of Wales' borders are coastal and therefore the country requires a strong planning policy. When the final version of PGW was released in May 1996, a further five paragraphs were added relating to coastal planning, but as can be viewed from Table 9.5, the national policy statements for the two countries were identical. It is interesting that the Welsh Office could state the government's position of coastal planning, protection and development within six paragraphs, whereas the version used in England contained 77 paragraphs.

GREEN BELTS

Green belt policy has been one of the few key planning policy areas where a distinctive and noticeable difference between England and Wales exists (see Table 9.6). Green belts have been in existence in England for almost fifty years but until 1999 there were no green belts in Wales. Attempts had been made at Welsh Office level and local authority level to designate green belts in Wales in both the 1950s and the early 1990s, but on both occasions progress had been thwarted. In their place, local authorities had relied on the designation of 'green wedges' and 'green barriers' in their development plans, thereby providing a flexible context to enable review of

Table 9.4 Comparison of national planning policies between Planning Policy Guidance Notes for England and Planning Guidance Wales: Conservation of the Natural and Built Environment

Paras.	Planning Guidance Wales	Planning Policy Guidance for England
92	Countryside	PPG7
93–4	Agricultural land	PPG7
95–112	Nature conservation	PPG7, PPG9
113	Habitats Directive	PPG9
114–15	Historic environment	PPG15
116–21	Listed buildings	PPG15
122–33	Conservation areas	PPG15
134–40	Archaeology	PPG16
National policy statements made within Planning Policy Guidance for England and similar statements identified in Planning Guidance Wales		
To take account of designations and weigh the need to encourage rural enterprise, the need to protect the landscape, habitats, etc., the quality of land for agriculture and other uses and the protection of other non-renewable resources (n/s)		
To protect the best agricultural land (para. 93)		
To strictly control agricultural dwellings and other house-building in the open countryside (para. 191)		
To protect designated sites and undesignated areas for nature conservation (para. 100)		
To state the criteria for strictly protecting Sites of Special Scientific Interest, and sites with additional national and international designations, including those protected by the Habitats Directive (para. 113)		
To make provision for the preservation and enhancement of conservation areas and other historic sites and buildings (para. 123)		
To protect listed buildings that possess outstanding architectural or historical features (para. 117)		
To reconcile development and archaeology and encourage early consultation between developers and planning authorities (para. 136)		
To protect, enhance and preserve sites of archaeological interest and their settings (para. 135)		

Source: English and Welsh national planning policy guidance notes

Note: n/s refers to 'no statement'

Table 9.5 Comparison of national planning policies between Planning Policy Guidance Notes for England and Planning Guidance Wales: The Coast

Paras.	*Planning Guidance Wales*	*Planning Policy Guidance for England*
141–6	The coast	PPG20
	National policy statements made within Planning Policy Guidance for England and similar statements identified in Planning Guidance Wales	
	To reconcile development with the need to protect, conserve and where appropriate, improve the natural character of the landscape, environmental quality, wildlife habitats, recreational opportunities for the coast (paras. 141/143)	
	To consider the impact of new coastal defence works on the environment (para. 146)	
	To set out the planning strategy and framework for coastal and estuary management plans (para. 143)	
	To identify areas at risk from flooding, by erosion or instability (para. 142)	

Source: English and Welsh national planning policy guidance notes

Table 9.6 Comparison of national planning policies between Planning Policy Guidance Notes for England and Planning Guidance Wales: Green Belts

Paras.	Planning Guidance Wales	Planning Policy Guidance for England
147–54 155–7	Green belts Inappropriate development	PPG2 PPG2
National policy statements made within Planning Policy Guidance for England and similar statements identified in Planning Guidance Wales		
To promote the re-use of redundant buildings in green belts (para. 156) To identify the general extent of green belt – to be altered only in extreme circumstances (para. 152) To define detailed green belt boundaries based on readily identifiable features (para. 152) To specify development appropriate to the green belt (para. 155) To implement a general presumption against inappropriate development (n/s)		

Source: English and Welsh national planning policy guidance notes

Note: n/s refers to 'no statement'

the green boundaries at every local plan review, something that green belt policy would not have provided. The reason for this relates to the possible location of green belts in Wales: the coastal plains of south-east and north-east Wales, that also happen to correspond to the preferred sites for inward investment and regional economic growth along the major transport arteries running east to west (see Tewdwr-Jones, 1997a; Phelps and Tewdwr-Jones, 1998).

Planning Guidance Wales was the first Welsh Office planning document that permitted local authorities to designate green belts in Wales. The approach, however, was one of local authority discretion in weighing-up environmental protection with economic development interests. The policy statement pointed out the factors to be borne in mind by authorities prior to green belt designation, and these appeared to go beyond the requirements for green belt extension in England. The Welsh Office called for green belt designation only where existing green wedge or green barrier policies within development plans were providing insufficient protection: the approach therefore seems to be 'a last resort'. Even more bizarre was the prospect of local authorities having to witness development within existing green wedge policy areas before green belt designation could be permitted, which may seem a classic case of 'Shutting the stable door after the horse has bolted'.

One prominent national policy statement missing from the Welsh version was the 'general presumption against inappropriate development', which was either a major error on the part of the Welsh Office drafters or else a deliberate move in recognition of the important economic activity that could be attracted to these areas to the environment, an issue that actually occurred in 1997 after the publication of the PGW in revised format (see Phelps and Tewdwr-Jones's 1998 discussion of the attraction of the Korean electronic company LG to south-east Wales). See Table 9.14 and discussion relating to the designation of major growth corridors in these areas.

ECONOMIC DEVELOPMENT

The government's policies relating to economic development across England and Wales are transposed into both Planning Guidance Wales and Planning Policy Guidance for England without any variation, as Table 9.7 illustrates. National policy statements to identify locations for new developments (especially in urban areas), and ensuring the vitality and viability of town centres and the rural economy, were all covered in the Welsh document. This included a policy curtailing the development of out-of-town retailing developments, first initiated in joint English and Welsh guidance in 1993. Since this time, the government has established a national sequential retail test to enable local authorities to assess retail developments by their proximity to town centres.

Table 9.7 Comparison of national planning policies between Planning Policy Guidance Notes for England and Planning Guidance Wales: Economic Development

Paras.	Planning Guidance Wales	Planning Policy Guidance for England
158–72	Industrial development	PPG4
173–86	Retailing and town centres	PPG6
187–8	Development in rural areas	PPG7
189	Agricultural development	PPG7
190	Re-use of rural buildings	PPG7
191–3	Agricultural/forestry dwell.	PPG3, PPG7

National policy statements made within Planning Policy Guidance for England and similar statements identified in Planning Guidance Wales

To provide a range of sites and identify specific locations for a range of developments (para. 158)

To encourage urban land to be re-used (para. 159) and to encourage development in locations which minimise travel/transport needs and congestion (para. 164)

To provide a clear strategy for town centres and retail development within the county (para. 176)

To encourage uses that will contribute to town centre vitality and viability (para. 174)

To consider traffic management including public transport facilities, provision and location of car parking, routes for pedestrians and cyclists, and access to town centre for disabled, traffic calming measures (para. 178)

To set out criteria for assessing out-of-town retail proposals, explaining how the local planning authorities will assess the impact of proposals on the vitality and viability of town centres, and how they will appraise the overall impact on travel (para. 179)

To promote diversification of the rural economy including agriculture (para. 187)

To consider the need for agricultural dwellings and other house-building in the open countryside (paras. 188/191/192/193)

To ensure re-use and adaption of rural buildings (para. 190)

Source: English and Welsh national planning policy guidance notes
Note: n/s refers to 'no statement'

CONTROL OF OUTDOOR ADVERTISEMENTS

The inclusion of a policy statement related to the display and location of adverts may not be a subject matter one initially thinks of as warranting a national approach (see Table 9.8). And yet the government has always held the opinion that it is important to control advertisements across England and Wales strictly to ensure that environmental and aesthetic safeguards remain in place. This national policy, and the control of advertisement regulations from which the policy is derived, has ensured effective limitation of the commercialisation of both town and country in England and Wales over the last 50 years. This policy even remained in place during the market-orientated and commercially minded deregulatory zeal of the Thatcherite governments of the 1980s and epitomises an area of planning regulation and control that was left in place at a time when other public sector planning controls were either being removed or else severely watered down.

TOURISM, SPORT AND RECREATION

Sport and recreation and tourism were two subjects covered by separate Planning Policy Guidance Notes in England, whereas the Welsh document devoted just six paragraphs to these policies. All principal national policy statements were replicated in the English and Welsh notes (see Table 9.9), with one exception: that dealing with the criteria for determining planning proposals for new large or innovative sports developments. This seems an odd statement to have excluded, particularly as local planning authorities in Wales are required to determine applications for planning permission for sports facilities, similar to English authorities. Wales does possess its own government-funded agency for the promotion of sport, the Sports Council for Wales, that does have a planning consultee role.

Local authorities are required to consult the Sports Council on any sports-related development proposals in their area, but the requirement to include the criteria by which those authorities would determine those planning applications is unusual in development plans. If anything, the placement of sports development criteria would seem to be a natural part of sports-related policies within development plans. Perhaps the Welsh Office assumed that Welsh local planning authorities would invariably include such criteria within their policies as a matter of course. Viewing this issue from the opposite perspective, it is questionable why the Department of the Environment in England should deem it necessary to explain the requirements of local government on planning for sport in this much detail.

ENERGY

Planning for energy, especially renewable energy developments, has featured prominently in media reporting of planning issues in Wales over the last ten years.

Table 9.8 Comparison of national planning policies between Planning Policy Guidance Notes for England and Planning Guidance Wales: Control of Outdoor Advertisements

Paras.	Planning Guidance Wales	Planning Policy Guidance for England
194–5	Control of outdoor adverts	PPG19
	National policy statements made within Planning Policy Guidance for England and similar statements identified in Planning Guidance Wales	
	To recognise the importance of advertisements to the national economy, while controlling design so as to not detract from the local vernacular and important built landscape features (para. 195)	

Source: English and Welsh national planning policy guidance notes

Table 9.9 Comparison of national planning policies between Planning Policy Guidance Notes for England and Planning Guidance Wales: Tourism, Sport and Recreation

Paras.	Planning Guidance Wales	Planning Policy Guidance for England
196–7	Tourism	PPG21
198–201	Sport and recreation	PPG17
National policy statements made within Planning Policy Guidance for England and similar statements identified in Planning Guidance Wales		
To address the environmental impact of tourist demand and ways in which any adverse effects can be moderated by restricting further expansion of tourist capacity, improve facilities for meeting existing demand and encourage alternative tourist destinations and attractions (para. 196)		
To examine ways in which tourism can contribute positively to other policy objectives (para. 197)		
To give a clear indication of the criteria to be applied in assessing the suitability of sites for large scale or innovative projects (n/s)		
To provide guidance on sport and recreation provision affecting all or significant parts of the country, especially major developments at suitable sites (paras. 199/200)		
To assess the need for recreational facilities (para. 198) and to protect open space with amenity or recreational value (para. 199)		

Source: English and Welsh national planning policy guidance
Note: n/s refers to 'no statement'

The development of wind turbine farms on remote hill-top locations in South Wales and Mid-Wales has caused a great deal of consternation on the part of rural communities that have objected to what they view as the blighting of the landscape. This has been particularly contested in the National Parks of rural Wales where the aesthetic qualities of the landscape have been perceived to be under threat from the large wind turbines.

The national planning policy position advanced by central government in the early 1990s was to encourage local government to permit applications for renewable energy, to meet an environmental obligation and to deregulate the energy industry. This policy was adopted as an overarching policy statement across England and Wales and was not rewritten in any substantive way for a Welsh audience (see Table 9.10). It is, perhaps, unfortunate that the most suitable locations for wind turbine farm developments in Wales correspond to the most sensitive landscape areas; namely, national parks and areas of outstanding natural beauty. The distinctiveness of the Welsh landscape may have required a more sensitive analysis of development proposals within these areas, but that did not lead to the development of a more Welsh landscape-friendly policy statement in Planning Guidance Wales. Renewable energy proposals are, in any case, subject to formal environmental assessment and the impact on the environment of any development proposal has to be assessed as part of the local authorities' duties of weighing up all relevant material consideration. However, this environment requirement is just one of many considerations to be taken into account by decision-makers. The heated debate in Wales during the early to mid-1990s could have prompted the Welsh Office to state the environmental issue more prominently within the Welsh policy. Had this occurred, it may have deflated a more contentious planning issue at the time.

WASTE TREATMENT AND DISPOSAL

Waste treatment and disposal is included within Planning Policy Guidance Note 23, *Planning and Pollution Control*, in England. 'Waste Treatment and Disposal' would actually be a more suitable title for the PPG, rather than 'Pollution Control', since one of the reasons why the PPG was released was to meet the UK government's obligations to implement European Union directives on a waste framework, and the note sets out policy on waste management in some detail. It is therefore surprising to note, as Table 9.11 reveals, that Planning Guidance Wales contained none of the key policy statements that existed in the English document. PGW's three paragraphs did mention the EU obligations but these are set in the context of the UK government's policy on waste management to promote reduction, re-use and recovery of sites, and to ensure that a sustainable approach occurs to deal with all of Wales' waste within Wales. Whether this provided the strategic

Table 9.10 Comparison of national planning policies between Planning Policy Guidance Notes for England and Planning Guidance Wales: Energy

Paras.	Planning Guidance Wales	Planning Policy Guidance for England
202–4	Energy	PPG22
	National policy statements made within Planning Policy Guidance for England and similar statements identified in Planning Guidance Wales	
	To consider the contribution that can be made to meeting renewable energy resources (para. 202) To reflect the nature and extent of resources in a particular area and other relevant planning considerations (para. 202) To provide renewable energy including general locations for significant projects (para. 203) To develop renewable energy sources that identify broad locations and specific sites suitable for various types of renewable energy installations (para. 204)	

Source: English and Welsh national planning policy guidance

Table 9.11 Comparison of national planning policies between Planning Policy Guidance Notes for England and Planning Guidance Wales: Waste Treatment and Disposal

Paras.	Planning Guidance Wales	Planning Policy Guidance for England
205–7	Waste treatment and disposal	PPG23
	National policy statements made within Planning Policy Guidance for England and similar statements identified in Planning Guidance Wales	
	To provide a strategic framework to meet the estimated need for disposal capacity. Strategic policies should show the broad area of search for landfill sites and take account of the availability of areas where incinerators could be located (n/s) To promote the use of completed landfill sites (n/s)	

Source: English and Welsh national planning policy guidance
Note: n/s refers to 'no statement'

POLLUTION

Table 9.12 Comparison of national planning policies between Planning Policy Guidance Notes for England and Planning Guidance Wales: Land Reclamation, Unstable Land, Contaminated Land and Flood Risk

Paras.	Planning Guidance Wales	Planning Policy Guidance for England
208	Land reclamation	PPG14
209–15	Unstable/contaminated land	PPG14
216–17	Flood risk	PPG14
National policy statements made within Planning Policy Guidance for England and similar statements identified in Planning Guidance Wales		
To take account of possible ground instability (para. 211)		
To ensure reclamation and use of unstable land (para. 212)		
To provide the criteria which will be used in determining planning applications, including conditions (para. 214)		

Source: English and Welsh national planning policy guidance

framework advocated in the English PPG is open to question, since the statement was made generally and did not adequately deal with implementation. This is yet another example of a detailed policy area covered by a lengthy PPG in England being replaced in Wales with just three short paragraphs that essentially cover the same broad issues.

LAND RECLAMATION, UNSTABLE LAND, CONTAMINATED LAND AND POLLUTION

The key policy statements covering land reclamation, unstable and contaminated land were replicated in the Welsh guidance (Table 9.12) as were those for pollution (Table 9.13). These comprised 14 paragraphs and matched the English policy guidance notes PPG14 and PPG23. No significant differences in PGW's sentiments were advanced compared to the English policy statements.

OVERVIEW

The findings from this policy research indicate that, generally, national policy statements within the planning system have been replicated between the English and Welsh planning guidance with very few exceptions. These statements do therefore conform to national overarching policies to be applied across England and Wales and, despite the existence of separate planning statements for Wales compared to those for England, the Welsh Office did largely implement the English-originated policies and replicated them in the 1996 released Planning Guidance Wales. Whether this was a deliberate action on the part of planning policy officers within the Welsh Office to meet a political agenda, or is simply the consequence of a lack of resources to consider alternative position statements, is difficult to extrapolate. The important point to consider is the fact that the national policy statements adopted by the Welsh Office in Wales have reinforced a national consistency remit, and directly or indirectly mitigated against the development of a sub-national peculiarly Welsh planning policy agenda.

Certain key issues can be drawn out, however. The first is that some national policy statements identified in the English documentation are absent from the Welsh guidance notes (for example, a presumption against development in green belts). It is difficult to assess the significance of this position, save for the suggestion that the Welsh Office may have deemed it fruitless to include certain statements within the Welsh policy because they could be taken for granted by local planning authorities. Alternatively, the lack of a national policy statement on such an important issue as green belt protection could indirectly lead to weakening of the policy position in Wales compared to that for England, and could undermine local planners' positions in planning control.

The second issue relates to the first. To what extent is it necessary for a

Table 9.13 Comparison of national planning policies between Planning Policy Guidance Notes for England and Planning Guidance Wales: Pollution

Paras.	Planning Guidance Wales	Planning Policy Guidance for England
218–21	Pollution	PPG23
	National policy statements made within Planning Policy Guidance for England and similar statements identified in Planning Guidance Wales	
	To strategically consider the location of potentially polluting development and sensitive development (para. 219)	
	To establish the criteria for potentially polluting development, especially industry within the special use classes, to meet economic needs (para. 220)	

Source: English and Welsh national planning policy guidance

central government department to cover all aspects of planning and to inform local planning authorities of detailed planning considerations? Within the Welsh guidance, certain national policy statements are absent, but are explicit in the English guidance notes. Without an explicit statement, local planning authorities in Wales may feel as though there is no requirement to consider particular issues, or else may deviate from the position explicitly set out in English policy. It begs the question of the degree to which local planning authorities are using central government national planning statements as explicit directives, as sources of information, or as mere guidance.

Third, and again relating to the previous point, the extremely noticeable difference in the amount and extent of national planning guidance contained in Planning Guidance Wales compared to Planning Policy Guidance for England questions the degree of national policy statement content of the documents. In certain topics, for example, coastal planning, pollution control and waste disposal, the key national policy statements are replicated in the Welsh guidance notes but only within a few relatively short paragraphs. The English notes, by comparison, devote complete documents to the topics. One feels as though the brevity of the Welsh versions are preferable. However, there has been a perception by planning professionals in Wales that the Welsh position is weak in the substantive policy content of these subjects simply because of the lack of the amount of guidance contained within Planning Guidance Wales. This illustrates an inability on the part of planners in Wales to distinguish between national policy statements and general national planning guidance, which might be a significant issue if planners are replicating the content (devised nationally) against the formulation of locally divergent planning policies.

Fourth, certain statements identified within both Welsh and English planning guidance notes must be regarded as overarching national statements. These include policies to promote sustainable development, the use of public transport, and market deregulation. However, these policies may not be regarded as national planning policies *per se*, but rather as central government policies. Clearly, certain statements can be traced back to other governmental policy sectors (telecommunications development and competitiveness), but others are far more detailed planning matters. Both types of national policy statements are included within the guidance notes and both PPG for England and PGW for Wales could therefore be said to have embodied the principles of national policy statements and national statements on the practice of local planning. Neither type of statement is distinguished explicitly within the guidance notes, and the Welsh Office and local planning authorities might be excused for failing to distinguish between national and local planning policy matters in their consideration of the contents of central government documents.

Fifth, despite political and public calls in the early 1990s to release separate national planning policy statements for Wales compared to those originating in England, Planning Guidance Wales of 1996 replicates the English position even on those policy sectors that could have warranted a distinctive approach. These sectors, including housing in the open countryside, settlement policies, design, coastal planning, and renewable energy, were not covered by Welsh planning policies but by the same national policy statements as those existing east of Offa's Dyke. If a distinctive policy position had been established by the Welsh Office within Planning Guidance Wales in 1996 in respect of these issues, some of the more contentious aspects of Welsh planning practice in the 1990s may have been avoided.

Finally, certain (albeit a few) sectoral issues did warrant distinctive and separate national policy statements in Wales compared to the position in England, and relate to green belts, economic development and transport. These are the subject of more detailed analysis in the next section.

THE DISTINCTIVENESS OF NATIONAL PLANNING POLICY STATEMENTS IN WALES

The previous section compared the national policy statements within Planning Guidance Wales with those identified by the Department of the Environment in England in its Planning Policy Guidance Notes. This final research section identifies those relatively few national policy statements that were identified within PGW but which were not evident in the English policy documents. This was necessary in order to assess the degree to which PGW did contain a distinctive sub-national policy content in parallel with the over-arching national policy statements applied across England and Wales.

The 221 paragraphs of national planning policy guidance contained within Planning Guidance Wales are divided into 15 sections and 35 pages, but analysis reveals a distinctive separate policy agenda for Wales in just 24 sentences (see Table 9.14). However, these statements do cover a number of policy sectors and some of these are of some significance.

The most noticeable policy areas displaying a distinctive Welsh approach relate to statements referring spatially to Wales. Planning Guidance Wales contained a black and white strategic planning map of Wales at the very start of the document that illustrated areas of growth, areas of restraint, major transport routes, and local government boundaries. While this figure provided an overall strategic planning picture of Wales, there were very few references to different parts of Wales in the accompanying text. As Table 9.14 indicates, these strategic planning references were made in discussion of transport policy (the strategic roads of the

Table 9.14 National policy statements identified in Planning Guidance Wales but not included in Planning Policy Guidance for England

Design
To take account of crime prevention measures in the design of new development

Transport
To consider the increasing impact of Cardiff International Airport in developing planning policies
To identify strategic roads suitable for the movement of freight
To consider re-opening rail lines and the provision of new stations
To provide enhanced bus services and facilities
To promote park-and-ride schemes
To designate disused rail alignments as open space corridors
To identify strategic roads in Wales as the A55, the M4 and the A465

Housing
To create a presumption against new settlements on greenfield sites in Wales
To assess the contribution of residential mobile homes in housing provision
To meet the accommodation needs of gypsies
To promote affordable housing

Conservation of the built and natural environment
To take account of the policies and recommendations of the Countryside Council for Wales in plan preparation and control
To undertake enhanced environmental assessment for development proposals in National Parks
To promote conservation of the National Parks over the promotion of opportunities for public understanding and enjoyment

The coast
To place a burden of proof on developers wishing to build major developments in coastal locations

Green belts
To designate green belts only in the more heavily populated parts of Wales which are subject to very significant pressures for development
To designate green belts in Wales only where existing green wedge or green barrier policies of development plans are not adequate to control development
To place a presumption against development in green belts unless in very exceptional circumstances where other considerations clearly outweigh the harm which such development would have on the green belt

Economic development
To place a presumption in favour of economic activity development in the existing urban locations, the valleys and the heavily populated coastal strips of South Wales and north-east Wales, and to designate these areas as 'major growth areas'
To consider the creation of urban villages that promote mixed use
To place a presumption against the development of new regional shopping centres of more than 500,000 square metres of gross floor space in Wales
To encourage the development of village shops

Waste disposal
To ensure waste is disposed of as close to the point of its generation as possible

Source: English and Welsh national planning policy guidance

A55, M4 and A465 where major growth would be located in the future, and the importance of Cardiff International Airport), and economic development policy (to locate strategically and have a presumption in favour of economic development in the coastal locations of North and South Wales (the major growth areas corresponding to the strategic highway networks mentioned above)). This has been a notable policy, since it is the only significant aspect of Planning Guidance Wales that appears to have been determined by the Welsh Office. It is even more noteworthy, however, given its importance for planning for inward investment opportunities, upgrading or improving the existing principal transport network along the coastal strips, and environmental protection of greenfield sites in these areas. In fact, one could go further and suggest that in view of its strategic significance and enhanced policy status within Planning Guidance Wales, the designation of these major growth areas in North and South Wales has had direct and indirect consequences for all other areas of planning policy and development locations.

It is interesting to note that the economic development quango, the Welsh Development Agency, is not mentioned at all in the economic section of Planning Guidance Wales, but it would be naive to think that this strategic growth policy had been developed by the Welsh Office in isolation from the WDA's strategy. In fact, the WDA's preferred location of all inward investment to Wales corresponds to these strategic growth corridors. Rather than the planning policy formulators of the Welsh Office developing this policy, the principal strategic planning element of Wales's national policy statement was largely determined by the Welsh Development Agency, and it is perhaps significant that the Welsh Office utilised the opportunity through its release of PGW to require local planning authorities to conform to this approach in formulating local policies and implementing local decisions.

Wales was also mentioned within Planning Guidance Wales in relation to the particular agencies or institutions that exist – for example, to take into account the policies and recommendations of the Countryside Council for Wales and the national parks. Outside this policy remit, certain policy sectors have been mentioned clearly and with a distinctive approach compared to those for England. Of note here are two policies. First, a presumption against new settlements on greenfield sites in Wales that preceded the policy position in England by some two years. And second, a presumption against the development of new regional shopping centres of more than 500,000 square metres of gross floor space in Wales. This was implemented to enable existing urban commercial centres and small market towns to remain viable. Associated with this policy, a further two areas subject to special mention are the promotion of urban villages and the encouragement of village shops, both of which were not mentioned in English planning guidance at the time of the release of Planning Guidance Wales, although they were included in a revised version of Planning Policy Guidance Note 7 on the countryside, released in England in February 1997.

The final policy area possessing a distinctive Welsh stamp is that for green belt designation. As mentioned previously, green belts had not existed in Wales prior to 1999, although Planning Guidance Wales allowed local planning authorities to designate parts of their areas as green belts for the first time. The designation in Wales is, however, a little different compared to that for England. The locations identified by PGW for possible green belt designation corresponded to the major growth areas suitable for economic development, and could also only be designated where existing green wedge or green barrier environmental protection policies of development plans were failing to control development adequately. It is not surprising, therefore, that local planning authorities have been reluctant to designate any parts of their areas as green belts since they are also conforming to the economic development national policy statements of Planning Guidance Wales to allocate these areas for major growth activity. We therefore have a clear contradiction between different policy statements within the one policy document, between the Welsh Development Agency strategic policy for inward investment and the environmentally aware prevention of the coalescence of neighbouring settlements. It is also worrying to note that PGW also placed a presumption against development in any green belts designated, but simultaneously called on local authorities to consider where other considerations (notably, economic) might outweigh the harm caused by development. The Welsh Office therefore adopted a caveat within its national policy statement on green belts to permit – in very exceptional circumstances – development where the benefit clearly overrode the impact on the environment.

CONCLUSIONS

The differences in national policy statements between Wales and England in the immediate pre-devolution period indicate the adoption in certain sectors of a distinctive Welsh approach to planning policy formulation compared to that for England. However, these statements only numbered a handful in comparison to the plethora of policies in all sectors that were joint overarching English and Welsh statements. The release of Planning Guidance Wales in 1996 occurred in the wake of political criticism of the 'Anglocentric' nature of the national policy statements. This research has indicated that it is predominantly the format of the statements that has changed, rather than the tenet of the policies for a Welsh audience. National policy statements in some of the more contentious sectors that the planning system in Wales has sought to ameliorate over the last few years – housing in the countryside, windfarm developments, protection of greenfields, coastal zone protection – have been identical to those for England. Where differences have occurred, this has been partly in reflection of the particular nuances of the institutional arrangements in Wales compared to those for England.

One clear policy difference is evident, however, and this seems to have dominated as the principal strategic policy statement for Wales: planning for inward investment along major transport arteries – the so-called major growth areas. This marked out national planning policy in Wales before 1999 compared to England, and even impacted on environmental protection policies (green belt designation). Uniquely, however, this policy had its origins in the policy strategy of a quango – the Welsh Development Agency – rather than a government department or amalgam of local planning authorities. By integrating the WDA's spatial strategy into the government's national planning policy statement, the Welsh Office created a distinctive system that was certainly not evident in the English regions (RDAs were designated in England in April 1999). This policy has also reiterated the perceived importance of a national planning guidance statement in focusing the spatial planning agendas of local government.

The position of Wales as a sub-national planning area within England and Wales was recognised in the mid-1990s by the release of separate national planning policy statements, but the degree to which this separatism created a distinctly separate approach to planning policy formulation in Wales was not evident; where it did exist the driving force was a government economic development agency. This approach has caused the continuation of a nationally consistent approach in planning policy formulation across England and Wales and its application by government departments in their monitoring of local government's development plans and planning decisions.

The planning policy formulation process in Wales in the early to mid-1990s was determined to a significant extent by central government's Planning Policy Guidance Notes for England in its quest for national consistency and certainty across England and Wales. The mid- to latter-1990s witnessed the separation of national planning guidance for Wales, but this documentation was still determined to a very large extent by the Planning Policy Guidance Notes for England. National consistency and certainty across the two countries, therefore, prior to devolution in 1999 was still being achieved.

The national consistency remit enjoyed by central government over these years largely militated against a sub-national alternative planning policy agenda promoted by local authorities and might even have been at variance with the locally formulated plan-led spirit of the Planning and Compensation Act 1991. Even the distinctive Welsh strategic policy agenda for economic development was directed by the Welsh Development Agency outside the discretionary powers of local authorities. The Welsh Office, by integrating the WDA strategy into its national policy statement, ensured that the locally led planning agendas conformed to the national approach. The ability of local planning authorities to provide alternative planning agendas to those formulated at the national level was, to all intents and purposes, circumscribed by central government agendas.

PART 3

Devolution, Distinctiveness and Planning Policy Development

This third and final part of the book considers how the planning polity is changing within Britain as a consequence of devolution, the carving out of distinctiveness in different spatial and geo-political regions, and the establishment of new forms of planning and policy-making processes. By unleashing the devolution genie from its bottle, the Blair government has enacted a widespread reform of the planning polity across Britain that seems almost unimaginable just five years ago. The establishment of a Scottish Parliament has resulted in a desire for new primary legislation and policy frameworks that reflect wider planning problems in Scotland. The National Assembly for Wales possesses policy-making powers and has been able to achieve a great deal in such a relatively short period of time. Within both countries, political assemblies are interested in carving out differentiation in their planning processes compared to that occurring in England.

The fragmentation of national planning policy across Britain as a consequence of devolution leaves fundamental questions about the form, shape and operation of a national consistency planning policy remit of the UK government. In particular, questions need to be considered on the future relationship between the UK government and the devolved national planning policy agendas of Wales and Scotland, and whether a UK government still possesses a national co-ordinating mandate over development and planning projects that are of national and regional significance.

Chapter 10 looks at how devolution in Wales has been progressed since 1999 by considering the form and function of devolution, the planning responsibilities and systems now in place, and the emerging policy agendas that are giving shape to a Welsh planning system. Chapter 11 considers the form of devolution in Scotland since 1999 by discussing powers and relationships, the legal and policy planning system, and the carving out of distinctiveness in policy development. Both countries appear enthusiastic to implement their own national spatial planning frameworks, and these are being designed to reach beyond the traditional land use boundaries of the formal and previous statutory planning systems. Changes are also earmarked for the local and regional levels within both countries, and we may well see the development of planning styles very different in each of the three British countries in future.

Chapter 12 considers how planning, as a function of governance, is now emerging in the early twenty-first century, what it means, and the expectations being placed on it from various sources, both within the formal political and administrative systems of government and also from agencies and institutions outside the planning process in devising their own spatial policy agendas. Planning now comprises several 'plannings', formed in a kaleidoscopic way across the governmental patchwork quilt of British politics and government. Chapter 13, finally, draws some conclusions from the work presented in the book. This discussion centres on planning polity relations across various scales of governance, but also considers some more theoretical and ideological questions concerning government approaches to the public sector, the relationship between different arms of the state, and the future regulatory form of a development plan and planning policy process.

CHAPTER 10

NATIONAL PLANNING POLICY AND DEVOLUTION IN WALES AFTER 1999

INTRODUCTION

As Chapter 4 indicated, the creation of the National Assembly for Wales in May 1999 was part of a series of constitutional reforms in the UK initiated by the Labour government after 1997. The Assembly, which has been awarded policy-making powers only, is still in its infancy, and any assessment of the perceived success of the new forum would be premature. Nevertheless, there are signs emerging that could give rise to the view that the Assembly will carve out a degree of distinctiveness in its approach to governance and substantive policy areas compared to that operating in England generally, and to the land use planning system in particular. This review paper charts the birth of the National Assembly for Wales, outlines its responsibilities and functions in relation to planning, and assesses what has happened 'on the ground' in its two and a half years of existence. Overall, the chapter portrays politicians and officials in the new governance framework searching for distinctiveness, inclusiveness and policy ownership; the task is to offer something different compared both to the system existing previously and to the ongoing processes of institutional restructuring underway in other parts of the UK. It situates planning within the crucible of decentralisation and devolution, since planning has been awarded a central facilitating role within the governance and restructuring process as part of the Welsh Cabinet's determination to deliver sustainable development in the twenty-first century.

Following its election to office in 1997, the Labour government set out a programme of constitutional reform and the devolution of power. Arrangements were proposed to secure greater accountability in the processes of government, including proposals for a Scottish Parliament (Scottish Office, 1997) and a Welsh Assembly (Welsh Office, 1997), a strategic planning authority and mayor for London, regional government and the establishment of regional development agencies in England. These specific proposals reflected different pressures from different parts of the UK political geography and the need to respond quickly to what would otherwise have remained a political vacuum over the effects of the 'hollowing out of the state' which had taken place over the previous 20 years (Ohmae, 1996). The emergence of the sub-national level has also occurred, partly by changes outside the UK, including globalisation (Brenner, 1999), changes in governance (Rhodes, 1997), and to developments within the European Union. Accompanying this restructuring was an enthusiasm for political change to realise greater democratic accountability throughout the UK (Lloyd and McCarthy, 2000) and within Wales (Jones and Balsom, 2000; Morgan and Mungham, 2000).

Outside these political and constitutional changes, reform has also been ongoing within the land use planning system. Planning, encompassing predominantly planning control and development plans, has been affected by numerous changes over the last 20 years. Amongst these have been a continued commodification of the planning process as part of a New Right agenda (Thornley, 1991; Allmendinger and Thomas, 1998), the enhancement of the European dimension of planning (Williams, 1996), and a regionalisation agenda (Murdoch and Tewdwr-Jones, 1999; see Chapter 7). Planning at the commencement of the twenty-first century should now be viewed as a much broader all-encompassing activity, since it serves a use to co-ordinate policy, cement partnerships, and facilitate much-needed change (Healey, 1998). This strategic co-ordinating planning role is very important for the evolving forms of devolved governance within the UK (Vigar et al., 2000).

In Wales, the National Assembly for Wales is a governmental body that possesses extensive discretionary powers over policy but no functions in passing primary legislation. Although the statutory basis of land use will remain unchanged, planning in this context is actually significant as a strategic enabling function, since it can inter alia, assist Wales's position in Europe, identify the national policy objectives for the Assembly for Wales as a whole, promote co-operation between different levels of government and agencies, and encourage the public and communities to possess some ownership or stake in the policy- and decision-making processes. The town and country planning process will therefore be at the heart of the devolved assemblies' abilities to set future policy for their spatial areas. This will be new territory for the planners and the politicians. It will not only be a case of trying to get some co-ordination and consistency, the Assembly also needs to create distinctive spatial agendas within the new governance of the UK.

All three demand-generators of political and institutional restructuring – ownership, inclusiveness and distinctiveness – are potentially at odds with each other, and will also yield significant changes to the planning process as a partnership process in unique forms of governance. The questions we need to pause to pose here relate to whether planning has the ability to keep pace with this restructuring process and with the demands on it 'to deliver', and with planning's transformation into a strategic enabling activity within a much broader framework of governance.

CONSTITUTIONAL REFORM IN WALES

The demand for an Assembly for Wales had a chequered history. The calls for Home Rule for Wales had long emanated from Welsh nationalists, and the then Labour government of 1978 agreed to hold referenda in Scotland and Wales to establish the principle of devolution. The result of the devolution referendum in 1979 indicated to particular strength for Home Rule; in fact, only 20 per cent of the voting Welsh population were in favour of the establishment of a Welsh Parliament (Osmond, 1994). The call for Welsh devolution returned to the mainstream political agenda in the 1990s and, as part of the Labour Party's modernisation programme, initially under John Smith and then Tony Blair, arrangements for constitutional reform in the UK formed the bedrock of the new political context (Allmendinger and Tewdwr-Jones, 2000a). After the May 1997 election when New Labour won with a landslide majority, proposals were put in train immediately for devolution referenda for Scotland and Wales.

In Wales, the White Paper, *A Voice for Wales*, offered the Welsh people an opportunity for them to have their own democratically elected Assembly within a strong United Kingdom (Welsh Office, 1997). The proposals differed markedly from those of the 1979 referendum. The offer here was not to create a Parliament with legislative powers, but rather an Assembly. The emphasis of the Welsh proposals was similar to that in Scotland (cf. Scottish Office, 1997); namely, initiating a process to fill a democratic deficit caused, among other things, by the proliferation of quangos in Wales put into place under the Conservative governments since 1979 (Morgan and Roberts, 1994), the determination of policy in Wales by secretaries of state representing English constituencies, and the loss of strategic policy-making functions – the creation of unitary authorities – through local government reorganisation in 1996 (Harris and Tewdwr-Jones, 1995). The principal element of the proposals was the transfer of the duties exercised by the Secretary of State for Wales to an elected National Assembly for Wales which would additionally take on the responsibilities for spending the £7 billion Welsh Office budget. The Assembly would establish policies and standards for public services in Wales, reform and oversee the work of the unelected public bodies, and implement secondary legislation only within a legislative framework established by Act of Parliament in Westminster. The Secretary of State for Wales's extensive responsibilities, transferred to the new Assembly in 1999, comprised economic development; agriculture, forestry, fisheries and food; industry and training; education; arts and culture; the built heritage; sport and recreation; local government; health and personal social services; transport and roads; housing; environment; and planning.

The Welsh proposals differ from those of Scotland in three important respects. First, Wales possesses an Assembly rather than a Parliament and in this respect can be more effectively viewed as a policy-making institution rather than a legislative body. Second, the people of Wales were not offered a chance to determine whether a Welsh Assembly should have tax-raising powers similar to Scotland. Third, the establishment of the Assembly has been accompanied by specific proposals for a simpler institutional framework, the major element of which has seen the creation of an economic powerhouse superquango combining the WDA, the Development Board for Rural Wales (DBRW) and the Land Authority for Wales (LAW). These three differences with Scotland were deeply contested in Wales in the run up to the devolution referendum, and could even explain the closeness in the result of the final vote. Unlike the clear majority 'yes' vote north of the border, the people of Wales were less convinced by the government's proposals. When the final vote was declared on the morning of 19 September 1997, the mandate to establish the Assembly cleared with an extremely fine majority of 6,721, with 50.3 per cent in favour and 49.7 per cent against, and a total turnout vote of over 1.1 million.

Despite the close vote, the referendum paved the way for the government to press on with the first stage of its constitutional reform programme. The result illustrated immense inter-regional differences: the eastern half of Wales bordering England, and the South and North Wales coastal belts, expressly saying 'no' (including the residents of the capital city, Cardiff), and the traditionally Welsh-speaking western half, together with the strongly Labour-supporting Glamorganshire valleys, saying 'yes'. At the time there was speculation that these spatial differences for future all-Wales policy-making (particularly with regard to planning, economic development and environmental protection) could lead to a great deal of uncertainty over the effectiveness of the Assembly's role as a national strategic policy-making institution after 1999 (Tewdwr-Jones and Lloyd, 1997); this has, however, proved to be unfounded to date.

PLANNING AND THE NATIONAL ASSEMBLY FOR WALES

The Government of Wales Act 1998 vested the National Assembly for Wales with a number of functions that impact upon land use planning. These include powers in relation to:

- Urban and rural regeneration
- Transport infrastructure projects
- Town and country planning policy
- Determination of planning appeals and call-in powers
- Environmental protection
- Conservation of the built and natural heritage

Uniquely, during the passing of the legislation in Parliament in 1998, the govern-ment inserted a clause into the bill requiring the Assembly itself to work in the inter-ests of sustainable development; Wales thus became the only area of the UK with such an objective legislatively enshrined into its functions. The statutory basis of planning is divided between the government, the National Assembly and local plan-ning authorities, although planning is a much broader policy-making function that can be used to ensure strategic collaboration and partnership between a diverse number of organisations. In this way, and following the government's determination to make the planning system more responsive to businesses and relevant to communities, the future framework and implementation of town and country plan-ning will actually be a matter for many governmental and non-governmental agen-cies.

The National Assembly possesses four broad strategic remits on the future formulation and implementation of planning policy (Tewdwr-Jones, 1998c):

1   To provide policy and guidance to ensure the planning system operated by the National Assembly, local planning authorities and other relevant agencies adheres to the principle of sustainable development.

2   To provide planning policy guidance that is relevant to the unitary authorities to enable them to implement planning locally, by ensuring best practice in the activities of local government.

3   To provide planning policy direction on certain issues of national importance to Wales.

4   To provide strategic policy-making co-ordination in relation to planning through planning policy promotion and strategic collaboration across various governmental levels and between agencies of governance, through national spatial policy co-ordination.

As discussed in Chapter 9, until very recently the planning process in Wales was marked by its similarity to processes in England. The Welsh Office, respons-ible for the provision of national planning policy to local authorities and the private sector, released guidance jointly with the Department of the Environment for England. This marked a determination on the part of central government to view planning in the two countries as practically identical. After 1996, however, the Welsh Office released separately formulated national planning policy guidance, even if the policy content between English planning and Welsh planning has remained broadly identical.

The planning framework that presently exists in Wales comprises national planning policy guidance issued by the Welsh Office within Planning Policy Wales and the accompanying Technical Advice Notes, regional planning guidance pre-pared at the sub-national level by consortia of local authorities within Strategic

Planning Guidance, and local planning policies prepared by local planning author-ities (the 22 unitary authorities and three national parks) within unitary development plans. While the National Assembly does not possess the power to amend primary legislation, members of the Assembly are able to amend secondary legislation and issue policy notes. This is extremely significant with regard to the planning system since most of the discretion lies not in law but in policy. The principal statute deter-mining the operation of the planning system in Wales will remain the Town and Country Planning Act 1990, as amended by the Planning and Compensation Act 1991. This has been accompanied by the provisions of the Government of Wales Act 1998 that require the Assembly to work in the interests of sustainable develop-ment. Accordingly, the potential now exists for the interpretation of the statute to be considered separately in Wales from that in England, and planning is an obvious area which has the potential to witness radical changes. It is at the national level of policy-making, through the release of amended national planning policy and policy co-ordination, that the whole planning framework in Wales could be amended.

THE ASSEMBLY IN ACTION: THE SEARCH FOR DISTINCTIVENESS

Once the Assembly was created in May 1999 discussions started to focus on exactly what the agenda might be for the National Assembly to consider, given that its overt responsibility was in relation to policy formulation (Osmond, 1998). The Assembly's first three-year strategic plan, *Made in Wales* (NAW, 2000d), estab-lished that, 'the immediate task is to demonstrate that the Assembly can deliver Welsh policies and programmes for the people of Wales' (cited in Harris, 2000). Mindful perhaps of the scepticism of the Welsh public towards the need for this new forum, the Assembly recognised that the Welsh aspect of public policy had to be strengthened in order to demonstrate (a) the Assembly's legitimacy, (b) the Assembly's powers, and (c) the development of a distinctive Welsh dimension to policies and programmes. In relation to planning, the National Assembly's Local Government, Environment, Planning, Housing and Transport Committee con-sidered a paper prepared by officials entitled *Approach to the Future of Land Use Planning Policy* (NAW, 1999e). It set out what powers the Assembly possessed in relation to planning, but noted that:

> Planning policy for Wales should no longer track DETR [English] priorities
> slavishly, nor should it diverge from GB policies unless this is for good reason.
> Both the process of developing planning policy, and its content, should be
> appropriate to Welsh circumstances.

> (NAW, 1999e)

The reaction from officials, therefore, was one of reluctance to establish a different or distinctive agenda from the outset without a demonstration for proven need. Clearly, there was no appetite to provide the newly elected politicians with a blank piece of paper and talk immediately of 'change'. If change was going to occur, it would be a piecemeal approach, and only where required. To inform this debate on whether there was a need for distinctiveness, the Assembly was awarded a budget to establish a Welsh Planning Research Programme. An early consultant's report to the Assembly on the scope of the Research Programme emphasised the need to give increasing emphasis to the distinctiveness of planning policy such that it can respond to the needs of Wales:

> The creation of the National Assembly for Wales provides a new political context and places an emphasis on the delivery of planning policy that is distinctive and directly relevant to Wales.
>
> (DTZ Pieda, 2000)

The report calls for the Research Programme to avoid duplicating work commissioned by the DETR in England, and pins down planning to three central themes: sustainable development, rural planning, and spatial planning. The report does not, however, set out a policy agenda, although attention is focused on particular circumstances to Wales that could give rise to the need to consider distinctive policy approaches. These comprise six issues:

- the Welsh language;
- the oft-conflicting goals of environmental protection and economic growth;
- the lack of a strong regional level of government in Wales and the existence of unitary authorities;
- the legacy of industrial decline;
- the changes within Welsh agriculture;
- regional economic disparities within Wales.

These issues are not necessarily unique to Wales, of course, but consultees to the report highlighted these issues as pressing within a Welsh context. Harris (2000) suggests that since these characteristics can be found in other parts of the UK, 'Even in combination, these do not only define Wales or what it is to be Welsh.' But this is a rather simplistic generalisation since the impacts of these issues have varying effects at different spatial scales. What has been required urgently, however, is the establishment of policies to address economic development, housing and transportation issues, in addition to a new context for European issues to be considered within Wales. These requirements have developed from external pressure for the most part, or perhaps have generated a need to respond to issues developed outside Wales.

THE DEVELOPMENT OF WELSH NATIONAL PLANNING POLICY

Green belt designation is just one example of a national planning policy issue that the Assembly members may wish to consider addressing further (Tewdwr-Jones, 1997a). But there are a number of other development issues that will need to be addressed at the all-Wales level; these include the siting of new regional airport, prisons, hospitals, major manufacturing plant, barrage developments, sport and recreational facilities, and the routing of new roads and railways. Many of these developments are currently addressed through lengthy and costly public inquiries. The government has indicated that it wishes to see these types of development considered through national, regional and local planning policy mechanisms in the future (DETR, 1998c). In England, for example, the Department for Transport, Local Government and the Regions intends to release a series of National Infrastructure Policy Statements on these topics. This is intended primarily to stop the English regions from entering into competition and wasteful bidding exercises for the same development. How does Wales wish to address major developments of national significance? It is certainly the case at the present time that the decisions lack a framework.

This is an area that all agencies, especially those with an economic development remit, need to consider further. In its monitoring of other agencies in Wales, the Assembly is adopting strategic and sustainable objectives in overseeing locational and investment decisions. Aside from the question of whether the future location of inward investment projects, for example, should be debated publicly, there exists the more general issue of what national policy direction Wales should head for. Until now that direction has been one of economic development, with the Welsh Office's policies and Welsh Development Agency's (WDA) objectives in some conformity to enable 'Team Wales' (the partnership approach) to deliver on economic growth. But with a new sustainable development remit, the Assembly will need to review national planning policies more prominently. The economic agenda in Wales, underlined by the creation of an enlarged WDA simultaneous to the creation of the democratic chamber, suggests a need to continue the momentum built-up over the last 20 years. It is for the National Assembly to consider how its national sustainable development objective can achieve a balance in policy aims and syntax while enabling the WDA and other relevant economic development partners to compete economically. But it will also be a requirement for these agencies themselves to consider how to (a) ensure economic development and planning policies are compatible and (b) foster strategic working across and between agencies.

What is clear in this period of transition is the need for a stronger form of national planning policy. This will be essential, not only to develop a Welsh-orientated planning policy system but also to be more transparent in meeting sustainable development objectives. Such a framework will also be desirable to ensure that a co-ordinating mechanism is set in place within which a range of organisations can develop compatible policies. The formulation of the National Development Plan for Wales recently to co-ordinate the bid to the European Commission for Objective 1 status indicates that moves towards this process are already being made (Wales European Task Force, 1999); one of the additional purposes of a stronger form of national all-Wales planning policy has been to promote Wales's interests in Europe and, indeed, the global economy (Tewdwr-Jones, 1998c).

An all-Wales national spatial development framework would be helpful in placing Wales on a European agenda. At the present time, Planning Policy Wales contains very few references to the European Union or the Structural Funds, even though their importance in developing the Welsh economy is beyond question. Scotland and the English regions are about to amend their planning policies to highlight more explicitly the European dimension. In future, they will highlight the areas of the country designated to receive EU funding through a range of Commission measures, to ensure that planning policies are then developed that co-ordinate physical land use and the resources and finances available for investment. Such a change is bound to benefit the Regional Development Agencies and Locate in Scotland in providing a competitive edge over Wales through a co-ordinated one-stop-shop policy mechanism.

In early 2000, the Assembly's Environment and Planning Minister decided that Wales should possess its own 'National Spatial Planning Framework' and initiated feasibility studies. During 2000 and 2001, work proceeded on addressing the methodological requirements of establishing such a framework (Cardiff University/ECOTEC, 2001). The new framework, called *Wales Spatial Plan: Pathways to Sustainable Development*, has to be in place by 2003. A consultation pre-draft was released in September 2001 and addresses issues relating to sustainable development, social disadvantage, and equality of opportunity, and has been prepared in partnership with business, local authorities, and the voluntary sector (NAW, 2001). The intention here is to co-ordinate the various spatial strategies and plans of disparate agencies and funding programmes, including the Sustainable Development Scheme, the Objective 1 Single Programming Document, the Transport Framework, and the Rural Development Plan. It aims to provide assistance for the planning policy but is also intended to provide regional and strategic direction, and link to European measures and initiatives such as the European Spatial Development Perspective.

The plan deliberately extends beyond the traditional land use only parameters of statutory planning, and the list of possible plan issues included within the September 2001 pre-draft indicate this wider remit (see Table 10.1).

Table 10.1 Possible issues for the Wales Spatial Plan

- identifying distinctive features and characteristics of Wales and the forces of change that may impact upon them;
- identifying the spatial effects of relevant land use and non-land use issues;
- looking at how to secure sustainable growth while protecting and enhancing the environment;
- promoting spatial balance appropriate to the different regions and areas within Wales;
- addressing the spatial consequences of globalisation;
- identifying broad measures of provision required for economic and housing development to support economic well-being and successful communities;
- identifying strategic areas of opportunity such as gateway locations, strategic sites, clusters of linked activities and centres of academic and specialist technical excellence;
- identifying factors which support balanced development, including telecommunications, energy and water supplies and inhibiting factors such as land form, land stability and flood risk;
- addressing distinct urban and rural issues and their interface, including regeneration, making best use of existing settlements to accommodate growth, securing viable and diverse rural economies and market towns;
- providing a framework for the designation of green belts in pressured areas;
- identifying how to make the best use of existing transport systems, identifying necessary and sustainable improvements for long distance links, the removal of bottlenecks, improved gateways, and accessibility;
- supporting local distinctiveness and cultural identities in Wales, including the well-being of the Welsh language;
- supporting the protection of statutorily designated areas, the countryside, landscapes, the historic environment, natural habitats, the undeveloped coast, and the best and most versatile agricultural land;
- safeguarding non-renewable resources, such as minerals, against alternative and inappropriate forms of development, and ensuring their prudent and efficient use;
- considering the implications of climate change;
- taking account of cross-border linkages and relationships to adjacent areas of England, to Ireland, and internationally.

Source: NAW (2001), figure 5

Consultation on this initial draft closed in mid-December 2001 and a final version is intended to be issued by December 2002. Simultaneous to the development of the Wales Spatial Plan, the Assembly has also been preparing a revision to its Planning Policy Wales (the original was first published as Planning Guidance Wales in 1996 and revised under its new title in 1999 and 2002; Welsh Office, 1999). The revised document is scheduled for release in 2002 and, in the autumn of 2001 Sue Essex, the Minister responsible for planning within the Assembly, stated that in future policy revisions would be released through Supplementary Policy Statements rather than being issued as a complete document revision. Another document, *Minerals Planning Policy Wales*, was released in December 2000 (NAW, 2000c).

The Assembly has also made its presence felt in relation to at least three key policy areas that planning intervenes in or co-ordinates: housing, economic development, and transport.

Housing has been one policy area that has been tackled relatively early in the life of the Assembly. Within a few months of being established, the Assembly published *A Framework for a National Housing Strategy for Wales* (NAW, 1999a), which considered the broad issues that need to be taken into account in developing a strategic approach to housing. Although the document contained a great deal of non-planning issues (such as effective management of the housing stock and social housing provision), there will be a knock-on impact on the planning system, including meeting housing growth expectations and in developing partnerships between various tiers of government and institutions. Once again we see an emphasis placed on generating effective procedures and strategies to formulate and implement housing policies within the new governance of Wales (see Smith *et al.*, 2000, for a comprehensive overview of agendas and possibilities in relation to housing). Given that a central theme of the Assembly's objective is to be inclusive, it will be interesting to see whether planning will be used at the community level to foster enhanced forms of participatory and consultative processes in line with the requirement for local authorities to produce community strategies under the Local Government Act 2000. With pressing housing problems in rural areas in particular requiring attention, such as the need for affordable housing provision and – possibly – second home controls (see Gallent and Tewdwr-Jones, 2000b), questions will emerge over the appropriateness of the planning system to provide wider social and cultural objectives. Although there remain limitations as to the legal nature of statutory land use planning (which can only be amended by legislature passed at Westminster), the policy element to planning for housing could change significantly. In November 2000 the Assembly produced the consultation paper *Better Homes for People in Wales* (NAW, 2000b) which contains proposals for the national housing strategy.

With proposals to enhance the Welsh Development Agency established alongside the creation of the National Assembly for Wales, it was no surprise that economic development would be one of the first policy areas addressed by the Assembly's politicians. The Assembly published a *National Economic Development Strategy for Wales* in 1999 (NAW, 1999b). This has been accompanied by the issuing of *A Sustainable Wales* (NAW, 2000a) document and, more specifically for rural areas, the *Rural Development Plan for Wales* (NAW, 1999c).

In transportation too, the Assembly has prepared a report, *The Transport Legacy in Wales* (NAW, 1999d), which is intended to consider the enhancement of public transport on the one hand and develop an integrated approach on the other. One of the first tasks the Assembly set itself was to develop more effective transportation links between the north and south of the country. The main strategic transport corridors currently run east to west, with the London to South Wales railway and M4 motorway in the south, the London–North Wales railway and A55 highway in the north, and the London–Aberystwyth railway in Mid-Wales. Wales also possesses three distinct privatised rail franchises which have also lacked co-ordination: Wales and the West, covering South Wales; the South Wales Valleys; and the North West, covering North Wales. The lack of effective north–south links has been a product of geographical constraints and political and industrial development decisions stemming from the nineteenth century. With the Assembly building located in Cardiff in the south, politicians have also expressed concern over the difficulty of North Wales and Mid-Wales Assembly members physically accessing the Chamber. It is not unusual, for example, for the journey from Holyhead to Cardiff by rail to take in excess of four hours, and to do so travellers have to travel via England and change trains once or twice en route. North–south links are likely to be selected for investment, upgrading and improvement in the next ten years. One concomitant affect of the review of the privatised rail franchises undertaken by the UK government in 2000 has been to reduce the number in Wales from three to one, covering the whole of Wales and the Borders. The Assembly is hoping that this will lead to the introduction of through services between North Wales and South Wales in the next two years.

On the whole, it is possible to identify a great deal of action on the part of the National Assembly in developing new policies and new policy frameworks at the national level over the last two and a half years. In the new world of openness and inclusiveness, the Assembly has prepared a number of national strategies and frameworks for public consultation with the intention of delivering a system of governance to meet the needs of Wales in a new political context. Aside from individual strategies for economic development, rural areas, housing and transport, the Assembly is also feeling its way to establish a new sustainable development co-ordinating tool, a national spatial planning framework – partly to address compatibility and integration issues, but partly to enable a Welsh voice to emerge internationally.

CONCLUSIONS

The driving force for constitutional reform in Wales has rested on the issue of enhancing the accountability of government to society and generating inclusiveness. This will be achieved by the setting up of new arrangements for representative democracy, and debate over the form and uniqueness of Welsh domestic policies in the National Assembly itself. Constitutional reform will have the effect of facilitating the democratic expression of different interest groups, while raising expectations across their respective constituencies. This will arise from the enthusiasm and momentum achieved by a National Assembly and is already evident in its first 18 months of operation. The devolution of responsibility within Wales will inevitably trigger different vested interests which may be territorial, sectional or sectoral in character, and many of these interests have been building up for some time under the centralised arrangements of the 1980s and 1990s. Such an outpouring of claim and attention seeking – legitimate or otherwise – will inevitably cause difficulties and pressures for the Assembly members. It will certainly bring about the danger of having to avoid increasing expectations on policy delivery, and the establishment of distinctiveness and differentiation in a changed political context.

This position is already a familiar problem to those involved in the operation of planning. Evidence suggests that when heightened expectations on the part of central and local government, developers, interest groups, and the public fail, there occurs a not unsurprising loss of faith in planning's ability to manage land use and development in the wider social interest (Mazza, 1995). The involvement and interest of a number of pressure groups and representative organisations is becoming more widespread in the planning system. The escalation of such narrow single-interest activity creates pressures on existing and newly emerging institutions that, if unprepared or not sufficiently strong, can have significant consequences for the very process of government itself (Rausch, 1995).

This raises questions about the abilities and trajectory of the National Assembly for Wales itself, but also of the planning system – the latter having already undergone a significant change in its scope and mode of operation as a consequence of ideological changes to the structures, financing and status of local government over the last 20 years or so (Thornley, 1991). Planning is now a fragmented activity, shared across various governance institutions and agencies both vertically and horizontally. While this may have been inevitable, it has also meant divergent views on the future of the planning system, including its scope and role in governance in the years ahead (Tewdwr-Jones, 1999c). The National Assembly for Wales has the ability to realise a more consistent and co-ordinated approach to planning in Wales in the future, involving the co-ordination and integration of governmental and non-governmental public sector interests and in generating discussion of carving out distinctiveness and differentiation in Wales. Such distinctiveness and inclusiveness could lead to more effective all-Wales planning policy agendas, that are distinct from those in England and Scotland on the one hand and potentially more opportunistic for a significant role in Europe on the other. With tensions continuing to increase within the ageing and, to some extent, outdated British planning process, the carving out of distinctiveness and differentiation in the planning systems in different parts of the UK will, in all likelihood, be a tortuous process.

CHAPTER 11

DEVOLUTION AND PLANNING POLICY DEVELOPMENT IN SCOTLAND AFTER 1999

.

INTRODUCTION

The expectation of Home Rule for Scotland was well establishment by the time the people of Scotland voted for a Scottish Parliament in September 1997. The perceived cultural, industrial, historical and economic distinctive of Scotland within the UK had already been defined. Legal and juridical systems were already separate from those of England and Wales by the time serious constitutional discussions pushing for the creation of a Scottish Parliament emerged in the late 1980s. The establishment of Scotland's Parliament in May 1999 signalled the promise of a more democratically legitimate governance north of the border. Planning had separated from the English and Welsh system both legally and in policy format prior to the Parliament being setting up, as was discussed in Chapter 5.

Over the last two years discussions have been underway as to whether the planning system can be made even more distinctive and what issues require addressing at a national (that is, all-Scotland level). A degree of optimism exists in Scotland about the future of planning, including determining what similar planning processes should remain in place compared to those south of the border, and what contextual factors need to be considered for planning's future relating to the changing nature of the state, the broadening out of governance, and the emergence of European spatial policy-making. This chapter outlines the current form of planning in Scotland, the impact the Scottish Parliament may have over planning, and what initiatives are currently underway to make the planning system more distinctive and inclusive in twenty-first century Scotland.

CONSTITUTIONAL REFORM IN SCOTLAND

The creation of the Scottish Parliament in May 1999 was the culmination of a 20-year campaign for Home Rule, that had a varied path socially, economically and politically (Mitchell, 1996; MacLean, 1999). The passing of the Scotland Act 1998 allowed for a parliament to be created that would have responsibility for all matters, the only exceptions being those defined as reserved matters that would remain the responsibility of the Westminster Parliament. Scotland's Parliament would have responsibility for education, local government, health, law and home affairs, economic development, the environment (including planning), sport, and the arts. Reserved powers at Westminster would comprise responsibility for defence, foreign affairs, social security, immigration and central economic policies (McCarthy and Newlands, 1999). The setting up of the Scottish Parliament democratises the Scottish Office (Lloyd and McCarthy, 2000), whose functions are now transferred to a 'Scottish Executive', while the Parliament itself (unlike the establishment of the National Assembly for Wales) would have both legal and policy-making abilities, in addition to reserve tax-raising powers.

PLANNING AND THE SCOTTISH PARLIAMENT

Prior to the establishment of the Scottish Parliament, Scotland already possessed a degree of distinctiveness, with separate legal arrangements, separate legislation, and policy documents, albeit all passed or released by the Westminster Parliament. In relation to planning, Scotland had possessed a uniqueness compared to the remainder of the UK, with regional government, regeneration policies undertaken by the Scottish Development Agency, the distinctive National Planning Guidelines, and regional reports (Wannop, 1980). However, many of these features were removed or watered down in the 1980s and 1990s as a consequence of a New Right legacy, intent on commodifying planning across the UK and creating certainty for developers on a national scale (Allmendinger and Thomas, 1998). As a consequence, the planning system in Scotland was not as distinctive as it had once been, leading Allmendinger (2001b, 2001c) to contend that Scotland has not actually been that distinctive from the rest of the UK in planning, despite both strong and weak claims to the contrary (Lyddon, 1980; Hague, 1990; cf. Hayton, 1996; Rowan-Robinson, 1997). Allmendinger (2001c: 51) notes that, 'Scottish planning is now much closer to its English counterpart than at any time.' Scotland, like England, now possesses a development plan system comprising structure plans and local plans; a development control system; national planning policy guidelines, deemed successful in offering an all-Scotland perspective on the future development and protection of the country (Land Use Consultants, 1999), but which are similar in form and scope to their English and Welsh counterparts (Hayton, 1996); and public consultation and a public service ethic within the planning process. In essence, statutory land use planning in Scotland is not that different to that in the remainder of the UK.

Land use planning is one of the legislative powers now devolved to the Scottish Executive, becoming the responsibility of the Environment and Transport Minister in July 1999. Following the election of the Blair government at Westminster, but prior to the creation of the Scottish Parliament, attention had focused on the future form and function of planning. At a planning conference in Edinburgh in February 1998, the then Minister for Planning, Calum MacDonald, announced that he wanted to 'help prepare the ground' for the Scottish Parliament by addressing a number of issues relating to the structure, policy and process of the planning system, intending to modernise it, and that he would consult with interested parties on these issues (Scottish Office, 1999). Consultations occurred with a number of organisations, including the Convention of Scottish Local Authorities, the Scottish Society of Directors of Planning and the Royal Town Planning Institute (RTPI) in Scotland, and a consultation paper was released in spring 1999 reflecting the discussion. This related to the statutory basis of planning in Scotland (the land use dimension), concerning development planning, planning control, and the planning service, and considered the opportunities for 'improving the effectiveness of planning within a more democratic, inclusive and accountable policy environment' (Lloyd and McCarthy, 2000: 254). This, after all, was the very purpose of establishing the Scottish Parliament, similar to the constitutional and devolution proposals for Wales and London (see Tewdwr-Jones, 1998c; Hebbert, 1999; Boyack, 1999).

Since the Scottish Parliament was elected aspects of planning have been considered, but these relate to the context of planning more than its content or purpose. Among the initiatives announced to date have been proposals for land reform and 'community planning' (Lloyd and Illsley, 1999; Lloyd and McCarthy, 2000). Nevertheless, and parallel to the contextual issues, there has been a vocal debate in Scotland on the future trajectory and style of planning north of the border, including calls for the establishment of a national physical plan (Hayton, 1997), enhanced regional planning (Tewdwr-Jones and Lloyd, 1997; Lloyd, 1999) and a stronger national framework for spatial planning (Goodstadt and U'ren, 1999). At a more abstract level, with a much broader definition of planning than its statutory core suggested within the Scottish Office's (1999) consultation paper, attempts are currently being made to consider the wider issues that planning either has a stake in or is affected by, and these relate to social, economic and environmental objectives. Essentially, these attempts are to broaden planning beyond its statutory land use core.

Over the last two years the development of government initiatives to modernise the planning system has been mirrored by an initiative led by the RTPI in Scotland to produce a 'National Spatial Planning Framework for Scotland'. The main ethos behind the Scottish Executive proposals for the future of planning and the RTPI's spatial planning framework has been (a) widening the scope of planning beyond its present narrow statutory definition, and (b) reconceptualising planning into a strategic co-ordinating activity involving a number of institutions and actors. The process of producing a modern planning system within a much broader spatial planning framework has occurred through a partnership of a number of interested agencies, although the method and approach chosen for the initiative has been – at the present time – unique to Scottish governance and Scottish planning.

This chapter considers how Scottish planning is developing in post-devolution Scotland. It considers two parallel developments: (1) short-term improvements to the effectiveness of planning, which are initiatives underway simultaneously in England and Wales and relate to planning's statutory core, and (2) the pressures and expectations within Scotland for the medium- to long-term carving out of distinctiveness and inclusiveness in the planning system compared either to the previous arrangements or else to the planning systems operating in England or Wales. The principal issues discussed here relate to the need to 'grasp the thistle' (Tewdwr-Jones, 2001b) and search for and define distinctiveness in planning. This includes not only assessment of what would be politically and professionally acceptable as distinctiveness, but also the pressures existing external and internal to Scotland on the need for distinctiveness and differentiation within planning. Furthermore, part of the distinctiveness agenda is bound up with the move from government to governance, and the development of strategic policy entrepreneurship involving a range of governmental, public, private and voluntary actors, all of whom now possess some stake in planning. This invariably modifies the procedural basis of planning as a policy-making and decision-making tool, but also broadens what we mean when we refer to 'planning'. The key questions we therefore need to consider are: does the creation of policy and agency co-ordination, new participatory processes, and differentiation in policy-making procedures, amount to 'distinctiveness' in planning, or is a more radical agenda required? These questions are addressed in the remainder of the chapter.

IMPROVING THE EFFECTIVENESS OF SCOTTISH PLANNING

A key priority of the Blair government since its election in May 1997 has been to 'modernise' the planning system so that it enables planning to contribute positively to the challenges of social and economic change and secures the delivery of sustainable development (DETR, 1998a; Tewdwr-Jones, 1998a; Allmendinger and Tewdwr-Jones, 2000a). As part of its modernising and open process towards planning, the Scottish Office established the 'Planning Audit Unit' to examine how local authorities' management of the planning control process could be enhanced with a view to achieving speedier planning decisions, an issue which ministers from both this government and the previous Conservative administration have been preoccupied with over the last ten years (Tewdwr-Jones and Harris, 1998). Furthermore, Scotland has also pursued a substantial ongoing programme of reform of planning procedures, similar to the form of review currently underway in England and Wales, with particular attention being given to the work of the Scottish Office Inquiry Reporters Unit (relating to planning appeal procedures and decisions) and ensuring that the planning service, like other local authority services, responds to the challenge of the government's 'Best Value' initiative.

The European dimension of planning was also another issue that the government, both north and south of the border, wanted to enhance further in relation to identifying the European 'root' of policies and in the development of the European Spatial Development Perspective (Faludi, 2000; R.H. Williams, 2000; Tewdwr-Jones, 2001a). EC Directives and regulations have already had a significant impact on planning at all levels of government in the UK through, for example, the introduction of environmental assessment procedures in planning decision-making in addition to other environmental regulations relating to sites of wildlife, birds and natural habitats (Tewdwr-Jones and Williams, 2001). Within the context of the UK's membership of the EU, the Scottish Executive and the Scottish Parliament will be able to scrutinise European legislation and consider how it will be transposed into domestic legislation. A recent DTLR research report on the impact of the EU on the UK planning system concluded that the Scottish national planning policy documents 'provide the most comprehensive information on EU policies of "special importance" to the planning system' (DETR, 1998h). Scotland was already ahead of both the English and Welsh planning policy documents in identifying a European dimension to national planning policies (Tewdwr-Jones *et al.*, 2000), and this has proved to be a useful basis upon which to explore an enhanced European component of Scottish planning policy (Scottish Office, 1999).

Another European matter that is influencing the form of planning in Scotland is the European Spatial Development Perspective (ESDP), which aims to provide a shared vision for the future pattern of development in the European Community. As a perspective rather than prescription, it is intended as an intergovernmental initiative, based on contributions from ministers from the Member States and the Commission. The ESDP provides a framework for co-operation on planning issues and, while these will be essentially taken forward through dialogue and debate, it is too early to say how these matters will emerge in practice; suffice to say that we are entering a new phase of European planning landscape (Tewdwr-Jones, 2001a).

THE FUTURE OF THE SCOTTISH PLANNING SYSTEM

The Scottish Office's consultation paper of January 1999 stated that the procedures of the Scottish Parliament and the working arrangements between the Scottish Executive and local government and other government agencies in Scotland would be 'essential in the development of a distinctly Scottish spatial planning framework' (Scottish Office, 1999). The Scottish Office has given some consideration to the trajectory of planning post-devolution, but the tone of subjects discussed seems to have been made with safety in mind, focusing on the form and structures of the present planning system and not straying into the realms of radic- ally different proposals. This is not necessarily a criticism of a lack of initiative on the Scottish Office's part; in the context of the edict, 'If it ain't broke, don't fix it', planning in Scotland does enjoy a relatively stable existence. The broad assump- tions made by the Scottish Office about the way in which the planning system might evolve under a Scottish Parliament were discussed in the results of the 1999 consultation document. It was concluded by the Scottish Executive that:

- there should be no substantial shift in responsibility between the national and local levels; so allowing planning to remain fundamentally a local authority activity;
- there should be better co-ordination of the work of the public and private sectors through the partnership approach;
- the area of planning in which the Scottish Executive and Scottish Parliament is likely to have greatest interest is the strategic policy level;
- any changes to planning should be consistent with ensuring a fair, open and participatory planning process, which offers the highest standards of integrity, probity, quality, service and Best Value for users of the system and local taxpayers.

The consensus for the future of planning in Scotland was essentially retention of the existing processes, but with more attention focused on improving efficiency, working arrangements, and local authority commitment and performance. Never- theless, the Executive did consider a number of options for the future structure and operation of the planning system that were rather more innovative than mere pro- cedural improvements. These amounted to considering two key issues:

- the scope of planning (broadening the definition of planning from its land use core);
- the interface between planning at the national and strategic levels and between planning and other activities supported by public sector agencies, and by the voluntary and private sectors (the possibility of a national spatial plan for Scotland and whether regional planning would be appropriate, together with the need for inclusiveness in policy-making).

Each of these issues was subject to consultation by the Scottish Office prior to the establishment of the Scottish Parliament and, following responses received from a wide range of bodies in Scotland with some stake in planning, the Scottish Execu- tive in December 1999 provided their decisions in relation to them. Each issue is important to consider here briefly, since these provide clues as to whether Scottish planning is going to become more distinctive or retain similarities to planning in England and Wales. This was how the Executive responded.

THE SCOPE OF PLANNING

The Scottish Executive took the view that the planning system in Scotland should be centred upon the statutory land use core of development plans and development control. This system, that has its roots in the 1940s, has been partly successful over the last 50 years when government at central and local levels have given it full backing (Vigar et al., 2000; Jones, 1996). Planning must take into account the need to promote sustainable development, and the full range of economic, social and environmental considerations, in formulating planning policies for each local area. The focus on land use systems, rather than economic, social and environmental needs per se, has served the UK well, in order to provide an effective framework for local planning decision-making and to determine the location of new developments and priorities in land use change, urban redevelopment and environmental protection.

Even though the Scottish Executive has embraced community planning to attempt to co-ordinate disparate local agencies involved in community development and community needs, this response was not quite along the lines of what planning means in a European context. This is true in respect of other European countries, planning systems, and with the European Spatial Development Perspective, which tends to look beyond mere land use considerations if planning is going to be something effective in promoting new development patterns, achieving economic growth, and securing sustainable development in the twenty-first century. There are, I dare say, certain opinions in government that suggest that there is actually no difference between statutory land use planning and spatial planning, but in reality the distinction is quite evident. It all depends on whether one believes in a narrow scope or broader scope for planning.

THE INTERFACE BETWEEN NATIONAL AND STRATEGIC PLANNING

The consensus of the Scottish Executive following its consultation document was that the present form of national planning policy guidelines (NPPGs), issued by its own planning department, would be usefully retained in order to support the preparation of structure and local plans. The idea about developing a national plan was viewed by consultees as 'unduly centralist and excessively rigid', although the Executive acknowledged that guidance produced by the Scottish Parliament and Executive, 'bringing together the various NPPGs and incorporating spatial issues more explicitly, might be attractive' (Scottish Office, 1999). So the introduction of a modified form of national planning policy, not as a fixed national blueprint document but as an overarching framework, was raised as a possibility. Such a document could inform future development in Scotland, provide some degree of consistency in the pursuit of sustainable development, and 'could be a vehicle for high level co-ordination of the objectives of the major agencies as they relate to development and land use' (ibid.).

The government considered that there was a case for revisiting the role of a complete national mosaic of structure plans; if the detail and locational specificity of national planning policy would change in future there would be less need for some structure plans and these could be replaced by unitary development plans at the level of individual local authorities.

For the most part, the Scottish Executive's review of planning in Scotland was similar to concerns raised and announced for modernising statutory land use planning in both Wales and the English regions (DETR, 1998c). The difference between the proposals in the three countries lies in the fact that there is a possibility that they will develop differently at different speeds, with differing priorities. This will enable some element of distinctiveness to be carved out in each of the countries. It seems that no one in Scotland is arguing for a radically different form of statutory planning from that existing at the present time. The case for distinctiveness or radical difference promoted by the planning profession itself, therefore, does not appear to be justified. It is interesting that the Scottish Office decided to press ahead with its review of planning, including addressing the scope of planning and the need for distinctiveness prior to the politicians within the Scottish Parliament considering the matter for themselves (or even being elected). Despite the fact that the question of change towards planning in Scotland was decided upon rather conservatively, some more radical proposals were nevertheless considered by the Scottish Executive in 1999, including broadening the scope of planning and the desirability of a national spatial plan. The Executive announced that broadening planning would not be desirable, but no firm proposals on the national spatial planning were taken forward in December 1999. With this in mind, the Royal Town Planning Institute in Scotland decided to take the initiative and press ahead with proposals to consider the feasibility of a national spatial planning framework for Scotland, while keeping the Scottish Executive informed of the initiative.

DISTINCTIVENESS IN SCOTTISH NATIONAL PLANNING POLICY

The key questions in relation to assessing the search for distinctiveness in planning in Scotland relate to the actual, as opposed to perceived, form planning will take under a Scottish Parliament, and its trajectory in the next few years. In particular, we need to consider how distinctive Scottish Planning is at the moment, and to what extent the government's proposals for improving or modernising the planning system actually make for a distinctive or different system. The key word here is 'distinctive'. By distinctive, are we referring to the fact that processes and systems are now formalised through democratic mandate by a legislature (and therefore might be identical to the situation in place prior to the creation of that legislature), or do we mean that processes and systems have become or are becoming different to that previously existing (under similar arrangements across countries)? This distinction – between the creation of new and different processes and the democratisation and transparency of existing processes – is an important issue in determining whether or not a substantially different set of proposals are likely to emerge and characterise Scottish planning in the next few years.

Allmendinger (2001c) has suggested that the scope for distinctiveness in the Scottish planning system is limited, highlighting the influence of New Labour as the principal political determinant of policy agendas in government both north and south of the borders and the limited opportunities under devolution to enact different processes, all of which might act as constraints to distinctiveness. Naturally, this is a far more pessimistic scenario than that adopted by other commentators over the last few years, all of whom are either actively involved in Scottish planning or have discussed the merits of devolution in relation to planning throughout the UK (see, for example, Tewdwr-Jones and Lloyd, 1997; Lloyd and Illsley, 1999; Lloyd and McCarthy, 2000). Clearly, there are forces acting both in favour of and against difference and distinctiveness in the Scottish planning system. Some of these forces relate to the recent development of policy under the Scottish Office and the Scottish Executive (Scottish Office, 1999), and the lack of time passing to make either sound judgements on the degree of difference or statements as to the reasons why distinctiveness has yet to emerge in a tangible form. Two years is a relatively short time in which the Scottish Executive should be judged on distinctiveness, and a more appropriate time should be one parliamentary term.

Perhaps the reason for Allmendinger's (2001c) pessimism towards the ability to carve out distinctiveness in planning relates to an inability to identify the degree to which Scotland in the years ahead will want to seize the initiative over Scottish spatial planning. Will Scotland be innovative at developing more distinctiveness in planning, and will Scotland be more opportunistic in taking changes currently occurring outside planning and tying them to ongoing changing governance within the country? Only time will tell, but there will be scope for argumentation by analysts in the years ahead on what exactly 'distinctive' and 'inclusive' mean; the signs are that some elements in Scotland will drive forward this new agenda. Commentators will be far more effective at drawing conclusions if they turn their attention towards identifying where the impetus for distinctiveness in planning is starting to come from.

Allmendinger (2001b, 2001c) has identified the asymmetrical nature of UK devolution, which allows different parts of the UK to evolve at their own pace but at the same time create pressure on other regions to 'catch up' with other more 'advanced' areas. In some devolved regions there is already some questioning over the degree to which certain regions are being seen to fall behind in carving out distinctiveness, with the use of competitive discourse in constitutional reform proposals (Tewdwr-Jones, 1999c). In Wales, for example, as was discussed in Chapter 10, the proposal to establish the National Assembly for Wales was couched in economic development terms, in the light of constitutional and political changes simultaneously occurring in both Scotland and the English regions (Tewdwr-Jones and Phelps, 2000). The government's White Paper for Welsh devolution made clear the case that Wales 'cannot afford to stand still' (Welsh Office, 1997: 11). Similarly, the proposals to establish Regional Development Agencies in England were set in the context of the need for the English regions to match the most successful features of regional economic development promotion in both Scotland and Wales (HM Government, 1997). As a result, the impact of institutional restructuring within different parts of the UK might actually promote an enhanced use of the planning system for promotional and competitive purposes between the agencies of governance within each country, and lead to demands for action to be taken rapidly to carve out distinctiveness. The impetus here might relate to either Scotland's voice within Europe, or Scotland's ability to attract inward investment on the global stage, and the 'assist role' the planning system could perform as a facilitating and marketing mechanism. In planning terms, Scotland is already viewed as being at the forefront of change; might Scotland use its unique position in relation to political devolution in the UK to advance itself internationally, within the context of European spatial planning?

The government has always believed that the planning system must be fit for purpose, to play its part in contributing to wider governmental objectives, especially in the promotion of the principles of sustainable development. The planning system can assist by:

- co-ordinating land use and transport;
- providing for economic development;
- assisting policies for social inclusion;
- safeguarding and enhancing the quality of cities, towns and countryside and the natural and historic environment.

The Scottish Executive believe that the planning system can make a more active input to sustainable development objectives, and this will require planning becoming a much broader, strategic and encompassing activity than its narrower statutory base. This will require better identification of cross-cutting issues, and ensuring consistency and coherence in policy-making and within the mechanisms for delivering them. For example:

- assisting housing and regeneration policies;
- supporting the rural development strategy and land reform programme;
- supporting environmental policies;
- assisting in the development of National Parks;
- exploring the relationship between land use planning and community planning;
- delivering Best Value in the quality and standard of the planning service and promoting Added Value.

At the present time, however, there is no reference to sustainable development in planning legislation (unlike the situation in Wales) and consideration is currently being given over to the provision of and need for sustainable development to be a statutory component of the planning framework.

The Scottish Executive has recognised that in order to deliver these sustainable development objectives a proper integration of policies is necessary. This requires a partnership approach with the key public, voluntary and private sector agencies and organisations and local communities themselves, and must occur at various levels of governance. To date, the Scottish Executive has been most active in fostering a wider planning agenda at the local level. The government recently published the report of the joint Scottish Office/COSLA Community Planning Working Group, *Community Planning*, which is intended to set out an agreed vision to promote the well-being of local areas in which the activities of key agencies can be co-ordinated. Five pathfinder areas for community planning have been identified and it will be important to draw upon the experience of these in determining the contribution of land use planning to the process. Once assessments are made on the effectiveness of these five projects, the Scottish Executive has stated that it is interested in considering the way in which community planning and development planning do and can interact.

On the whole, one can say that the whole planning ethos in Scotland, even prior to the creation of the Scottish Parliament, has been essentially positive. Initiated by the Scottish Office and taken over by the Scottish Executive, there has been a wide-ranging and informed debate among a number of varied stakeholders on the future of planning in Scotland. From this debate, a rather conservative stance emerged on proposals for the future of planning post-devolution, mainly centred on retention of the statutory core of land use planning but with improved procedures. In terms of more innovative proposals, the changes which have emerged – community planning, European spatial planning, policy co-ordination – have developed gradually, possibly more out of the need for co-ordination and governance working rather than a concern *prima facie* with planning. Different agencies in Scotland with a planning remit have recognised the need to be part of the strategic policy entrepreneurship process, and to be seen to be part of that process. The ability of the Scottish Parliament to provide this harnessing role for the institutions of planning across Scotland does make Scotland unique, certainly compared to the style of government operating in the early 1990s. But whether this is a strong or weak strategic harness is a mute point (Lloyd, 1997). The problem relates more to the need to stop one agency of government dominating the agenda.

GENERATING POLICY ENTREPRENEURSHIP

Lloyd and McCarthy (2000: 252) have identified this new form of governance working or policy entrepreneurship and, following Parry (1997), describe the Scottish Parliament as being characterised by 'a professionally based stasis where professional classes and elites seek to use their influence to maintain their privilege and influence'. So, the processes of governance under a Scottish Parliament, and within the planning system in particular, promote a situation where the varied agencies of the state are required to tap in to the policy-making structures in a much more open, strategic and compatible way than previously. As Hassan (1999) has suggested, the new Scottish Parliament is promoting a style of government where the rules are agreed nationally and are then implemented by other agencies of the state. Does this – the establishment of strategic policy-making compatibility processes – give rise to innovation and distinctiveness in Scottish planning? One can say that, compared to previously, agencies of the state with varied planning remits are certainly being more innovative in their style of policy-making and consultation, and for the present time this is a distinctive approach that has not yet materialised in such an advanced form either in the English regions or in Wales, even though there are moves afoot in both countries to consider this need. The evidence suggests, in actuality, that strategic policy entrepreneurship is a not a distinctive feature of Scottish devolution but rather a by-product or perhaps a feature of twenty-first-century governance in the UK at all levels of the state. Scotland's distinctiveness in adopting this style of working at the present time may therefore be rather short-lived.

The Scottish reforms to planning have tended to concentrate on improving existing mechanisms, and finding new ways for planning stakeholders to consult each other and interact. Both these elements give rise to distinctiveness, compared to the processes existing previously, although neither are unique to planning. In June 2001, however, the Scottish Executive did release a consultation document on the future of the planning system that considered, again, the issue of national planning policy, strategic planning, and development plans. Before going on to address this document and drawing some conclusions towards the end of this chapter, I wish to consider one final initiative that might have a significant impact on Scotland's attempt to differentiate itself from the rest of the British planning polity. This initiative has emanated more from the Royal Town Planning Institute in Scotland, planning stakeholders and planning researchers in Scotland rather than the Scottish Executive, although the latter has taken an interest in the proposals.

THE NATIONAL SPATIAL PLANNING FRAMEWORK FOR SCOTLAND

The concept of a National Spatial Planning Framework (NSPF) for Scotland was first initiated by the RTPI in Scotland. A similar feasibility process into establishing a National Spatial Planning Framework for the whole of the UK had been started by the RTPI in 1995 (Shaw, 1999; Upton, 2001; Wong, 2001), but with devolution becoming a reality during the course of this project it was decided to consider the feasibility of preparing a similar document for Scotland, in parallel to that currently underway in Wales (see Chapter 10). A NSPF for Scotland would provide a common vision for future spatial development and territorial management and could prove to be a major contribution to achieving sustainable development. Such a vision would deliberately go beyond the statutory core of the planning system and would provide a corporate spatial framework to guide the future development of all sectors' interests and areas of activity. It was intended for the NSPF to provide an effective tool for strong and accountable political leadership on matters of spatial development, thereby avoiding vested interests, and would simultan-eously provide a link upwards to European Union and UK policies and form an overarching perspective downwards for sub-national and regional issues within Scotland. It was never intended as a blueprint plan, but rather as a means of creat-ing and supporting policy synergy (policy entrepreneurship) between public, private and voluntary sectors and organisations.

Following the Scottish Executive statement in 1999 that a modified form of national planning policy might be feasible in the future, the RTPI in Scotland com-menced a process to consider the feasibility of a National Spatial Planning Frame-work in late 1999 by bringing together a number of key professional planning representatives and planning academics from Aberdeen, Dundee, Heriot-Watt, and Strathclyde universities. It was decided that scoping papers devoted to key topics would be requested initially to identify which issues warranted attention within a National Spatial Planning Framework, those issues that were distinctly Scottish, and the issues at the UK national and EU levels that might have an impact on Scot-tish planning policy. The baseline research papers included the following topics:

*   the European context;
*   the UK context;

- National Planning Guidelines;
- urban regeneration;
- social inclusion;
- rural and primary resources issues;
- private investment considerations.

These papers were prepared by planning academics and representatives of the Scottish universities in the first instance and were subject to consultation and comment from a number of planning, government agency, voluntary and private sector individuals who had been invited to join an RTPI Steering Group. Following amalgamation and editing of the scoping papers, a formal consultation paper was prepared for release in summer 2000. This document was then circulated to relevant government agencies, the voluntary sector, local government and the private sector over the summer months. The three main issues identified by the Steering Group in the scoping paper in the summer of 2000 were identified as the need for (a) a national overview, (b) a corporate framework, and (c) a broader scoping document.

First, there was a need for a coherent national spatial overview for Scotland. This was considered desirable as (a) there have been many recent changes to the government of Scotland which affect the way spatial decisions are made at a national level, and (b) there is a lack of a suitable national policy framework which is causing many shortfalls in achieving established aims of such decision-making. Second, the purpose of the proposed form of National Spatial Planning Framework would be to provide a corporate spatial framework to guide the development of all sectors' interests over an extended period without being a blueprint plan. It would help Scotland to meet many of its international obligations and to serve the community more effectively. Third, in terms of the scope of the document, it would also have the purpose of stipulating key central policy aims, such as promoting sustainable development, national regeneration priorities, the sustainable use of resources for regeneration, and social inclusion and social justice. It would also address policy linkage, especially at the EU and UK levels, and achieve policy integration to ensure coherence between policy systems and consistency of approach and practice. Similarly it would provide a context for investment and act as a financial resource framework. It would operate beyond a narrow concept of land use planning and would, rather, be focused on spatial scale, developing a land resource theme but also going on to take both a sustainable development theme and a spatial and institutional systems theme, ensuring the key motivator was land, while placing sustainability at the forefront of policy development and ensuring that all policy-making agencies with a stake in planning (i.e. the 'implementers') were integral to the document's objectives.

The consultation process came to a close in 2000 and the next stage is underway to identify options for the form which the National Planning Framework should take and then test them for performance against criteria which the response to the consultation paper will help to establish. At this stage, the process concentrates on the philosophy of a national spatial approach, rather than the form of a NSPF. Clearly, this document has the potential to forge distinctiveness in planning in Scotland, although it may be some way off in formulation, style and even political commitment. What is important at this stage is ensuring commitment from various parties towards the philosophy of a National Spatial Planning Framework. As such, it is more related to convincing planners of a need to think differently (as is happening in Wales and London), to capitalise on the opportunities that devolution offers, and to bolster planning's role as a strategic facilitating mechanism.

THE POSSIBILITY OF REFORM: THE FUTURE OF STRATEGIC PLANNING

In June 2001, the Scottish Executive released a consultation document entitled *Review of Strategic Planning* (Scottish Executive, 2001). The document, that predates the Green Paper in England by six months, proposes a radical overhaul of development plans and national planning policy in Scotland. This is in marked contrast to the more conservative proposals put forward in the 1999 document and reflects the changing enthusiasm within Scotland to carve out more distinctiveness. The proposals could be far reaching as far as the planning polity are concerned.

With regard to national planning policy, the Executive would like to replace National Planning Policy Guidelines with 'National Planning Policy Statements', focusing more on issues of national and regional significance. It is further proposed that, possibly, a national spatial plan could be produced, similar to that currently being prepared in Wales (the Wales Spatial Plan). Among the issues suggested by the Executive for possible inclusion within this national document, are:

- settlement patterns, land resources and infrastructure capacity;
- population and household change, including the spatial dimension of social justice;
- economic prospects and the implications for planning;
- environmental challenges and the role of the planning system;
- strategic priorities for transport and other infrastructure investment.

This is a clear attempt to extend the land use boundaries of planning into other areas. The consultation document also addresses the future of development plans and the provision of strategic policy-making. The present system of structure plans and local plans across Scotland are earmarked for abolition. In their place, the

Executive would like to retain two tiers of plans for the four major cities and their city-region hinterlands (Glasgow, Edinburgh, Dundee and Aberdeen): these would be called 'Strategic Development Plans' for strategic policies and 'Local Development Plans' for detailed local policies. Outside these four cities, it is proposed that one tier of plan exist: to be called 'Development Plans'.

The Executive proposes that all development plans in future should address the following key issues as parameters:

- *Diversity:* the structure and components of the system should reflect the diversity in geography, the differing characteristics of communities and variation in the scale/nature of development pressures in Scotland.
- *Consistency:* within this diversity there should be more consistency in the content of plans.
- *Focus:* the priority is for development plans to be clear on what they can deliver and concentrate on doing that well.
- *Subsidiarity:* planning policies should be formulated and planning decisions taken at the level of individual councils unless there are strong reasons for a framework that transcends local authority areas.
- *Inclusion:* development plans must be based on wide consultation with local communities, agencies, as well as the private sector.
- *Responsiveness:* the system must be sufficiently flexible to address new and emerging issues with speed and confidence.
- *Certainty:* plans must be more directional and much clearer about the nature/scale of development and how it should be carried out in a way that is sustainable and reflects Scotland's distinctive natural and cultural heritage.

Here, then, we are starting to witness an element of distinctiveness in the planning polity north of the border, and a clear departure on the system and formulation of development plans in Scotland compared to those for England and Wales. Further proposals, including the results of the 2001 consultation exercise, were due to be released in spring 2002.

CONCLUSIONS

Wales has taken the initiative earlier than Scotland in relation to the creation of a National Spatial Planning Framework, but both countries are interested in considering planning issues beyond a traditional narrow statutory land use boundary. There has clearly been a consensus in Scotland towards a recognition of spatial planning in European terms, the history of which goes back over ten years when national planning policy guidance appeared to be more receptive towards European planning issues than its English and Welsh counterpart (Tewdwr-Jones *et al.*, 2000). There has also been a degree of pressure on the need for some form of collaborative and inclusive working between different agencies of the state possessing some direct or indirect responsibility for planning. This has been as much to do with the need for compatibility of policy agendas from a managerial perspective as it has in relation to creating a distinctive new approach to planning. It also reflects the degree to which Scottish governance has fragmented during the 1980s and 1990s and the extent to which planning, broadly defined, has been shared between various institutions and agencies and stretched across different tiers of government, causing the need for integration.

Planning now comprises several 'plannings', and government determination to improve the efficiency and effectiveness of planning as a public service, including its further development as a commodity, should not be confused with planning lacking an ability to perform wider social, economic, or environmental intervention. This planning is different; it is not the narrow statutory form of planning involving development planning and planning control, but rather a much broader activity used as a co-ordinating mechanism to achieve policy entrepreneurship across government agencies and tiers of the state.

Scotland, similar to Wales, currently enjoys a degree of optimism that implies that the new democratic forums will lead to a real difference, not just of style but substance too. Yes, it does relate directly to nationalism and a desire to be different from the rest of the UK. But what is of more concern is the need for Scotland to be confident enough to determine the shape of planning for herself, without constantly following a London-led agenda. Allmendinger (2001c: 46) concludes by stating that, for the reasons he outlines, his probable future vision of planning post-devolution in Scotland 'is more likely to be frustration at the inability of the Scottish Parliament to deliver a sufficiently distinctive approach to planning'. What has been lacking to date is debate on the meaning of distinctiveness, and the range of actors within Scotland – other than the Scottish Parliament – who can contribute to the development of distinctiveness in planning.

Scotland is already developing – in a piecemeal fashion – distinctiveness in planning compared both to what went before and also to what is happening elsewhere in the UK. New forms of co-ordination and participation make for differentiation, with planning playing a central role in facilitating these processes. More radical proposals to the planning polity will lead to a difference compared to the systems operating in England and Wales and, within three years of the establishment of a Scottish Parliament under three First Ministers, that is an admirable start. But we should not expect central government alone to take up the challenge, either for planning or for governance, in the devolved administrations. The challenge exists for all agencies, institutions and participants in planning. The RTPI in

Scotland, in partnership with a range of agencies and planning researchers, has shown the rest of the country what can be achieved if the enthusiasm and commitment is there to debate distinctiveness. Ultimately, it seems, the search for distinctiveness in planning rests with the planning profession itself in Scotland, and in its ability to enter into dialogue with and convince major government players. The chances of planning carving out a greater central role as a distinctive and worthwhile activity in the future governance of Scotland rest with planners themselves in promoting the proactive element of their work and being able to respond to the challenges for change that appear there for the taking.

CHAPTER 12

PLANNING POLICY WITHIN NEW FORMS OF GOVERNANCE

INTRODUCTION

Chapters 10 and 11 considered the development and implementation of devolution in Wales and Scotland after 1999. Chapter 7 explained the enhancement of regional planning across Britain, and Chapter 4 highlighted political and governmental commitments to devolution and decentralisation in Northern Ireland and in London. With so much devolution occurring to the planning polity, it is questionable whether Britain now possesses a national town and country planning system at all, since so much is changing spatially and within policy-making institutions and processes across different parts of the country. The planning polity now comprises at least four different systems within the four countries of the UK.

Britain still possesses a UK government, of course, and policies are formulated within UK government on certain topics for application across the whole of Great Britain and Northern Ireland, and planning's importance within government and politics has not been underestimated. But to what extent can the UK government now claim a remit over securing national consistency and co-ordination within the planning policy, a remit it has possessed for over 50 years? This is the theme of this chapter.

The importance of the UK national planning context is recognised in facilitating government policy objectives relating to the economy, society, and the environment, and in delivering European Union commitments. The development of more effective planning frameworks through the modernisation agenda and an enhanced European context will strengthen the spatial policy processes within the new structures of governance currently being put into place as part of the implementation of devolved assemblies in Scotland, Wales, Northern Ireland, the English regions and London. While this dual-push is occurring towards European spatial planning and devolution and decentralisation, we need to assess whether a UK-wide approach to planning will be required in future and how UK national policies and decisions could potentially impact upon devolved forms of spatial planning processes.

The government's review of the planning system, published by the Department for Transport, Local Government and the Regions in 1998 (DETR, 1998c), emphasised that the basic principles of the planning system do not need to be fundamentally altered, although certain dimensions are presently missing. These missing dimensions include the European context for planning at national and regional levels, a clearer statement of intent on nationally significant development projects, the strengthening of regional policy-making, and the use of modern economic instruments through taxation and subsidy. The future of the planning system Green Paper released in December 2001 advocated the replacement of the current form of development plans and the formulation of enhanced regional strategies in England. National planning policy would increasingly focus on nationally and regionally significant projects and policies (DTLR, 2001b).

The present process of national planning policy, unique to each of the three British countries, is likely to be retained, but with an opportunity for the Scottish Parliament and National Assembly for Wales to develop further their own national policy perspectives divergent to that presently laid down in England. Wales has already started to strengthen its national spatial policy by preparing the Wales Spatial Plan (NAW, 2001). In Scotland, similar proposals are being advanced to create a national spatial planning framework there. England retains its narrow land use focused national planning policies (the PPGs) but has no plans to develop anything stronger at the all-England level, preferring to rely on broader regional spatial strategies. In future, the ODPM will essentially concentrate on improving the provision of national planning policy to the English regions, while the Scottish Executive has already discussed the possibility of reviewing the planning system in Scotland (Scottish Office, 1999). Review of the national planning policies in Wales are also now underway, to coexist with the Wales Spatial Plan.

Although the UK government has indicated that European, national, regional and local levels of planning will provide a strong context for spatial policy formulation and delivery in future, it remains uncertain as to the position of a UK perspective. The Royal Town Planning Institute has recently progressed a feasibility study into the provision of a UK National Spatial Planning Framework (Wong, C. et al., 2000), although given commitments towards devolution this might be running counter to political thought and developments. For the moment, however, the UK possesses a kaleidoscopic framework of planning policy processes with the word 'national' meaning different things in different contexts, both geographically and politically. This is also compounded by a simultaneous emphasis on transnational and supra-national spatial planning developments (Alden, 2001b; Tewdwr-Jones, 2001a).

BROADER POLICY CONTEXTS FOR BRITISH PLANNING

Before going on to consider the nature of current and potential future UK planning requirements that could impact on any new national spatial planning agendas formulated within the devolved nations of Britain, it is first necessary to highlight the range of political, economic, social and environmental contexts within which planning is situated. As was remarked in the Preface at the outset of this book, planning is only one component of a much broader UK policy perspective on the future growth, development and protection of the country. It is affected by forces outside the UK (notably international obligations, EU directives, and so on) as much as by pressures internal to the UK. What we possess in Britain from a legislative viewpoint is a planning process that is quite tightly defined, focusing on the physical or land use implications of broader sectoral policies relating to, for example, social inclusion, equality, economic prosperity, and environmental protection. This has been both a curse and a blessing over the last 50 years.

It has enabled professional planning officers to restrict their advice and the political deliberations of elected members to a narrow remit recognised by law. But it has also resulted in frustrations amongst the users of planning, especially the public (eager, perhaps, to utilise planning for community benefit or the amelioration of social problems), developers (eager to consider financial and resource matters as part of the planning process within a changing property market), other third party interests (attempting to identify the planning implications of their policies and strategies relating to health, social services, and education), and government (attempting to implement policies to either stimulate economic growth and competitiveness or social and community inclusion). Ask any official within local government or central government to comment on the nature of enquiries and complaints from members of the public and they will reel off a list of issues that the law considers to be not necessarily planning matters and ones that are difficult to integrate within development plans and planning control. These frustrations seem to be increasing, and the present town and country planning system is creaking under the weight of pressure for reform emanating from disparate interests.

A further problem relates to the various ways in which planning can be defined and viewed. As a statutory function, it involves the preparation of planning policies and the control of development at various government tiers. More broadly, planning can also be viewed as a strategic co-ordinating mechanism for a range of public and private organisations. Planners working within public and private entities can work both within the narrower statutory definition of planning to assist the amelioration of economic, social and environmental problems (for example, through the formulation and implementation of development plans) and within sectoral and fiscal programmes intended to facilitate equality and economic growth (for example, through EU programmes and structural funds). What we refer to today as planning is a much broader, all-encompassing activity to that developed in the post-war period. Nevertheless, despite the complexity associated with a broadening of the definition of planning, and the activity of planning now stretching across a range of governmental and non-governmental organisations as part of the onset of governance, the essential purpose of planning in the UK – regardless of territory – has remained relatively unchanged since 1947.

The UK planning system is intended to provide guidance, control and incentive in the use and development of land. As this remit has gone unchanged, the economic, social and environmental contexts that call for planning intervention have changed markedly over the last 50 years and are constant concerns. For example, the UK government's international commitments toward sustainable development have necessitated planners reconciling environmental protection and enhancement with economic prosperity and rising living standards. Similarly, the push towards social inclusion within Europe has placed another tier of expectations on the planning system. These issues have been merely bolted onto the 1947-style statutory land use planning system. It is little wonder that the planning system is viewed as increasingly unresponsive to business and other interests.

To summarise these issues, as a consequence of devolution, the broadening of planning as a state function, and the emergence of a governance framework responsible for spatial planning policies and decision-making, the UK no longer possesses a UK planning system. It never did, save for the fact that the law in all parts of the kingdom related to the narrow planning remit of land use and development. The fragmentation of spatial planning policies within the UK – to Scotland (initially through the release of National Planning Guidelines and their successors since 1974 and more recently through the establishment of a Scottish Parliament); to Wales (initially through the provision of Planning Guidance Wales since 1996 and more recently through the establishment of a Welsh Assembly); to Northern Ireland (through the operation of the planning polity within a single government department and more recently through the early work of the Northern Ireland Assembly) – has intensified the differences and potential for distinctiveness within, in planning terms, a dis-United Kingdom. What now remains of the UK or British planning system are two features:

1   The broader political context for spatial planning and land use decision-making that each of the devolved administrations can address only insofar as they are affected by them.
2   International obligations and commitments signed up to by the UK government that each of the devolved administrations need to take into consideration.

In each case, the responsibility revolves around the relationship between the devolved administration and Westminster and Whitehall, where new forms of working, partnership, and concordats now exist to retain some linkages between the various arms of the state. Whether these make for loose bonds or weak threads is a mute point, depending on your perspective towards the necessity or undesirability of a national and co-ordinated planning polity.

A Future Remit for National Planning Policy

In 1998, the Royal Town Planning Institute in its examination into the feasibility of a UK National Spatial Planning Framework identified a number of objectives for national planning:

1   to safeguard national interests and resources;
2   to make or identify inter-regional development choices;
3   to ensure inter-regional consistency of policy;
4   to establish good planning practice;
5   to reinforce the role of the planning system as an essential guiding framework for making development decisions.

Policy choices within these objectives can rest with national planning policy guidance, either at the UK level or through separate documents released by each of the devolved administrations. The key issue surrounding the development of UK national planning objectives is whether a UK tier of government is required to promote and implement them, or whether they can be transposed into principles formulated and monitored by each of the devolved assemblies. In particular, at what level is it appropriate to formulate policy responses to provide:

1   a national perspective on the directions of change that are occurring;
2   the need for new directions;
3   the resource priorities;
4   inter-regional balances.

A number of interrelated contextual UK national issues will also impinge on national planning policies developed within the devolved nations. These were identified by the Royal Town Planning Institute in 1998 as further explored in the commissioned report. These covered five areas:

1   *Demographic, Household and Housing Issues:* demographic and household change within the UK; demographic projections; household projections; housing provision (see Breheny, 1999).
2   *Environmental Resources and Energy:* air emissions and quality; land use, landscapes and soil; water resources and consumption; biodiversity; waste and minerals; energy (see Nadin, 1999).
3   *Social Exclusion:* work exclusion; trends in employment and unemployment; forms of employment; exclusion from learning; welfare policy; family, health

and cultural exclusion; demographic and legal exclusion; regional-urban-rural differentials; concentrations of poverty and exclusion (see Turok *et al.*, 1999).

4   *The Economy and Employment:* new technology; trade relationships; evolving and upgrading infrastructure; consumer preferences, rising incomes and improved knowledge; emerging policy regimes (fiscal, monetary, regulatory, state distribution); self-employment and small firm development; privately owned, publicly regulated companies; geography of economic decline within the UK; changes in employment, supply and demand (see Townroe, 1999).

5   *Land Use and Transportation:* increasing car dependence; levels of mobility and car ownership; reduction in vehicle occupancy and use of public transport; dispersion of cities and closure of facilities; concentration of activities in smaller units; peripheral development – edge cities; green belt pressures; freight distribution and logistics; the motorway network; road pricing possibilities; rail services and the revitalisation of the railways; integrated transport policies and programmes; congestion costs of transportation; environmental pollution (see Banister, 1999).

These might be regarded as the macro-political issues requiring action, intervention or co-ordinating by central government, but clearly other issues constantly emerge in response to changing socio-economic issues and to respond to global events. Associated with the implementation of the above issues, Alden (1999) identified 13 objectives that require a national context and perspective at the UK level. Although it is possible to distinguish these as UK national issues, there are alternative perspectives on them insofar as they impact upon or are impacted upon by the devolved administrations and the legislative and/or policy processes now in place:

*   to provide a national strategic vision for the UK within a global economy with planning as an important element of this vision;
*   to provide an overarching view of national plans or perspectives being produced in Scotland, Wales and Northern Ireland, and the amalgam of regional plans in England;
*   to meet the UK government's international obligations;
*   to consider the interface with EU spatial development policy and initiatives, particularly access to structural funds;
*   to consider the interface with EU spatial planning systems and policies (for example, transnational co-operation);
*   to promote and consider the implications of global and transnational and cross border issues;
*   to inject spatial considerations into macro-economic and social policies of central government;

- to address major planning, development or infrastructure projects which can only be decided at a national level and which are outside the scope of locally orientated development plans;
- to promote consistency in planning practice across the nation;
- to establish and promote norms and standards of best planning practice across the nation;
- to provide a framework for local government and planning practitioners through national guidance, to promote certainty and support for planning decisions;
- to promote innovation and good practice in planning practice through advice notes;
- to address strategic planning issues which contain important national dimensions, priorities and policy options.

It is contended that only the first eight objectives actually require a UK national perspective, since the last five can be effectively covered by the devolved administrations and other relevant agencies and organisations in their support for good government. Each of these eight objectives are highlighted below:

TO PROVIDE A NATIONAL STRATEGIC VISION FOR THE UK WITHIN A GLOBAL ECONOMY WITH PLANNING AS AN IMPORTANT ELEMENT OF THIS VISION

Driven by economic growth forces and competitiveness and cohesion within the European Union, the future will be a planned future. The UK government will respond accordingly through economic and trade policies, with the devolved administrations transposing this context into national perspectives and strategic planning policies. The vision is not so much a blueprint but a constantly evolving objective. This will also be related through the UK government's response to the ESDP and Europe 2000+ and other EU initiatives in the Commission's attempts to achieve a balanced and sustainable development of the EU territory.

TO PROVIDE AN OVERARCHING VIEW OF NATIONAL PLANS OR PERSPECTIVES BEING PRODUCED IN SCOTLAND, WALES AND NORTHERN IRELAND, AND THE AMALGAM OF REGIONAL PLANS IN ENGLAND

This is essential in the promotion and delivery of economic development and to reduce the prosperity gap within the UK. Each of the nations will produce their own statements for future development and growth, but the UK government has indicated within the Memorandum of Understanding published in October 1999 (HM Government, 1999) that economic growth will be co-ordinated through London on such issues as multiple bidding for Foreign Direct Investment. This is intended to prohibit competitive stances and turf wars between Scotland, Wales, Northern Ireland and the English regions. Other policy sectors that might require similar attention through concordats include transnational transportation networks between the nations, major airport development, and social exclusion. These directly impact on the spatial distribution of economic activity within the UK.

TO MEET THE UK GOVERNMENT'S INTERNATIONAL OBLIGATIONS

The UK government is obliged to make commitments at the international level, and this includes government policies at international summits (for example, Kyoto) and within the European Commission and the transposition of EC Directives. EC Directives are required to be transposed into domestic legislation and this will in future be a matter for the legislative bodies. The October 1999 Memorandum of Understanding also covered statutory European links, although the devolved administrations are free to establish policy and organisational links with Brussels.

TO CONSIDER THE INTERFACE WITH EU SPATIAL DEVELOPMENT POLICY AND INITIATIVES

The UK government signed up to the European Spatial Development Perspective in 1997. This aims to take into account the progressive economic integration and related co-operation between Member States, the growing importance of local and regional communities and their role in spatial development, and the anticipated enlargement of the EU and the development of closer relations with neighbours. This is encouraging the UK government to consider the development of a balanced and polycentric urban system and a new urban–rural relationship; the securing of parity of access to infrastructure and knowledge, and the sustainable development, prudent management and protection of nature and cultural heritage. This commitment will not necessarily relate to existing political and administrative boundaries within the UK. Imbalances within the UK stemming from EU policies will also need to be considered by the UK government in the allocation of UK resources.

TO CONSIDER THE INTERFACE WITH EU SPATIAL PLANNING SYSTEMS AND POLICIES (FOR EXAMPLE, TRANSNATIONAL CO-OPERATION)

The financing of new development by the European Commission is intended to address regional welfare disparities within the EU. The financial mechanisms offered from the EU include the structural funds, Common Agricultural and Common Fisheries Policies, and the INTERREG and Article 10 initiatives to promote transnational co-operation. The UK government will be required to assist regions and localities in accessing EU funding. At the present time this is under-

taken in England by the Government Regional Offices and by the national government bodies in Scotland and Wales. This is essentially a UK remit, although the
implementation and operation of EU accessing has been devolved to a sub-UK
tier. Parts of the ESDP will also impose obligations on the UK government that will
affect the devolved administrations, including attempts to achieve a better
spatial balance in economic and social cohesion; to achieve a more balanced
urban and regional competitiveness; to achieve better accessibility, especially in
peripheral regions; to reinforce EU border regions and their cities; and to develop
Euro-corridors.

TO INJECT SPATIAL CONSIDERATIONS INTO MACRO-ECONOMIC AND SOCIAL POLICIES OF CENTRAL GOVERNMENT

Planning is concerned with space and land use, although macro-economic policies
and social programme have a spatial dimension too. National fiscal policies in relation to taxation and public expenditure programmes could affect more or less pros-
perous regions. Additionally, national sectoral programmes such as transport,
health and energy could also possess a spatial dimension. The Scottish Executive
has its own tax-raising powers, but Scotland will nevertheless be subject to influence from Whitehall public expenditure programmes.

TO ADDRESS MAJOR PLANNING PROJECTS WHICH CAN ONLY BE DECIDED AT A NATIONAL LEVEL AND WHICH ARE OUTSIDE THE SCOPE OF LOCALLY ORIENTATED DEVELOPMENT PLANS

The Modernising Planning statement of January 1998 first indicated the UK
government's intention to release more national infrastructure statements on those
issues that cannot be decided regionally or locally, although it failed to define
'national' in this context. The topics highlighted for addressing through future policy
statements included major transport routes, large inward investment schemes, and
airport and port development. In addition to infrastructure decisions, major planning
projects could also include large-scale developments funded through the UK
National Lottery or Millennium Commission, the Private Finance Initiative, energy
companies, the Ministry of Defence, and incentives offered by regional development agencies for inward investment. A consultation paper was released in January
2002 on the subject of national infrastructure project policy and this indicates the
government's desire to progress its future national direction on this remit.

NATIONALLY RELEVANT ISSUES WITHIN PLANNING AND DEVELOPMENT

Alden (1999, 2001a, 2001b), stemming in part from his work for the RTPI on a UK national spatial planning framework in 1998, also highlighted a number of projects that would need to be addressed at the UK level. Again, some of these can be addressed within each UK nation where funding is allocated separately by possibly autonomous agencies:

- Prison development
- Defence establishment
- Flagship sport and cultural development
- *Ad hoc* national competitive bidding projects
- Hospitals
- Airport
- Major roads
- Rail links
- Foreign Direct Investment
- Coastal management
- Estuary development
- Power stations and other energy supply institutions
- Housing development
- Minerals sites
- Reservoirs and water supply
- Waste disposal
- Education and training
- Social cohesion/exclusion programmes

These are some of the issues that will be covered by the proposed national infrastructure policy statements. It is interesting to note here that the government will be entering a new period of open government by establishing definitive policies for these developments, rather than relying on *ad hoc* and pragmatic policy as and when a decision needs to occur. From the parameters provided by these policies, the government intends to rely on parliamentary powers and Acts of Parliament to propose and instigate projects. This will remove uncertainty out of the process and lead to faster decision-making for the projects under consideration.

The change in policy directly stemmed from the government's experience with the Terminal Five Inquiry at Heathrow Airport that lasted seven years and cost millions of pounds. Following the inquiry, as is usually the form in these cases, a report or recommendation was submitted to a government minister by an independent inspector for that minister to take the decision ultimately on whether to grant planning permission or not. Central government ministers have long been in a no-win situation with regard to call-in applications for developments of this scale, since they frequently are caught between having to determine which sets of national interests should be prioritised. In the case of the Terminal Five, there was a great deal of environmental pressure over the development and concern that the project would be sacrificing government environmental principles in order to implement a project in the national economic interest.

By enacting parliamentary procedures rather than public inquiries, government ministers will rely on the full scrutiny of parliament to consider the developments that will be sponsored, supported or opposed publicly by political parties. This may seem as though developments will not be able to be scrutinised in such depth as would otherwise happen at an inquiry, and certainly the government will have to consider how this expert examination could be achieved, otherwise accusations could be made that ministers are avoiding rigorous scrutiny intentionally for certain sensitive or controversial projects. It remains to be seen how this would work in practice, although there have been prominent developments approved via parliamentary bills in the recent past, including the Channel Tunnel rail link and the Cardiff Bay barrage.

It is difficult to see, nevertheless, how all national infrastructure projects could be approved through this approach. Take, for example, a large-scale inward investment project. Should a global electronics firm suddenly court national and regional governments in Europe in their search for a suitable site to employ 5,000 workers, the speed with which a planning decision could be made in Britain is handicapped depending on which scrutiny method is employed. Global or multinational companies are used to the rival bidding evident in European regions from national and regional government representatives, eager to attract − and to be seen to be attracting − prestigious foreign direct investment (Phelps and Tewdwr-Jones, 2001). Projects are won on a range of criteria relating to financial incentives, site suitability, proximity to market, proximity to labour supply, transportation and environmental issues, and so on. The only uncertain element in the process is what happens after the projects are won by national and regional governments on the bidding criteria: the requirement for planning approval. In the early to mid-1990s, central government circumscribed this dilemma by imposing centralised planning solutions that effectively usurped local planning, environmental and democratic concerns (see Phelps and Tewdwr-Jones, 2000; Tewdwr-Jones and Phelps, 2000).

A national infrastructure policy statement would require strategic sites being identified in advance, and fast-track planning permissions delivered in a matter of weeks, if regions are going to be effective in the inward investment bidding wars between nations. There is nothing inherently wrong with this approach if that is the policy objective at the outset. Maybe such strategic sites could be promoted as 'Business Planning Zones' (one of the proposals within the future of planning Green Paper of December 2001) where regulatory mechanisms are abandoned for the purposes of economic development. But the strategic selectivity adopted by multinational companies in their choice of a final site suitable for their plant may result in their 'wish list' being different to what is on offer through planning and grant incentives. The site may be inappropriate, or it may be in the wrong location for the firm's needs (a good illustration of this in practice was when the UK government in the early 1990s offered an inward-investing Asian electronics company a brownfield site on the east of an urban area that possessed a positive planning framework, only for the company executives to prefer a greenfield site on the west side of the urban area; see Phelps and Tewdwr-Jones, 1998, 1999).

Here, then, we return to the problematic issue of asking to what extent a policy within the flexible British planning system can ever be applied rigidly. National infrastructure policy statements will undoubtedly create more certainty in the process, assist in the development of a positive planning framework, and reduce both bureaucracy and financial waste. But they may not completely eradicate funding problems or 'little local difficulties' within planning that occur when the market's desires interact with the state's policy and decision parameters.

FROM GOVERNMENT TO GOVERNANCE: REASSESSING PLANNING POLICY CONFLICT

Britain has now entered a long and overlapping period of governmental and political modernisation, instigated by the Blair government's commitments to constitutional reform, openness, inclusiveness, joined-up thinking, and an apparent 'third way' in politics (Giddens, 1998). The government's manifesto promises to commence a comprehensive period of devolution for Scotland, Wales, Northern Ireland, and London have been mirrored by proposals to enhance the regional level of governance, modernise both the planning system and local government, while simultaneously committing the government to an enhanced form of integration with the European Community. Land use planning had certainly felt the impact of political, socio-economic and environmental restructuring during the 1980s (Thornley, 1991; Cullingworth, 1999) and the early 1990s (Tewdwr-Jones, 1996a; 1999a), but the proposals of the late 1990s and early twenty-first century amend the process fundamentally. The proposals to alter the planning polity, the administrative and political framework within and across which planning is situated, have created additional and significant changes to the role of planning and its status as a governmental process.

The world has changed considerably in a short space of time, and town and country planning is a very different activity today from that which emerged in the post-war period; significantly, for this discussion, it is no longer solely the preserve of either central government or local government. Town and country planning is now a process that is shared between and across central government, local government, innumerable public organisations, and the private sector. It is important to recognise that when we discuss sub-national systems of governance responsible for planning, we are referring 'not just to the formal agencies of elected local political institutions which exert influence over the pattern of life and economic make-up of local areas' (Painter and Goodwin, 1996: 636), but additionally to a wide range other agents including central government, supra-national institutions, and quasi-governmental, voluntary and private sector organisations, all of which possess some stake in the policy process (Healey, 1997). Together, these agents can form unique systems of local governance (Rhodes, 1996).

Planning as a 50-year-old statutory process in the UK merely facilitates development on the one hand, and regulates development to protect the environment on the other. But this simplistic description masks the evolving nature of the state and of government since the latter 1990s and planning's role within that process. Planning as a truly partnership activity is prominent in government; for that, we should be thankful. The political turnaround from the Thatcherite stance towards land use planning as a state function in the 1980s is a consequence of the recognition on the state's part of how planning can assist numerous levels of government, government agencies and other actors in achieving or realising their strategic and local objectives. But it would be wrong to view planning in the same way as that that existed in the 1970s or early 1980s; essentially, a new planning system has been created to sit alongside the established statutory process. The number of organisations existing in the UK that possess planning duties in one form or another as part of the new governance in the country suggests that it is more important than ever for the government, and the new devolved assemblies, to generate effective national and regional strategic planning co-ordination.

Contrary to popular opinion, town and country planning is not simply a process that controls the use and development of land. Admittedly, the planning control function remains a bedrock for planning professionalism, but we should not believe that planning control *is* planning (Tewdwr-Jones, 1999b). Planning at the commencement of the twenty-first century should be viewed as a much broader all-encompassing activity, since it exists to co-ordinate policy, cement partnerships, and facilitate much-needed change (Healey, 1998). This strategic co-ordinating planning role is very important for the evolving forms of devolved governance within the UK. In Wales, for example, as was discussed in Chapter 10, the National Assembly for Wales possesses extensive discretionary powers over policy but no functions in passing primary legislation. Although the statutory basis of land use will remain unchanged, 'planning' in this context is actually significant as a strategic enabling function, since it can assist Wales's position in Europe, identify the national policy objectives for the Assembly for Wales as a whole, promote co-operation between different levels of government and agencies, and encourage the public to possess some ownership or stake in the policy- and decision-making processes. That is exactly what is occurring in the development of the Wales Spatial Plan.

The town and country planning process will therefore be at the heart of the devolved assemblies' abilities to set future policy for their spatial areas. This will be new territory for the planners and the politicians. It will not only be a case of trying to get some co-ordination and consistency, the assemblies also need to create distinctive spatial agendas within the new governance of the UK.

Political and institutional restructuring also encourages high expectations of delivery at all levels of governance. This will not only impact on future national and regional policy-making but also on the relationship between the devolved governance and local areas and communities. Already in England and Wales, under the provisions of the Local Government Act 2000, local authorities are implementing community planning as a way of tackling social exclusion, urban regeneration, and public involvement in decision-making, by the development of community strategies to sit alongside planning policies (Lloyd and Illsley, 1999). Who would have foreseen that just 15 years ago? The unique forms of governance emerging at the present time are also expected to create an element of inclusiveness in communities.

Political and institutional restructuring inevitably involves questions concerning policy ownership, policy inclusiveness and policy distinctiveness, all of which are potentially at odds with each other. All these will also yield significant changes to the planning process as a partnership process in unique forms of governance. The questions we need to pause to pose here relate to the ability of the British planning system (in all its subtleties) to keep pace with this restructuring process and with town and country planning's transformation from an end product into a strategic enabling or means-based activity within a much broader framework of governance. I am not convinced at the present time that planning professionals in practice have woken up to this fact.

The planning system will sit across this multifarious planning polity and, aside from the tensions and conflicts inherent within this complex structure, two other sets of seemingly irreconcilable dimensions exist. These are, first, the vested interests that may be summarised as territorial, social, sectoral and policy-based in character. And second, there are the networks of partnerships, collaboration and concordats that are arranged across both the planning polity and the vested interests, in order to achieve implementation. The key issue for policy-makers from now on will be how to reconcile the apparent irreconcilable tensions inherent within the new governance of planning and how to meet the perceived high expectations from a range of government tiers, agencies, organisations, businesses and the public on why planning exists and what planning, and indeed the new political processes more generally, is expected to deliver (Tewdwr-Jones, 1999a, 1999c, 2001a).

Devolution and agency fragmentation actually promotes consideration of space and territory (Vigar and Healey, 1999) through the championing of differences between regions in order to achieve a competitive edge, or financial support, or achieve investment potential over their regional (and political) rivals (Phelps and Tewdwr-Jones, 1999). In terms of planning delivering for business and investment purposes, will we see increasingly in the future the capacity for customised spaces (Peck, 1996) and customised policies being developed for strategic development purposes tailor-made through territorially specific planning polities?

The proposals to establish the Welsh Assembly, for example, were couched in regional economic development terms. As a consequence of constitutional and political changes occurring simultaneously in both Scotland and England, the government's White Paper for Welsh devolution made it clear that Wales 'cannot afford to stand still' (Welsh Office, 1997: 11). In a similar vein, the proposals to establish Regional Development Agencies in England were set in the context of the need for the English regions to match the most successful features of regional economic development promotion in Scotland and Wales (HM Government, 1997). Therefore, the impact of state restructuring within the UK might actually promote an enhanced use of the planning system for promotional or competitive purposes between the agencies of governance within the four countries. This move, which will occur at the national and regional scale, will be bound to have an impact on the form, purpose and policy-making processes of the planning polity at the local and community levels.

THE COMPETING CLAIMS ON PLANNING POLICY

The implementation of community strategies by local authorities under the Local Government Act 2000, and the proposals for Local Development Frameworks to form the implementation arm of such strategies under the December 2001 Green Paper's proposals, epitomises what is occurring to the planning polity in the restructuring process at the local level. This involves fostering enhanced participatory measures and partly using the planning system and/or planning methods to achieve community inclusiveness. This is very laudable and is particularly useful if it serves the purpose of encouraging a greater number of individuals and organisations to participate in the policy-making process at the neighbourhood level.

There are, nevertheless, problems in implementing community strategies in association with planning. First, there is the possibility that adopting a community plan for all or part of each local authority area will be viewed as a panacea to resolve every community's ills (in other words, it raises expectations on local authority delivery, but that may not be a bad thing); second, there is a possibility that tensions will occur between the expectations placed on the community planning initiative and other strategic or policy documents, formulated through other means or else that may have emerged from separate series of negotiation and consultation mechanisms either at the local level or by other levels of governance.

These problems can be resolved easily providing participants are informed of the purpose and role of the initiative within the wider policy-making machinery; but the difficulties will only be accentuated if a too-heavy reliance is placed on community planning as a separate policy process to the frameworks in existence within and pursued by other agencies of governance (Tewdwr-Jones, 1999c). Meeting state objectives at the local level is a case in point, and exemplifies the tensions that can exist between local government acting as the agents of central government in policy implementation or as separately elected autonomous agencies with their own policy agenda (Rhodes, 1980). This dilemma was described by Bulpitt (1983) as a 'dual tension' between high politics (national agenda setting) and low politics (policy implementation). It is apparent that such dualist tensions will emerge in the expectations placed on the new structures of governance, and particularly affects planning.

This suggests that a dual push of expectation will occur whenever planning is changed structurally and substantively, and involves the broadening of the institutional framework of planning policy-making (the planning polity) while broadening the substantive notion of what planning is supposed to achieve. As I have remarked elsewhere (Tewdwr-Jones, 1999c, 2001c), it seems that a two-level development is occurring: from an institutional perspective, the policy interpretation of the statutory function of planning has shifted towards an enabling role, both for the private sector and for the other agencies of governance; from a political perspective, the planning process has also been affected by political, socio-economic and environmental changes outside planning. These are important points to bear in mind. They are ongoing processes of modernisation, reform and restructuring that constantly impinge upon and reshape planning and the planning polity. When changes occur to the planning polity (either to the system itself or to the agencies charged with formulating, operationalising, or utilising the system), deeper questions need to be asked about planning's future.

A great potential now exists under devolution for each of the four countries of the UK to develop very different planning systems even without statutory powers to implement radical planning reform. These changes can be as equally caustic as the impact caused by statutory changes. Even within three years of devolution, this has not gone unnoticed in each of the countries where suggestions are already being advocated to supposedly improve policy-making and governance, partly intended to establish clearly definable separate agendas unique to those countries com- pared to the status quo (for example, see Osmond (1998) in relation to Wales, and McCarthy and Newlands (1999) in relation to Scotland).

CONCLUSIONS

This chapter has reviewed the future of a UK planning system and planning polity during a process of institutional, governmental and political restructuring. I have attempted to pin down this restructuring, to make sense of the institutional context of political reform, and to assess what the implications of changes to the structure and function of planning may mean for different tiers of government and gover- nance. There is a future for national planning policy, particularly in relation to inter- national commitments, macro-economic and social policies, national security issues, and the design and implementation of national infrastructure projects. But this future is a different planning future from that we have all been used to for the last 50 years. The nature, role and function of the state and government has shifted irreversibly, and planning – as an element within that changing structural process – has been altered fundamentally too.

I conclude this chapter considering some key interrelated points. These issues place the previous discussion about the future of the national planning polity within a broader political and institutional governmental context that attempts to consider planning as part of a wider process of change. They are replicated from a previous publication but remain relevant today (Tewdwr-Jones, 1999c):

1   Planning as a governmental process of the state has been transformed to become a function of governance.
2   In calling for a degree of compatibility across the new agencies responsible for the governance of planning it is necessary to consider the nature of hori- zontal relations between local agents of governance.
3   Compatibility across local agencies of governance also needs to be inter- preted by assessment of the vertical relations between the other tiers of governance, since it is at these processes where degrees of power and responsibility and state objectives lie.
4   The surface relations and interactions and shared understanding between the

agencies of governance are underpinned at the subsurface level by political interaction and strategic behaviour.

5   All the local, regional and national agencies of governance within the planning polity will possess varied remits, agendas and objectives that could make compatibility difficult to achieve; such potentially conflicting remits will not disappear as a consequence of the perceived compatibility of agendas.

6   A desire to produce one type of framework or strategic document, such as community planning or a statutory development framework, could well satisfy a planning desire at the local level but will only be one of the aspects of the interagency collaborative effort that will require addressing.

7   The notion of broadening the communicative culture across agencies of local and regional governance is desirable but should not be underestimated through the political and institutional perspective of what planning is there to achieve and who it serves.

8   Enhancing local and neighbourhood forms of policy-making will only be successful if participants are informed in advance of what exactly the purpose is of the exercise: is it for the purpose of administrative co-ordination, participation, policy agenda-setting, support, or forum soundings?

Each of these raises the spectre of high expectations, and local desires could well clash with higher planning polity desires at some point.

CHAPTER 13

CONCLUSIONS

INTRODUCTION

This book has sought to analytically combine political ideology, multi-level government activity and planning practice as a distinctive contribution to research in the field of town and country planning. This has necessitated undertaking empirical research to assess practically the impact of changing government relationships. The analysis concentrated on central government and its national planning policy guidance on sub-national planning policy formulation since the introduction of the plan-led planning system by the Planning and Compensation Act 1991. Relationships between central government and local government, central government and regional governance, and central government and national policy agendas have been scrutinised, while discussing the evolving nature of both politics and governance and the planning system.

The research focused on multi-levels of governmental activity in the field of planning policy development, but this has occurred within a broader theoretical debate that sought to identify whether the national, regional, and local planning policy nuances that accompanied both the plan-led system and devolution have been a continuation of Thatcherite New Right ideology in the previous five years in particular. A key question posed was whether rule of law was extended into the town and country planning function.

The objective for this research, identified in Chapter 1, sought to assess whether:

1   The planning policy formulation process operated in Britain since the early 1990s has been determined to a significant extent by central government's national planning policy in its quest for national consistency and certainty across England, Scotland and Wales.

2   The national consistency remit enjoyed by central government militated against any sub-national alternative planning policy agenda promoted by local authorities and was at variance with the locally formulated plan-led spirit of the Planning and Compensation Act 1991.

Within this objective, I also identified a number of questions to progress in the research:

1   How has central government used its legal planning remit to provide national

consistency and certainty while promoting locally and regionally led planning agendas within local government and regional governance respectively?

2   To what extent do the changes to the English, Scottish and Welsh planning process since the early 1990s actually provide for sub-national and local authority policy alternatives in formulating planning policies in the spirit of devolution, decentralisation, and the plan-led legislation?

3   What have been the political ways in which both the Conservative and Labour governments created new forms of national control over the formulation of local and regional policy agendas; did these in the spirit of New Right and New Labour ideology, and how might answers to these questions assist us in conceptualising the planning relationship between different levels of government?

The approach discussed in this book has been to attempt to answer these questions through a detailed examination of the theoretical and practice-related literature on two paradigmatic levels.

First, a micro-political examination of planning policy formulation, including a detailed assessment of the planning relationships between central government, devolved administrations, regional governance, and local government, and the degree of discretion available at the sub-national to counteract or reinterpret guidance and policy published at the national level. This has been useful to provide an indication of the nature of planning policy formulation in the mid- to late 1990s, and to begin to understand the complexities, differences and requirements of planning policies between different agencies of government, and to assist in identifying problems between achieving national consistency, certainty, and local discretion in policy-making.

Second, a macro-political examination of the ideological framework of planning and its manifestation as a political process, including assessment of the nature of New Right thinking utilised in the planning system in the 1980s, the impact of this ideology on planning policy development within government, and the degree to which these ideological strands were continued by the Major and Blair governments in their approach to the planning polity and the planning system. This was enlarged on in Chapters 3 and 4, that sought to analyse the transition of government between Thatcher, Major and Blair, but lacked thorough empirical testing or theorising within planning, and it was thought that the results of the research discussed in the book would be of some assistance in making a distinctive contribution to this debate.

This final chapter concludes by providing two extended discussions of these two paradigmatic levels of thinking.

NATIONAL CONSISTENCY, CERTAINTY AND LOCAL DISCRETION

The government's employment of consistency in planning policy formulation since the early 1990s has resulted in the development of a planning policy process as one overarching framework across England, Scotland and Wales. Central government's introduction of the plan-led planning system in the Planning and Compensation Act 1991 was based on a desire for more certain conditions for developers and the general public. The quest for certainty in planning policy formulation necessitated, at its simplest level, the production of mandatory district-wide plans by the district level of local government. At the more detailed level, the quest for certainty directly translated into the plan preparation process by the government requesting local authorities to prepare policies within their plans that indicated, in more secure and certain language, the spatial areas where development and regeneration was considered desirable, or possible, and the spatial areas where the natural and built environment should be protected and conserved from development.

This quest for certainty in planning policy-making found expression through central government's regional offices, the Scottish Office and the Welsh Office, increasing their monitoring role of local authorities' development plans more prominently than hitherto. The regional offices were given authority to highlight areas of inconsistency both within plans and between plans and national planning policy guidance, and policies that lacked certainty in policy expression. In relation to a desire for national consistency, the quest for certainty by the government led to the utilisation of national planning policy to ensure that local policies were in conformity with those of central government.

However, despite research evidence proving the hypothesis correct, further research evidence indicates that for planning practitioners themselves this was not an issue of particular concern. The aggregate research data presented in Chapter 6 indicates that despite the high degree of intervention occurring by central government in their use of national planning policy guidance to monitor local planning policies, the respondents did not believe this to be particularly significant. At a more detailed level, the results of the West Dorset research, in Chapter 8, indicate that the significance of intervention was, however, noticeable, but this did not seem to cause problems for local policy-makers who – in the majority of cases – readily amended their local policies to be in conformity.

Before considering this new picture of planning in England, Scotland and Wales it is first necessary to return to the questions posed earlier, in Chapter 4, that relate to the nature of consistency, certainty and discretion under the plan-led planning system. The three questions posed were:

1   Did the legislation and policy operating prior to 1992 permit either (a) the
      local authority discretion in the interpretation of planning laws and policies
      conferred by the state or (b) the individual officer discretion to decide each
      case on its merits based on professional judgement?

2   Does the plan-led legislation, by introducing greater certainty in the process,
      limit in any way the discretionary powers of the local planning authority, of the
      individual planning officer, or both?

3   Does the plan-led legislation, by introducing greater certainty in the process,
      limit discretionary powers of the authority or officer to either interpret the laws
      and policies or to depart from the laws and policies to a greater extent than
      was previously the case?

THE PLAN-LED PLANNING SYSTEM AND PLANNING POLICY FORMULATION

The Planning and Compensation Act 1991 sought to generate greater certainty in
the statutory planning process. The first principal effect was to remove the discretion available to local authorities to determine whether or not local development
plans should be prepared for their areas. The Act made district-wide local plan
preparation a statutory, mandatory requirement. The second principal effect was to
reduce the discretionary powers available to the individual officer to decide each
case on its merits. The Act statutorily requires decision-makers to follow the policies in the development plan in the first instance and then to consider all other relevant material considerations. The development plan is therefore to be used as a
starting point; individual officers can no longer rely on professional judgement to
determine whether material considerations within the plan should be applied.

The third principal effect was to alter the distinction between discretion and
regulation in the interpretation of legislation and policies. Local authorities' and
individual professional officers' discretion in interpreting laws and guidance is
retained post-1991. However, there has been an indirect change to this discretionary role. As a consequence of a policy requirement, introduced within national
planning policy in association with the statutory amendments, local authorities must
now give prominence to central government's national planning policies both in
development plan formulation and in planning policy implementation.

Central government's new statutory and policy requirements have, therefore,
altered the discretionary role of both local authorities and individual professional
planning officers. With regard to the distinction between professional and administrative discretion (discussed in Chapter 2), the legal and policy changes have
resulted in a shift of discretion. The imposition of mandatory requirements on local
authorities has created an increase in administrative discretion at the expense of
professional discretion. The existence of local plans and policies and national

planning policy ensures that the individual's freedom in discretionary judgement is either removed or significantly reduced. The ability of the professional officer to rely on professional judgement as a justification for his or her action can no longer be relied upon, since the availability of professional discretion to determine actions and decisions has been circumscribed by central government's legal and policy requirements. While some commentators in professional planning circles may lament this loss, it does actually create greater accountability and provide less uncertainty for user groups, objectives that both the Major and Blair governments have sought in introducing legislative and procedural changes.

CERTAINTY WITH FLEXIBILITY

The most noticeable issue to emerge from this study concerns the positioning of certainty with flexibility in planning policy formulation and syntax. This issue strikes to the very heart of the ideological ethos behind the plan-led system. As discussed in Chapter 3, it attempts to reflect the introduction of a rule of law within government's policies as one of the principal tenets of New Right ideology by insisting that local plan policies provide an almost inflexible rigid local regulatory process. This has not altered fundamentally under the Blair government since 1997, although the emergence of the regional agenda and possible reforms to the planning policy in the next few years could alter this ethos markedly.

The 1991 Act and the regional agenda are also noteworthy since they appear to enhance the weight given to local and regional planners' determination processes and policy-making powers, thereby bolstering the position of local government rather than central government. This seems to contradict another tenet of New Right ideology utilised by both the Thatcher and Major governments: centralisation. If local planning authorities do attempt to provide a rigid inflexible policy based on their own local needs and assessment, the certainty with flexibility statement would create a wholly localised planning agenda, and thereby water down all other planning actors' positions, including central government's use of national planning policy in policy formulation and regional office monitoring. We know in practice that this bolstering of local policies has occurred, but there have been other requirements to alter the direction of the UK government over local and regional planning agendas.

Certainty with flexibility therefore promotes rule of law but simultaneously attempts to reduce regulation and blueprint planning. A dilemma therefore exists between local certainty that central government expects in its interpretation of the plan-led system, and the certainty that might be expected in providing clear unambiguous statements that are of use to the users of planning.

The underlying question that remains, therefore, is to what extent should this be a matter of concern? From the ease with which they amended their policies,

West Dorset planners did not seem terribly concerned that significant parts of their local planning policy formulation agenda were pre-determined by the contents of national planning policy rather than by localised problems. If the planners did view the contents of national planning policy statements and the government office's comments not as interference in local policy-making but simply as a resource base to get a local plan in place quickly, the origins of policy statements are not a matter to seem to warrant much concern. Similarly, it is telling from the results of the regional research that local authorities are requesting more national policy, rather than less, in the carrying out of their functions. Either one could say that this leaves professional planning at the local level as a fundamentally weak profession, full of people with low intellectual ability and low innovation to enable them to establish their own spatial agendas, or else it suggests that local policy-makers do not attach any political significance whatsoever to the policies they are being asked to formulate, consider and implement.

Turning attention to the flexibility part of certainty with flexibility, if commentators were concerned at the prospect of the 1991 Act reducing flexibility in the planning process, this concern was justified – but it did not occur at the level originally thought. Greater development plan coverage ensured that certainty would be afforded to developers and the public in assessing local authorities' policies and decisions. In addition, by making the plan the first consideration among many, greater certainty would be afforded to the development control process to ensure that decisions were not *ad hoc* or discretionary, and that they were accountable to local people. But the resultant legal and policy position was only a partial move at introducing a rule of law to reduce flexibility. Statutory land use planning in Britain had not switched overnight from being a flexible, discretionary system to a prescribed, regulatory process. The changes have been far more subtle. If anything, the new system has created a mixture of discretion and regulation; more certainty but not a blueprint overriding all other factors. Policies and decisions could still be implemented in the light of current circumstances, thus emphasising flexibility.

CONSISTENCY, CERTAINTY AND DISCRETION: DEFINING 'OPERATIONAL DECISIONS'

The theoretical discussion advanced in Chapter 2 concerning Faludi's decision-centred view of planning is useful here to provide a context for the fuzziness between certainty and flexibility. A local plan contains policies that provide a strategy of certainty at the local level by indicating what is and is not acceptable development, but plans are being formulated on the basis of not only local choice but a national planning policy agenda too. So while the plan provides a degree of certainty in the local planning authority's expression, it does not necessarily mean that these local commitments (or 'operational decisions', to use Faludi's terminology (1987: 117)) will be implemented. The implementation task will depend on the commitment possessed, relationships of and tensions between the local planning authority and central government, and could vary from case to case. Therefore, while central government issues a specific programme of policies through national planning policy guidance, it is unable to implement those policies directly since the implementation task rests with an independently elected lower tier of government. The process of implementing national planning policies therefore has to be delegated to local government, or other agencies. Central government initiates the legislation and sets out through national planning policies the course of action to be taken or considered, but delegates the implementation of law and interpretation of policy to local government.

As discussed in Chapter 2, although the operational decisions for central government in this instance involve the decision to mandatory delegate, for local government the operational decision is to take account of central government's laws and policies in carrying out their decision-making duties. There is clearly a difference between how both levels of government define this operational decision. Central government's operational decision is to expect its policies to possess a degree of commitment on local planning authorities in taking decisions in particular ways and to mandatorily enforce them to produce statutory local plans; local government's operational decision, on the other hand, is to recognise the existence of central government's planning policies and its own local policies as only guides in taking decisions. There can, therefore, be a world of difference between the plan or policy as a definite commitment, and the plan or policy as an aid to refer to in taking action. Additionally, there is a world of difference between producing a rational plan and in taking a rational decision in the light of a plan's existence. The change in procedure brought about by the 1991 Act has essentially resulted in central government providing more guidance and direction to local planning authorities on how they should interpret national planning policy in implementing the new statutory provisions. Central government may argue that this enhanced guidance role has been necessary to provide information to local planning authorities to avoid uncertainty in implementing the 1991 Act. But it could also be viewed as unnecessary interference on the part of central government on the activities and practice of local government.

Central government also possesses a clear view of the function of local planning policy under the plan-led planning system. Flexibility is an essential prerequisite of formulating a plan since it can then respond to changing circumstances and to take account of any uncertainty surrounding planning decisions. This function has not changed since 1947, and remains in place today even under the provisions of the Planning and Compensation Act 1991. The local plan, therefore, does not possess any 'superior wisdom' (Faludi, 1987: 126), since policies provide an indication only for a decision; it is not a blueprint, although the plan's status has undoubtedly been enhanced since the introduction of the plan-led legislation. Faludi has been particularly concerned with the operational decisions planning agencies develop, although he has failed to recognise how discretion can be defined according to the different perspectives of each agency, or level of government operating within policy formulation. Therefore, while operational decisions might relate to a mandatory task, or the expectation that a decision will be made in a particular way, they can equally mean something that should be seen to be taken account of, not necessarily followed. In relation to statutory planning in the UK and using this distinction, there is clearly a gap between central government expecting its national planning policies to be followed and local government merely taking central government's planning agenda and its own local plan policies into account when formulating policies. This debate is equally as relevant for the new devolved assemblies and their relationships to local authorities within their countries.

Following this debate, the next section goes on to assess the macro-political context of planning changes that occurred under the Major and Blair governments, to identify what political ideology the micro-political planning changes occurred within.

POLITICAL IDEOLOGY AND CHANGE WITHIN PLANNING POLICY DEVELOPMENT

Let us move the debate at this point to broader issues concerning the political ideology of the Major and Blair governments towards planning since the early 1990s. If commentators were searching for evidence of Major's political ideology and leadership style once he was elected Prime Minister in November 1990, the planning system provided one of the first opportunities to gauge the transition. The move to a legislative plan-led process (until then, the local choice concept had only been advocated through central government policy advice) and the initial endorsement of sustainability would be tested through new planning legislation in Major's first parliamentary session as premier. The resultant statute, the Planning and Compensation Act 1991, made widespread reforms to the planning process but had particular effects on the provision of statutory planning. Some elements of the Thatcher government's 1989 White Paper (HM Government, 1989) relating to development plans were included in the bill. As discussed in Chapter 5, the most important reforms concerned the speeding-up of development plan preparation, to remove the need for Secretary of State approval of structure plans, to require district authorities to mandatorily prepare district-wide local plans for the whole of their administrative areas, and to increase the weight afforded to development plan policies for decision-making purposes (the so-called Section 54A requirement). These changes, that could be labelled the most significant changes to the planning process for over forty years, appear to strengthen local authority planning powers and reduce centralised control of local planning issues. Although there was nothing in the legislation that was not wholly unexpected, the government's posit-ive stance towards planning was noteworthy. After the planning profession's demoralising and battering period in the 1980s under Thatcherism, the new commitment did generate renewed optimism on the part of local authority planners. Questions were asked as to whether this would perhaps start to reverse the market dominance of planning. Following the implementation of the environmental legislation in 1990, the government also amended the primary legislation to permit sustainability issues to be at the core of planning's concerns, reflecting a recogni-tion that global environmental change could also be tackled at the local level of the state. The environmental agenda and the pro-planning legislation both seemed to provide a distinct reversal of Thatcherite ideology towards planning's role in enabling the market.

Central government did seem to be paying more attention to the activities and efficiency of local government; planning, as one administrative function of local government, has been directly affected by this change of ethos. Local government started to become more efficient in its statutory duties and is operating within 'Citizen's Charter' and 'Best Value' parameters set by both central government and government agencies. Once again, this reflects a reversal of the Conservatives' position on planning and local government in the 1980s, and possibly extends the New Right ideology into new territories. It is to these New Right principles that this chapter now turns, to identify the extent to which the three tenets of Thatcherism – market orientation, centralisation and rule of law – continued or were amended by both the Major and Blair governments.

MARKET ORIENTATION

Thornley (1991) claims that the consistent thrust of Thatcherism during the 1980s was a shift towards market mechanisms. As Gamble states:

> It is taken as axiomatic that markets are inherently superior to any other way of organising human societies. The problem is seen to be creating the conditions in which markets can function and removing whatever obstacles exist to their operation.
>
> (Gamble, 1988: 38)

Changes to the market emphasis of the 1980s started to arise when the govern-ment accepted, through the Rio Earth Summit, that economic growth was not a sufficient condition for achieving a high quality of life (Healey, 1992), and, superficially at least, the balance between markets and plans once again shifted in favour of the latter. The presumption in favour of the development plan introduced by the 1991 Act meant that a check was put in place on the free market by regulatory processes, with policy-makers and decision-makers finding that the relationship between the two were, essentially, a balancing exercise.

Central government national planning policy released through the 1990s, and since 1997 by the Labour government, has provided a clear reminder of the need for the planning system not to hinder the markets. Indeed, the most recent Green Paper on the future of the planning system released in England in December 2001 seems to have been formulated with this objective in mind. Furthermore, proposals to introduce Business Planning Zones combine planning with market-orientated procedures (in much the same way as Enterprise Zones and Simplified Planning Zones in the 1980s). It is a proper function of the planning system to intervene in the market if harm is being created in some way on the public good. Business Planning Zones are a prime example of how the present government would like to have its cake and eat it: committed to environmental protection and sustainability, but nevertheless overtly concerned about the country's economic performance and dominated with a concern for economic growth. This is not a criticism; it merely reflects how the planning polity is now expected to sit in the middle of an extremely precarious balancing act.

This balancing act between the environment and the market has also been reflected in other initiatives. The Thatcherite market legacy continued primarily in urban regeneration. Under Major, three Enterprise Zones and one Urban Development Corporation were designated between 1990 and 1997. The principle of competitiveness (HM Government, 1994) was also a continuing element in urban regeneration initiatives through City Challenge and Single Regeneration Budget funding. Even the launch of the UK's National Lottery in 1994 and the establishment of the Millennium Commission extended this competitiveness ethos, with a proportion of proceeds from the lottery being available for urban planning-related projects promoted by public–private partnership bidding to a government-appointed panel of experts. Successful projects must demonstrate an ability to generate private sector funding and develop a partnership approach. Labour has extended this ethos with Public–Private Partnership (PPP), a controversial policy that has included ministers attempting to apply it to the London Underground investment.

These initiatives provide a clear reflection of the political ideology existing at this time: a balance between the market and the environment; a degree of power returned to the local level but the parameters of the power resting in the hands of either central government or a government agency. Chapter 9 provided a useful illustration of this with the revelation that the Welsh Development Agency had formed the key organisation leading attempts to create distinctive spatial policies for Wales within an agenda set by the UK government. If one compares this approach to the plan-led system, it reflects how central government utilises national planning policy, through monitoring by regional offices, to ensure that local government sufficiently reflects the national agenda in its dilemmas over striking a market and environmental balance. Furthermore, both the Major and Blair govern-ments have amended the rules, funding mechanisms, and policy requirements to circumscribe the autonomous abilities of local authorities, but often with the coer-cion of local actors themselves. It will be interesting to see whether a similar approach emerges in the English regions as it emerged in Wales in the relation-ships between regional spatial plans and the policies of the Regional Development Agencies.

Overall, therefore, in the mid-1990s there was little diminution in the role of the centre. The British planning system is (and has been since inception) highly centralised. But what seems to have happened since 1990 are two things. First, increased and standardised central input into local (and since 1997 regional) policy and its interpretation, along with an (as yet) unachieved local framework of plans that translate the policies. Second, an increased role for local people in questioning their local authorities' operations and policy-making has encouraged an illusion of local influence against a reality of central control within a dictated set of parameters for local policy-making.

CENTRALISATION

The approach to development planning since 1990 has not seen a complete rever-sal of the market-led Thatcher approach (Healey, 1992) but rather a gradual move away from the explicit flexibility inherent within British planning at that time. The plan-led approach introduced the need for local planning authorities to adopt dis-trict-wide plans and can be traced back to the problems associated with the more laissez-faire approach of the 1980s. Healey (1992) points to the government's need to accommodate its commitment to sustainable development at the Rio Earth Summit, and this simply could not have been achieved by the planning system of the 1980s since it required a strong centrally led sustainable development strategy with opportunities for locally led initiatives within that strategy. Since Labour took office, this tendency has been institutionalised and the government is a leading player at international climate conferences.

The intention of government through the introduction of the plan-led Planning and Compensation Act 1991 was undoubtedly to strengthen the role of the devel-opment plan in local decision-making to achieve greater certainty for plan users. Nevertheless, planners, the public and the development industry have placed more emphasis upon the plan leading to delays in plan preparation and lengthy public inquiries. This, in turn, has encouraged both Conservative and Labour ministers to talk of inefficient planning authorities, a desire to speed up the process, and concern at planning becoming a block on business and economic growth. These concerns also seem to underlie proposed changes to the planning polity announced by the government in England, Wales and Scotland in 2001.

Local authorities' development plans and regional planning policies are required to be consistent with national objectives if the planning system is to work. The increased weight afforded to the development plan and local authority decision-making, and to regional planning policies, is therefore not as locally or regionally orientated as we might first conclude. Local and regional policies have to be consistent with national policies, and where there is inconsistency developers may use this as grounds to 'out-trump' the provisions of those policies. This, in turn, results in a planning system which is heavily dependent on the priorities of central government and causes difficulties for local authorities, regional agencies, and others wishing to take any alternative policy line. It also raises legitimate questions on whether this system creates a plan-led planning system at all, since plans and policies may over time be regarded as out of date, irrelevant to the development demands of an area, or inconsistent with central government's planning priorities. Such nuances that have accompanied the legal and policy requirements of the plan-led system and the regional renaissance have, to some extent, resulted in an increase – rather than decrease – in the centralised planning policy regime.

RULE OF LAW

A rule of law sets out a framework that is known and agreed beforehand and within which subsequent decisions must conform (Thornley, 1993). The aim of this rule in central government during the 1980s was to decrease local discretion and shift any costs of dispute directly onto the interested parties themselves rather than the community. Davies (1996) has concluded that development control decisions are based on administrative discretion rather than legal rule, and it was this discretionary element that the Thatcher governments sought to reduce. The environmental commitments enforced on the government and the plan-led system reorientated the process. While still wishing to minimise local discretion, and maintain and build upon the rule of law, the 1980s approach was no longer feasible to the same extent. It simply occurred in different ways.

The switch in emphasis to centrally controlled, locally formulated development plans was not the only area where a rule of law has been evident during the Major and Blair years. Consultation procedures in plan preparation have been reduced to speed-up the policy adoption process and have thereby minimised public involvement while creating greater certainty for those who are still involved in the process. On the whole, the rule of law approach of the 1980s is virtually unrecognisable in the early years of the twenty-first century. From a limited amount of central policy, but with much more central control in favour of the market under the Thatcher administrations, England, Scotland and Wales now possesses a plethora of policy and a system that makes it much more certain that the central advice has to be followed at the local and regional scales. Devolution to Scotland and Wales at least offers an alternative approach, if local and regional actors want to be assertive. The indications are that changed directions and different ideo-logical expectations towards planning and what it could achieve will only come about as a consequence of pressures outside the planning profession and outside local government. The 1980s mentality of local planners waiting to be told what to do by central government has hardly diminished, even within these devolved and decentralised days.

The image of a locally orientated plan-led system and a regionally sensitive policy framework are both clear departures from the market-orientated, project-led approach of the 1980s. But, to some extent, the effect has been different from the image. Centralised control increased under John Major at the expense of the market, and the local, once again, lost out in terms of influence. Under Tony Blair, the setting up of devolved and decentralised policies and governmental frame-works has occurred within agendas set nationally. The difference between the 1980s and the present time concerns the philosophical underpinnings of the reasons for centralisation and intervention; since the latter 1990s the imperative has been political necessity.

CONCLUSIONS

This book has been concerned with the nature of the planning polity since 1990 and the conflicts between different tiers of government that form the planning polity. These tensions have been caused by the release and use of national plan-ning policy in the plan-led planning system and the expectations on the part of local and regional actors to mark out differentiation and distinctiveness from a national approach. At the same time, central government has utilised new means to ensure that its agenda is not only taken into account at the local and regional levels, but followed. In order to assess these relationships, it was necessary to set two paradigmatic levels for analysis: a micro-political context to assess the prac-tical and professional nature of planning in Britain from an operational perspective that could focus in on the nature of national consistency, regional certainty and local discretion in practice, and a macro-political context to assess the political ideology utilised by central government to account for the changes made to planning and to the roles awarded to different levels of government. To some degree, both contexts overlap, but are also distinctive. This has resulted in a more comprehensive picture being portrayed of planning in England, Scotland and Wales since the early 1990s than would otherwise have been the case, but it has also allowed for different perspectives and academic critiques of planning-thinking to be combined for analytical purposes. This has certainly made the book a challenging (and rather complex) academic project.

The subject chosen for study is an issue of concern to practitioners and academics in the field of planning but – more generally – is also of interest to political scientists and students of government. It has debated a particularly narrow area of governmental activity but a subject that strikes to the very heart of the planning system and one that seems to be at the core of the tensions between the UK government, local government, and its devolved and decentralised assemblies that involve issues relating to policy-making and political conflict. As a transitory subject, planning will always produce intriguing nuances that are worthy of further in-depth study; the proposed reforms to planning will continue this assessment by others interested in the subject. This book has taken over nine years to produce, but more work is required to monitor the operational decisions within the planning polity, to assess the tensions between one level of planning policy and another, and the ideologies and practices utilised by different levels of government to enforce change.

REFERENCES

Adam Smith Institute (1983) *Omega Report: Local Government Policy*, ASI, London.

Adler, M., Asquith, S. (1981) *Discretion and Welfare*, Heinemann, London.

Alden, J. (1991) *Strategic Planning Guidance in Wales*, Paper in Planning Research 122, Department of City and Regional Planning, University of Wales Cardiff.

Alden, J. (1992) 'Strategic planning guidance in Wales', *Town Planning Review*, 63(1), 429–32.

Alden, J. (1999) 'Scenarios for the future of the British planning system', *Town Planning Review*, 70(3), 385–407.

Alden, J. (2001a) 'Devolution since Kilbrandon and scenarios for the future of spatial planning in the United Kingdom and European Union', *International Planning Studies*, 6(2), 117–32.

Alden, J. (2001b) 'Planning at a national scale: a new planning framework for the UK', in J. Alden, L. Albrechts, A. da R. Pires (eds), *The Changing Institutional Landscape of Planning*, Ashgate, Aldershot, 55–82.

Alden, J., Albrechts, L., Pires, A. da R. (eds) (2001) *The Changing Institutional Landscape of Planning*, Ashgate, Aldershot.

Alden, J., Offord, C. (1996) 'Regional planning policy', in M. Tewdwr-Jones (ed.), *British Planning Policy in Transition: Planning in the 1990s*, UCL Press, London.

Alexander, E. (1997) 'A mile or a millimetre? Planning theory gap', *Environment and Planning B: Planning and Design*, 24(1), 3–6.

Allmendinger, P. (1996) *Thatcherism and Simplified Planning Zones: An Implementation Perspective*, Oxford Brookes University, School of Planning Monograph, 2.1.

Allmendinger, P. (1997) *Thatcherism and Planning: The Case for Simplified Planning Zones*, Ashgate, Aldershot.

Allmendinger, P. (2001a) *Planning in Postmodern Times*, Routledge, London.

Allmendinger, P. (2001b) 'The future of planning in a Scottish Parliament', *Town Planning Review*, 72(2), 121–48.

Allmendinger, P. (2001c) 'The head and the heart: national identity and urban planning in a devolved Scotland', *International Planning Studies*, 6(1), 33–54.

Allmendinger, P. (2002) *Planning Theory*, Palgrave, Basingstoke.

Allmendinger, P., Barker, A. (2001) 'Attitudes towards planning in a devolved Scotland', *Regional Studies*, 35(8), 759–64.

Allmendinger, P., Chapman, M. (eds) (1999) *Planning Beyond 2000*, John Wiley and Sons, Chichester.

Allmendinger, P., Tewdwr-Jones, M. (1997a) 'Mind the gap: planning theory-practice and the translation of knowledge into action', *Environment and Planning B: Planning and Design*, 24(6), 802–6.

Allmendinger, P., Tewdwr-Jones, M. (1997b) 'Post-Thatcherite urban planning and politics: a Major change?', *International Journal of Urban and Regional Research*, 21(1), 100–16.

Allmendinger, P., Tewdwr-Jones, M. (2000a) 'New Labour, new planning? The trajectory of planning in Blair's Britain', *Urban Studies*, 37(8), 1379–402.

Allmendinger, P., Tewdwr-Jones, M. (2000b) 'Spatial dimensions and institutional uncertainties of planning and the "new regionalism" ', *Environment and Planning C: Government and Policy*, 18, 711–26.

Allmendinger, P., Tewdwr-Jones, M. (eds) (2002) *Planning Futures: New Directions for Planning Theory*, Routledge, London.

Allmendinger, P., Thomas, H. (eds) (1998) *Urban Planning and the British New Right*, Routledge, London.

Ambrose, P. (1986) *Whatever Happened to Planning?*, Methuen, London.

Amin, A. (1999) 'An institutional perspective on regional economic development', *International Journal of Urban and Regional Research*, 23, 365–78.

Amin, A., Thrift, N. (1992) 'Neo-Marshallian nodes in global networks', *International Journal of Urban and Regional Research*, 16, 571–87.

Amin, A., Thrift, N. (1995) 'Globalisation, institutional "thickness" and the local economy', in P. Healey, S. Cameron, S. Davoudi, S. Graham, A. Mandani-Pour (eds), *Managing Cities: The New Urban Context*, John Wiley and Sons, Chichester.

Anderson, J. (1990) ' "The New Right", enterprise zones and urban development corporations', *International Journal of Urban and Regional Research*, 14, 468–89.

Anderson, P., Mann, N. (1997) *Safety First: The Making of New Labour*, Granta, London.

Argyris, C., Schon, D. (1978) *Organizational Learning: A Theory of Action Perspective*, Addison-Wesley, Reading, Mass.

Assembly of Welsh Counties (1991) The Structure of Local Government in Wales: The Assembly's Response to the Consultation Paper Issued by the Secretary of State, Assembly of Welsh Counties, County Hall, Cathays Park, Cardiff CF1 3NE.

Assembly of Welsh Counties (1992) Strategic Planning Guidance in Wales: Overview Report, Assembly of Welsh Counties, County Hall, Cathays Park, Cardiff CF1 3NE.

Assembly of Welsh Counties (1993) Strategic Planning Guidance in Wales, Assembly of Welsh Counties, County Hall, Cathays Park, Cardiff CF1 3NE.

Bailey, J. (1980) *Ideas and Intervention: Social Theory for Practice*, Routledge, London.

Baker, M. (1998) 'Planning for the English regions: a review of the Secretary of State's Regional Planning Guidance', *Planning Practice and Research*, 13, 153–69.

Baker, M. (1999) 'Intervention or interference? Central government involvement in the plan-making process in some English regions', *Town Planning Review*, 70(1), 1–24.

Baker, M., Deas, I., Wong, C. (1999) 'Obscure ritual or administrative luxury? Integrating strategic planning and regional development', *Environment and Planning B: Planning and Design*, 26, 763–82.

Baker, M., Wong, C. (1997) 'Planning for housing land in the English regions: a critique of household projections and Regional Planning Guidance', *Environment and Planning C: Government and Policy*, 15, 73–87.

Baker, P. (1995) 'The labours of Hercules', *Planning Week*, 2, 3.

Banfield, E. (1974) *Unheavenly City Revisited*, Little Brown and Co., Boston, Mass.

Banham, R., Barker, P., Hall, P., Price, C. (1969) 'Non-plan: an experiment in freedom', *New Society*, 20 March.

Banister, D. (1999) 'Planning more to travel less: land use and transport', *Town Planning Review*, 70(3), 313–38.

Batchler, J., Turok, I. (eds) (1997) *The Coherence of EU Regional Policy*, Jessica Kingsley Publishing, London.

Batey, P.W.J., Breheny, M.J. (1982) *The History of Planning Methodology: A Framework for the Assessment of Anglo-American Theory and Practice*, Department of Geography, University of Reading, Reading Geographical Papers No. 79.

Berry, J., Brown, L., McGreal, S. (2001) 'The planning system in Northern Ireland post-devolution', *European Planning Studies*, 9(6), 781–91.

Bishop, K., Tewdwr-Jones, M., Wilkinson, D. (2000) 'From spatial to local: the impact of the EU on local authority planning in Britain', *Journal of Environmental Planning and Management*, 43(3), 309–34.

Blair, T. (1996) *New Britain: My Vision of a Young Country*, Fourth Estate, London.

Blowers, A., Evans, B. (eds) (1997) *Town Planning in the 21st Century*, Routledge, London.

Blundell, J. Gosschalk, B. (1997) *Beyond Left and Right*, Institute of Economic Affairs, London.

Bomberg, E. (1996) *Green Parties and Politics in the European Community*, Routledge, London.

Booth, P. (1996) *Controlling Development: Certainty and Discretion in Europe, the USA and Hong Kong*, UCL Press, London.

Boyack, S. (1999) 'Planning and the parliament: challenges and opportunities', in E. McDowell, J. McCormick (eds), *Environment Scotland: Prospects for Sustainability*, Ashgate, Aldershot.

Boyne, G., Griffiths, P., Lawton, A., Law, J. (1991) *Local Government in Wales: Its Role and Functions*, Report prepared by the Welsh Unit for Local Government, Polytechnic of Wales, Joseph Rowntree Foundation, York.

Boyne, G., Law, J. (1993) 'Bidding for the local government franchise: an evaluation of the contest in Wales', *Local Government Studies*, 19(4), 537–57.

Bradbury, J., Mawson, J. (eds) (1997) *British Regionalism and Devolution: The Challenges of State Reform and European Integration*, Jessica Kingsley Publishing, London.

Bradshaw, J. (1992) 'Social security', in D. Marsh, R. Rhodes (eds), *Implementing Thatcherite Policy: Audit of an Era*, Open University Press, Buckinghamshire.

Breheny, M.J. (1983) 'A practical review of planning theory', *Environment and Planning B: Planning and Design*, 10, 101–15.

Breheny, M.J. (1991) 'The renaissance of strategic planning?', *Environment and Planning B: Planning and Design*, 18, 233–49.

Breheny, M.J. (1999) 'People, households and houses: the basis to "the great housing debate" in England', *Town Planning Review*, 70(3), 275–94.

Brenner, N. (1999) 'Globalisation as reterritorialisation: the re-scaling of urban governance in the European Union', *Urban Studies*, 36, 431–51.

Brindley, T., Rydin, Y., Stoker, G. (1989) *Remaking Planning: The Politics of Change in the Thatcher Years*, Unwin Hyman, London.

British Property Federation (1986) *The Planning System: A Fresh Approach*, BPF, London.

Bruton, M., Nicholson, D. (1985) 'Strategic land use planning and the British development plan system', *Town Planning Review*, 56(1), 21–40.

Bruton, M., Nicholson, D. (1987) *Local Planning in Practice*, Hutchinson, London.

Bull, D. (1980) 'The anti-discretion movement in Britain: fact or phantom?', *Journal of Social Welfare Law*, 3, 65–84.

Bulpitt, J. (1983) *Territory and Power in the UK: An Interpretation*, Manchester University Press, Manchester.

Bulpitt, J. (1986) 'The Thatcher Statecraft', *Political Studies*, 14(6), 47–61.

Burns, D., Hambleton, R., Hoggett, P. (1994) *The Politics of Decentralisation*, Macmillan, London.

Cabinet Office (2000) *Reaching Out: The Role of Central Government at the Regional and Local Levels*, Performance and Innovation Unit, Cabinet Office, London.

Campbell, J. (1994) *Edward Heath: A Biography*, Papermac, London.

Cardiff University (1997) *Slimmer and Swifter: A Critical Examination of District Wide Local Plans and UDPs*, Report produced by Stephen Crow, Alison Brown, Sue Essex, Huw Thomas and Chris Yewlett, RTPI, London.

Cardiff University/ECOTEC (2001) *Comparative Spatial Planning Methodologies*, Cardiff University, Cardiff.

Centre for Policy Studies (1980) *A Bibliography of Freedom* (2nd edn), CPS, London.

Chambers, L.D., Taylor, M.A.P. (eds) (1999) *Strategic Planning: Processes, Tools and Outcomes*, Ashgate, Aldershot.

Chapman, W. (1995) 'PPGs: The Government's View', Paper presented to the PPGs of the Year Conference, Royal Town Planning Institute, London, May.

Church, A. (1986) 'Urban regeneration in London Docklands: a five year policy review', *Environment and Planning C: Government and Policy*, 6, 218–37.

Clavel, P. (1983) *Opposition Planning in Wales and Appalachia*, University of Wales Press, Cardiff.

Cloke, P. (ed.) (1992) *Policy and Change in Thatcher's Britain*, Pergamon Press, Oxford.

Cloke, P. (1996) 'Housing in the open countryside: windows on "irresponsible" planning in rural Wales', *Town Planning Review*, 67(3), 291–309.

Cloke, P., Little, J. (1990) *The Rural State? Limits to Planning in Rural Society*, Clarendon Press, Oxford.

Clotworthy, J., Harris, N. (1996) 'Planning policy implications of local government reorganisation', in M. Tewdwr-Jones (ed.), *British Planning Policy in Transition: Planning in the 1990s*, UCL Press, London.

Constitution Unit, The (1996) *Regional Government in England,* The Constitution Unit, University College London, London.

Cooke, P. (1983) *Theories of Planning and Spatial Development*, Hutchinson, London.

Cooke, P. (ed.) (1989) *Localities*, Unwin Hyman, London.

Cooke, P. and Morgan, K. (1993) 'The network paradigm: new departures in corporate and regional development', *Environment and Planning D: Society and Space*, 11, 543–64.

Cooke, P. and Morgan, K. (1998) *The Associational Economy: Firms, Regions and Innovation*, Oxford University Press, Oxford.

Council of Welsh Districts (1991) The Structure of Local Government in Wales: Response to the Welsh Office Consultation Document, Council of Welsh Districts, 10–11 Raleigh Walk, Atlantic Wharf, Cardiff CF1 5LN.

Cowell, R., Murdoch, J. (1999) 'Land use and the limits to (regional) governance: some lessons from planning for housing and minerals in England', *International Journal of Urban and Regional Research*, 23(4), 654–71.

Crewe, I. (1994) 'Electoral behaviour', in D. Kavanagh, A. Seldon (eds), *The Major Effect*, Macmillan, London.

Crookston, M. (1998) 'Regional policy and the great housing debate', *Town and Country Planning*, July, 213–15.

Cross, D.T., Bristow, M.R. (eds) (1983) *English Structure Planning*, Pion, London.

Crow, S. (1995) 'Third party rights: will they work and do we need them?', *Journal of Environment and Planning Law*, 47(5), 376–87.

Crow, S. (1996) 'Lessons from Bryan', *Journal of Planning and Environment Law*, 48, 359–69.

Crow, S. (1999) *Chairman's Report, Examination in Public for Regional Planning Guidance for the South East*, DETR, London.

CSD (Committee for Spatial Development) (1999) *European Spatial Development Perspective*, CEC, Luxembourg.

Cullingworth, J.B. (ed.) (1999) *British Planning*, Athlone Press, London.

Cullingworth, J.B., Nadin, V. (2002) *Town and Country Planning in Britain* (13th edn), Routledge, London.

Darke, M., McLoughlin, B., Thompson, R., Thornley, J. (eds), *Aspects of Structure Planning in Britain*, Research Paper No. 20, Centre for Environmental Studies, London (pp. 131–55).

Davidoff, P., Reiner, T.A. (1962) 'A choice theory of planning', *Journal of the American Institute of Planners*, 28, 108–15.

Davies, H.W.E. (1996) 'Planning and the European question', in M. Tewdwr-Jones (ed.), *British Planning Policy in Transition: Planning in the 1990s*, UCL Press, London.

Davies, H.W.E. (1999) 'The planning system and the development plan', in J.B. Cullingworth (ed.), *British Planning: 50 Years of Urban and Regional Policy*, Athlone Press, London.

Davies, H.W.E., Edwards, D., Hooper, A.J., Punter, J.V. (1989) *Planning Control in Western Europe*, HMSO, London.

Davies, H.W.E., Edwards, D., Rowley, A. (1986) *The Relationship between Development Plans, Development Control and Appeals*, Department of Land Management and Development, Faculty of Urban and Regional Development, University of Reading, Working Paper 10.

Davis, K.C. (1971) *Discretionary Justice*, University of Illinois Press, Urbana.

Deakin, N., Edwards, J. (1993) *Enterprise Culture and the Inner City*, Routledge, London.

Deas, I., Ward, K. (2000) 'The song has ended but the melody lingers on: RDAs and the lessons of the urban development corporations', *Local Economy*, 14, 114–32.

Delafons, J. (1998) 'Reforming the British planning system 1964–65: the Planning Advisory Group and the genesis of the planning act of 1968', *Planning Perspectives*, 13, 373–87.

Denman, D. (1980) *Land in a Free Society*, Centre for Policy Studies, London.

DETR (1997) *Building Partnerships for Prosperity*, Consultation Paper, DETR, London.

DETR (1998a) *Modernising Local Government: In Touch With the People,* Consultation Paper, DETR, London.

DETR (1998b) *Modernising Local Government: Local Democracy and Community Leadership*, Consultation Paper, DETR, London.

DETR (1998c) *Modernising Planning: A Policy Statement*, DETR, London.

DETR (1998d) *Modernising Planning: Improving Arrangements for the Delivery of Local Plans and Unitary Development Plans*, DETR, London.

DETR (1998e) *New Leadership for London: The Government's Proposals for a Greater London Authority*, Consultation Paper, DETR, London.

DETR (1998f) *Planning for the Communities of the Future,* Consultation Paper, DETR, London.

DETR (1998g) *The Future of Regional Planning Guidance*, Consultation Paper, DETR, London.

DETR (1998h) *The Impact of the EU on UK Planning*, DETR, London.

DETR (1998i) *A Mayor and Assembly for London*, DETR, London.

DETR (1999) *Modernising Planning: A Progress Report*, DETR, London.

DETR (2000a) *Development Plans: PPG12*, Stationery Office, London.

DETR (2000b) *Quality and Choice: A Home for All*, Consultation Paper, DETR, London.

DETR (2000c) *Regional Planning: PPG11*, Stationery Office, London.

DETR (2000d) T*he Way Forward for Housing*, Consultation Paper, DETR, London.

DETR (2000e) *Transport 2010: The Ten Year Plan for Transport*, DETR, London.

Diamond, D. (1979) 'The uses of strategic planning: the example of the national planning guidelines in Scotland', *Town Planning Review*, 50(1), 18–25.

Di Maggio, P. (1993) 'On metropolitan dominance: New York in the urban network, in M. Shelter (ed.), *Capital of the American Century: The National and International Influence of New York City*, Russell Sage Foundation, New York.

DoE (1977) *Memorandum on Structure Plans and Local Plans: Circular 55/77*, HMSO, London.

DoE (1978) *The Form and Content of Local Plans: Circular LP1/78*, HMSO, London.

DoE (1985) *Development and Employment: Circular 14/85*, HMSO, London.

DoE (1990) *Structure Plans and Regional Planning Guidance: PPG15*, HMSO, London.

DoE (1992a) *Development Plans: A Good Practice Guide*, HMSO, London.

DoE (1992b) *Development Plans and Regional Planning Guidance: PPG12*, HMSO, London.

DoE (1993) *Enquiry into the Planning System in North Cornwall District*, HMSO, London.

DoE (1995) *The Effectiveness of Planning Policy Guidance Notes*, DoE, London.

DoE (1996) *Town Centres and Retail Development: PPG6*, HMSO, London.

DoE (1997) *Speeding Up the Local Plan Process*, Consultation Paper, DoE, London.

DoE/DoT (1994) *Transport: PPG13*, HMSO, London.

DoE/Welsh Office (1986) *The Future of Development Plans*, Consultation Paper, DoE, London.

DoE/Welsh Office (1988) *Planning Policy Guidance and Minerals Planning Guidance: Circular 1/88*, HMSO, London.

DoE/Welsh Office (1992a) *Coastal Planning: PPG20*, HMSO, London.

DoE/Welsh Office (1992b) *General Policy and Principles: PPG1*, HMSO, London.

DoE/Welsh Office (1992c) *Industrial and Commercial Development and Small Firms: PPG4*, HMSO, London.

DoE/Welsh Office (1993) *Town Centres and Retail Development: PPG6*, HMSO, London.

DRDNI (2000) *Shaping Our Future: The Regional Development Strategy for Northern Ireland*, Department for Regional Development in Northern Ireland, Belfast.

Driver, S., Martell, L. (1998) *New Labour*, Polity Press, Bristol.

Driver, S., Martell, L. (2000) *New Labour*, Polity Press, Cambridge.

DTI (1985) *Burdens on Business: Report of a Scrutiny of Administrative and Legislative Requirements*, HMSO, London.

DTLR (2001a) New Parliamentary Procedures for Processing Major Infrastructure Projects, Consultation Paper, DTLR, London.

DTLR (2001b) Planning: Delivering a Fundamental Change, Consultation Paper, DTLR, London.

DTLR (2001c) Planning Gain, Consultation Paper, DTLR, London.

DTZ Pieda (2000) *Land Use Planning Research Scoping Study Final Report*, DTZ Pieda, Cardiff.

Dworkin, R. (1977) *Taking Rights Seriously*, Duckworth, London.

Edgar, E. (1983) 'Bitter Harvest', *New Socialist*, September/October.

Edwards, J.A., Thomas, W. (1974) Llantrisant New Town: The Case Against, Heads of the Valleys Standing Conference.

Edwards, M. (2000) 'Towards a joined-up London', *Planning in London*, 32(1), 41–2.

Edwards, M., McCafferty, A. (1992) '1991: a time to reflect', *Estates Gazette*, no. 9223.

Etzioni, A. (1968) *The Active Society*, Collier-Macmillan, London.

European Commission (1991) *Europe 2000*, CEC, Luxembourg.

European Commission (1994) *Europe 2000+*, Office for Official Publications of the European Communities, Luxembourg.

European Commission (1999) *European Spatial Development Perspective*, Office for Official Publications of the European Union, Luxembourg.

Evans, R. and Harding, A. (1997) 'Regionalisation, regional institutions and economic development', *Policy and Politics*, 25, 19–30.

Faludi, A. (1973) *Planning Theory*, Pergamon Press, Oxford.

Faludi, A. (1986) *Critical Rationalism and Planning Methodology*, Pion, London.

Faludi, A. (1987) *A Decision-Centred View of Environmental Planning*, Pergamon Press, Oxford.

Faludi, A. (2000) 'The European Spatial Development Perspective: what next?', *European Planning Studies*, 8(2), 237–50.

Faludi, A. (2001) 'The European Spatial Development Perspective and the changing institutional landscape of planning', in J. Alden, L. Albrechts, A. da Rosa Pires (eds), *The Changing Institutional Landscape of Planning*, Ashgate, Aldershot.

Faludi, A., Mastop, J.M. (1982) 'The IOR School: the development of a planning methodology', *Environment and Planning B: Planning and Design*, 9, 241–56.

Fischer, F., Forester, J. (eds) (1993) *The Argumentative Turn in Planning and Policy Analysis*, UCL Press, London.

Flynn, A., Leach, S., Vielba, C. (1985) *Abolition or Reform? The Greater London Council and the Metropolitan Counties*, Allen and Unwin, London.

Foley, P. (1998) 'The impact of the Regional Development Agency and Regional Chamber in the East Midlands', *Regional Studies*, 32(8), 777–82.

Forester, J. (1989) Planning in the Face of Power, University of California Press, Berkeley, Calif.

Friedmann, J. (1973) *Retracking America: A Theory of Transactive Planning*, Doubleday Anchor, Garden City, N.Y.

Friedmann, J. (1987) *Planning in the Public Domain*, Princeton University Press, Princeton, N.J.

Friend, J. (1983) 'Reflections on rationality in strategic choice', *Environment and Planning B: Planning and Design*, 9, 241–56.

Friend, J. (1989) 'The strategic choice approach', in J. Rosenhead (ed.), *Rational Analysis for a Problematic World*, John Wiley and Sons, Chichester.

Friend, J., Hickling, A. (1987) *Planning Under Pressure*, Pergamon Press, Oxford.

Friend, J., Jessop, N. (1969) *Local Government and Strategic Choice*, Pergamon Press, Oxford.

Friend, J., Power, Yewlett, C.J.L. (1974) *Public Planning: the Inter-Corporate Dimension*, Tavistock, London.

Gallent, N., Tewdwr-Jones, M. (2000a) 'Rural housing', in B. Smith, T. Stirling, P. Williams (eds), *Housing in Wales*, CIT Wales, London.

Gallent, N., Tewdwr-Jones, M. (2000b) *Rural Second Homes in Europe: Examining Housing Supply and Planning Regulation*, Ashgate, Aldershot.

Gallent, N., Tewdwr-Jones, M. (2001) 'Second homes and the UK planning system', *Planning Practice and Research*, 16(1), 59–69.

Gallent, N., Tewdwr-Jones, M., Higgs, G. (1998) 'Planning for residential tourism in rural Wales', in G. Day and D. Thomas (eds), *Contemporary Wales*, University of Wales Press, Cardiff.

Gamble, A. (1984) 'This lady's not for turning: Thatcherism mark III', *Marxism Today*, July.

Gamble, A. (1988) *The Free Economy and the Strong State*, Macmillan, London.

Game, C. (1997) 'How many, when, where and how? Taking stock of local government reorganisation', *Local Government Policy Making*, 21(4), 3–9.

Gatenby, I., Williams, C. (1992) 'Section 54A: the legal and practical implications', *Journal of Planning and Environment Law*, 42(2), 110–20.

Gatenby, I., Williams, C. (1996) 'Interpreting planning law', in M. Tewdwr-Jones (ed.), *British Planning Policy in Transition: Planning in the 1990s*, UCL Press, London.

Giddens, A. (1998) *The Third Way*, Polity Press, London.

Glasson, J. (1978) *An Introduction to Regional Planning*, UCL Press, London.

Goodstadt, V. (2001) 'The need for effective strategic planning: the experience of Glasgow and the Clyde Valley', *Planning Theory and Practice*, 2(2), 215–21.

Goodstadt, V., U'ren, G. (1999) 'Which way now for Scottish planning?', *Planning*, 22 January, 11.

GOSW (Government Office for the South West) (1997) *Annual Report 1996/97*, GOSW, Bristol.

Greed, C. (1996a) *Implementing Town Planning*, Longman, Harlow.

Greed, C. (1996b) *Investigating Town Planning*, Longman, Harlow.

Griffiths, R. (1986) 'Planning in retreat? Town planning and the market in the 1980s', *Planning Practice and Research*, 1, 3–7.

Hague, C. (1990) 'Scotland: back to the future for planning', in J. Montgomery and A. Thornley (eds), *Radical Planning Initiatives*, Gower, Aldershot.

Hague, C. (1997) 'In search of the Scotland 2020 vision', *Town and Country Planning*, 66(11), 307–8.

Ham, C., Hill, M. (1985) *The Policy Process in the Modern Capitalist State*, Wheatsheaf, Sussex.

Hambleton, R., Mills, L. (1993) 'Local government reform in Wales', *Local Government Policy Making*, 19(4), 45–55.

Harding, A., Evans, R., Parkinson, M., Garside, P. (1996) *Regional Government in Britain: An Economic Solution?*, Policy Press, Bristol.

Harding, A., Wilks-Heeg, S., Hutchins, M. (1999) 'Regional Development Agencies and English regionalism: the question of accountability', *Environment and Planning C: Government and Policy*, 17, 669–83.

Harlow, C., Rawlings, R. (1984) *Law and Administration*, Weidenfeld and Nicolson, London.

Harris, M. (1998) 'New Labour: government and opposition', *Political Quarterly*, 70(1), 42–51.

Harris, N. (2000) 'Creating a "distinctively Welsh" planning system', *Planning Wales*, 3 September, pp. 9–11.

Harris, N., Tewdwr-Jones, M. (1995) 'The implications for planning of local government reorganisation in Wales: purpose, process and practice', *Environment and Planning C: Government and Policy*, 13(1), 47–65.

Harvie, C. (1991) 'English regionalism: the dog that never barked', in B. Crick (ed.), *National Identities*, Blackwell, Oxford.

Hassan, G. (1999) 'The new Scottish politics', in G. Hassan (ed.), *A Guide to the Scottish Parliament: The Shape of Things to Come*, Centre for Scottish Public Policy, Edinburgh.

Hayek, F. von (1960) *The Constitution of Liberty*, Routledge and Kegan Paul, London.

Hayton, K. (1996) 'Planning policy in Scotland', in M. Tewdwr-Jones (ed.), *British Planning Policy in Transition: Planning in the 1990s*, UCL Press, London.

Hayton, K. (1997) 'Planning in a Scottish Parliament', *Town and Country Planning*, 66(11), 45–7.

Hayward, R., McGynn, S. (1995) 'The town centres we deserve? Guidance for planning, design and management', *Town Planning Review*, 65(3), 321–8.

Headicar, P. (1995) *PPG13: Can the Honeymoon Begin Without a Bride?*, Oxford Brookes University, School of Planning Monograph 1.2.

Healey, P. (1979) 'Networking as a normative principle with particular reference to local government and land use planning', *Local Government Studies*, 5, 55–68.

Healey, P. (1983) *Local Plans in British Land Use Planning*, Pergamon Press, Oxford.

Healey, P. (1990) 'Development plans and markets', *Planning Practice and Research*, 7(2), 13–20.

Healey, P. (1992) 'The reorganisation of state and market in planning', *Urban Studies*, 29, 411–34.

Healey, P. (1993) 'The communicative work of development plans', *Environment and Planning B: Planning and Design*, 20(1), 83–104.

Healey, P. (1997) *Collaborative Planning: Shaping Places in Fragmented Societies*, Macmillan, London.

Healey, P. (1998) 'Collaborative planning in a stakeholder society', *Town Planning Review*, 69(1), 1–21.

Healey, P. *et al.* (1985) The Implementation of Planning Policies and the Role of Development Plans, Report to the Department of the Environment, Oxford Polytechnic, Oxford.

Healey, P., McDougall, G., Thomas, M.J. (1982) *Planning Theory: Prospects for the 1980s*, Pergamon, Oxford.

Healey, P., McNamara, P., Elson, M., Doak, A. (1988) *Land Use Planning and the Mediation of Urban Change*, Cambridge University Press, Cambridge.

Hebbert, M. (1999) *London*, John Wiley and Sons, Chichester.

Hedley, G. (1984) 'Enterprise Zones in Britain: the form and consequences of the planning scheme', *Planning Practice and Research*, 7(3), 13–20.

Herbert-Young, N. (1995) 'Reflections on Section 54A and "plan-led" decision-making', *Journal of Planning and Environment Law*, 48, 292–305.

Hetherington, P. (1998) 'Prescott gets half a cake', *The Guardian*, 20 November, p. 23.

Hirst, P. (1989) *After Thatcher*, Collins, London.

HM Government (1967) *Wales: The Way Ahead*, HMSO, London.

HM Government (1979) *Central Government Controls Over Local Authorities*, Cmnd. 7634, HMSO, London.

HM Government (1985) *Lifting the Burden*, Cmnd. 9571, HMSO, London.

HM Government (1989) *The Future of Development Plans*, Cmnd. 569, HMSO, London.

HM Government (1990) *This Common Inheritance*, Cmnd. 1200, HMSO, London.

HM Government (1994) *Competitiveness*, HMSO, London.

HM Government (1996) *Rural England*, HMSO, London.

HM Government (1997) *Building Partnerships for Prosperity*, White Paper, Stationery Office, London.

HM Government (1998) *A New Deal for Transport*, White Paper, Stationery Office, London.

HM Government (1999) *Local Leadership, Local Choice*, White Paper, Stationery Office, London.

Hogg, S., Hill, J. (1995) *Too Close to Call: Power and Politics – John Major and Politics in No. 10*, Little, Brown and Company, London.

Hogwood, B.W. (1996) *Mapping the Regions: Boundaries, Coordination and Government*, The Policy Press, Bristol.

House of Commons Environment Transport and Regions Select Committee (1998) *First Report: Regional Development Agencies*, The Stationery Office, London.

House of Commons Select Committee on Scottish Affairs (1972) *Land Resources in Scotland*, Volume 1, HMSO, London.

House of Commons Welsh Affairs Committee (1993) *Rural Housing*, Volume 1, HMSO, London.

House of Commons Welsh Affairs Committee (1997) *Devolution, Governance and the Welsh Assembly,* Volume 1, HMSO, London.

Hudson, R., Dunford, M., Hamilton, D., Kotter, R. (1997) 'Developing regional strategies for economic success: lessons from Europe's economically successful regions', *European Urban and Regional Studies*, 4, 365–73.

Hull, A. (2000) 'Modernizing democracy: constructing a radical reform of the planning system', *European Planning Studies*, 8(6), 767–82.

Hull, A., Vigar, G. (1998) 'The changing role of the development plan in managing spatial change', *Environment and Planning C: Government and Policy*, 16, 379–94.

Imrie, R., Thomas, H. (1993) 'The limits of property-led regeneration', *Environment and Planning C: Government and Policy*, 11(1), 87–102.

Imrie, R., Thomas, H. (eds) (1998) *British Urban Policy and the Urban Development Corporations* (2nd edn),, Sage, London.

Insight Social Research (1989) *Local Attitudes to Central Advice*, J. Sainsbury, London.

Jackson, P. (1992) 'Economic policy', in D. Marsh, R. Rhodes (eds), *Implementing Thatcherite Policies: Audit of an Era*, Open University Press, Milton Keynes.

Jacobs, J. (1965) *The Death and Life of Great American Cities*, Penguin, Harmondsworth.

Jacobs, J. (1970) *The Economy of Cities*, Jonathan Cape, London.

Jacques, M., Hall, S. (1997) 'Blair: is he the greatest Tory since Thatcher?', *The Observer*, 13 April, p. 14.

Jarvis, R. (1996) 'Structure plans and strategic planning guidance in Wales', in M. Tewdwr-Jones (ed.), *British Planning Policy in Transition: Planning in the 1990s*, UCL Press, London.

John, P., Whitehead, A. (1997) 'The renaissance of English regionalism in the 1990s', *Policy and Politics*, 25, 7–17.

Johnson, C. (1991) *The Economy Under Mrs. Thatcher 1979–90*, Penguin, London.

Johnston, R., Pattie, C. (1996) 'Intra-local conflict, public opinion and local government restructuring in England 1993–95', *Geoforum*, 27(1), 97–114.

Jonas, A., Ward, K.G. (1999) 'Towards new urban and regional policy frameworks for Europe: competitive regionalism "bottom up" and "top down" ', Paper presented to the 6th International Conference of the Regional Studies Association, University of the Basque Country, Bilbao, Spain, September.

Jones, A. (1996) 'Local planning policy: the Newbury approach', in M. Tewdwr-Jones (ed.), *British Planning Policy in Transition: Planning in the 1990s*, UCL Press, London.

Jones, G., Stewart, M. (1983) *The Case for Local Government*, Allen and Unwin, London.

Jones, J.B., Balsom, D. (eds) (2000) *Road to the National Assembly for Wales*, Cardiff: University of Wales Press.

Jones, M. (1999) 'The regional state and economic regulation: regional regeneration or polit-ical mobilisation?', Paper presented to the 6th International Conference of the Regional Studies Association, University of the Basque Country, Bilbao, Spain, Sep-tember.

Jones, M. (2001) 'The rise of the regional state in economic governance: "partnerships for prosperity" or new scales of state power?', *Environment and Planning A*, 33, 1185–211.

Jones, M., MacLeod, G. (1999) 'Towards a regional renaissance? Reconfiguring and rescal-ing England's economic governance', *Transactions of the Institute of British Geo-graphers*, 24, 295–314.

Jones, R. (1982) *Town and Country Chaos*, Adam Smith Institute, London.

Jones, T. (1997) *Remaking the Labour Party: From Gaitskell to Blair*, Routledge, London.

Jowell, J. (1973) 'The legal control of administrative discretion', *Public Law*, 178–219.

Kavanagh, D. (1994) 'A Major agenda?', in D. Kavanagh and A. Seldon (eds), *The Major Effect*, Macmillan, London.

Kavanagh, D., Seldon, A. (eds) (1989) *The Thatcher Effect*, Oxford University Press, Oxford.

Kavanagh, D., Seldon, A. (eds) (1994) *The Major Effect*, Macmillan, London.

Keating, M. (1997) 'The invention of regions: political restructuring and territorial government in Western Europe', *Environment and Planning C: Government and Policy*, 15, 383–98.

Keeble, L. (1969) *The Principles of Town and Country Planning*, Estates Gazette, London.

King, D. (1987) *The New Right: Politics, Markets and Citizenship*, Macmillan, London.

Kitchen, T. (1997) *People, Politics, Policies and Plans*, Paul Chapman Publishing, London.

Labour Party (1991) *Devolution and Democracy*, Labour Party, London.

Labour Party (1995) *A Choice for England Consultation Paper*, Labour Party, London.

Labour Party (1997) *Because Britain Deserves Better*, Labour Party, Labour.

Lawless, P. (1983) *Britain's Inner Cities*, Harper and Row, London.

Layfield, Sir F. (1990) 'Material considerations in planning: the law', *Journal of Planning and Environment Law*, Occasional Paper 17, 6–16.

Leach, S., Stewart, J., Walsh, K., Gibson, J. (1992) *The Heseltine Review of Local Govern-ment: A New Vision or Opportunities Missed?*, INLOGOV, Birmingham.

Leadbetter, C. (1998) 'A hole at the heart of the Third Way', *New Statesman*, 8 May, 32–3.

Lindblom, C.E. (1959) 'The science of muddling through', *Public Administration Review*, 19, 79–88.

Lloyd, M.G. (1996) 'National Planning Guidelines and development plans in Scotland', *Local Government Studies*, 22(4), 262–72.

Lloyd, M.G. (1997) 'Structure and culture: regional planning and institutional innovation in Scotland', in R. MacDonald, H. Thomas (eds), *Nationality and Planning in Scotland and Wales*, University of Wales Press, Cardiff.

Lloyd, M.G., Illsley, B. (1999) 'Community planning for a Scottish Parliament: necessary but not sufficient', *Town Planning Review*, 70(4), 409–17.

Lloyd, M.G., McCarthy, J. (2000) 'The Scottish Parliament, regulation and land use planning', *European Planning Studies*, 8(2), 251–6.

Lloyd, P.E. (1999) 'The Regional Development Agencies and social inclusion: widening the agenda', *Environment and Planning C: Government and Policy*, 17(6), 701–13.

Local Government Association (1999) *Memorandum to the House of Commons Select Committee on Environment, Transport and the Regions*, House of Commons, London.

Lock, D. (1998) 'Compassion finds a sustainable slant', *Planning*, 1 May, 14.

Lovering, J. (1997) *Misleading and Misreading Wales: The New Regionalism*, Papers in Planning Research 166, Department of City and Regional Planning, Cardiff University.

Lovering, J. (1999) 'Theory led by policy? The inadequacies of the "new regionalism" (illustrated from the case of Wales)', *International Journal of Urban and Regional Research*, 23, 379–95.

Lovering, J. (2001) 'The coming regional crisis (and how to avoid it)', *Regional Studies*, 35(4), 349–54.

Low, N. (1991) *Planning Politics and the State*, Unwin Hyman, London.

Lunch, P. (1999) 'New Labour and the English Regional Development Agencies: Devolution as Evolution', *Regional Studies*, 33(1), 73–8.

Lyddon, D. (1980) 'Scottish planning in practice: influences and comparisons', *The Planner*, 66(3), 66–7.

Lyddon, D. (1985) 'Planning and recovery: an alternative route', *The Planner*, 71(2), 26–30.

MacDonald, R., Thomas, H. (eds) (1997) *Nationality and Planning in Scotland and Wales*, University of Wales Press, Cardiff.

MacGregor, B., Ross, A. (1995) 'Master or servant? The changing role of the development plan in the British planning system', *Town Planning Review*, 66(1), 41–59.

MacKinnon, D., Phelps, N.A. (2001) 'Regional governance and foreign direct investment: the dynamics of institutional change in Wales and North East England', *Geoforum*, 32(2), 255–69.

MacLean, E. (1999) 'A brief history of Scottish Home Rule', in G. Hassan (ed.), *A Guide to the Scottish Parliament: The Shape of Things to Come*, Centre for Scottish Public Policy, Edinburgh.

MacLeod, G. (1997) ' "Institutional thickness" and industrial governance in Lowland Scotland', *Area*, 29(4), 299–311.

MacLeod, G., Goodwin, M. (1999) 'Space, scale and strategy: rethinking urban and regional governance', *Progress in Human Geography*, 23, 503–27.

McAuslan, P. (1981) *The Ideologies of Planning Law*, Pergamon Press, Oxford.

McCarthy, J., Newlands, D. (eds) (1999) *Governing Scotland: Problems and Prospects*, Avebury, Aldershot.

McCormick, J. (1991) *British Politics and the Environment*, Earthscan, London.

McDougall, G. (1983) 'The interactional approach to organisations and planning: a critique', in I. Masser (ed.), *Evaluating Urban Planning Efforts*, Gower, Aldershot.

McIntyre, D. (1995) 'Making sense of a mystery', *The Independent on Sunday*, 26 November, 7–8.

McKinsey Global Institute (1998) *Driving Productivity and Growth in the UK Economy*, McKinsey Global Institute, London.

McLoughlin, J.B. (1969) *Urban and Regional Planning: A Systems Approach*, Faber and Faber, London.

McNeill, D. (2001) 'Barcelona as imagined community: Pasqual Maragall's spaces of engagement', *Political Geography*, 26(3), 340–52.

McNeill, W.V., Gordon, M. (2001) 'Shaping our future? The regional strategic framework for Northern Ireland', *Planning Theory and Practice*, 2(1), 31–52.

Major, J. (1999) *John Major: The Autobiography*, HarperCollins, London.

Marquand, D. (1996) 'The Blair paradox', *Prospect*, May, 19–24.

Marsh, D. (1991) 'Privatisation under Mrs. Thatcher', *Public Administration*, 69, 245–58

Marsh, D., Rhodes, R.A.W. (eds) (1992) *Implementing Thatcherite Policies: Audit of an Era*, Open University, Milton Keynes.

Martin, D. (1992) 'Europe 2000: Community actions and intentions in spatial planning', The Planner/Proceedings of the Town and Country Planning Summer School, 27 November.

Mawson, J. (1997a) 'New Labour and the English regions: a missed opportunity?', *Local Economy*, 194–203.

Mawson, J. (1997b) 'The English regional debate: towards regional governance or government?', in J. Bradbury, J. Mawson (eds), *British Regionalism and Devolution: The Challenges of State Reform and European Integration*, Jessica Kingsley Publishing, London.

Mawson, J. (1998) 'English regionalism and New Labour', in H. Elcock, M. Keating (eds), *Remaking the Union*, Frank Cass, London.

Mawson, J., Spencer, K. (1997) 'The origins and operations of the Government Offices for the Regions', in J. Bradbury, J. Mawson (eds), *British Regionalism and Devolution: The Challenges of State Reform and European Integration*, Jessica Kingsley Publishing, London.

Mayor of London (2001) *Towards the London Plan*, Greater London Authority, London.

Mazza, L. (1995) 'Technical knowledge, practical vision and the planner's response', *Town Planning Review*, 66(4), 389–410.

Minay, C. (1992) 'Developing regional planning guidance in England and Wales', *Town Planning Review*, 63(1), 415–34.

Mitchell, J. (1996) *Strategies for Self-Government: The Campaign for a Scottish Parliament*, Polygon, Edinburgh.

Morgan, K. (2001) 'The new territorial politics: rivalry and justice in post-devolution Britain', *Regional Studies*, 35(4), 343–8.

Morgan, K., Mungham, G. (2000) *Redesigning Democracy*, Seren Press: Bridgend.

Morgan, K., Roberts, E. (1994) *The Democratic Deficit: A Guide to Quangoland*, Paper in Planning Research 144, Department of City and Regional Planning, University of Wales Cardiff.

Morgan, R., Alden, J. (1974) *Regional Planning: A Comprehensive View*, Leonard Hill, Leighton Buzzard.

Murdoch, J., Abram, S., Marsden, T. (1999) 'Modalities of planning: a reflection on the persuasive powers of the development plan', *Town Planning Review*, 70(2), 191–212.

Murdoch, J., Norton, A. (2001) 'Regionalisation and planning: creating institutions and stakeholders in the English regions', in J. Alden, L. Albrects, A. da Rosa Pires (eds), *The Changing Institutional Landscape of Planning*, Ashgate, Aldershot.

Murdoch, J., Tewdwr-Jones, M. (1999) 'Planning and the English regions: conflict and convergence amongst the institutions of regional governance', *Environment and Planning C: Government and Policy*, 17, 715–29.

MWWSPG (2000) Mid and West Wales Strategic Planning Statement, Mid and West Wales Strategic Planning Group, Carmarthen.

Nadin, V., Stead, D. (1999) 'Environmental resources and energy in the UK: the potential role of a national spatial planning framework', *Town Planning Review*, 70(3), 339–62.

NAW (1999a) *A Framework for a National Housing Strategy for Wales*, National Assembly for Wales, Cardiff.

NAW (1999b) *National Economic Development Strategy for Wales*, National Assembly for Wales, Cardiff.

NAW (1999c) *Rural Development Plan for Wales*, National Assembly for Wales, Cardiff.

NAW (1999d) *The Transport Legacy in Wales*, National Assembly for Wales, Cardiff.

NAW (1999e) *Approach to the Future of Land Use Planning Policy*, National Assembly for Wales, Cardiff.

NAW (2000a) *A Sustainable Wales*, National Assembly for Wales, Cardiff.

NAW (2000b) *Better Homes for People in Wales*, National Assembly for Wales, Cardiff.

NAW (2000c) *Minerals Planning Policy Wales*, Stationery Office, London.

NAW (2000d) *Made in Wales*, National Assembly for Wales, Cardiff.

NAW (2001) *Wales Spatial Plan: Pathways to Sustainability*, National Assembly for Wales, Cardiff.

Neill, W.J.V., Fitzsimons, D.S., Murtagh, B. (1995) *Reimaging the Pariah City: Urban Development in Belfast and Detroit*, Avebury, Aldershot.

Needham, B. (1982) *Choosing the Right Policy Instruments*, Gower, Aldershot.

Newman, P. Thornley, A. (1996) *Urban Planning in Europe*, Routledge, London.

Norton, P. (1990) *Legislatures*, Oxford University Press, Oxford.

Norton, P., Aughey, A. (1981) *Conservatives and Conservatism*, Temple Smith, London.

Nott, S.M., Morgan, P.H. (1984) 'The significance of Department of the Environment Circulars in the planning process', *Journal of Planning and Environmental Law*, 36, 623–32.

Nuffield Foundation (1986) A Committee of Inquiry appointed by the Nuffield Foundation on the Town and Country Planning system, Nuffield Foundation, London.

NWPG (2000) *Regional Planning Guides for North Wales*, North Wales Planning Group, Wrexham.

Ohmae, K. (1996) The End of the Nation State, HarperCollins, London.

Osmond, J. (ed.) (1994) *A Parliament for Wales*, Gomer, Bridgend.

Osmond, J. (ed.) (1998) *The National Assembly Agenda: A Handbook for the First Four Years*, Institute of Welsh Affairs, Cardiff.

Paddison, R. (1997) 'The restructuring of local government in Scotland', in J. Bradbury, J. Mawson (eds), *British Regionalism and Devolution: The Challenge of State Reform and European Integration*, Jessica Kingsley Publishing, London.

Page, E. (1985) 'State development and local government: a comparative study', Paper presented to the XIII World Congress of the International Political Science Association, Paris, July (cited in R.A.W. Rhodes (1988), *Beyond Westminster and Whitehall: Sub-Central Governments of Britain*, Unwin Hyman, London).

Painter, J., Goodwin, M. (1996) 'Local governance, the crises of fordism and the changing geographies of regulation', *Transactions of the Institute of British Geographers*, 21, 635–48.

Parry, R. (1997) 'The Scottish Parliament and social policy', *Scottish Affairs*, 19, 14–21.

Peck, F.W. (1996) 'Regional development and the production of space: the role of infrastructure in the attraction of new inward investment', *Environment and Planning A*, 28, 327–39.

Pennance, F.G. (1967) *Housing, Town Planning and the Land Commission*, Hobart Paper No. 40, Institute for Economic Affairs, London.

Pennington, M. (2000) *Planning and the Market*, Athlone Press, London.

Pennington, M. (2002) 'A Hayekian liberal critique of collaborative planning', in P. Allmendinger, M. Tewdwr-Jones (eds), *Planning Futures: New Directions for Planning Theory*, Routledge, London.

Perryman, M. (1996) *The Blair Agenda*, Lawrence and Wishart, London.

Phelps, N.A., Tewdwr-Jones, M. (1998) 'Institutional capacity building in a strategic policy vacuum: the case of the Korean company LG in South Wales', *Environment and Planning C: Government and Policy*, 16(6), 735–55.

Phelps, N.A., Tewdwr-Jones, M. (1999) 'Competing through planning', *Environment and Planning B: Planning and Design*, 26(2), 159–61.

Phelps, N.A., Tewdwr-Jones, M. (2000) 'Scratching the surface of collaborative and associative governance: identifying the diversity of social action in institutional capacity building', *Environment and Planning A*, 32, 111–30.

Phelps, N.A., Tewdwr-Jones, M. (2001) 'Globalisation, regions and the state: exploring the limits of economic modernisation through inward investment', *Urban Studies*, 38(8), 1253–72.

Pickvance, C. (1991) 'The difficulty of control and the ease of structural reform: British local government in the 1980s', in C. Pickvance, E. Preteceille (eds), *State Restructuring and Local Power: A Comparative Perspective*, Pinter, London.

Poulton, M.C. (1991a) 'The case for a positive theory of planning, Part I: what is wrong with planning theory?', *Environment and Planning B: Planning and Design*, 18, 225–32.

Poulton, M.C. (1991b) 'The case for a positive theory of planning, Part II: a positive theory of planning', *Environment and Planning B: Planning and Design*, 18, 263–75.

Powell, K. (2001) 'Devolution, planning guidance and the role of the planning system', *International Planning Studies*, 6(2), 215–22.

Powell, W., Di Maggio, P. (eds) (1991) *The New Institutionalism in Organisational Analysis*, University of Chicago Press, Chicago.

Poxon, J. (2000) 'Solving the development plan puzzle in Britain: learning lessons from history', *Planning Perspectives*, 15, 73–89.

Prior, A. (2000) 'Development plans', in P. Allmendinger, A. Prior, J. Raemaekers (eds), *Introduction to Planning Practice*, John Wiley and Sons, Chichester.

Purdue, M. (1989) 'Material considerations in planning: an ever expanding concept?', *Journal of Planning and Environment Law*, 41, 156–61.

Purdue, M. (1994) 'The impact of Section 54A', *Journal of Planning and Environmental Law*, 46, 399–407.

Quinn, M. (1996) 'Central government planning policy', in M. Tewdwr-Jones (ed.), *British Planning Policy in Transition: Planning in the 1990s*, UCL Press, London.

Quinn, M. (2000) 'Central government planning policy', in P. Allmendinger, A. Prior, J. Raemaekers (eds), *Introduction to Planning Practice*, John Wiley and Sons, Chichester.

Raco, M. (1999) 'Assessing "institutional thickness" in the local context: a comparison of Cardiff and Sheffield', *Environment and Planning A*, 30, 975–96.

Raemakers, J., Prior, A., Boyack, S. (1995) *A Review of the Emerging New Scottish National Planning Series*, Royal Town Planning Institute, London.

Rausch, J. (1995) *Demosclerosis: The Silent Killer of American Government*, Random House, New York.

Rawnsley, A. (2000) *Servants of the People*, Hamish Hamilton, London.

Reade, E. (1987) *British Town and Country Planning*, Open University, Milton Keynes.

Redwood, J. (1994) *An Environmental Statement for Wales*, Welsh Office, Cardiff.

Rees, G., Lambert, J. (1979) 'Urban development in a peripheral region: some issues from South Wales', Paper presented at the Centre for Environmental Studies Conference on Urban Change and Conflict, University of Nottingham, January.

Regional Policy Commission (1996) *Renewing the Regions*, Sheffield Hallam University, Sheffield.

Rein, M., Schon, D. (1993) 'Reframing policy discourse', in F. Fischer, J. Forester (eds), *The Argumentative Turn in Policy Analysis and Planning*, UCL Press, London.

Rhodes, R.A.W. (1980) 'Some myths in central–local government relations', *Town Planning Review*, 51, 270–85.

Rhodes, R.A.W. (1981) *Control and Power in Central–Local Government Relations*, Gower, Aldershot.

Rhodes, R.A.W. (1988) *Beyond Westminster and Whitehall: Sub-Central Governments of Britain*, Unwin Hyman, London.

Rhodes, R.A.W. (1992) 'Changing intergovernmental relations', in P. Cloke (ed.), *Policy and Change in Thatcher's Britain*, Pergamon, Oxford.

Rhodes, R.A.W. (1996) 'The new governance: governing without government', *Political Studies*, XLIV, 652–67.

Rhodes, R.A.W. (1997) *Understanding Governance: Policy Networks, Governance, Reflexivity and Accountability*, Open University Press, Milton Keynes.

Riddell, P. (1983) *The Thatcher Government*, Martin Robinson, Oxford.

Riddell, P. (1994) 'Major and parliament', in D. Kavanagh, A. Seldon (eds), *The Major Effect*, Macmillan, London.

Roberts, P. (1996) 'Regional Planning Guidance in England and Wales: back to the future?', *Town Planning Review*, 67(1), 97–109.

Roberts, P., Lloyd, M.G. (1999) 'Institutional aspects of regional planning, management and development: models and lessons from the English experience', *Environment and Planning B: Planning and Design*, 26, 517–31.

Roberts, P., Lloyd, M.G. (2000) 'Regional Development Agencies in England: new strategic regional planning issues?', *Regional Studies*, 34(1), 517–31.

Roberts, P., Thomas, K., Williams, G. (eds) (2000) *Metropolitan Planning in Britain: A Comparative Study*, Jessica Kingsley Publishing, London.

Robinson, F., Shaw, K. (2001) 'Governing a region: structures and processes of governance in North East England', *Regional Studies*, 35(5), 473–8.

Robinson, M. (1992) *The Greening of British Party Politics*, Manchester University Press, Manchester.

Roderick, P. (1994) 'Central Government Planning Policy', Paper presented to the Planning Policy in the 1990s Conference, Department of City and Regional Planning, University of Wales Cardiff, Cardiff, March.

Rogers, S. (1998) *Community Planning and Engagement*, INLOGOV, Birmingham.

Rowan-Robinson, J. (1997) 'The organisation and effectiveness of the Scottish planning system', in R. MacDonald, H. Thomas (eds), *Nationality and Planning in Scotland and Wales*, University of Wales Press, Cardiff.

Rowan-Robinson, J., Lloyd, M.G. (1991) 'National Planning Guidelines: a strategic opportunity wasting away?', *Planning Practice and Research*, 6(3), 16–19.

Rowan-Robinson, J., Lloyd, M.G., Elliot, R.G. (1987) 'National planning guidelines and strategic planning', *Town Planning Review*, 58(4), 369–81.

Rowan-Robinson, J., Ross, A., Walton, W. (1995) 'Sustainable development and the development control process', *Town Planning Review*, 66(3), 269–86.

Royal Institution of Chartered Surveyors (1986) *A Strategy for Planning*, RICS, London.

Royal Town Planning Institute (1997) *Slimmer and Swifter*, RTPI, London.

Royal Town Planning Institute (1998) *Members' Survey: What Do We Need to Do to Ensure the Future of Planning and the Planning Profession?*, Priority Search Ltd, London.

Rydin, Y. (1993) *The British Planning System: An Introduction*, Macmillan, London.

Saunders, P. (1984) *Urban Politics: A Sociological Interpretation*, Hutchinson, London.

Savage, S., Robbins, L. (eds) (1991) *A Nation of Homeowners*, Unwin Hyman, London.

Schon, D. (1982) 'Some of what a planner knows', *Journal of the American Planning Association*, 48, 352–64.

Schon, D. (1983) *The Reflective Practitioner: How Professionals Think in Action*, Basic Books, New York.

Scott, A.J. (1983) 'Industrial organisation and logic of intra-metropolitan location, I: theoretical considerations', *Economic Geography*, 59, 233–50.

Scott, A.J. (1986) 'Industrial organisation and location: division of labour, the firm and spatial processes', *Economic Geography*, 62, 215–31.

Scott, A.J. (1998) *Regions and the World Economy: The Coming Shape of Global Production, Competition and Political Order*, Oxford University Press, Oxford.

Scott, A.J., Roweis, S.T. (1977) 'Urban planning theory and practice: a reappraisal', *Environment and Planning A*, 9, 1097–119.

Scottish Executive (2001) *Review of Strategic Planning*, Consultation Paper, Scottish Executive, Edinburgh.

Scottish Office (1997) *Scotland's Parliament*, Cm. 3658, Stationery Office, London.

Scottish Office (1999) *Land Use Planning Under a Scottish Parliament*, Scottish Office, Edinburgh.

Seldon, A. (1997) *Major: A Political Life*, Weidenfeld and Nicolson, London.

SEWSPG (2000) *Strategic Planning Guidance for South East Wales*, South East Wales Strategic Planning Group, Rhymney.

Sharpe, L.J. (ed.) (1979) *Decentralist Trends in Western Democracies*, Sage, London.

Shaw, M. (1999) 'A national spatial planning framework for the UK', *Town Planning Review*, 70(3), 271–4.

Shirlow, P. (2001) 'Devolution in Northern Ireland/Ulster/The North/Six Counties: delete as appropriate', *Regional Studies*, 35(8), 743–52.

Siegan, B. (1972) *Other People's Property*, Lexington Books, Lexington, Mass.

Smith, R., Stirling, T., Williams, P. (eds) (2000) *Housing in Wales: The Policy Agenda in an Era of Devolution*, Chartered Institute of Housing/Housing Studies Association, Coventry.

Sorenson, A.D. (1982) 'Planning comes of age: a liberal perspective', *The Planner*, 68(6), 184–5.

Sorenson, A.D. (1983) 'Towards a market theory of planning', *The Planner*, 69(3), 78–80.

Sorenson, A.D., Day, R.A. (1981) 'Libertarian planning', *Town Planning Review*, 52, 390–402.

Stoker, G., Mossberger, K. (1995) 'The post-Fordist local state: the dynamics of its development', in J. Stewart, G. Stoker (eds), *Local Government in the 1990s*, Macmillan, Basingstoke.

Storper, M. (1997) *The Regional World: Territorial Development in a Global Economy*, Guilford Press, New York.

Switzer, J.F.Q. (1984) 'The duty of the Secretary of State for the Environment', *Journal of Planning and Environment Law*, 36, 72–6.

SWWSPG (2000) *Regional Planning Guidance (South West Wales)*, South West Wales Strategic Planning Group, Carmarthen.

Taussik, J. (1992) 'Development plans: implications for enhanced status', *Estates Gazette*, 9235, 5 September.

Taylor, N. (1998) *Urban Planning Theory Since 1945*, Paul Chapman Publishing, London.

Tewdwr-Jones, M. (1993) *Material Considerations in Planning*, Paper in Planning Research 134, Department of City and Regional Planning, University of Wales Cardiff, Cardiff.

Tewdwr-Jones, M. (1994a) 'Policy implications of the "plan-led" planning system', *Journal of Planning and Environment Law*, 46(7), 583–94.

Tewdwr-Jones, M. (1994b) 'The development plan in policy implementation', *Environment and Planning C: Government and Policy*, 12(2), 145–63.

Tewdwr-Jones, M. (1994c) 'The Government's Planning Policy Guidance', *Journal of Planning and Environment Law*, 46(2), 106–16.

Tewdwr-Jones, M. (1995) 'Development control and the legitimacy of planning decisions', *Town Planning Review*, 66(2), 163–81.

Tewdwr-Jones, M. (ed.) (1996a) *British Planning Policy in Transition: Planning in the 1990s*, UCL Press, London.

Tewdwr-Jones, M. (1996b) 'Introduction: land use planning after Thatcher', in M. Tewdwr-Jones (ed.), *British Planning Policy in Transition: Planning in the 1990s*, UCL Press, London.

Tewdwr-Jones, M. (1996c) 'Reflective planning theorising and professional protectionism', *Town Planning Review*, 67(2), 235–43.

Tewdwr-Jones, M. (1997a) 'Green belts or green wedges for Wales? A flexible approach to planning in the urban periphery', *Regional Studies*, 31(1), 73–7.

Tewdwr-Jones, M. (1997b) 'Land use planning in Wales: the conflict between state centrality and territorial nationalism', in R. MacDonald, H. Thomas (eds), *Nationality and Planning in Scotland and Wales*, University of Wales Press, Cardiff.

Tewdwr-Jones, M. (1997c) 'Plans, policies and intergovernmental relations: assessing the significance of national planning guidance in the planning system in England and Wales', *Urban Studies*, 34(1), 141–62.

Tewdwr-Jones, M. (1998a) 'Planning modernised?', *Journal of Planning and Environment Law*, 50(6), 519–28.

Tewdwr-Jones, M. (1998b) 'Rural government and community participation: the planning role of community councils', *Journal of Rural Studies*, 14(1), 51–62.

Tewdwr-Jones, M. (1998c) 'Strategic planning', in J. Osmond (ed.), *National Agenda for Wales Assembly Handbook*, Institute of Welsh Affairs, Cardiff.

Tewdwr-Jones, M. (1999a) 'Discretion, flexibility, and certainty in British planning: emerging ideological conflicts and inherent political tensions', *Journal of Planning Education and Research*, 17(2), 244–56.

Tewdwr-Jones, M. (1999b) 'Reasserting town planning: challenging the image and representation of the planning profession', in P. Allmendinger, M. Chapman (eds), *Planning Beyond 2000*, John Wiley and Sons, Chichester.

Tewdwr-Jones, M. (1999c) 'Reconciling competing voices: institutional roles and political expectations in the new governance of planning', *Town Planning Review*, 70(4), 417–23.

Tewdwr-Jones, M. (2001a) 'Complexity and interdependency in a kaleidoscopic spatial planning landscape for Europe', in J. Alden, L. Albrechts, A. da Rosa Pires (eds), *The Changing Institutional Landscape of Planning*, Ashgate, Aldershot.

Tewdwr-Jones, M. (2001b) 'Grasping the thistle: the search for distinctiveness in the devolved Scottish planning system', *International Planning Studies*, 6(2), 199–213.

Tewdwr-Jones, M. (2001c) 'Planning and the National Assembly for Wales: generating distinctiveness and inclusiveness in a new political context', *European Planning Studies*, 9(4), 553–62.

Tewdwr-Jones, M. (2002) 'Personal dynamics, distinctive frames and communicative planning', in P. Allmendinger, M. Tewdwr-Jones (eds), *Planning Futures: New Directions for Planning Theory*, Routledge, London.

Tewdwr-Jones, M., Allmendinger, P. (1998) 'Deconstructing communicative planning: a critique of Habermasian collaborative planning', *Environment and Planning A*, 30(11), 1975–91.

Tewdwr-Jones, M., Bishop, K., Wilkinson, D. (2000) ' "Euroscepticism", political agendas and spatial planning: British national and regional planning policy in uncertain times', *European Planning Studies*, 8(5), 655–72.

Tewdwr-Jones, M., Gallent, N. (2000) 'Planning strategically for housing growth', in B. Smith, T. Stirling, P. Williams (eds), *Housing in Wales*, CIT Wales, London.

Tewdwr-Jones, M., Harris, N. (1998) 'The New Right's commodification of planning control', in P. Allmendinger, H. Thomas (eds), *Urban Planning and the British New Right*, Routledge, London.

Tewdwr-Jones, M., Lloyd, M.G. (1997) 'Unfinished business', *Town and Country Planning*, November, 302–4.

Tewdwr-Jones, M., McNeill, D. (2000) 'The politics of city-region planning and governance: reconciling the national, regional and urban in the competing voices of institutional restructuring', *European Urban and Regional Studies*, 7, 119–34.

Tewdwr-Jones, M., Phelps, N.A. (2000) 'Levelling the uneven playing field: inward investment, interregional rivalry and the planning system', *Regional Studies*, 34(5), 429–40.

Tewdwr-Jones, M., Thomas, H. (1998) 'Collaborative action in local plan making: planners' perceptions of "planning through debate" ', *Environment and Planning B: Planning and Design*, 25(1), 127–44.

Tewdwr-Jones, M., Williams, R.H. (2001) *The European Dimension of British Planning*, Spon Press, London.

Thatcher, M. (1992) 'Don't undo my work', *Newsweek*, 27 April.

Thew, D., Watson, D. (1988) 'Unitary development plans: the West Midlands experience', *The Planner*, 74(11), 19–23.

Thomas, H. (1994) 'The New Right, "race" and planning in Britain in the 1980s and 1990s', *Planning Practice and Research*, 9(4), 353–66.

Thomas, H. (1996) 'Public participation in planning', in M. Tewdwr-Jones (ed.), *British Planning Policy in Transition: Planning in the 1990s*, UCL Press, London.

Thomas, H., Lo Piccolo, F. (2000) 'Best Value, planning and race equality', *Planning Practice and Research*, 15(1/2), 79–94.

Thomas, H.D., Minett, J.M., Hopkins, S., Hamnett, S.L., Faludi, A., Barrell, D. (1983) *Flexibility and Commitment in Planning*, Martinus Nijhoff, The Hague, Boston and London.

Thomas, K. (1997) *Development Control*, UCL Press, London.

Thomas, K., Kimberley, S. (1995) 'Rediscovering regional planning? Progress on Regional Planning Guidance in England', *Regional Studies*, 29(5), 414–21.

Thomas, K., Roberts, P. (2000) 'Metropolitan strategic planning in England: strategies in transition', *Town Planning Review*, 71(1), 25–50.

Thompson, R. (1987) 'Is faster better? The case of development control', *The Planner*, 73(9), 11–15.

Thornley, A. (1991) *Urban Planning Under Thatcherism: The Challenge of the Market* (1st edn), Routledge, London.

Thornley, A. (1993) *Urban Planning Under Thatcherism: The Challenge of the Market* (2nd edn), Routledge, London.

Thornley, A. (1996) 'Planning policy and the market', in M. Tewdwr-Jones (ed.), *British Planning Policy in Transition: Planning in the 1990s*, UCL Press, London.

Tiesdell, S., Allmendinger, P. (2001) 'Neighbourhood regeneration and New Labour's third way', *Environment and Planning C: Government and Policy*, 19, 903–26.

Tomaney, J, Ward, N. (2000) 'England and the "new regionalism" ', *Regional Studies*, 34(5), 471–8.

Tompsett, R. (1994) 'English Welsh on guidance for Wales', *Planning Week*, 2(41), 10–11.

Townroe, P. (1999) 'Rising real incomes and enough jobs: the contribution of a British national spatial planning framework', *Town Planning Review*, 70(3), 295–312.

Turok, I. (1992) 'Property-led urban regeneration: panacea or placebo?', *Environment and Planning A*, 29, 361–79.

Turok, I., Kearns, A., Goodlad, R. (1999) 'Social exclusion: in what sense a planning problem?', *Town Planning Review*, 70(3), 363–84.

Upton, R. (2001) 'Devolution and the future for "British" planning systems: future directions for Wales and the UK regions?', *International Planning Studies*, 6(2), 223–31.

Urban Task Force (1999) *Towards an Urban Renaissance*, Spon Press, London.

Vigar, G. (2002) *The Politics of Mobility*, Spon Press, London.

Vigar, G., Healey, P. (1999) 'Territorial integration and "plan-led" planning', *Planning Practice and Research*, 14(2), 153–69.

Vigar, G., Healey, P., Hull, A., Davoudi, S. (2000) *Planning, Governance and Spatial Strategy in Britain*, Macmillan, Basingstoke.

Wakeford, R. (1993) 'Planning Policy Guidance: what's the use?', *Housing and Planning Review*, April/May, 14–18.

Waldegrave, W. (1987) Speech to the Planning Inspectorate, Tollgate House, Bristol, April 1997.

Wales European Task Force (1999) *National Development Strategy for Wales*, Welsh Office, Cardiff.

Walters, A.A. (1974) 'Land speculator: creator or creature of inflation', in A.A. Walters, F.G. Pennance, W.A. West, D.R. Denman, B. Bracewell-Milnes, S.E. Denman, D.G. Slough, S. Ingram (eds), *Government and the Land*, Institute of Economic Affairs, London.

Wannop, U. (1980) 'Scottish planning practice: four distinctive characteristics', *The Planner*, May, 64–5.

Wannop U. (1995) *The Regional Imperative*, Jessica Kingsley Publishing, London.

Wannop, U., Cherry, G. (1994) 'The development of regional planning in the United Kingdom', *Planning Perspectives*, 9(1), 29–60.

Webb, D. Collis, C. (2000) 'Regional Development Agencies and the "new regionalism" in England', *Regional Studies*, 34(9), 857–64.

Welsh Office (1981) *Historic Buildings and Conservation Areas – Policy and Procedure: Circular 61/81*, HMSO, London.

Welsh Office (1986) *Housing for Senior Management: Circular 30/86*, HMSO, London.

Welsh Office (1988a) *The Valleys Programme*, HMSO, London.

Welsh Office (1988b) *The Welsh Language: Development Plans and Development Control: Circular 53/88*, HMSO, London.

Welsh Office (1990) *Planning and Archaeology*, HMSO, London.

Welsh Office (1992a) Development Plans and Strategic Planning *Guidance in Wales: PPG12 Wales*, HMSO, London.

Welsh Office (1992b) *Land for Housing: PPG3*, HMSO, London.

Welsh Office (1993a) *Development Control – A Guide to Good Practice*, Welsh Office, Cardiff.

Welsh Office (1993b) *Local Government in Wales: A Charter for the Future*, HMSO, London.

Welsh Office (1995a) *Planning Guidance Wales: Planning Policy*, Draft Consultation Paper, Welsh Office, Cardiff.

Welsh Office (1995b) *Planning Guidance Wales: Unitary Development Plans*, Draft Consultation Paper, Welsh Office, Cardiff.

Welsh Office (1996a) *Planning Guidance Wales: Planning Policy*, HMSO, London.

Welsh Office (1996b) *Planning Guidance Wales: Unitary Development Plans*, HMSO, London.

Welsh Office (1997) *A Voice for Wales*, Cm 3718, The Stationery Office, London.

Welsh Office (1999) *Planning Guidance Wales: Planning Policy, First Revision*, Stationery Office, London.

West Dorset District Council (1994) *West Dorset Local Plan Deposit Version*, WDDC, Dorchester.

West Dorset District Council (1995) *West Dorset Local Plan Pre-Inquiry Changes*, WDDC, Dorchester.

White, A. (2000) 'Accountability and regional governance: the emerging role of regional chambers in England', *Local Economy*, 14(4), 329–45.

White, S., Tewdwr-Jones, M. (1995) 'The role and status of supplementary planning guidance', *Journal of Planning and Environment Law*, 48(6), 471–81.

Willets, D. (1992) *Modern Conservatism*, Penguin, Harmondsworth.

Williams, G. (1999a) 'The metropolitan framework for planning and governance', in P. Roberts, K. Thomas and G. Williams (eds), *Metropolitan Planning in Britain: A Comparative Study*, Jessica Kingsley Publishing, London.

Williams, G. (1999b) 'Metropolitan governance and strategic planning: a review of experience in Manchester, Melbourne and Toronto', *Progress in Planning*, 52(1), 1–70.

Williams, G., Strange, I., Bintley, M. and Bristow, R. (1992) *Metropolitan Planning in the 1990s: Unitary Development Plans*, Department of Planning and Landscape Occasional Paper, University of Manchester.

Williams, R.H. (1996) *European Union Spatial Policy and Planning*, Paul Chapman Publishing, London.

Williams, R.H. (2000) 'Constructing the European Spatial Development Perspective – for whom?', *European Planning Studies*, 8(3), 357–65.

Wilson, B. (1990) 'Planning policy guidance', *Town and Country Planning Summer School Proceedings/The Planner*, 75(46), 85–7.

Winkler, J.T. (1977) 'The corporate economy: theory and administration', in R. Scase (ed.), *Industrial Society: Class, Cleavage and Control*, Allen and Unwin, London.

Wong, C. (2001a) 'Constructing a national spatial planning framework', *Town Planning Review*, 72(1), iii–vii.

Wong, C. (2001b) 'The case for a UK spatial planning framework', *Town Planning Review*, 72(1), 000–0.

Wong, C., Ravetz, J., Turner, J. (2000) *The United Kingdom Spatial Planning Framework: A Discussion*, RTPI, London.

Yiftachel, O. (1989) 'Towards a new typology of urban planning theories', *Environment and Planning B: Planning and Design*, 16, 23–39.

Ying Ho, S. (1997) 'Scrutiny and direction: implications of government intervention in the new development plan process in England', *Urban Studies*, 34(8), 1259–74.

Young, H. (1994) 'The prime minister', in D. Kavanagh and A. Seldon (eds), *The Major Effect*, Macmillan, London.

INDEX

Note: page numbers in *italics* denote tables or figures